# Transcultural Research – Heidelberg Studies on Asia and Europe in a Global Context





For further volumes:
http://www.springer.com/series/8753

Isabella Löhr • Roland Wenzlhuemer
Editors

# The Nation State and Beyond

## Governing Globalization Processes in the Nineteenth and Early Twentieth Centuries

Springer

*Editors*
Isabella Löhr
History Department
Heidelberg University
Heidelberg
Germany

Roland Wenzlhuemer
EXC "Asia and Europe"
Karl Jaspers Centre
Heidelberg
Germany

ISSN 2191-656X ISSN 2191-6578 (electronic)
ISBN 978-3-642-32933-3 ISBN 978-3-642-32934-0 (eBook)
DOI 10.1007/978-3-642-32934-0
Springer Heidelberg New York Dordrecht London

Library of Congress Control Number: 2012951616



Printed on acid-free paper

Springer is part of Springer Science+Business Media (www.springer.com)

# Contents

## Part III Education



## Part IV Borders

# Notes on Contributors

**Tomoko Akami** is a fellow at the Research School of Asia and the Pacific, and senior lecturer at the School of Culture, History, and Language at the College of Asia and the Pacific at the Australian National University. She specialises in history of international relations. She has recently embarked on a project on the health governance of the League of Nations and the Japanese empire. Her publications include *Internationalizing the Pacific* (London 2002), and her two monographs on Japan's news agencies and foreign policy are forthcoming shortly.

**James Casteel** is a historian of modern and contemporary Europe and is cross-appointed to the Institute of European, Russian, and Eurasian Studies, and the program in religion at the College of the Humanities at Carleton University, Ottawa, Canada. He also serves as the assistant director of the Max and Tessie Zelikovitz Centre for Jewish Studies. He is currently completing a book manuscript entitled *Between Empire and Utopia: Russia in the German National Imaginary, 1881–1956.*

**Klaus Dittrich** is assistant professor in the Department of Korean History at Korea University in Seoul, South Korea. He received his doctorate from the University of Portsmouth (United Kingdom) with a dissertation entitled *Experts Going Transnational: Education at World Exhibitions during the Second Half of the Nineteenth Century*. He has been a postdoctoral fellow at the Research Institute of Comparative History and Culture at Hanyang University in Seoul. He is currently preparing a new research project on the European and American community in Korea around 1900.

**Heather Ellis** is a lecturer and researcher in British history at the Centre for British Studies, Humboldt University, Berlin. Her doctoral thesis, completed at Balliol College, Oxford in 2009, examined the relationship between generational conflict and university reform in Britain against the background of the American and French Revolutions. It is due to be published as a monograph with Brill later in 2012. She is currently working on a book project which will explore the relationship between masculine identity and the development of scientific culture and authority in nineteenth and early twentieth-century Britain. She has published widely on the history of education, masculinity, and adolescence in eighteenth, nineteenth, and twentieth-century Britain.

**E. Thomas Ewing** is a professor in the Department of History and associate dean for research and graduate studies at the College of Liberal Arts and Human Sciences at Virginia Tech. His education includes a BA from Williams College and a PhD in history from the University of Michigan. His publications include, as author, *Separate Schools: Gender, Policy, and Practice in the Postwar Soviet Union* (2010) and *The Teachers of Stalinism. Policy, Practice, and Power in Soviet Schools in the 1930s* (2002); as editor, *Revolution and Pedagogy. Transnational Perspectives on the Social Foundations of Education* (2005), and as co-editor, with David Hicks, *Education and the Great Depression. Lessons from a Global History* (2006).

**Madeleine Herren** is full professor of history and co-director of the Cluster of Excellence "Asia and Europe in a Global Context" at Heidelberg University. Her fields of interest cover European and global history of the nineteenth and twentieth centuries, the history of international organisations, the development of transnational networks and border-crossing civil society activities, research on encyclopaedia, information transfer and information cultures, historiography and transcultural methodologies of history in the digital century. Recent publication: Madeleine Herren, Martin Rüesch, Christiane Sibille, *Transcultural History*, Berlin 2012.

**Isabella Löhr** is assistant professor at the History Department of Heidelberg University. Her doctoral thesis explored the global implementation of intellectual property rights since the nineteenth century. Her monograph *Die Globalisierung geistiger Eigentumsrechte. Neue Strukturen internationaler Zusammenarbeit, 1886–1952* was published by Vandenhoeck and Ruprecht in 2010. She is currently working on a book project which examines transnational advocacy networks of academic refugees in the twentieth century. Her fields of interest include processes of globalisation and transnationalisation, the social history of international organisations, internationalists and of border-crossing civil society networks in the twentieth century.

**Simone Müller-Pohl** (FU Berlin) is assistant professor of history at the John F. Kennedy Institute for North American Studies. She works on the global communication system of the late nineteenth and early twentieth centuries. In her dissertation, *The Class of 1866 and the Wiring of the World. Telegraphic Networks in Maritime Space*, she analysed the individual actors of the global submarine cable system as actors of globalisation and illustrated how their global imaginaries shaped concepts of *Weltcommunication.*

**Thies Schulze** is research fellow in contemporary history at the Cluster of Excellence "Religion and Politics in Pre-Modern and Modern Cultures," Westfälische Wilhelms-Universität Münster. His PhD thesis on *Dante Alighieri as a Symbolic*

*National Figure in Italy (1793–1915*) was published in 2005. He has published various journal articles in fields such as the history of diplomacy in the twentieth century, the history of "fascist" movements in Europe, the history of nationalism, and the history of the Roman Catholic Church. His current book project will examine the attitude of the Catholic Church towards modern nationalism, both analysing the Vatican's perspective on nationalist movements and conflicts of nationalities in border regions between the two world wars.

**Guido Thiemeyer**, born in 1967, is a professor of contemporary history at the University of Cergy-Pontoise. His main fields of interest are international economic and political relations, internationalism in the nineteenth century, and European Integration history.

**Norman Weiß** is an interim professor of international and European law at the Helmut Schmidt University/University of the Federal Armed Forces Hamburg, and a researcher at the Human Rights Centre of the University of Potsdam. His doctoral thesis (1999, Peter Lang 2000) dealt with the constitutional complaint under German constitutional law; his habilitation (2007, Springer 2009) examined the powers of international organisations. He recently edited a book on the relationship between judicial redress and the rule of law (Nomos 2011), and co-edited a book on the global challenges the United Nations has to meet (Potsdam University Press 2011). He has published widely on the protection of human rights and on minority issues.

**Roland Wenzlhuemer** received a doctoral degree in history from Salzburg University, Austria, in 2002. The desire to combine social and cultural approaches and to institutionally transgress disciplinary boundaries took him to postdoctoral research positions at interdisciplinary institutes such as the Centre for Modern Oriental Studies and the Centre for British Studies at Humboldt University in Berlin. Since 2008 he has been leading an independent research group within the Cluster of Excellence "Asia and Europe in a Global Context" at Heidelberg University.

# Chapter 1
# Introduction: The Nation State and Beyond. Governing Globalization Processes in the Nineteenth and Early Twentieth Centuries

**Isabella Löhr and Roland Wenzlhuemer**

**Abstract** The history of globalisation is anything but a no-frills affair that moves smoothly along a clear-cut, unidirectional path of development and eventually leads to seamless global integration. Consequently, scholarship in the social sciences increasingly argued against equating the history of globalisation processes and transcultural entanglements with the master narrative of the gradual homogenisation of the world. A strong common ground these concepts share is the objective of transcending the national as an analytical category and replacing it by focusing on interaction and flows, transfers, and exchanges as the core categories in the study of history. Examining the shifting patterns of global connections has, therefore, become the main challenge for all those who seek to understand the past, the present, and the future of modern societies. And this challenge includes finding a place for the nation state—a form of social organisation that no longer seem to fit into the new analytical framework despite its obvious historical and current significance. Against this background, the introductory chapter argues that the authors assembled in the volume suggest another reading of the role and significance of the nation state in the development of the modern world. The studies presented here argue that looking at the nation state from the perspective of global entanglements gives way to its interpretation as a dynamic and multi-layered structure that partakes in globalisation processes and plays different and at times even contradictory roles at the same time. Accordingly, it is not the nation state that ceases to exist, due to increasing processes of global exchange, but a certain perspective on the nation state which can no longer be upheld.

I. Löhr (✉)
History Department, Heidelberg University, Heidelberg, Germany
e-mail: isabella.loehr@zegk.uni-heidelberg.de

R. Wenzlhuemer
EXC "Asia and Europe", Karl Jaspers Centre, Heidelberg, Germany
e-mail: wenzlhuemer@asia-europe.uni-heidelberg.de

I. Löhr and R. Wenzlhuemer (eds.), *The Nation State and Beyond*, Transcultural Research – Heidelberg Studies on Asia and Europe in a Global Context,
DOI 10.1007/978-3-642-32934-0_1, © Springer-Verlag Berlin Heidelberg 2013

## Globalization

The history of globalization is anything but a no-frills affair that moves smoothly along a clear-cut and unidirectional path of development and eventually leads to seamless global integration. Following this, authors such as Sebastian Conrad and Andreas Eckert have argued against equating the history of globalization processes and transcultural entanglements with the master narrative of the gradual homogenization of the world.[1] In a similar manner, Ian Clark observed for the twentieth century that the willingness of states either to enhance or to boycott processes of global integration by means of specific policy strategies can both foster global integration and trigger dissent and resistance to a considerable degree.[2] Against this background, Michael Geyer and Charles Bright proposed a double-layered understanding of the development of the modern world. They suggested making a distinction between empirically describable processes of integration and fragmentation on the one hand and globality on the other as the basic condition which ultimately frames and embeds all actions taken within the "human community"[3] – whether or not they generate, reshape, transform or dissolve encounters, contacts, interaction and exchange. The "global age", as Geyer and Bright have put it, describes the horizon within which we live and act under global conditions, which continuously and irrevocably create path dependencies with a global reach. In turn, the historical actors retain the possibility to decide between different forms and varying degrees of integrative dynamics or a struggle for partial autonomy when it comes to political and economic sovereignty and questions of identity.[4]

Departing from this particular dialectic of integration and fragmentation and assuming that the development of the modern world can only be understood adequately as both a connected and a decentralized process, consideration should be given as to how such a macro-perspective on the history of a global modernity can be adequately reflected in the empirical research on globalization and global integration since the modern period. In recent years, the term globalization has increasingly been used as a kind of shorthand in several disciplines within the social sciences and the humanities: it gives expression to the analytical challenge of studying the plurality of actors, places and decision-making levels that appear when attention is increasingly directed towards border-crossing or border-ignoring flows of people, goods and information. In this sense, the shorthand 'globalization' points to the impossibility of continuing to work with theoretical approaches based on clear-cut differentiations between centre and periphery, the evaluation of primary and secondary acting groups and clear analytical distinctions between the political, the economic, the social and the cultural field which for a long time served as the main frame of reference in the analysis of inter-societal relationships. On the

[1] Conrad and Eckert 2007, p. 21.

[2] Clark 1997.

[3] Manning 2003, p. 15.

[4] Geyer and Bright 1995.

other hand, however, the use of a shorthand often entails difficulties of mutual understanding. At times, the term *globalization* is used in an all-encompassing, almost arbitrary way and its meaning has, therefore, become more and more elusive. Attempts to define the term by stating what it does not refer to have rightly been criticized. Complaints have been raised about the blurring of the term as soon as globalization is not applied to something specific but used to subsume nearly all phenomena that somehow transcend state borders. Frederick Cooper, for example, considers globalization to be a "powerful juggernaut"[5] and vehemently criticizes the notion's universality. His criticism mainly concentrates on its unsuitability as an analytical tool because in his view it provides only vague explanations of how and why different world regions were connected. Primarily, Cooper goes on, the term contributes to concealing both the understanding of concrete mechanisms that trigger cultural flows or movements of people and the understanding of institutions for regulating them. Instead, he seeks to draw attention to the limits of interrelations over long distances and argues for a close look at specific countermovements and processes that resist or at least redirect spatial interrelations, and thereby lead to the emergence of new patterns of re-territorialization.[6]

Where Cooper campaigns for exact analysis and close descriptions of processes of exchange and entanglement between regions and continents, strong arguments remain for the term *globalization* not to be abandoned. In contrast to other notions that describe long-term macro-processes – for example modernization, industrialization or urbanization – globalization is the only approach which bundles up together all kinds of research that treat interaction between societies as the default condition. We should, however, heed Cooper's advice not to equate processes of global integration with teleological notions of universalization and homogenization and steer clear of such quasi-deterministic interpretations of globalization which sometimes even entail visions of a world society or a world government.[7] Rather, the term should be clearly defined in a way that permits it to be used as an analytical tool in hands-on empirical research, while at the same time providing a level of abstraction that allows for a more general diagnosis of modern socio-cultural trajectories. We suggest the following: in a nutshell, globalization comprises the process of the gradual detachment of patterns of socio-cultural interaction from geographical proximity. Only in very rare and isolated cases of globalization processes will such a detachment eventually lead to the correlation between socio-cultural interaction and geographical proximity becoming superseded. Usually, this correlation is merely weakened to different degrees and at different paces. Despite the word's etymological roots, globalization does not automatically (or necessarily) aim at covering the whole globe. Instead, the root "global" refers to the increasing number of personal or institutional connections that transcend local horizons and let actors across the entire globe interact with each other. In this

[5] Cooper 2001, p. 191.

[6] Ibid, pp. 189–213.

[7] Anghel et al. 2008; Krücken 2009; Lechner 2009.

regard, globalization processes add more and more global connections to the mix of personal and institutional relations that constitute the networks of historical actors. It is important to see that globalization evolves not in a deterministic but often in an erratic fashion as it does not aim at systematically establishing a particular order but rather at departing from an established pattern.

Looking at the other end of the process, this also means that globalization can be understood as a default mode of the development of human interaction. And yet, of course, processes of globalization have not always been equally pronounced and influential. At various times they have either been painstakingly slow and almost imperceptible, or have gained sudden momentum and become historically potent – for instance, at the beginning of the sixteenth century that saw European colonial and economic expansion and brought a long period of almost undetectable movement in this regard to an end.[8] From there followed alternating phases between a slowing-down of the processes, the disintegration of certain world regions and at the same time an almost incredible acceleration of the process as has been observed from the middle of the nineteenth century onwards.[9] These phases are typically the ones most readily perceived in the field of global history and, therefore, historians have usually tried to define globalization on the basis of them alone. Here, however, we suggest looking at globalization from a more holistic perspective that acknowledges that the process can only be understood by looking beyond its high-speed phases and by bearing in mind the various opposing forces that aim at a reversal of the process.

Following this (or a related) definition of the term, globalization signifies both a multitude of entangled processes of the transformation of social relations as well as an analytical perspective that guides research on a global past and acknowledges the non-linearity of the aforementioned processes along with the alternation between phases of slow, fast or reversed global integration. Globalization as a perspective, therefore, draws on the simultaneity and the multitude of global encounters and searches for the interfaces, conflicts and unexpected consequences that occur when processes of global integration are juxtaposed by reverse tendencies that advocate the correlation between social relations and notions such as ethnicity, nationality or religion (to name but a few examples). In this perspective, the term has at least two additional benefits. First, it makes us aware that at least since the middle of the nineteenth century interaction has inevitably taken place in a framework of a global reach so that, conversely, each measure designed either to reinforce or reduce connectivity should be interpreted as a reaction to the overarching global conditions the historical actors could not escape from but had to deal with. Second, the term subsumes and nominates these various processes of global integration that are decentralized in character and sometimes even contradictory, that can influence each other but are not driven by some universal force or

[8] Hopkins 2002, pp. 11–46; Gunn 2003; for studies covering the early modern and the modern era see for example: Darwin 2008; Fernandéz-Armesto 2007; Wendt 2007.

[9] Bayly 2004; Osterhammel 2009.

directed by certain groups and that can lead to fragmentation and integration all at the same time.[10] If we assume the interconnection of groups, cultures and states on a global scale to be among the main constituent features of societies since the modern period, we face a number of tricky questions: how does the nation state fit into this opposing and at the same time closely connected interplay of globalization and fragmentation? How did state and non-state actors handle problems with a transnational reach? Who were the driving forces that either strengthened or slowed down processes of exchange and interconnection? Which aims and interests did the main acting groups pursue? Did a certain institutional and organizational framework develop so as to legalize and standardize interactions across national borders and to make them more predictable? And how did the nation states react towards the flows of information, technology, knowledge, commodities or capital, which did not stop at their borders? At the end of the day, this means that historians of globalization and a global past need to look attentively beyond the nation state just as they should by no means completely jettison it as an analytical framework from the outset.

## Beyond the Nation State

In their well-known work on the transformation of sovereignty to rest with a new and anonymous apparatus of global rule that they called *Empire*, Michael Hardt and Antonio Negri subjected the political consequences of globalization processes and global markets to a critical analysis. They directed the reader's attention to flows of capital, to new forms of supranational manifestations of political power and to border-crossing cultural practices of what they baptized *biopower*, in consequence of which the modern nation state no longer seems to be the principal framework of political sovereignty. Rather, Hardt and Negri detect a "new form of sovereignty",[11] that has been de-territorialized, de-centralized and, thus, has a weakening effect on the capability of nation states to exercise power and control. This diagnosis of an ongoing transformation of global power relations implicitly conveys a distinct historical master narrative about the development of global entanglements and globalization processes. The claim that the sovereign powers of the territorially-defined nation state currently become more and more porous and will finally be superseded by non-territorial forms of political control, relies on two central assumptions: that during the last two centuries the nation state has, indeed, been the principal driving force behind the creation of the modern world; and that only recently have alternative forms of cross-border interaction above and beyond the national framework started to challenge its political agency and supersede its economic, social and cultural monopoly.

[10] Osterhammel and Petersson 2005, p. 24.

[11] Hardt and Negri 2000, p. XI.

In the last few years, however, historians have provided much empirical evidence to question this master narrative. Taking up Hardt and Negri's argument that national sovereignty was not limited exclusively to the national territory as imperial nation states ruled foreign territories "through a system of channels and barriers that alternately facilitated and obstructed the flows of production and circulation",[12] historians started to focus on the interplay of nation-building and globalization processes and directed their attention to space as one principal analytical category. The paradigmatic discussions subsumed under the umbrella term *spatial turn* are closely related to the increasing attention the social sciences and humanities have thus begun to pay to globalization processes since the end of the Cold War.[13] While some contemporary observers have suggested that the tremendous technological improvements and acceleration in realms such as telecommunication and transport have led to the collapse of space-time relations[14] and thus to a loss of space,[15] social scientists and historians of a global past have articulated serious doubts in this regard. Rather than falling in step with ideas that reflect the short-term consequences (and perceptions) of informationalization, a majority of social scientists, and – a little later – historians, started to work with actor-based approaches and methods of network analysis. Thus acknowledging the existence of a plurality of spaces according to the plurality of spatial frames of reference, set up by the historical actors themselves, social scientists and historians turned their attention to analytically coming to terms with this often confounding notion.[16] Many of these spaces were created by the emergence of a variety of local, regional, transnational or transcultural interconnections resulting from global flows of money, goods or people. What is characteristic of the networks that arise from these connections is that they are no longer congruent with an established form of organizing social relations that we have been familiar with since the nineteenth century – namely with the nation state as the principal analytical framework within which modern societies may be studied and described.

Much research has been done on the historicity of the modern nation state and its formative impact on the social, economic and political constitution of modern societies. For a long time, historians have styled the nineteenth and the first half of the twentieth century as the time of the nation state.[17] Although historical

---

[12] Ibid., p. XII.

[13] Döring and Thielmann 2008; Harvey 2006; Warf and Arias 2009.

[14] See the related concepts of "convergence of time and space" (Janelle), "time-space distanciation" (Giddens), "time-space compression" (Harvey, Stein) or the "disempowerment of space" (Sonnemann). Janelle 1969; Giddens 1981, 1984; Harvey 1990; Stein 2001, p. 106; Sonnemann 1990, p. 21.

[15] See, for instance, a recent study by Regine Buschauer that looks at the recurrence of discourses on "annihilated" (German: "vernichtet"), "dead" ("getötet"), "disappeared" ("verschwunden") or "lost" ("verloren") space in the context of several technological transformations. Buschauer 2010, p. 17.

[16] See Wenzlhuemer 2010; Holton 2005.

[17] Iggers and Wang 2008.

sub-disciplines such as imperial or economic history pointed out that the setting-up of a territorially-defined national entity took place simultaneously with the transgression of national borders in the course of the expansion of European imperialism and the establishment of international value creation and commodity chains, curiously enough, these insights did not find their way into mainstream historical research.[18] By putting emphasis on the attempts to divide the world up into clearly definable geographical entities and political spheres of influence in the course of the nineteenth century, nationalization processes were placed centre stage. Starting from the assumption that the modern world has been shaped by the clash of national interests, the mainstream of historical research was preoccupied with the study of patterns of nationalization, of the establishment of national borders and of the subsequent development of national agendas that appeared to be highly incompatible – the Great War was interpreted only as the last proof of this historical master narrative. By assigning political power to spatially defined entities, historical research provided a clear political geography and, thus, delineated national territories as the principal backcloths of socio-cultural life in modern societies "where decision space, the writ of effective legislation, shared the same boundaries with identity space, the extended turf that claimed citizens' loyalties".[19] Thus caught up in what has become known as methodological nationalism,[20] post-war historiography continued the historiographical traditions of the late nineteenth century. For a long time it positively sidelined more constructivist approaches that perceived national entities only as quasi-erratic consequences of the territorialization of political or economic power or as only one possible construction of social or cultural affiliations.

Only in the wake of the extensive debates on the nature of globalization processes initiated in the social sciences since the beginning of the 1970s did historians eventually begin to take an interest in all kinds of entanglements and flows that transgress national boundaries. As a consequence, various methodological and analytical approaches for the study of this subject matter have been developed in recent years.[21] Interestingly, the wish to overcome the constraints of national histories seems to unite historians from right across the discipline regardless of their regional or subject specializations. Some observers even point out that one strength of current historical research on globalization processes and global entanglements can be found in its very openness and the refusal to put forward fixed definitions of its central terms and concepts at such an early point in time.[22] This works in favour of an ongoing experimental phase that aims at exploring the suitability of new topics and perspectives. Consequently, global history is a field

[18] O'Rourke and Williamson 2000; O'Brien 1997; Pomeranz and Topik 2006.

[19] Maier 2006, p. 35.

[20] Chernilo 2007; Marjanen 2009; Wimmer and Glick Schiller 2002.

[21] To name but a few examples: Hopkins 2006; Manning 2003; Vries 2009; Hughes-Warrington 2005.

[22] Hadler and Middell 2010, p. 23f.

of research on the move. But while it is still open for discussion about historiographical precursors, subjects, periodization or methods,[23] unity prevails as regards one central aspect: research on subjects with a global reach usually builds on the shared notion that the modern world has been shaped by connections and interactions that did not only cross long distances but also cultural borders in a way that cannot be grasped within the bi- or multilateral models that conventional histories on political or economic developments propose.[24] This shared focus on global connections and interactions forms the core of the field and holds it together. None the less, different approaches within this common framework have already started to emerge. Even though individual strains such as entangled history,[25] cultural encounters,[26] transcultural history,[27] transnational history[28] or the concept of translocality[29] tend to differ mainly in the weighting of individual aspects of global history, their existence is testimony to the rapidly growing sophistication of the field. For instance, while transcultural history emphasizes the transgression of cultural and social boundaries and highlights regimes of circulation, studies on translocality strongly emphasize the detachment of culture from a politically circumscribed space in favour of a new set of socio-cultural connections emerging within the spatial frame of reference set up by mobile historical actors.[30]

Still, there is a strong common ground these concepts share, namely the objective to transcend the national as an analytical category and to replace it by focusing on interaction and flows, transfers and exchanges as the core categories in the study of history. Examining the shifting patterns of global connections – established and transformed by the movement and exchange of people, goods and information – has, therefore, become the main challenge for all those who seek to understand the past, the present and the future of modern societies. And this challenge includes finding a place for the nation state – a form of social organization that does not seem to fit into the new analytical framework any more despite its obvious historical and current significance.

[23] Bentley 2003; O'Brien 2006; Middell 2005; Osterhammel 2008.

[24] See for example McNeill and McNeill 2003. See also Patrick Manning's definition of world history: "To put it simple, world history is the story of connections within the global human community", in: Manning 2003, p. 3.

[25] Gruzinski 1999; Lepenies 2003; Randeria 2002.

[26] Bentley and Ziegler 2000.

[27] Herren et al. 2012 (forthcoming); Bose and Manjapra 2010.

[28] Iriye and Saunier 2009; Patel 2009; Tyrrell 2007.

[29] Freitag and von Oppen 2010.

[30] Ibid.; Herren et al. 2012 (forthcoming).

## Bringing the State Back In: Actors and Their Networks

Noticing that constant flows of people, goods and information beyond national borders render the nation state much more porous than state-centred approaches in historiography and the social sciences have long suggested, some researchers felt this permitted them to speak of the decline and even the vanishing of the nation state.[31,32] Against these assumptions, the authors assembled in this volume suggest another reading of the role and significance of the nation state in the development of the modern world. As soon as we accept space not as a prerequisite but consider it as a very particular product of cross-bordering entanglements and connections, the nation state does not disappear but becomes one – sometimes more, sometimes less powerful – possible way of organizing social, political, economic and cultural relations in space. Accordingly, it is not the nation state that ceases to exist owing to increasing processes of global exchange but a certain perspective on the nation state which can no longer be upheld. The studies presented here argue that looking at the nation state from the perspective of global entanglements gives way to its interpretation as a dynamic and multi-layered structure that partakes in globalization processes and plays different and at times even contradictory roles at the same time. On the one hand, states have a leading part to play as they design national and international strategies, rules and policy measures with transregional scope in order to deal with global movements of people, goods and information across their national territory; on the other hand, governmental authorities depend on the delegation of competence by means of international agreements. Supreme state authority over its actors involved in globalization processes has become weakened by technical innovations (*E. Thomas Ewing* in this volume), processes of standardization (*Norman Weiß*), the emergence of multinational corporations and supranational institutions (*Simone Müller-Pohl* and *Guido Thiemeyer*) or the constant global flows of both money (*Madeleine Herren*) and knowledge (*Heather Ellis, Klaus Dittrich, James Casteel*).[33] Consequently, the nation state now appears as an analytical framework that opens up a variety of different perspectives on the question of how private and state actors have tried to manage the complicated and often opaque interdependence of regional, national, transnational and global spaces.[34] Vice versa, however, we can analyze the several roles the nation state has played in globalization processes: the nation state as a means to control the political, social, economic and cultural life of a certain territory (*Tomoko Akami, James Casteel, Thies Schulze*), as an instrument to enable or prevent global flows by

---

[31] The phrase has been borrowed from Evans et al. 1985.

[32] Hardt and Negri 2000; Zürn 2005.

[33] Geyer and Paulmann 2001; Löhr 2010; Murphy and Yates 2009.

[34] See also Brenner 1999; Middell and Naumann 2010.

opening or closing national borders (*Guido Thiemeyer*, *Norman Weiß*, *Simone Müller-Pohl*, *Klaus Dittrich*), or as a certain spatial pattern that is influenced by and at the same time has to compete and to come to terms with alternative spatial frames of reference (*Madeleine Herren*, *E. Thomas Ewing*, *Heather Ellis*). Lastly, as far as the contemporaneous perception of imperialists goes, the concept of the nation state stood at the heart of every empire. Imperialist policies, therefore, always need to be seen as being nationalist at the same time and cannot be understood without taking the notion of the state very seriously (*E. Thomas Ewing*, *Tomoko Akami*, *James Casteel*).

As soon as we characterize processes of global integration by the simultaneity of the dissolution of clear spatial hierarchies and reverse developments to extend national, imperial or colonial regimes of power, conflicting ideas of how state and non-state actors are to regulate and control globalization processes come to the fore. But how can we integrate state and non-state actors in such an analytical framework without ignoring their very different access to power, resources and competences? The seeming contradiction of emphasizing the important role of both states as well as transnational groups in the governing of globalization processes can be overcome by putting the historical actors back into the focus of our research. Every single one of these actors maintained a host of affiliations with other people. The pattern of these affiliations reflects the social and personal position of the actor just as it mirrors his or her private and professional requirements (as *Heather Ellis* shows regarding British-German academic relations). The social networks that arise from such patterns of affiliations can, accordingly, look very different. They can largely stay within the territorial (or sovereign) boundaries of a state or they can transgress these boundaries (as *Thies Schulze* argues with regard to the Roman Catholic Church). In the case of historical actors of globalization, often both situations can be seen: coming back to the above definition of globalization, one could say that parts of these actors' networks have already lost any correlation with geographical (or, in this case, national) proximity, while other parts have not. Every so often, actors of globalization in the nineteenth and twentieth centuries will – through their networks – maintain close ties with national as well as transnational groups. It is important to see that this relationship works both ways. On the one hand, it is, of course, useful to be well-connected in both national and transnational regard (as *Klaus Dittrich* emphasizes for the case of the French education expert Ferdinand Buisson). On the other, however, membership in such groups also entails adherence to certain rules and the acceptance of particular forms of sovereignty. Thus, states – which thrive on networks just as non-state organizations do – as well as transnational groups of actors gain a degree of power over their members. This can lead to the emergence of a very particular ethos of transnational professional elites beyond political or national loyalty (as *Simone Müller-Pohl* shows for the case of a transnational cable community). Therefore, the capability of states and non-states to govern and control processes of globalization crystallize in the historical actors and their myriad parallel affiliations. Accordingly, it is they who should stand at the core of our investigations.

## Governing Globalization Processes

This volume sets out from the assumption that the intensification of various kinds of relationships on a global scale shaped the development and perception of modern society to a considerable extent. Because of the increasing density of social, economic, cultural and political interactions across national borders since the nineteenth century, many people living at the time did not necessarily perceive the nation state as their main point of reference. Rather, alternative spatial frames of reference were set up – economic, social, cultural, political or legal ones. These rival spatial orders crossed national boundaries on a regional, transnational or supranational level and became numerous and significant enough to have a formative influence on actors in realms such as culture, society or economics. By examining the emergence of a first set of formal and informal rules, norms and standards during the nineteenth and early twentieth century, the authors in this volume explore the processes of negotiation between private interest groups, the public and the state in (and between) different world regions. In doing so, they pay explicit attention to the double role of the nation state as one principal actor behind newly emerging regulatory regimes and, at the same time, as the subject of technical, cultural, social and economic flows above and beyond political boundaries. The contributions in this volume all conceptualize globalization instead as an analytical perspective that guides historical research on a global past and acknowledges the mostly dialectic interplay between conflicting interests of state, non-state or imperial groups of actors.

The contributions assembled in this volume explore four different aspects of the interplay of national and transnational actors: economies, technologies, education and borders. Looking from such different angles, the authors use their case studies as magnifying-glasses on globalization. The chapters are intended to jettison the vague application of this term in favour of a clear-cut empirical analysis of the phenomena subsumed under the idea of global integration and fragmentation. They offer a precise description of the composition, aims and interests of the acting groups, of their affiliations, their networks and of their social, political or professional requirements. These shaped the way in which historical actors reacted to the opportunity (or the necessity) to expand their scope of action beyond the political and socio-cultural borders of the nation state. The selection of topics mirrors some of the core fields of actions that have driven the dynamics of global entanglements forward since the middle of the nineteenth century: the integration of global markets and the setting-up of supranational institutions because of a regularized and standardized flow of money across national and institutional borders; the acceleration of communication with other world regions with all its consequences for the social, cultural and economic life of national societies and the concomitant need to create international standards in the fields of communication, transport, trade and rights; education as one of the prominent examples for the development of international expert elites caught between their responsibilities to the nation and to an international community; and the inexhaustible topic of borders and border regions that testifies to the impossibility of describing the modern world in terms of clearly definable territorial units. Highlighting both the contradictions and the similarities in the phenomena under investigation, the chapters manage to apply globalization as both an analytical concept and a valuable approach that allows a precise and thorough analysis of processes of exchange and entanglement in the late nineteenth and early twentieth centuries.

*Guido Thiemeyer* and *Madeleine Herren* open the discussion by looking at the strategies and consequences which emerged in the course of the increasing dependence of financial markets and the creation of international organisations to solve these practical challenges. Both authors critically question the nineteenth-century master narrative that describes states as self-enclosed entities, concentrated exclusively on territorial expansion and the creation of a national infrastructure within their own territory. Rather than agreeing with interpretations of international relations as being characterized exclusively by national rivalry and trials of strength, both authors suggest a much more complex reading of the relationship between state(–formation), global entanglements and national rivalry during the nineteenth and the first half of the twentieth century. By introducing states as complex structures that used dependence on international organisations to follow their own interests, they scrutinize national sovereignty as a key category in nineteenth- and twentieth-century historiography. On the one side, the authors view governmental authorities as independent agents who were quite aware of the dependence of their economies on international organizations and networks dealing with economic questions. On the other side, however, they direct our attention to the subversive power of international institutions and networks to influence national policies and to de-territorialize the conjured political order of national entities.

*Guido Thiemeyer* examines the efforts to coordinate European monetary policy within the framework of the Latin Monetary Union – a specialized international organization founded in the 1860s and based on bimetallism, a monetary standard that relates currency value both to a certain quantity of gold and silver coins with fixed rates of exchange and to the French Franc as pivotal currency. Taking a close look at the driving forces behind monetary integration, the chapter embeds economic internationalism in an open analytical framework that widens its perspective beyond an exclusive focus on market forces. By including the political and cultural motives of state delegates, diplomats and the economic elites, *Thiemeyer* draws a differentiated picture. Of course, industrialization, the emergence of global markets and the liberalization of trade triggered international cooperation in this field. To this end, the Latin Monetary Union served as a means to facilitate economic interaction and to make the development of transnational markets more predictable. But at the same time, the Union turned out to be a double-edged sword: on the one hand, it became an instrument of French foreign policy to extend its power to set economic standards and, thus, to increase its claim to political and economic leadership within continental Europe; on the other, however, the Union substantially increased economic and political interdependences between the involved states and, thus, eventually led to a certain loss of state sovereignty that in some cases may even have limited national decision-making powers to a considerable extent. Still, *Thiemeyer* shows that despite these delicate side-effects, economic internationalism was deeply rooted in shared global visions such as, for instance, bourgeois liberalism and its notions of civilization, freedom and progress as common objectives of state and non-state elites for the future development of European societies.

The article by *Madeleine Herren* reverses this perspective: whereas *Thiemeyer* approaches international monetary cooperation from the perspective of the states in question, *Herren* understands the global as a genuinely independent space full of tensions and contradictions that can only be adequately investigated through a close analysis of the numerous, not necessarily coherent cross-border entanglements and agencies of state and private actors. Her chapter, therefore, focuses on international networks and organizations and their particular agency to challenge national master narratives during the first half of the twentieth century. In order not to fall back upon notions that construe the international realm as the sum of national histories and inter-national cooperation, *Herren* introduces a transcultural approach, which concentrates on the driving forces of the transgression of social, cultural and ruling orders. This emphasis on the often informal and not immediately discernible border-crossing agencies directs our attention towards the instability and volatility of global entanglements in comparison to the institutionalized and historically well-consolidated appearance of the national. But, as the chapter shows, it is even more complicated: on the one hand, global entanglement constitutes a phenomenon in its own right and consequently historians have to develop an analytical toolbox that is capable of explaining globalization forces and grasping the dialectic dynamic of global integration and fragmentation so as to comprehend the global profile and the very specific scope of action that border-crossing agencies develop in distinct historical contexts; on the other hand, the way in which international organizations operate illustrates that the nation state remains one of the key elements in processes of global exchange and interaction. The example of the international transfer of money and the role of the Bank for International Settlements therein shows us that border-crossing entanglements definitely followed a political rationale of their own. But translating this rationale into practice makes them dependent on the consent (or at least passive support) of actors and institutions on a national scale that control large parts of the economic and political infrastructure. Therefore, as *Herren* argues, historians of a global past face the task of making a critical analysis of historical phenomena which seemingly do not fit into established narratives of either nationalization or globalization.

Taking telecommunication as the starting point, the section on technologies presents the technological backgrounds of the swift increase in international agreements and organizations since the 1860s. The telegraph, as a new communication technology invented in the middle of the nineteenth century, provides an insightful example for the disintegrating and at the same time integrating effects of what Michael Geyer and Charles Bright called the "global age". The telegraph made intensified interaction over great distances possible and, thus, induced people at the time to examine closely how to handle the potentials, limits and risks associated with the restructuring of global communication. Whilst *Norman Weiß* sheds light on the motives of sovereign states to develop standard-setting procedures and to create an institution with its own powers and competencies, *E. Thomas Ewing* and *Simone Müller-Pohl* focus on private actors and their networks: they introduce us to the complexities and often unintended consequences that new technological tools could entail for states, colonial administrations and professionals in the nineteenth century. As an example, a study of telegraphy highlights both the struggles of state and imperial authorities to regain control over communication flows across their territory as well as the emergence of new acting groups and their competing claims to appropriate the new technologies as a powerful instrument for turning existing territorial orders and socio-political relationships upside down.

*Norman Weiß* discusses the International Telegraph Union (ITU) as an excellent example of technical cooperation being institutionalized in an international organization that eventually formed a force of global integration on its own and led to the development of 'global governance *avant la lettre*'. *Weiß* points us to the evolution of distinct institutions of technical cooperation during the nineteenth century, starting with the international regimes controlling the Rhine and the Danube. The ITU serves as an example of the subsequent foundation of numerous international administrative unions. Triggered by the emergence of new transport and telecommunication technologies, they mirrored the pragmatically facilitated cross-border interaction by providing a framework of rules not only governing transnational trade but also minimizing transaction costs and spurring commercial-industrial, cultural and social activities between states and regions. The chapter argues, however, that the ITU gathered a momentum of its own as soon as standard-setting procedures and intergovernmental bargaining processes were officially institutionalized and the international bureau of the ITU received its own competences. *Weiß* demonstrates that the ITU regulated global flows of information and goods and thus transformed social and political relations to a considerable extent: it contributed to a weakening of state authorities and gradually reached a higher level of integration between governmental interests. Consequently, international organizations became central authorities to govern technical, economic and social entanglements and to mediate conflicts between state and non-state agents.

With a regional focus on the Middle East, *E. Thomas Ewing* leads us out of the European state system into the colonial periphery and thus into the sites of contested sovereignty and power struggles. He discusses the telegraph as an instrument that brought Europe and Asia closer together and, thereby, also caused conflicts over the political side-effects of the new technology in respect to the shifting balance of power in the Ottoman Empire, Persia and Egypt. The case of telegraphy reminds us of the potential ambiguity of globalization processes. The telegraph detached flows of information from material carriage and ended the correlation between communication times and geographical distance. It was, therefore, a principal tool of globalization. At the same time, however, it became a crucial tool in local and regional conflicts over the extension and limits of colonial rule; indeed, it accelerated these conflicts. Telegraph wires became tangible symbols of imperial power (the case of Egypt), anti-colonial resistance or nationalization processes (the Persian and the Ottoman cases). The local presence, visibility and, at times, vulnerability of an inherently global technology contributed to the regionalization of globalization processes which then fitted in with specific historical path dependencies serving processes of global integration and fragmentation all at the same time.

Analyzing the same technology for the same period but in the different regional setting of the Atlantic world, *Simone Müller-Pohl* illustrates once more that globalization processes do not necessarily entail the homogenization of the world. Rather, the same technological invention can lend itself to very different processes of the social and economic reformation of modern societies. Directing our attention towards the relatively small group of cable agents and their border-crossing engagements since the 1850s, *Müller-Pohl* explores the complex relationship between nation states, cable professionals acting on a transnational scale and a new communication technology with a global reach. This relationship eludes comprehension when explained only in the framework of national interests. In place of this, the chapter conceptualizes the cable professionals as global players beyond the nation state who primarily served their own interests while constantly lobbying the British and other national decision-makers in order to maintain a favourable environment for their business interests. Seen through the eyes of the cable agents, the involved states turned into agents themselves within the system of international ocean telegraphy and had to position themselves strategically in relation to the cable agents' capability to act on the national, transnational and global scale at the same time. Consequently, *Müller-Pohl* interprets their turn to nationalism after the 1880s more as a strategic decision expressing their perception of the state as a useful tool to work with to the advantage of their business interests.

The section on education takes up the thread of actors and their networks. Unlike the preceding sections, which elaborate on both the benefits and problems of the internationalization of common technological or economic needs and on the relationship between private and governmental actors, these two chapters ask how groups of actors caught in between the complex interdependence of regional, national and transnational spaces on the one side, and social, cultural and professional scales on the other, managed to negotiate these seemingly different domains. By analyzing professional and elite networks of education experts at the end of the nineteenth century, *Heather Ellis* and *Klaus Dittrich* make us aware of the important role that social and cultural path dependencies played as soon as professional elites, with their centuries-old traditions of network-building, self-perception and mechanisms of inclusion and exclusion, had to cope with conflicting demands: to participate in international gatherings and to perform within the framework of a transnational professional ethos with a rich tradition, to influence the border-crossing flow of information, to start international cooperation under the auspices of governmental authorities and to perceive themselves as national citizens who act for the benefit of their nation state. Consequently, *Heather Ellis* and *Klaus Dittrich* further explore the tensions which arose from the simultaneity of global integration and national fragmentation in particular during the late nineteenth century. Both chapters discuss the way national elites engaged in international and transnational cooperation and how they made sense of their missions within the framework of the "global age". By highlighting the multiple patterns of professional and personal affiliations of educational experts and university staff they expose complex world views that did not necessarily perceive the identification with national interests and policy goals on the one hand and the sense of belonging to a transnational elite on the other as being mutually exclusive. Both articles produce convincing evidence of the historical agents' awareness that they were part of multiple regimes of power, control, regulation and cooperation and of their ability to act on several spatial levels at the same time.

In her investigation of British-German academic networks in the nineteenth century, *Heather Ellis* applies the idea of a genuinely transnational space to a subject that has so far been analyzed predominantly through the lens of national history. Instead of seeing the modern university as a prototypical by-product of nationalization processes since the nineteenth century, *Ellis* suggests to overcome, at least in this particular field, the master narrative of national British-German rivalry in favour of another trajectory, namely the early modern 'republic of letters' paradigm – academic networks and scholarly connections between individual academics, students and institutions beyond the national. Taking these networks as a distinct unit of study, the chapter finds a transnational space of scholarly exchange. By emphasizing concrete agents and their interests, *Ellis* sketches a certain academic space of interaction that refutes the popular assumption of scholarly exchange and interaction predominantly taking place within the limits of a territorially defined political order. Instead, the chapter highlights the importance of notions such as social prestige and intellectual reputation, the influence of personal contacts and the preserving powers of already existing traditions of scholarly exchange in this regard. Unlike many existing studies on cultural transfers between Great Britain and Germany, this perspective highlights the particular importance of the actors' mental maps. Assuming that the national and the transnational contexts collapse in the actors themselves and their numerous affiliations, the chapter negotiates the obstacles of methodological nationalism. However, *Ellis* does not argue in favour of a total neglect of the impact of national interests and politics on higher education. More precisely, she interprets British and German attempts to nationalize higher education since the late nineteenth century as a political response by governmental circles to growing cross-border contact between higher-education institutions and to the inherent dynamism in higher education to weaken the concept of the university as a national or imperial institution.

Digging into the multi-faceted meaning of world exhibitions, *Klaus Dittrich* argues in a similar vein by presenting us with a striking example of how a host of different affiliations could be united within one professional biography. His actor-centred perspective on the French education expert Ferdinand Buisson highlights the seemingly effortless ways in which expert elites both represented national interests and at the same time envisioned and endorsed international cooperation. By referring to three different conceptual frameworks – cultural transfers, imperial societies and governmental internationalism – *Dittrich* identifies three motives behind Buisson's active support of and participation in the educational sections of several world exhibitions: to learn for his own institutions, to represent French achievements on the international scene and to promote educational internationalism as the essential counterpart to the advancement of the national education system. *Dittrich* interprets the world exhibitions as a prototypical manifestation of what Jacques Revel called the *jeux d'échelles*[35]: they are events where national, transnational and global spaces collapse and where the actors, analogously, carry out an ambiguous performance that makes it impossible to classify them as belonging exclusively to one spatial framework. Rather, these actors constitute an elite with both national affiliations and global reach that actively advanced globalization processes by reconciling them with national interests.

The final section ultimately leads us back to our starting point: the global horizon of the nation state as it is reflected in a plurality of competing spaces that organize the social, cultural, economic and political life of modern societies on different scales and each time with different scopes of action. The three contributions in this section approach the plurality of spaces from their point of intersection: borders are closely linked to competing regimes of territoriality and they are constructed and described in line with the prevailing discourses on the benefits and costs of border-crossing interaction. Taking Japan, Siberia, Germany and border regions in South Tyrol and Alsace-Lorraine as examples, *Tomoko Akami*, *James Casteel* and *Thies Schulze* give plenty of empirical evidence for the main hypothesis of this volume that the integrative dynamic of exchange and interdependence brings the historical agents closer together even over long distances while at the same time people perceive the need to distance themselves from other social units and in consequence constantly renew differences on a national and regional scale. The three chapters reflect this multi-layered process on three different levels. While *Tomoko Akami* interprets the gradual transformation of Japan into a formal empire as a distinct strategy to manage and control the global condition of East Asia in the interwar years, *James Casteel* examines a sort of imagined imperialism. Digging into the imperial ambitions of German experts to influence social and economic orders in Siberia and thus beyond their own territory, he illuminates their mental maps of the global and their perception of threats, critical junctures and potentials which accompany economic dependence on other parts of the world. *Thies Schulze* inverts the perspective and explores the dependence of regional politics on international rivalry by looking at the tensions which emerged in the course of the reordering of the political map in the aftermath of the Great War.

*Tomoko Akami* looks at the role imperial ambitions played in the process of governing global entanglements and globalization processes. In her contribution, Japan serves as a case study for a critical assessment of the relationship between nation states and empires. The observation that powerful modern nation states in many cases also stood at the centre of empires leads *Akami* to perceive nation states and empires as one analytical unit. A close investigation of how globalization processes were managed, enhanced or slowed down must also consider empires

[35] Revel 1996.

as distinct structures for governing transnational issues by extending the political sphere of influence beyond the national territory. In this perspective, the chapter introduces asymmetrical political and economic power relations as a main feature of the critical investigation of processes of global integration and fragmentation. However, *Akami* detects such asymmetries not primarily in the colonized territories, but rather directs our attention towards the ways imperial structures can influence the development of governance structures within imperial societies. The chapter argues that colonial patterns very much influenced ideas and institutions of the governance of global flows within the (former) colonial metropolis. Using Meiji Japan as her example, *Akami* tracks the close interrelations between the rhetoric of state sovereignty and the gradual establishment of formal colonies as Japan's main strategy to secure its sovereignty from other empire's advances. Looking at the interwar years, the chapter challenges the narrative which interprets Japan's aggression in Manchuria at the beginning of the 1930s as a dialectic between nationalism and internationalism or Japan's withdrawal from the League of Nations as the beginning of international isolationism. Rather, seeing imperial expansion and national isolation as two sides of the same coin, the chapter interprets the Japanese case as paradigmatic for a fundamental shift in the way global issues were managed.

Following this, *James Casteel* discusses the consequences of economic globalization processes on the imperial ambitions of national actors in pre-war Germany. The chapter contextualizes a group of German social scientists' and economists' idea of imperial expansion in broader trends of global economic integration at the turn of the nineteenth century. It provides a good example of how global integration, national imaginations and imperial empowerment went hand in hand. *Casteel* argues that the German observers' fantasies of how to develop Siberia economically and how they might extend control over the territory, were it to fall into their possession, can only be understood properly when considering the consequences of the development of global markets on power relations and on the self-perception of the involved agents. Attempts to assert national sovereignty and Germany's rapidly changing status as expanding industrial power were irrevocably rooted in an increasingly competitive and globally connected world. Observers of the time were quite aware that global flows of goods and the concomitant transnational interdependencies fundamentally changed the relationship between territories and peoples – a transformation that could potentially undermine national loyalty. While it was important, on the one hand, to exploit new markets to keep the economy running, *Casteel* argues that on the other hand the German observers were critically aware of the economic dependence on Russia that this could lead to. In this context, their attitude towards the Russian empire mirrored perfectly the dialectical tension, inherent in the global horizon of the nation, that found expression in welcoming but at the same time inspecting with scepticism Germany's political and economic entanglement in the wider world. The Russian empire remained in a highly ambiguous position as both an object of European economic domination and an ally in a broader European civilizing mission in Asia.

The closing chapter by *Thies Schulze* follows a twofold aim: it presents struggles over regional hegemony as a consequence of the political reordering of global space and introduces a new actor who has hitherto been mostly overlooked in discussions about the interrelatedness and tensions of national, transnational and global strategies for governing globalization processes. With the Roman Catholic Church *Schulze* introduces an agent of universal nature which is normally perceived as a genuinely global player in terms of its global presence as well as its religious and moral orientation that is accompanied – at least nominally – by a neutral status towards political issues and clashes of interest. In challenging this perception, *Schulze* directs our attention towards the Church's inner structures and describes the Catholic Church as a multifaceted organization composed of a wide range of different, more or less formalized personal networks anchored in different spatial contexts and different networks of social affiliations to regional or national authorities. In this way, the Catholic Church can be interpreted as a dynamic organization, simultaneously entangled on the regional, the national and the global level. Depending on the distinct historical contexts and compositions of the respective networks under scrutiny, the Catholic Church contributed to processes of regionalization, nationalization and global convergence. For the interwar years, *Schulze* discusses two case studies where the Catholic Church was involved in struggles over national hegemony and regional autonomy in border regions. The conflict over the language used for religious instruction in primary schools in South Tyrol and the protest movement in Alsace-Lorraine at the beginning of the 1920s against the change from denominational to interdenominational schools gives evidence that the Catholic Church could not avoid getting involved in serious struggles over national minority rights and considerably shaped these conflicts by advocating its own causes. The chapter employs the nation state as an analytical framework that opens up a variety of different perspectives on how state and non-state actors tried to manage the complicated connections and dependencies between the regional, the national and the transnational space.

What do we learn from all these case studies? First of all, the historical studies presented challenge our conception of nineteenth- and twentieth-century history. They invite us to question the methodological assumptions modern historiography is based upon. The case studies provide plenty of empirical evidence that highlights how misleading it is to style globalization as having a clear place in a clear historical sequence – a sequence that starts with the predominance of the national during the nineteenth century, followed by its gradual collapse during the World Wars and ends with the increasing interdependence of world regions, societies and social sub-systems in the post-war period. Instead of this, the articles assembled in this volume argue in manifold ways that the development of global orders and the increasing interdependence of state and private actors heavily depended on national and imperial entities which favoured technological innovations, the creation of governance structures, the development of transnational experts and professionals and a broad sector of private and governmental cooperation. Once more, the chapters underline Michael Geyer and Charles Bright's conception of the nineteenth century as a "global age", which we fail to understand when concentrating exclusively on state and state formation. The same is true for the formative impact of international institutions on the governing of border-crossing flows of goods, money and information in the post-war period. These developments can only be contextualized sufficiently when taking into consideration the institutional structures for international cooperation set out by these early international organizations and agreements.

The focus on the historical actors and their manifold and sometimes seemingly contradicting affiliations should lead us to make further and more thorough enquiries about how globalization processes were perceived by those who were witness to them at the time: why do we still continue to highlight nationalization processes as the core development of the nineteenth century when at the same time there is plenty of evidence that the historical actors knowingly navigated through a much more complicated world? Or do these findings mirror primarily the world-views of elite networks rather than those of ordinary people? The chapters in this volume make it strikingly clear that our historiographical thinking and writing is still very much impressed by the power that both the nation state and nationalism could, at times, wield, culminating in the two World Wars of the twentieth century. As justified as the persistence of such a framework might be, historical research should be absolutely aware, when dealing with conceptions of the past, of both the role and consequences of policies of remembrance and cultural commemoration.

## Bibliography


Anghel, Remus Gabriel, et al. eds. 2008. *The Making of World Society. Perspectives From Transnational Research*. Bielefeld: Transcript Verlag.

Bayly, Christopher A. 2004. *The Birth of the Modern World, 1780–1914. Global Connections and Comparisons*. Maiden, MA: Blackwell Publishing.

Bentley, Jerry H. & Herbert F. Ziegler. 2000. *Traditions and Encounters: A Global Perspective on the Past*. Boston: McGRaw Hill.

Bentley, Jerry H. 2003. "World History and Grand Narrative." In *Writing World History 1800–2000 (Studies of the German Historical Institute London)*, edited by Benedict Stuchtey and Eckhardt Fuchs, 47–65. London: Oxford University Press.

Bose, Sugata and Kris Manjapra, eds. 2010. *Cosmopolitan Thought Zones: South Asia and the Global Circulation of Ideas*. New York: Plagrave Macmillan.

Brenner, Neil. 1999. "Beyond State-Centrism? Space, Territoriality, and Geographical Scale in Globalization Studies." *Theory and Society* 28, 39–78.

Buschauer, Regine. 2010. *Mobile Räume: Medien- und diskursgeschichtliche Studien zur Tele-Kommunikation*. Bielefeld: Transcript.

Chernilo, Daniel. 2007. *A Social Theory of the Nation-State. The Political Forms of Modernity Beyond Methodological Nationalism*. London: Routledge.

Conrad, Sebastian and Andreas Eckert. 2007. "Globalgeschichte, Globalisierung, multiple Modernen: Zur Geschichtsschreibung der modernen Welt." In *Globalgeschichte. Theorien, Ansätze, Themen*, edited by Sebastian Conrad et al. Frankfurt am Main: Campus Verlag.

Cooper, Frederick. 2001. "What is the Concept of Globalization Good for? An African Historian's Perspective." *African Affairs* 100, 189–213.

Clark, Ian. 1997. *Globalization and Fragmentation. International Relations in the Twentieth Century*. Oxford: Oxford University Press.

Darwin, John. 2008. *After Tamerlane. The Global History of Empire*. London: Penguin Books.
Döring, Jörg and Tristan Thielmann, eds. 2008. *Spatial Turn. Das Raumparadigma in den Kultur- und Sozialwissenschaften*. Bielefeld: Transcript.
Evans, Peter B. et al. eds. 1985. *Bringing the State Back In*. Cambridge: Cambridge University Press.
Fernandéz-Armesto, Felipe. 2007. *Pathfinders. A Global History of Exploration*. Oxford: Oxford University Press.
Freitag, Ulrike & Achim von Oppen. 2010. "'Translocality': An Approach to Connection and Transfer in Area Studies." In: *Translocality. The Study of Globalising Processes From a Southern Perspective*, edited by Ulrike Freitag, 1–24. Leiden: Brill.
Geyer, Michael H. and Charles Bright. 1995. "World History in a Global Age." *American Historical Review* 97, 1034–1060.
Geyer, Michael H. and Johannes Paulmann, eds. 2001. *The Mechanics of Internationalism. Culture, Society, and Politics from the 1840 s to the First World War*. Oxford: Oxford University Press.
Giddens, Anthony. 1981. *A Contemporary Critique of Historical Materialism. Volume 1: Power, Property and the State*. London: Macmillan.
Giddens, Anthony. 1984. *The Constitution of Society*. Cambridge: Polity Press.
Gruzinski, Serge. 1999. *La pensée métissage*, Paris: Fayard.
Gunn, Geoffrey C. 2003. *First Globalisation. The Eurasian Exchange, 1500–1800*. Lanham: Rowman & Littlefield.
Hadler, Frank and Matthias Middell. 2010. "Auf dem Weg zu einer transnationalen Geschichte Ostmitteleuropas." *Comparativ. Zeitschrift für Globalgeschichte und vergleichende Gesellschaftsforschung* 20 (1/2): 8–29. Leipzig: Leipziger Universitätsverlag.
Hardt, Michael and Antonio Negri. 2000. *Empire*, Cambridge, MA: Harvard University Press.
Harvey, David. 1990. "Between Space and Time: Reflections on the Geographical Imagination." *Annals of the Association of American Geographers* 80 (3): 418–434.
Harvey, David. 2006. "Space as a Keyword," In *David Harvey: A Critical Reader*, edited by Noel Castree and Derel Gregory, 270–293. Oxford: Blackwell.
Herren, Madeleine, et al. Forthcoming. *Transcultural History. Theories, Methods, Sources*. Heidelberg: Springer.
Holton, Robert J. 2005. *Making Globalization*. New York: Palgrave Macmillan.
Hopkins, Anthony G. 2002. "The History of Globalization – and the Globalization of History." *Globalization in World History*, 11–46. London: Pimlico.
Hopkins, Anthony G., ed. 2006. *Global History. Interactions Between the Universal and the Local*. New York: Palgrave Macmillan.
Hughes-Warrington, Marnie, ed. 2005. *Palgrave Advances in World Histories*, Basingstoke: Palgrave Macmillan.
Iggers, Georg G. and Q. Edward Wang. 2008. *A Global History of Modern Historiography*. Harlow: Pearson Longman.
Iriye, Akira and Pierre-Yves Saunier, eds. 2009. *The Palgrave Dictionary of Transnational History*. Basingstoke: Palgrave Macmillan.
Janelle, Donald G. 1969. "Spatial Reorganization. A Model and Concept." *Annals of the Association of American Geographers* 59, 348–364.
Krücken, Georg, ed. 2009. *World Society. The Writings of John W. Meyer*. Oxford: Oxford University Press.
Lechner, Frank J. 2009. *Globalization. The Making of World Society*. Malden, MA: Wiley-Blackwell.
Lepenies, Wolf. 2003. *Entangled Histories and Negotiated Universals. Centers and Peripheries in a Changing World*. Frankfurt am Main: Campus.
Löhr, Isabella. 2010. *Die Globalisierung geistiger Eigentumsrechte. Neue Strukturen internationaler Zusammenarbeit, 1886–1952*. Göttingen: Vandenhoeck & Ruprecht.

Maier, Charles. 2006. "Transformation of Territoriality, 1600–2000." In *Transnationale Geschichte. Themen, Tendenzen und Theorien*, edited by Gunilla Budde et al., 32–55. Göttingen: Vandenhoeck & Ruprecht.

Manning, Patrick. 2003. *Navigating World History. Historians Create a Global Past*. New York: Palgrave Macmillan.

Marjanen, Jani. 2009. "Undermining Methodological Nationalism. Histoire croisée of Concepts as Transnational History." In *Transnational Political Spaces. Agents – Structures – Encounters*, edited by Mathias Albert et al., 239–263. Frankfurt am Main: Campus.

McNeill, John R. and William H. McNeill. 2003. *The Human Web. A Bird's Eye View of World History*. New York: W.W. Norton.

Middell, Matthias. 2005. "Universalgeschichte, Weltgeschichte, Globalgeschichte, Geschichte der Globalisierung – ein Streit um Worte?." In *Globalisierung und Globalgeschichte*, edited by Margarete Grandner et al., 60–82. Vienna: Mandelbaum.

Middell, Matthias and Katja Naumann. 2010. "Global History and the Spatial Turn: From the Impact of Area Studies to the Study of Critical Junctures of Globalization." *Journal of Global History* 5, 149–170.

Murphy, Craig N. and JoAnne Yates. 2009. *The International Organization for Standardization (ISO): Global Governance Through Voluntary Consensus*. London: Routledge.

O'Brien, Patrick. 1997. "Intercontinental Trade and the Development of the Third World Since the Industrial Revolution." *Journal of World History* 8 (1) 75–133.

O'Brien, Patrick. 2006. "Historiographical Traditions and Modern Imperatives for the Restoration of Global History." *Journal of Global History* 1 (1) 3–39.

O'Rourke, Kevin and Jeffrey G. Williamson. 2000. *Globalization and History. The Evolution of a Nineteenth Century Atlantic Economy*. Cambridge, MA: MIT Press.

Osterhammel, Jürgen and Niels P. Petersso. 2005. *Globalization: A Short History*. Princeton, NJ: Princeton University Press.

Osterhammel, Jürgen. 2008. "Alte und neue Zugänge zur Weltgeschichte." *Weltgeschichte*, edited by Jürgen Osterhammel, 9–32. Stuttgart: Steiner.

Osterhammel, Jürgen. 2009. *Die Verwandlung der Welt. Eine Geschichte des 19. Jahrhunderts*. Munich: Beck.

Patel, Kiran Klaus. 2009. "'Transnations Among Transnations?' The Debate on Transnational History in the US and Germany." *American Studies* 53, 451–472.

Pomeranz, Kenneth and Steven Topik. 2006. *The World That Trade Created. Society, Culture, and the World Economy*. New York: M.E. Sharpe.

Randeria, Shalini. 2002. "Entangled Histories of Uneven Modernities: Civil Society, Caste Solidarities, and the Post-Colonial State in India." In *Unraveling Ties. From Social Cohesion to New Practices of Connectedness*, edited by Yehuda Elkana, 284–311. Frankfurt am Main: Campus Verlag.

Revel, Jacques, ed. 1996. *Jeux d'échelles: la micro-analyse à l'éxpérience*. Paris: Gallimard.

Risse-Kappen, Thomas, ed. 1995. *Bringing Transnational Relations Back in: Non-State Actors, Domestic Structures and International Institutions*. Cambridge: Cambridge University Press.

Sonnemann, Ulrich. 1990. "Die Ohnmacht des Raums und der uneingestandene Fehlschlag der Zeitentmachtung. Zur Aporetik des Staus." In *Zeit-Zeichen. Aufschübe und Interferenzen zwischen Endzeit und Echtzeit*, edited by Georg Christoph Tholen and Michael Scholl, 17–28. Weinheim: Bundesrepublik Deutschland: VCH, Acta Humaniora.

Stein, Jeremy. 2001. "Reflections on Time, Time-Space Compression and Technology in the Nineteenth Century." In *Timespace. Geographies of Temporality*, edited by Jon May and Nigel Thrift, 106–119. London: Routledge.

Subrahmanyam, Sanjay. 1997. "Connected Histories: Notes Towards a Reconfiguration of Early Modern Eurasia." *Asia Studies* 31, 735–762.

Tyrrell, Ian. 2007. *Transnational Nation. United States History in Global Perspective Since 1789*. New York: Palgrave MacMillan.

Vries, Peer, ed. 2009. *Global History, Österreichische Zeitschrift für Geschichtswissenschaft* 20 (2).

Warf, Barney and Santa Arias, eds. 2009. *The Spatial Turn: Interdisciplinary Perspectives*. London: Routledge.

Wendt, Reinhard. 2007. *Vom Kolonialismus zur Globalisierung. Europa und die Welt seit 1500*. Paderborn: Schöningh.

Wenzlhuemer, Roland. 2010. "Globalization, Communication and the Concept of Space in Global History." *Historical Social Research – Historische Sozialforschung. Global Communication: Telecommunication and Global Flows of Information in the Late 19th and Early 20th Century*, 19–51. Cologne: Zentrum für Historische Sozialforschung.

Wimmer, Andreas and Nina Glick Schiller. 2002. "Methodological Nationalism and Beyond: Nation-State Building, Migration and the Social Sciences." *Global Networks* 4 (2) 301–334.

Zürn, Michael. 2005. *Regieren jenseits des Nationalstaates. Globalisierung und Denationalisierung als Chance*. Frankfurt am Main: Suhrkamp.

# Part I
# Economies

# Chapter 2
# The "*Forces Profondes*" of Internationalism in the Late Nineteenth Century: Politics, Economy and Culture

**Guido Thiemeyer**

**Abstract** The decades before 1914 have often been described as the period of internationalism. This is the concept mainly used by historians to describe the internationalisation of economy and culture in the second half of the nineteenth century. This article will examine the driving forces behind internationalism by using the example of the Latin Monetary Union which was founded in 1865 through an international treaty between France, Belgium, Italy, and Switzerland and was the first international monetary union in history. The Latin Monetary Union is an important subject for the interrelatedness of the political sphere and the economic sector because it is an early example of governments trying to intervene into (monetary) markets and trying to shape them to their needs. This, however, met with serious obstacles. The Latin Monetary Union therefore illustrates the struggle between the political and economic sectors and their respective systems of governance. The driving forces behind international monetary internationalism will be analysed on three levels: they have a political, an economic, and a cultural dimension. On the political level the article will ask what are the intentions and motives of the principal actors in monetary internationalism. Who were the actors and what did they intend by promoting monetary union? How did they negotiate the balancing act between diplomacy and monetary policy? On the economic level I will enquire into the role of international markets for monetary integration. Was monetary integration—as economic theory argues—a result of dynamic transnational markets leading inevitably to a single international currency? And the third part will deal with cultural aspects of monetary internationalism. What were the cultural aspects of monetary internationalism?

G. Thiemeyer (✉)
Geography and History Department, University of Cergy-Pondoise, Cergy, France
e-mail: guido.thiemeyer@u-cergy.fr

I. Löhr and R. Wenzlhuemer (eds.), *The Nation State and Beyond*, Transcultural Research – Heidelberg Studies on Asia and Europe in a Global Context,
DOI 10.1007/978-3-642-32934-0_2, 

## Introduction

The decades before 1914 have often been described as the period of internationalism. This is the concept mainly used by historians to describe the internationalisation of economy and culture in the second half of the nineteenth century.[1] Political scientists instead tend to define it as the second phase of globalisation in an economic, cultural and social respect.[2] Internationalism, however, seems to be the more precise term because it was the contemporaneous notion as to describe the phenomenon whereas globalisation could lead to the misleading interpretation that the internationalisation in this period is more or less the same as globalisation is today. There is at least one important difference between the two: whereas historians have shown that internationalism before 1914 in the long run led to a strengthening of the nation state, most political scientists and economists agree that the nation state would be dissolved by globalisation.[3]

But even though the phenomenon of internationalism has been an important subject in historical research for a few years now, we do not know what it really means. We know, however, that internationalism is a broad phenomenon that developed certain specifications in different sectors. Political internationalism aimed at the foundation of political institutions and international organisations in a wider sense. Sometimes this led to the establishment of an international office with a staff of its own, in other cases institutions were set up only by an international treaty establishing common rules or standards. Economic internationalism was instead characterised through the transnational entanglement of markets for capital, products and – to a lesser extent at that time labour. Because of the improvement and development of infrastructure, markets more and more transcended political and cultural borders and in this way became international. Cultural internationalism can be characterised as the internationalisation of customs, habits and values. European nations but also the USA were convinced that their way of living was a model for other peoples in other parts of the world and to some extent this was accepted as an ideal of civilisation by other cultures.

This article will examine the driving forces behind internationalism by using the example of the Latin Monetary Union which was founded in 1865 through an international treaty between France, Belgium, Italy and Switzerland and was the first international monetary union in history.[4] This monetary Union was based on bimetallism, which means that the currencies of the member countries relied on

[1] Herren 2000; Geyer and Paulmann 2001; Osterhammel and Petersson 2003; on financial systems in particular Redish 2006; Thiemeyer 2009.

[2] Holton 2005, pp. 28–54.

[3] For the debate: Ambrosius 2009; Henrich-Franke et al. 2007, pp. 221–230.

[4] Esslen 1926; from an economic point of view: Zellfelder 1991; Ibid. 1995, pp. 213 f.; Willis 1901; van der Rest 1881, p. 5; Kleinmann 1892; Brossault, Eric 1903; Greul 1926; Niederer 1976; Ratcliffe, “Latin Monetary Union”; Bartel 1977; Bitar 1953; Herren 1999; in spite of plagiarism: Koch-Mehrin 2001; Einaudi 2001.

both gold and silver coins with an identical power to pay debts and conclude transactions, having a fixed legal price for gold in terms of silver of 1:15.5. Britain and the German Reich (from 1871) by contrast had officially adopted the monometallic gold standard which meant that silver was not legal tender for transactions. Prussia and most German states before 1870 had adopted the monometallic silver standard. The Latin Monetary Union is an important subject for the interrelatedness of the political sphere and the economic sector because it is an early example of governments trying to intervene into (monetary) markets and trying to shape them to their needs. This, however, met with serious obstacles. The Latin Monetary Union is therefore an important example of the struggle between the political and economic sectors and their respective systems of governance.

From a methodological point of view the model of driving forces in history can be traced back to the concept of the "*Forces Profondes*" developed by the French scholars Pierre Renouvin and Jean-Baptiste Duroselle.[5] In this context the "Forces Profondes" designated material and spiritual structures influencing and shaping human behaviour in history. According to Renouvin, history is influenced by long-term structures as for instance geographical preconditions, economic structures, mental activities and shared values which contribute to the framework of human life. We can therefore also speak of material and mental structures shaping human activity in a double sense. On the one hand, these structures initiate human activity, on the other, however, they can be restrictive to human action in the sense that individuals can only act within this framework of structures. The driving forces behind international monetary internationalism will be analysed on three levels: they have a political, an economic and a cultural dimension. On the political level the article will ask what are the intentions and motives of the principal actors in monetary internationalism. Who were the actors and what did they intend by promoting monetary union? How did the relationship stand between diplomacy and monetary policy? On the economic level I will enquire into the role of international markets for monetary integration. Was monetary integration – as economic theory argues – a result of dynamic transnational markets leading inevitably to a single international currency? And the third part will deal with cultural aspects of monetary internationalism. What were the cultural aspects of monetary internationalism?

## Economic Driving Forces of Monetary Internationalism

A monetary union is first of all an economic institution and as such economic structures and motives have played a major role in monetary internationalism. Whilst the treaty of the so-called Latin Monetary Union was signed in December 1865, monetary integration had actually begun earlier. When in 1832 Belgium was

[5] Renouvin 1954; Renouvin and Duroselle 1970, pp. 2 ff.; Thobie 1985; Soutou 2000.

founded as a new nation state, discussions opened concerning a monetary system. Should Belgium develop a new system on its own or would it be better to adopt one of the existing monetary systems?[6] In the end, the Belgian government decided to adopt the French monetary system, based on the French Franc, for several reasons: firstly, the French monetary system was based on the decimal system which was easy to handle in everyday life. Secondly, influential commercial interest groups in the south of the country pleaded for the French system because it would facilitate economic relations with northern France. This decision was even more remarkable from a political point of view; the French Government of Louis Philippe wanted to avoid any suspicion that the Belgian uprising against the Netherlands was supported by France and therefore avoided any political intervention. The Belgian decision in favour of the French Franc as national currency was therefore motivated by economic pragmatism; political or cultural reasons, the currency as a symbol of national sovereignty for instance, did not play any role.

The situation was quite similar in 1848, when Switzerland adopted the French system.[7] Since 1758 cantons like Berne, Solothurn, Basle and Lucerne had coined Francs and with the foundation of the 'République Helvétique' under Napoleon the French currency became legal tender. After the foundation of the Swiss Federation in 1848, discussion followed on the question of the monetary standard. While the eastern part of Switzerland supported the adoption of a single silver standard corresponding to the Austrian monetary system, the western part of the country was in favour of the French bimetallic system. The latter was adopted on 7 May 1850 and named the 'Franc Suisse'. The coins were identical to the French and Belgian ones with the only exception that the Swiss subdivision of smaller coins was called 'Rappen' instead of 'centimes'. Again, as in Belgium before, only economic motives seemed to have played a role.

A little bit more complicated was the situation in Italy.[8] In 1861, when the nation state came into being, the Italian peninsula was economically very heterogeneous and exchanges between the Italian states relatively infrequent. Sardinia-Piemont, which was to become the nucleus for the Italian nation state, was economically and politically oriented towards France, the south of Italy had close contacts with England, whereas Lombardia and Veneto looked to Austria. Consequently the currencies used were different as well; until 1860 there were nine banks issuing their own coin on the Italian peninsula. In 1862 a currency reform was put in place and again the French system became the prototype for the Italian currency system. The only difference from Belgium and Switzerland was that the Italian currency got a name of its own, Lira, although in fact it was a copy of the French Franc. Belgian, Swiss, French and Italian coins were freely accepted in all four countries and a de-facto monetary union developed between 1832 and 1862 without any political cooperation among the respective governments.

---

[6] Janssens 1976.

[7] Paillard 1909; Hagenbach 1929.

[8] di Mattia Rom, Bari 1990; Theurl 1992, p. 86.

Why did this monetary union come into being?[9] From an economic point of view, the rapidly growing international trade played a predominant role: it led to a modernisation of the national economies in which money became more and more important as an exchange instrument in cross-border transactions. As a consequence, three major currency areas developed throughout Europe in the 1860s, the first based on the monometallic gold standard with the British Sterling as its centre, the second on the monometallic silver standard with the German states as its core region and thirdly the bimetallic de-facto monetary union with the French Franc as pivotal currency. As with all markets, monetary markets tend to monopolise because actors try to reduce their transaction costs. Consequently, there is a certain tendency in international trade towards using one single currency for cross-border transactions, a phenomenon, that was also observed by the French member of parliament, Charles Louvet: "Monetary internationalism is a consequence of free trade and of the irresistible movement which pushes nations to associate with each other through the strongest solidarity of all, the solidarity of industry and trade, of wealth and well being."[10]

Consequently, from an economic point of view, monetary internationalism was the result of the liberalisation of trade within the framework of industrialisation. The rapid growth of international trade was based on innovative developments in the European infrastructure of transport and communication. The monetary union that came into being between 1832 and 1862 was a result of this development. Economic structures, however, do not explain the treaty of the Latin Monetary Union in 1865, and to understand this, we have to take into account the political aspects of monetary internationalism.

## Political Diving Forces of Monetary Internationalism

In the mid 1860s the de-facto monetary union that had come into being between 1832 and 1862 ran into trouble. The reason for this was the gold-rush of the middle of the century that took off with the discovery of gold mines in California (1847) and Australia (1851), and resulted in a significant increase of gold on markets for precious metals around the world. The problem for the Latin Monetary Union was that the fixed exchange rate between gold and silver of 1:15.5 was no longer valid on the markets, even though the monetary system was based on this relationship, and the governments of the Latin Monetary Union were obliged to sell or buy gold and silver at this fixed price. As a result, traders sold their silver coins in Paris for gold, transferred this gold to the London market and sold it at extraordinary profit. The problem for France was that silver coins disappeared from circulation; between

[9] Haberler 1964; Flandreau 1995, pp. 13–21.

[10] Annales du Sénat et du Corps Législatif, vol. VIII (1866), 13 June 1866, p. 11 (annexe) quoted after Einaudi 2000, p. 288.

1855 and 1860 the country lost about 10 % of its silver coins. This in turn was detrimental to everyday life, because it was silver coins which were mostly used for smaller transactions. On 25 May 1864 the French government reduced the proportion of silver in 20 and 50 centimes coins from 900 to 835. In January 1861 the Swiss government had done the same, but reduced the standard from 900 to 800. The Belgian government instead waited for the markets to calm down and then strove to adapt to the new circumstances. All these actions helped to overcome the downward revaluation of gold but had an important disadvantage: the monetary union based on the identity of national coins was destroyed. The French minister of Finance Achille Fould concluded:

> Ces modifications, effectuées sans concert préalable, ont eu l'inconvénient de donner carrière à un commerce illicite très préjudiciable aux intérêts des gouvernements. [...] Ces mesures restrictives sont de nature à jeter du trouble dans les relations internationales et il serait de l'intérêt de tous les gouvernements de les faire disparaître. J'ai pensé qu'il serait possible d'assister à ce résultat par la voie diplomatique et en réglant d'une manière uniforme par une Convention spéciale la fabrication et la circulation des monnaies fractionnaires dans chacun des pays intéressés.[11]

Here we find the initial political interest of the Latin Monetary Union. After the uncoordinated actions against the depreciation of gold the national governments realised the economic and political significance of the de-facto monetary union. On 11 February 1865, therefore, the French government invited the governments of Belgium, Switzerland and Italy to a conference in Paris in order to re-establish the common monetary standard. After brief discussions on 23 December 1865, an international treaty was signed that re-established the monetary union. From this perspective the Latin Monetary Union was a diplomatic step to overcome the troubles of the international monetary system in the 1860s.

But this is just one part of the story. Article 12 of the treaty for the Monetary Union offered membership to all those countries that were willing to adopt the rules of the monetary union.[12] Just before the negotiations with Belgium, Italy and Switzerland, discussions had taken place within the French government on the enlargement of the monetary union that would not only be advantageous for France but for Europe as a whole.

"Il est évident", the Finance Minister, Achille Fould, wrote in a letter to the Ministry of Foreign Affairs,

> qu'il y aurait d'incontestable avantages à créer en Europe une vaste circulation monétaire, se rattachant à un même système, et identique dans la valeur réelle et nominale. Cette circulation ne tarderait pas à s'assimiler celle des autres pays, et l'on pourrait entrevoir l'époque où, sous influence d'un même régime monétaire, les paiements en numéraire seraient soustraits aux conditions essentiellement variables du change.[13]

---

[11] MAE Convention Monétaire de 1865. 1865–1880, vol. 602/3, dossier 2, no. 2, Ministre des Finances à Ministre des Affaires Etrangères, 19.01.1865.

[12] Text of the treaty in: Knipping 1996, pp. 291–301.

[13] MAE Convention Monétaire de 1865. 1865–1880, Boite 602/3, dossier 2, no. 6, Le Ministre des Finances à Ministre des Affaires Etrangères, 18.05.1865.

This shows that the principal aim of the treaty of 1865 was not only to re-establish the existing monetary union, which had been destroyed by external factors (i.e. the gold rush), but to create a European monetary union. This was a completely new concept, emerging not primarily out of economic structures as had the monetary union existing up to 1865, but out of political motives. This is confirmed by a letter from Achille Fould to the Emperor Napoleon III. on 14 April 1866: The aim of the French initiative, he explained, was "an international enactment which may bring important advantages in the commercial communications of more than 66 millions souls, which, in spite of the diversity of language and of nationality, are united under a monetary system whose name and origin remain French"[14] With more pathos, this was taken up by Félix de Parieu[15] in the French *Revue Contemporaine*: "Le Franc peut donc avoir de grande chance d'être un jour tout au moins une des syllabes fondamentales dans une langue universelle des valeurs."[16] The extension of the Latin Monetary Union, therefore, had two underlying motives: firstly, to facilitate and support the commercial relations between European countries by establishing a common European currency; secondly, the new European currency should be based on the French monetary system and this again would give France a natural leadership within this union.

Monetary union had thus become an instrument of French foreign policy in order to establish economic leadership in continental Europe. This corresponds to the general aim of French foreign policy under Napoleon III. Since the early 1860s, the French Emperor tried to assert French hegemony throughout Europe by diplomatic means. First of all, he tried to prevent the rise of Prussia and a likely German unification. But leadership in this context had not only to be asserted through traditional instruments of diplomatic and military force, but also through setting formal and informal rules and norms in infrastructures, weights and measures in order to make the national system a mandatory regulation on the international level. This is what political theory nowadays calls "soft power", that is the ability to reach national interests through co-operation and attraction instead of force and violence. But this was just one aspect. The Latin Monetary Union can be considered as an integral part of the French economic ideology of that time, which became known as "Saint Simonism".[17] This was based on a specific combination of social politics and *laissez-faire* liberalism in which the state was not intended to act as an entrepreneur but rather to secure the economy´s infrastructure in a wider sense. This meant not only the construction of roads, railways and canals, but the government was also supposed to provide the economy with cheap loans and provide collateral for

---

[14] Report addressed to his Majesty the Emperor by his Excellency the Minister of Finance, 14.04.1866, in: International Monetary Conference 1879, p. 786.

[15] Félix de Parieu was one of the most influential personalities in the Second Empire. As Vice-President of the Council of State from 1865 to 1870 he exerted considerable influence on French monetary policy.

[16] de Parieu 1866.

[17] Cf. Ratcliffe 1985; Smith 1982, pp. 248–265; Schieder 1984.

business enterprises. The same applied to the Monetary Union: the French government did not intervene directly in the economy but instead facilitated international trade by reducing transaction costs.

On 5 December 1866, therefore, the French Foreign Ministry sent a circular letter to all diplomatic missions and embassies in Europe inviting the diplomats to forward the text of the Monetary Union treaty to all governments with special reference to article 12 and the invitation to join the Union.[18] This French initiative met with considerable interest. Sweden and the other Scandinavian countries had been interested in the French system since the early 1860s. One of the country´ s leading monetary expert had appealed to the government in a report to adopt the French standard and to give up the existing silver standard. The same applied in Denmark where the government was preparing the introduction of gold coins which were identical in composition, weight and measure with the French ten-franc coin.[19] But not only Scandinavia, Austria too was interested in the French initiative. After the defeat by Prussia in 1866, the Austrian Government had decided to leave the monetary treaty with Prussia and Baron von Hock, a leading expert in questions of monetary affairs, recommended that the French government be contacted in order to explore the conditions under which Austria might join the Latin Monetary Union.[20] Negotiations started on 23 July 1867 in Paris where von Hock presented a draft treaty to the French delegation under the leadership of Félix de Parieu. Interestingly, Prussia also entered into negotiations about joining the Latin Monetary Union and in March 1867 the French Minister for Foreign Affairs submitted a note to the Prussian Ambassador in Paris asking the German state to join the Union. In Berlin this approach led to discussions between Prime Minister Otto von Bismarck and his Finance Minister von der Heydt. Whilst Bismarck, for political reasons, showed some interest in the French approach, von der Heydt argued that this step would require monetary reform in Prussia something which would be impossible with preparations taking place for monetary integration among the German states.[21] Further negotiations were also held with the Holy See which submitted its request for membership of the Monetary Union in May 1867. These negotiations proved to be very complicated, mainly for political reasons since Italy as a member of the Monetary Union tried to prevent the Vatican from joining because of the still lingering 'Questione Romana', the situation whereby the Italian

---

[18] MAE Convention monétaire de 1865, 1865–1880, vol. 602/603, doss. 2, no. 4. Le Ministre des Affaires étrangères à Berne, Turin/Bruxelles, 01.02.1867.

[19] MAE, Direction Commerciale. Questions monétaires. Convention de 1865 et de 1867, vol. 604, no. 205 Légation de France en Suède à MAE, 29.8.1968; MAE, Direction Commerciale. Questions monétaires. Convention de 1865 et de 1867, vol 604, no. 209, Légation de France en Danemark à MAE, 14.09.1968.

[20] MAE Direction Commerciale. Convention monétaire de 1865 et de 1867, Vol. 603. Négociations monétaires entre la France et l'Autriche, 23.07.1867.

[21] Cf. for details: Thiemeyer 2002.

government did not accept the papal supremacy over the City of Rome.[22] Apart from these, Spain and even Venezuela showed their interest in joining the Latin Monetary Union.

All in all, the French initiative for monetary leadership in continental Europe seemed to be very successful. The only state that openly rejected the proposal was Russia. In spite of this considerable interest, however, the initiative failed for an unexpected reason: as said before, the Latin Monetary Union that had come into existence with the treaty of December 1865 was based on bimetallism, and all the nations interested in joining the Union did so expecting that they would have to adopt a bimetallic system, too. But this was highly improbable. At the very time the foreign ministry sent the circular letter to the European states, the French political and economic elite were discussing the monetary standard of France.[23] Some of the most influential actors in this system openly argued that the two metal standard should be abandoned and a monometallic gold standard be adopted. During the negotiations with Belgium, Switzerland and Italy in December 1865 the French government was the only one wanting to keep bimetallism, whereas all the other governments were in favour of introducing the gold standard as monetary system. The French delegation, however, based on its economic power, had asserted the bimetallic system, if on condition that there should be further discussions among the member countries on this particular question. The decisive question of the monetary standard, therefore, was still unresolved when France asked the other nations to join the Union. This was the exact point the Belgian Finance Minister, Hubert Frère-Orban, hinted at in a letter to his French colleague: "Cette considération ne portera-t-elle pas le cabinet des Tuileries à penser avec moi qu'il y a là une question préalable à résoudre, avant de recommander aux autres états l'accession à la convention?"[24] This turned out to be the decisive reason for the failure of the French initiative. Even though many European states and even Great Powers like Austria had showed considerable interest in the French proposal, all negotiations – with the only exception of Greece which joined the Union in January 1869 – failed utterly. From today´s perspective it is quite astonishing to see that the French government had started an initiative for monetary (and political) leadership in Europe without having the domestic preconditions to support it.

Regarding the underlying question of the driving forces of internationalism this episode clearly shows that the 'internationalisation' of monetary markets was not only driven by market forces but also by governments. The French government had decided to enlarge the Latin Monetary Union in order to support its principal aim in foreign policy, hegemony over continental Europe, by means of economic, i.e. monetary instruments. The French government, however, was not the only one to

---

[22] MAE Direction Commerciale. Convention monétaire de 1865. 1865–1877. vol. 601, dossier 3, no. 61, Ministre des Affaires Etrangères à Berne, Bruxelles, Florence, 29.05.1867.

[23] Einaudi 2000, passim.

[24] MAE Convention Monétaire de 1865. 1865–1880, vol. 602/603, doss. 2, no. 47, Frère-Orban à Ministère des Affaires étrangères, 23.12.1866.

attempt this. The United Kingdom and the U.S. (from 1878) acted quite similarly. From a political point of view, therefore, internationalism had become an instrument of foreign policy.

But this is just one aspect. Another is that monetary internationalism not only supported foreign policy but could also prove harmful to the sovereignty of the nation state. This was the situation in the mid-1870s when the Latin Monetary Union was confronted with serious problems. One of them was the introduction of the "Cours Forcé" in Italy (1866) and France (1871).[25] Following the wars of 1866 (Italy) and 1870/71 (France) neither country was capable any longer of securing the changeability of their respective currencies into gold and silver through their national banks. This was not only detrimental to their own currencies which lost in value, but also to the other countries of the Latin Monetary Union, Belgium and Switzerland in particular, who found themselves flooded with Italian 5-franc silver coins.[26] The LM U convened a number of conferences on this subject until the Italian government was forced to give up the Cours Forcé under pressure from the other states of the monetary union in 1879. Even though the abolition of the Cours Forcé had been the political aim of all Italian governments since 1866, the decisive impetus for monetary reform in Italy now came from outside, from the countries of the monetary union. One of the leading Italian experts on monetary questions, Luigi Luzzatti, commented in the newspaper *Opinione* on 15 January 1879:

> I delegati nostri a titolo di transazione proposero il ritiro dei piccoli biglietti, cioè concedettero meno. Ma non si avvidero che introducendo nella Convenzione Internazionale l'obligo di ritirare i piccoli biglietti e di non emettere di nuovi, impegnavano la sovranità nazionale in un punto che si sottrae per l'indole sua a vincoli somiglianti. Ora il Governo italiano, se lo credeva conveniente, poteva annunziare la sua volontà di ritirare i piccoli biglietti e di sostituirvi gli spiccioli; ma dall'annunzio di questo suo disegno alla stipulazione internazionale vi è il tratto che corre fra l'equità e la debolezza.[27]

In Italy this decision was perceived as a serious intervention into national sovereignty.

Another example is Belgium which for several reasons wanted to leave the monetary union in 1885. After a short but intense discussion in Brussels, the government decided to remain in the union because the economic disadvantages which might ensue in the event of a dissolution of the monetary union were so enormous. Decisive arguments were brought forward by the chamber of commerce in Antwerp: the transnational trade, it argued, with France had been extremely intense on all levels. "Le papier belge, en effet, a toujours été très estimé en France et les maisons de banque ou de commerce le conservaient volontiers en portefeuille."[28] Since the political debate about the Belgian retreat from the Latin

[25] Mertens 1944; di Mattia 1982, p. 189; Romanelli 1979, pp. 80 f.

[26] Einaudi 1997.

[27] Luigi Luzzatti in: *L'opinione*, 15.01.1879; quoted after Luzzatti 1935, p. 127.

[28] MAE Direction Commerciale. Question Monétaire. Union Latine. Convention de 1885, Consulat Général de France en Belgique (Anvers) à MAE, 20.11.1885.

Monetary Union, however, Belgian traders had been confronted with serious trouble. The Belgian Franc devalued considerably and the National Bank was forced to raise interest rates, both having marked negative impact on external trade. Again the question was to decide between serious economic disadvantages or political freedom and national sovereignty. The Belgian liberal Hubert Frère-Orban noted on this occasion:

> Ce n'est pas, messieurs, qu'en exprimant le regret de voir cesser l'Union, je partage la frayeur que quelques-uns paraissent éprouver à l'idée de cette rupture. Cette Union a incontestablement ses avantages, mais elle offre aussi des inconvénients. De très bons esprits sont opposés à de semblables conventions; ils sont convaincus qu'un pays ne doit pas abandonner son indépendance monétaire; et à voir ce qui se passe aujourd'hui, je serais presque tenté aujourd'hui de partager cette manière de voir.[29]

These examples show the other side of political internationalism in the second half of the nineteenth century. On the one hand, monetary internationalism provided a new instrument for governments, as for instance the French, for exerting power in Europe by setting standards in measures, weights and currency. Even though the French government by the end of the 1860s had failed to impose the French monetary standard on Europe because of domestic problems the concept was successfully adopted by Great Britain, Germany and – later – the United States. On the other hand, monetary internationalism created a multitude of mutual interdependencies between the countries involved. In monetary matters in particular, national governments were no longer sovereign, but subject to decisions taken in other nations under different conditions. The contemporaries recognised this difficult interrelatedness only very slowly. With remarkable clarity it was summarised by the head of the French consulate-general in Leipzig in a note to the French Ministry for Foreign Affairs:

> Ces exemples prouvent qu'une convention monétaire internationale implique ou suppose une foule d'homogénéités et de solidarités *impossibles* entre les parties contractantes. Toute pacte de cette nature, en effet, ne forme qu'un chaînon de la grande chaîne qui unit les contractants, et la moindre secousse qui vient ébranler la situation de l'un d'entre eux, sera immédiatement et par ricochet ressentie, par tout les autres. Survienne dans l'un des pays alliés une guerre ou une mauvaise récolte, les intérêts de l'Etat directement atteint seront affectés les premiers, mais l'impression électrique de la catastrophe se communiquera nécessairement aux autres.[30]

All in all, internationalism in the second half of the nineteenth century was not only driven by economic market forces but also by political interests. Foreign ministries and diplomats tried to extend their means to assert national interest. Even though this turned out to be quite successful in the case of the Latin Monetary Union, the same Union also showed the consequences of these actions. This led to a

[29] Chambre des Représentants 1885, p. 1781.

[30] MAE Direction Commerciale. Questions monétaires et financières. Conférence de 1881, vol. 612, Consulat Général de France à Leipzig à MAE, 30.11.1880.

closer interrelationship between the countries, in some cases even to a restriction of national sovereignty.

## Cultural Driving Forces of Monetary Internationalism

These economic and political structures met with and were reinforced by a general tendency supporting internationalism out of cultural motives, and with this I come to my third level of analysis. The cultural driving forces of monetary internationalism relied on a set of shared values, goals and practices among actors involved in the political and economic processes in the second half of the nineteenth century. These shared values are what engender community among individuals. They create a common ideology and thus a common goal for political and economic action. From a constructivist historian's perspective, these common ideologies are created in permanent collective bargaining processes on the basic questions of a society in a transnational public sphere. This public sphere is created through media (in the nineteenth century first of all newspapers) but also in parliamentary debates and, last but not least, international conferences on monetary questions. In the period in question, i.e. between 1865 and 1914, there were at least ten international conferences dealing with monetary affairs, most of them taking place in Paris which had become the capital of monetary internationalism at this time. Those shared values and common ideologies manifested themselves in a couple of key words frequently used in the opening addresses of the conferences, dealing with the general framework of the deliberations with mostly political and technical questions of international finance.

One of these key words frequently used in the context of monetary integration in the framework of monetary internationalism is 'civilisation'. The French government, as all European governments, considered itself civilised, first and foremost in contrast to other peoples, particularly in Africa and Asia. This was the reason why the French government in its initiative for European monetary unification in 1866 aimed at a "circulation monétaire uniforme entre tous les états civilises".[31] Membership in the monetary union was to be restricted to those countries that were 'civilised', and more than this, monetary integration, from this point of view, itself became a symbol of civilisation. For the English newspaper *The Times* the foundation of the Latin Monetary Union therefore was "a most important step in the process of European civilisation".[32] This was confirmed by the US representative to the international monetary union in 1879, Senator Robert Fenton, who said in his opening remarks:

[31] MAE Convention monétaire de 1865, 1865–1880, Vol. 602/603, doss. 2, no. 4. Le Ministre des Affaires étrangères à Berne, Turin, Bruxelles, 01.02.1867.

[32] "Monetary Convention," in: *The Times*, 08.09.1866, p. 8.

> It marks the beneficent advance of civilisation that the commercial relations of different countries grow nearer and firmer year by year. Thus we come to see more clearly the community of interest among nations, and are wisely prompted to cultivate more and more friendly intercourse. Among the measures to this end we cannot be insensible to the benefits which would flow from a uniform basis as to international coin-metal exchanges.[33]

As a reason for the Spanish application for membership the Spanish Minister of Finance declared in 1868:

> Everything that facilitates trade and relations between nations constitutes an immense benefit, fertilising the seeds of wealth, improving the position of citizens and reaffirming civilization and freedom. Adopting the monetary system of the international convention, Spain opens her arms to her sister states in Europe and gives a new and evident proof of her unshakable resolve to unite with them, to enter the assembly of free peoples.[34]

From this point of view membership in the Latin Monetary Union was not only important for political and economic reasons but also became a symbol of membership among the free and civilised nations. This idea of civilisation was closely linked to another key word supporting monetary internationalism in this period, 'progress'. This was a recurring theme for the whole period characterising not only technical achievements but also the construction of societies by means of scientific knowledge. Science was considered the key instrument to understand and shape the world. This underlying attitude was supported by the bourgeois ideology of liberalism as for instance when the Belgian delegate to the international monetary conference in 1878 declared:

> This conference proves how easily a number of nations can assemble together to discuss the interests which are common to them. I doubt not that this precedent will bear fruit, but if I may be allowed here to express a desire ... it is that the labours of future conferences ... may be directed, not with a view to government interference, but by liberal aspirations. There still exist in the world – and I do not think a single country is exempt from them – a multitude of measures, restrictive of liberty ... It is to make them disappear that the combined efforts of nations should tend.[35]

From this perspective, monetary internationalism was part of a huge project: the transformation of the world into a single society based on scientific knowledge under the auspices of bourgeois liberalism. National monetary systems were considered restrictive to economic and political liberty. Their abolition could be achieved by us of a single international currency constructed by the people and not by governments.

---

[33] International Monetary Conference 1879, p. 4.

[34] French Embassy in Spain to the Minister of Foreign Affairs, 05.11.1868, quoted after Einaudi 2000, p. 289.

[35] International Monetary Conference 1879, p. 125.

## Conclusion: Driving Forces of Internationalism in the Late Nineteenth Century

Monetary internationalism in the late nineteenth century relied on three essential driving forces: in the economic sector, emerging transnational markets led to a unification of currencies through markets. This was a process that had already started in the 1830s, when Belgium had adopted the French monetary system chiefly for economic reasons. The same applied to Switzerland (1848) and Italy (1861). Seen from this angle, rapid industrialisation in combination with path-breaking developments in infrastructure led to the internationalisation of trade. Consequently, there was a strong development in the monopolisation of currency markets, leading in the 1860s to three major currency areas in Europe: one adhering to the monometallic gold standard with British Sterling as its centre, one following the monometallic silver standard with Germany as its core region and a third, the bimetallic Latin Monetary Union with the French Franc as pivotal currency. Economic integration through transnational markets, therefore, played an important role.

This development affected national politics in a double sense, on the one hand, governments and diplomats tried to use currencies for their particular interests as such for example when the French ministry for foreign affairs asked the European governments to join the Latin Monetary Union in December 1866, this was an instrument for asserting political leadership in continental Europe. This was a new development of the nineteenth century, prior to which there had been a sharp partition between the political and the economic sectors of international relations. The emerging international markets, however, provided diplomats with new tools they willingly adopted: the principal idea was to impose the French national standards for weights and measures and currencies on continental Europe and thereby create an economic union under French leadership. The attempt failed, however, because of domestic problems in the Second Empire in the late 1860s. Perhaps to the surprise of most diplomats, the new instruments turned out to be ambivalent. On the one hand, they extended the possibilities for diplomatic action; on the other hand they proved to be harmful for national sovereignty. This was the case for Italy, which was obliged to give up the Cours Forcé in 1879 after considerable pressure from the member states of the Latin Monetary Union. Another example is given by Belgium which planned to leave the monetary union in 1885, but refrained from doing so after pressure from several chambers of commerce interested in cross-border trade with France. But nevertheless, diplomatic actors, foreign ministries and diplomats were important driving forces for monetary internationalism.

There is, however, a third important driving force at the cultural level. Both economic markets and diplomatic actions were supported by a set of shared values held by the European elite of the time. They found their concrete expression in the notions of civilisation and progress. The organisation of an international monetary system was part of a European mission to civilise the world. It was closely combined with the idea of scientific progress, i.e. the shaping of the world through the instruments of science.

## Bibliography


Ambrosius, Gerold. 2009. *Liberale versus institutionelle Integration von Wirtschaftspolitiken in Europa. Das 19. und das 20. Jahrhundert im systematischen Vergleich*. Baden-Baden: Nomos.

Bartel, Robert J. 1977. "International Monetary Unions: The Nineteenth Century Experience," *Journal of European Economic History* 3, 689–704.

Bitar, YassarYves. 1953. *Les Unions monétaires*. Damas: Université Catholique de Louvain.

Blaum, Kurt. 1908. *Das Geldwesen der Schweiz seit 1789*, Straßburg: K.J. Trübner.

Brossault, Eric. 1903. *Histoire de l'union monétaire latine*. Ph.d Thesis, Université de Rennes.

Chambre des Représentants, ed. 1885. *Annales Parlementaires, Séance du 11 Août 1885 (Salle du Sénat)*, Brussels.

Einaudi, Luca. 1997. "Monetary Unions and Free Riders. The Case of the Latin Monetary Union (1865–1878)." *Rivista di Storia Economica*, 327–362.

Einaudi, Luca. 2000. "From the Franc to the 'Europe': The Attempted Transformation of the Latin Monetary Union into a European Monetary Union, 1865–1873." *Economic History Review* 53 (2) 284–308.

Einaudi, Luca. 2001. *Money and Politics. European Monetary Unification and the International Gold Standard, 1865–1873*. Oxford: Oxford University Press.

Esslen, Joseph B. 1926. "Münzbund"in: *Handwörterbuch der Staatswissenschaften*, vol. VI, 664–668. Jena: G. Fischer.

Esslen, Joseph B. 1995. "Lateinische Münzunion." In *Von Aktie bis Zoll. Ein historisches Lexikon des Geldes*, edited by Michael North, 213 f. Munich: C.H. Beck.

Flandreau, Marc. 1995. *L'Or du Monde. La France et la stabilité du système monétaire international, 1848–1873*. Paris: Éd. l'Harmattan.

Geyer, Martin and Johannes Paulmann, eds. 2001. *The Mechanics of Internationalism. Culture, Society, and Politics from the 1840s to the First World War*. Oxford: Oxford University Press.

Greul, Robert. 1926. *Die Lateinische Münzunion. Eine Völkerrechtsgeschichtliche Studie*. Berlin: Dümmler.

Haberler, Gottfried. 1964. "Integration and Growth of the World Economy in Historical Perspective." *The American Economic Review* 65, 1–22.

Hagenbach, Paul. 1929. *Die Entwicklung zur Goldwährung in der Schweiz*. Weinfelden: A.G. Neuenschwander.

Henrich-Franke, Christian et al., eds. 2007. *Internationalismus und Europäische Integration im Vergleich. Fallstudien zu Währungen, Landwirtschaft, Verkehrs- und Nachrichtenwesen*. Baden-Baden: Nomos.

Herren, Madeleine. 1999. "L'Union Monétaire Latine, la guerre et la Suisse," *Relations Internationales* 99, pp. 269–288.

Herren, Madeleine. 2000. *Hintertüren zur Macht. Internationalismus und modernisierungsorientierte Außenpolitik in Belgien, der Schweiz und den USA 1865–1914*. Munich: Oldenbourg Verlag.

Holton, Robert J. 2005. *Making Globalization*. New York: Palgrave Macmillan.

International Monetary Conference held in Paris in August 1878, under the Auspices of the Ministry of Foreign Affairs of the Republic of France; in Compliance with the Invitation Extended to certain Governments of Europe by the Government of the United States, in Pursuance of the Second Section of the Act of Congress of February 28, 1878. Washington: Government Print. Off, 1879.

Janssens, Valéry. 1976. *Le Franc Belge, un siècle et démi d'histoire monétaire*. Brussels: Services inter-entreprises.

Kauch, P. 1950. *La Banque nationale de Belgique, 1850–1918*, Brussels: Imprimé pour la Banque nationale de Belgique à l'occasion de son centenaire.

Kleinmann, E. 1892. *La conférence monétaire de Bruxelles et l'union latine*. Paris.

Knipping, Franz, ed. 1996. *Das System der Vereinten Nationen und seine Vorläufer, vol. 2: Vorläufer der Vereinten Nationen. 19. Jahrhundert und Völkerbundzeit*. Bern: Stämpfli.

Koch-Mehrin, Silvana. 2001. *Historische Währungsunion zwischen Wirtschaft und Politik. Die Lateinische Münzunion 1865–1927*, Baden-Baden: Nomos.

Luzzatti, Luigi. 1935. *Memorie, vol. 2: 1876–1900*. Bologna: N. Zanichelli.

di Mattia, Renato. 1982. "Moneta, Credito e Finanza." *1861–1887. Il Processo di unificazione nella realtà del paese. Atti del L Congresso di Storia del Risorgimento Italiano*. Rome.

di Mattia, Renato, ed. 1990. *Gli Istituti di Emissione in Italia. I tentativi di unificazione 1843–1892*. Rome: Laterza.

Mertens, Jacques. 1944. *La Naissance et le Développement de l'Etalon-or, 1696–1922*. Paris: Presses universitaires de France.

Niederer, Albert. 1976. *Die Lateinische Münzunion. Ausstellungskatalog*. Hilterfingen: Helvetische Münzenzeitung.

Osterhammel, Jürgen and Niels P. Petersson. 2003. *Geschichte der Globalisierung. Dimensionen, Prozesse, Epochen*, Munich: Beck.

Paillard, Georges. 1909. *La Suisse et l'Union monétaire latine*. Lausanne: Payot.

de Parieu, Félix. 1866. "L'Union monétaire de la France, de l'Italie, de la Belgique et de la Suisse, le 'Münzverein' latin." *Revue Contemporaine* 15, 636.

Ratcliffe, Barrie M. 1985. "Latin Monetary Union." In *Historical Dictionary of the French Second Empire, 1852–1870*, edited by William E. Echard, 342–343. Westport CT: Greenwood Press.

Ratcliffe, Barrie M. 1985. "Saint Simonism," In *Historical Dictionary of the French Second Empire, 1852–1870*, edited by William E. Echard, 595–598. Westport CT: Greenwood Press.

Redish, Angela. 2006. "Recent Contributions to the History of Monetary and International Financial Systems: A Review Essay." *European Review of Economic History* 10, 231–248.

Renouvin, Pierre, 1954. "L'histoire contemporaine des relations internationales. Orientation de recherches." *Revue Historique* 211, 233–255.

Renouvin, Pierre & Jean-Baptiste Duroselle. 1970. *Introduction à l'histoire des Relations Internationales*. Paris: Librairie Armand Colin.

Report addressed to his Majesty the Emperor by his Excellency the Minister of Finance, 14.4.1866, in: International Monetary Conference held in Paris in August 1878, Washington 1879, p. 786.

van der Rest, E. 1881. "L'union monétaire latine, son origine et ses phases diverses," *Revue de droit international* 13, 5.

Romanelli, Raffaele. 1979. *L'Italia Liberale (1861–1900)*. Bologna: il Mulino.

Schieder, Wolfgang. 1984. "Sozialismus." *Geschichtliche Grundbegriffe*, vol. 5, 941–944. Stuttgart: Klett.

Smith, William H.C. 1982. *Napoleon III*. Paris: Hachette.

Soutou, Georges Henri. 2000. "Die französische Schule der internationalen Beziehungen." In *Internationale Geschichte. Themen, Ergebnisse, Aussichten*, edited by Wilfried Loth and Jürgen Osterhammel, 31–45. Munich: Oldenbourg

Theurl, Teresia. 1992. *Eine gemeinsame Währung für Europa. 12 Lehren aus der Geschichte*. Innsbruck: Österr. Studien-Verl.

Thiemeyer, Guido. 2002. "Napoleon III, Otto von Bismarck und die Lateinische Münzunion 1865–1867." *Bankhistorisches Archiv* 28, 1–20.

Thiemeyer, Guido. 2009. *Internationalismus und Diplomatie. Währungspolitische Kooperation im europäischen Staatensystem 1865–1900*. Munich: Oldenbourg.

Thobie, Jacques. 1985. "La dialectique forces profondes – décision dans l'histoire des relations internationales." *Relations Internationales* 41, 29–38.

Willis, Henry P. 1901. *A History of the Latin Monetary Union*. Chicago: University of Chicago Press.

Zellfelder, Friedrich. 1991. "Der Lateinische Münzbund. Grundlagen, Entstehen und Scheitern." In *Währungen der Welt*, vol. I, edited by Jürgen Schneider, 105–121. Stuttgart: Steiner.

# Chapter 3
# "They Already Exist": Don't They? Conjuring Global Networks Along the Flow of Money

**Madeleine Herren**

**Abstract** Internationalism, a concept of the nineteenth-century, still shapes the way globalisation is discussed in the twenty-first century. This essay explains why internationalism contributed to a powerful discourse on international organisations, based on national comparability, and how twenty-first century research on international relations still follows the path of nineteenth-century internationalists. The paper elaborates what the nineteenth-century master narrative of international organisations omitted. The numerous lists of organisations published since the nineteenth century hide, astonishingly enough, the role of money. The border crossing and networking function of money, the financial aspect of the building of international organisations and their contribution to the global economy constitute a neglected topic in this field. Introducing the role of money as an obvious border-crossing element, this paper first of all raises methodological concerns. The main question is to what extent the understanding of international organisations as border-crossing versions of national associations overlooked crucial functions of the international institutions. Taking the Bank for International Settlements as an example, the approach asks whether international organisations represent a specific form of porosity within the international system, an idea that is constantly and inevitably locked in a struggle with historical forms of nationalism and methodological nationalism in modern historiography.

M. Herren (✉)
History Department, EXC "Asia and Europe"
University of Heidelberg, Heidelberg, Germany
e-mail: madeleine.herren@zegk.uni-heidelberg.de

I. Löhr and R. Wenzlhuemer (eds.), *The Nation State and Beyond*, Transcultural Research – Heidelberg Studies on Asia and Europe in a Global Context,
DOI 10.1007/978-3-642-32934-0_3, © Springer-Verlag Berlin Heidelberg 2013

## Introduction

In 1908, the Austrian pacifist Alfred Hermann Fried published a small booklet entitled "Das internationale Leben der Gegenwart" (International Life Today).[1] The preface showed Fried's quality as a master of rhetoric: he translated the list of newly created international institutions into the preferred nineteenth-century master narrative – the geographical map. He conceived his booklet as a travel guide and called it a "Baedeker für das internationale Land". Following this territorial narrative, the international landscape was shaped by multilateral treaties on distant topics, such as combating plant diseases, protecting seals in the Bering Sea, or the international agreement on Swiss neutrality in 1815. As landmarks, Fried added the so-called Public International Unions, and finished with the numerous treaties the Hague Peace Conferences had approved in 1899 and 1907. The land Fried proposed to discover was therefore primarily ruled by international law, multilateralism and the sovereign state. Its explorers were members of a globally active international civil society who described themselves as internationalists.

With Internationalism, a concept that interested the nineteenth-century much in the way globalisation is of interest to the twenty first century, Fried presented a perfect combination of mainstream nationalism and a border-crossing, international exchange of ideas, commodities and concepts. As a precaution, his preface denied all constructivist aims, rejoicing instead that the international organisation of the world already existed – even the notion of already existing *networks* of international organisations appeared. The question is: did they?

No, they didn't. This essay explains why Fried's imaginary world gave shape to a powerful discourse on international organisations, based on national comparability, and how twenty first-century research on international relations still follows nineteenth-century internationalists. As a next step, this paper will elaborate what the nineteenth-century master narrative of international organisations omitted. The numerous lists of organisations published since the nineteenth-century hide, astonishingly enough, the role of money. The border-crossing and networking function of money, the financial aspect of the building of international organisations and their contribution to the global economy constitute a neglected topic in this field. These aspects are mentioned neither in the various nineteenth century publications, nor in modern histories of international organisations.[2] However, the methodological consequences of hiding the role of money can be considered as being even more important than highlighting a neglected field of research. Introducing the role of money as an obvious border-crossing element, this paper first of all raises

---

[1] Fried 1908a; for Fried's publication output see Fried 1908b; for his biography see Schönemann-Behrens 2004; Göhring 2006.

[2] Of course, international organisations with financial aims have their institutional histories. See e.g. histories about the Bretton Woods system, or the Bank of International Settlements. However, the question of financing is not even discussed in the case of the League of Nations. See the most detailed history of the League written by Walters 1960.

methodological concerns. The main question is to what extent the understanding of international organisations as border-crossing versions of national associations overlooked crucial functions of the international institutions. The approach presented asks whether international organisations represent a specific form of porosity within the international system, an idea that is constantly and inevitably locked in a struggle with historical forms of nationalism *and* methodological nationalism in modern historiography.

Where nineteenth-century internationalists respected the role of international law, Kantian cosmopolitanism, and advanced the history of the success of the now globally spreading Western idea of civil association, this article uses a transcultural approach and focuses on the porosity of borders by investigating the role of money. The idea is to gain an understanding of international organisations without just presuming the meaning of "international" to be a more or less successful connection of national parts to form a global puzzle. At first glance, however, this approach seems counterproductive to the topic addressed. Instead of Fried's international land, fragile international organisations surface from the past, unprotected by national laws, and therefore without the (economic) rights accorded to national associations. As one follows this path, the problem of missing source material, well known to historians of international organisations, intensifies. Indeed, in the turmoil of two world wars, archives were destroyed or just disappeared. For this investigation, source material has been based on the archives of the Bank for International Settlements (BIS) for several reasons: first of all, the BIS *is* an international organisation *and* a financial institution at the same time. Second, the archives of this institution based in Basel are accessible and have been unaffected by war. Third, for the short but decisive time between 1932 and 1945, the BIS played a certain role as the international organisations' bank. It is important to note that the BIS began business with international organisations from a state of financial embarrassment. Today "the world's oldest international financial institution",[3] the BIS got off to a difficult start, far from the founders' aims: the reason for its foundation, the international administration of reparations, had disappeared in the blast of the global economic crisis when the bank began to operate in 1930. In the available BIS histories, the business conducted for international organisations is therefore not of central interest, neither for researchers, nor in the history of archival preservation. For a complete financial history of international organisations, the BIS collection therefore needs additional material for each organisation mentioned. However, aiming at new insights beyond Fried's well-known narrative, this article presents a pilot project in the direction of a transcultural history of international organisations and reveals in a first part the underlying sketches of Fried's still influential mental map. In a second section, the role of the BIS explains why money helps to shape a new history of international organisations. This part regards money as an information carrier, giving an insight into the specific problems of international organisations during times of crisis and war. The section further explains

[3] "BIS History – Overview," (http://www.bis.org/about/history.htm).

what kind of information arrived in Basel, and on the basis of these findings, the conclusion looks at the consequences of an approach which replaces a territorial with a relational understanding of international organisations.

This paper aligns with the debate on the porosity of borders and the ambivalent position of international organisations as transgressive agencies on one side and entities clearly defined by topics and national membership in their own profile on the other side. The costs of border-crossing and the financial side of international organisations are a rather underestimated aspect of research – several contributions in this volume, however, confirm the attractive, sometimes even unintended bundling of financial flows by international organisations as one of the fields beyond the nation state – where even the nation state maintained an interest.

## Fried's Imaginary World and Its Methodological Deconstruction

At the turn of the twentieth century, Fried was just one among a growing community of well-known authors who described themselves as internationalists whilst carefully cultivating platforms of international self-presentation. Fried was the founder of several pacifist organisations, a committed member of the Esperanto movement,[4] and a close collaborator with the female public relations star Bertha von Suttner. These communities constantly produced promotional publications, and almost all preferred a narrative in which lists of international conferences, or organisations, or treaties emphasised internationalism as a quantity of countable items with strong entrenchment in national territories. For nineteenth-century internationalists, patriotism was part of internationalism, and the opening of international offices proved the appeal of each respective nation state. The concept of internationalism spread quickly since internationalists maintained a kind of "quotation cartel", which was substantially enlarged by the establishment of the Nobel Prize in 1900. Fried quoted and commented on each move of his British alter ego, the journalist and pacifist William T. Stead. He published together with the Belgian group around Paul Otlet and Henri La Fontaine, and his "Who is Who of the Peace Movement" gave visibility on a personal basis to the internationalists' networks on a personal basis under the umbrella term of peace.[5] Following the idea of an international civil society based on personal border- crossing connections, the value of this network of internationalists increased with the inclusion of non-Western members. However, the aim of the authors presenting these networks focused on their territorial foundation, not on the members' autonomy or their motivation to join the group, or on an understanding of the international organisation as a political agent in its own right. In Fried's "Who is Who" the Japanese members of the Interparliamentary Union, the international organisation

[4] Fried 1912.

[5] Fried 1913, pp. 311–422.

of parliamentarians, provided evidence for the global spread of the successful concept of Western internationalism, and not a merging of different cultural traditions.

A global search shows many more publications of this type; however, we will not venture too far in exploring the development of a global quotation cartel shortly after the turn of the century. Founded in 1907, *The American Journal of International Law* played a comparable role. Besides the industrious Fried, many other people participated in the dynamics of networking, presenting biographies only vaguely related to peace.[6] These multilayered personalities established their social standing with a flood of publications, mostly following the positivist master narrative of their time. All these "annuaire de la vie internationale", "anales de la corte de Justicia centro Americana", "catalogue of treaties", lists of international congresses and conferences[7] successfully established an understanding of internationalism that still influences research on global governance and international organisations today. The existence of international networks, which Fried announced, much later characterised the research of Wallace and Singer in the 1970s, but also influenced Craig Murphy's Gramscian approach, and John Boli's sociological research on NGOs.[8] Whatever we can say about global connections within, beyond and after the nation state, existence was granted to everything that could be formally counted, following the example of national statistics. The "order of things" followed the gospel of statistics, the magic of the ever-growing number connected to increasing modernisation and the only ostensibly absurd transformation of nationalism into globalism. This bourgeois internationalism of the nineteenth and early twentieth centuries carefully avoided its coincidence and affinity with anarchism and different forms of socialist internationalism, both created contemporaneously. Rather, for this positivist bourgeois internationalism, border-crossing networks constituted a substantial part of a successful nation's expansionism. The counting of organisations went along with their territorial foundation – Fried and his colleagues did not use the image of the map, the metaphor of the traveller and the idea of an "international land" accidentally. Along the same lines, nineteenth-century internationalists carefully avoided highlighting the transgressive aspect of their approach – which is one more reason why a constructivist methodology needs to illuminate the hidden places and white spots of Fried's "international land".

Looking beyond the pretended existence of global networks by means of a deconstructivist approach, the question arises of what should be regarded as border-crossing agencies. As a first step, instead of self-contained entities, e.g.

[6] To give an example, Gilbert Bowles (1869–1960), an American missionary in Japan, published a Japanese-English Peace Journal ("Heiwa"), but was also involved in tuberculosis prevention and the education of the blind; Shavit 1990, p. 55.

[7] As an example see Baldwin 1907. Baldwin died in 1927; as a professor at Yale Law School, Governor of Connecticut and member of the Supreme Court he had shaped substantially the understanding of American internationalism – and, of course, was mentioned in Fried's "Who is Who" (Fried 1913, p. 323).

[8] Murphy 1994; Boli and Thomas 1999; Archer 1992.

international institutions and treaties, this paper suggests concentrating on border-crossing aspects not as peripheral but as decisive parts beyond national historiography and national expansionism. The proposed sea change goes hand in hand with a historiography described as transcultural. Conceptually connected to Ortiz and Welsch, transcultural history introduces a global view of the past by focusing on processes of border crossing. Instead of attaching the past to clearly defined entities such as eras, territories, nations, classes and states, transcultural history focuses on incompatibilities, tensions and disputes which develop whenever people, objects, concepts and ideas cross the ruling orders of their respective time. The reaction to crossing borders – which are of course not just national borders – reflects the acceptance or rejection of entanglements in the society concerned.

According to this definition, transcultural history is first of all a *method*, a helpful analytical tool, which, by focusing on culture as an umbrella term, helps to overcome methodological nationalism even in cases where 'foreign' cultures are not involved. Rather, this approach presumes to see the impulse for the heartbeat of development and change in the disturbing awareness of another world which exists outside the respective mind maps. This foreign dimension becomes substantial every time limits and borders are established or changed. Each generation has found different answers for this tension between border-protected local identities and the lure of global openness. In almost every imaginable case, passing over borders is therefore much more than just a question of travelling and always influences both those who stay and those who leave.[9]

Take the example of international organisations established from 1850 to 1939: the transcultural approach accentuates the obvious imbalance between their structural functions and their political use in the internationalists' endlessly long lists. Despite being celebrated as a guarantee for universal peace, international organisations are highly unstable entities. In regard to international law, an West-Eastern imbalance unfolded in an unexpected direction: every foreign post office and international sanitation committee in the Ottoman empire, the lighthouses in North Africa and the foreign cemeteries in Japan and China were better protected by international law than an international organisation located in Berne, Brussels, or Paris. To put it otherwise, Fried highlighted the role of the European governments, and thus always preferred the part of the world where international organisations had their weakest influence.

The asymmetry between a limited scope of action and the conjured value of international organisations gains even more importance when the law of association is involved. In the nineteenth-century, not a single European law of association may

[9] According to this definition, transcultural history encompasses (a) events and practices intended to enhance self-representation on a global stage (e.g. world fairs), (b) shifting objects of contested origin (spoils of war), or valued for their foreign character, forms of standardisation as reading for shifting concepts (Esperanto, road signs, pictograms), (c) border-crossing information and its financing, the question of transgression costs, (d) institutions and movements with the opportunity for global membership, (e) places and space with extraterritorial and international character, (f) people living transboundary lives under different labels. See Herren et al. 2012 (forthcoming), p. 7.

be examined in which the specific needs of international actors are appropriately mentioned. Sadly enough, it was first of all the German National Socialist regime which was interested in this matter. Aiming at a specific law for international organisations under totalitarian rule,[10] NS authors investigated international and national laws and discovered that since the nineteenth-century associations followed exclusively national rules. International associations remained in an uncertain legal state, a fact which accentuates the refusal of territorial rights to international organisations. Fried's "international land" therefore appears as a no-man's land. The existence of an international civil society was hinged on weak, legally unprotected international institutions.

In times of war and occupation, this white spot also opened up ambivalent opportunities: international associations were unstable entities, but not subject to the restrictions of national associations, e.g. the exclusion of women and foreigners from political associations. Their informal status guaranteed a certain openness towards border-crossing influences. On the other hand, legal non-existence strengthened the influence of the state (whenever an international entity gained formal importance, a multilateral treaty was needed), but became chiefly an economic problem for those non-governmental groups that had to run an international office or secretariat in accordance with national laws.

Not having legal status became, firstly a problem in regard to the transfer of money. The numerous lists of all kinds of international actors produced in the nineteenth and early twentieth centuries have a blind spot concerning questions of financial transfers. In the nineteenth-century mind map, with its silver- and gold-bullion-based financial system, money is virtually the best example of a still nationalist but also transgressive, border-crossing element, which needed multilateral cooperation in monetary unions but pretended to be spent by an "invisible hand".[11] However, the contemporary discourse on international organisations carefully established a distance between internationalism and its economic foundations. Definitions highlighted the difference between multinational firms and international organisations. Internationalists celebrated the small and discreet administration even in the case of Public International Unions, the forerunner of today's IGO, while pacifists framed an argument from the obvious imbalance of the states' military investment compared to the money available for global governance.[12]

The role of money therefore underlines and challenges the nineteenth-century narrative from two sides: the method of a territorial listing of organisations has a rather weak explanatory value; furthermore, the conjured existence of national and Western associations increasing to become a border-crossing flood is

---

[10] Questions related to this matter were discussed in a special journal published during World War II in German, French and Italian: *Archiv für das Recht der Internationalen Organisationen* 1940–1943.

[11] The Latin Monetary Union is a good example of an international organisation which constantly denied being an international organisation. For this see Guido Thiemeyer's contribution in this volume.

[12] E.g. Poinsard 1901.

not convincing, due to the fact that these organisations had weak economic foundations, lacked territorial rights and therefore had an unstable, ephemeral institutional structure. Using a transcultural approach, the question of financing gains visibility as an important aspect omitted by nineteenth-century internationalists. A history of international organisations told from the perspective of border crossing and presuming "transgression costs" promises new insights. In contrast to nineteenth-century historiography, a transcultural approach defines the significance of international organisations beyond legitimising stable entities within the territoriality of the nation state. In fact, the option of acting across borders and presuming (national) borders as aiming at but not embodying non-porosity might provide new insights into how a global multitude of actors developed and – as a reference to the contemporary situation – how they managed, enforced or disappeared in times of transition and crisis. This approach at least seems helpful for the situation after World War I, when the League of Nations introduced a new era of border-crossing institutions, when the number of international organisations increased substantially and the urgent need to end economic crises fostered national *and* border-crossing planning.[13]

## Flows of Money, Flows of Information. The Secret History of Transgression Costs and the Example of the Bank for International Settlements

### *The Bankers of International Organisations*

Opened in 1930 and since then located in Basel, the Bank for International Settlements was established to execute the Young Plan for German reparation payments. To the present day the BIS coordinates the central banks' policies and makes foreign currency and gold transactions. In the 1930s, it also acted as trustee for certain international loans. The BIS is not and was never a commercial bank; it is an international organisation without supranational functions but with an extra-territorial status.[14] In the BIS' structure the representation of national banks is crucial while private customers do not exist. As mentioned several times in BIS correspondence, the bank did not even have a vault because there was no money or gold to put in one.

[13] For an overview see Herren, Sibille and Meigen (http://www.lonsea.de).

[14] Article 10 of the relevant treaty explicitly protected the BIS against expropriation and confiscation, but also against embargo and limitation of the import and export of gold and foreign currency. See Abkommen (20.01.1930), (http://www.admin.ch/ch/d/sr/0_192_122_971/index.html).

The institutional history of the BIS is a well-researched field.[15] However, three instances of interference with the history of international organisations are rarely mentioned: first, because of the global economic crisis, the BIS' main task, the administration of international loans, simply disappeared. In 1932, the Lausanne conference decided on suspension of the World War I reparation payments, leaving the BIS with the administration of an instalment (never paid) in German bonds. While economies returned to national confinement, the BIS needed new fields of action. Second, the BIS remained the only agency imaginable that could handle money for international organisations in the 1930s by earmarking gold. Following this strategy, the BIS never became involved in the physical transfer gold. In fact, an agreement with the participating national banks allowed the BIS to identify (i.e. earmark) and reserve gold in these banks' vaults. This special function made discreet transfers possible without leaving the circle of adept financial experts. Third, the interest of the BIS in new fields of action answered the need of international organisations, whose financing by membership fees from different nations had come under pressure when states established exchange controls and limited the transfer of money in the aftermath of the global economic crisis.

When asked for empirical evidence concerning money transfers for international organisations, BIS archivists did not believe that anything of this sort was available. Theoretically, they were right. The bank was created to fulfil limited purposes, namely to stabilise national economies in Europe in order to protect the world economy. In doing so, the BIS worked first of all as a bank. Its character as an international organisation played a certain role in its recognition as an extraterritorial entity. Under the special economic and political circumstances of the 1930s, however, the BIS raised its profile as an international organisation. Although the BIS was founded to solve a European problem – the payment of German reparations – transcultural cohesion developed on a global scale: the BIS corresponded with the Indian central bank,[16] and even made advances to the National Bank of China in London.[17]

The BIS source material confirms the problems and difficulties faced by international organisations when almost all nations established exchange controls in the course of economic crisis and war. But the material does not confirm the disappearance of international border-crossing activities. In contrast to the weak legal position of international organisations and the increasing fortification of national borders, some international organisations developed an astonishing scope of action through the channels of the BIS. This aspect of activities, however, has remained virtually unnoticed in historiography. On the one hand, the destruction and looting

---

[15] Toniolo and Clement 2005; UEK (ed.), *Die Schweiz und die Goldtransaktionen im Zweiten Weltkrieg*, Zürich 2002.

[16] Bank for International Settlements Archive, Basel (henceforth BISA), 6/48, International Payments under World Postal Agreement.

[17] BISA 2/104, Bank of China 01.06.1936 – 31.10.1936.

of the archives of international organisations[18] made the reconstruction of this part of their history difficult. Even more, assuming the end of internationalism occurs with the outbreak of war, this periodisation nicely introduces a clean break separating the complex border-crossing entanglements of the 1930s from the United Nations' world order established after World War II. The BIS itself verified the assumption of an almost complete destruction of border-crossing networks during World War II by closing the corresponding files in the early 1950s.

Why then insist on a reconsideration of World War II entanglements? Currently, growing interest in complex border-crossing activities has triggered a lively debate on the so-called "third United Nations" within the UN Intellectual History Project.[19] From a historical point of view, the promising approach of reconsidering a global civil society by overcoming the formal separation between NGO and IGO entails further aspects: namely the questions of how these forms of entanglement act in times of crisis and war, how in times of political tensions national and supranational concepts interact, and, lastly, what kind of transgression costs and financing are involved.

Back to the 1930s, and presuming border-crossing entanglements are a historical rationale rather than a rare exception, the BIS files confirm an even-increasing significance of porous borders and transgressive dynamics during the War. International organisations, governmental or private, shared the fate of having a weak and unstable institutional structure. But in the hands of international civil servants and busy internationalists, international organisations turned into useful tools for border-crossing activities. The new platforms opened up a scope of action not accessible to national organs. They therefore became precious, even for those who did not believe in the League of Nations' cosmopolitanism at all. To put it differently: entanglements did not work in the way described by Fried, namely as a sum of national activities, but gained profile as an agency, doing things, which, from an institutional point of view, historians would never expect to find. As a further difference to Fried's scheme, the transcultural platform which surfaces from the BIS material has a highly ambivalent political profile. As elaborated below, the BIS attracted and served, among others, different Red Cross agencies and the Jewish Agency. It also facilitated the financial takeover of the Danube Commission by the National Socialist regime. Transcultural entanglements therefore developed a political rationale of their own, providing access to a global scope of action that was highly attractive for very different reasons.

---

[18] Herren 2002.

[19] Weiss et al. 2009.

## *The Bank's Participation in Visions of Global Governance: Contacts with the International Chamber of Commerce*

Indeed, two groups of international clients showed up in Basel. One relied on the BIS because of the sheer impossibility of transferring money across borders in the usual way, since almost all states inaugurated a severe regime of exchange control. The other group imagined it could overcome national control and fostered the idea of global connectivity. Sometimes agencies belonged to both groups, and practical reflections on banking under the pressure of war merged with visions of global governance. We might even think about the BIS itself, which, founded as a European organisation, now became a global player, corresponding with the Chinese ambassador, placing European money in the US, arguing with the Reserve Bank of India about the transfer of money from the British sterling block into earmarked gold, and discussing the problem of which institution should handle the costs of telegraphic information about prisoners of war between Japan and the US through the intermediary of the Red Cross in Geneva. Behind all these practical reflections, including the price of grain in Greece, the BIS attracted a certain type of organisation, namely those whose interests developed in a supranational context in a more prospective and utopian way.

Before explaining the practical work done by the BIS, it is important to show how the handling of transgression costs became part of a supranational world order's conceptual scheme. From this point of view, the rather precocious rapprochement of the International Chamber of Commerce (ICC) is crucial. To the BIS, the ICC was presented as an agency influencing "world public opinion", as a tool to "improve the conditions of international trade by direct ententes and without the interference of public authority".[20] When George L. Ridgeway published his still useful history of the ICC in 1938, he evoked his close relationship to Pierre Quesnay, Leon Fraser and Per Jacobsson,[21] the leading managers of the BIS. The ICC, one of the most powerful international organisations with a surprisingly low presence in today's research literature, shaped the international discourse on trade with the publication of numerous studies and opulent congress activities.[22] The affiliation between the ICC and BIS did not exclude totalitarian regimes. Although this part of ICC history needs further investigation, the asserted distance from governmental control turned into sometimes hidden forms of cooperation. In the German case, the regional group of the ICC was related to the

[20] BISA 6/19, Report on the International Chamber of Commerce. The file "Relations with International Chamber of Commerce 01.08.1930 – 31.12.1974" has a substantial gap between 1939 and 1947.

[21] Ridgeway 1938, p. x. The French citizen Pierre Quesnay (1895–1937) was a BIS director; the American Leon Fraser directed the BIS 1933–1935; Per Jacobsson entered the BIS as an economic adviser in 1931, and was "the intellectual driving force of the Bank" as Toniolo explains (Toniolo and Clement 2005, p. 287).

[22] For a rough survey see League of Nations 1938, pp. 337–338.

*Reichswirtschaftsministerium*. However, during the war, the ICC transferred its seat from Paris to Stockholm, the domicile of the president, Jan Sigfrid Edström. Better known as one of the presidents of the Olympic committee, Edström, chairman of Swedish General Electric, personally oversaw discrete but powerful networks. He had connections with the International Organisation of Industrial Employers, where he had served as a committee member;[23] he combined sports connections, trade and money. Edström cultivated personal connections with the Swedish monarchy and during the war remained a frequently spotted guest in the United States.[24] Through these functions he knew the elites of internationally active industrialists, and belonged to border-crossing networks which extended to the League of Nations' financial and economic department and the International Labour Organisation. The case of the ICC indeed shows that border-crossing flows of money went beyond financial aspects and literally crossed the borders of ideological and conceptual confinement, since connections also included the International Labour Organisation, and the world peace movement. These connections added, however, did not prevent close relations with totalitarian regimes, which gained visibility at the Berlin conference of the International Chamber of Commerce in 1937.

## *International Relief Union – and the Red Cross: How Much the BIS Knew About International Organisations*

Our second example of BIS connections with the multilayered field of international organisations seems less important and beyond the BIS' interests. The International Relief Union, founded in 1927 and located in Geneva and Paris, was devoted to disaster management and published a "revue pour l'étude des calamités". In July 1940, shortly after the German occupation of Paris, and after the BIS temporarily transferred its seat to Château d'Oex for fear of a German invasion of Basel, the secretary general of the International Relief Union wanted its rather small fortune of 400,000 Swiss Francs placed in safe custody. The Union, located at 122, Rue de Lausanne in Geneva, in the same beautiful building as the International Committee of the Red Cross (ICRC), had handed over managing control to its Italian president, Senator Giovanni Ciraolo during the war. Contacts with the BIS therefore went via Italian connections provided by the BIS General Secretary, Raffaele Pilotti, while the intermediary of the banking business was an investment-banking house in Milan.[25] The Union did not belong to the rich or powerful organisations, but had a global asset allocation with Argentine titles in the US, Indian loans in London, and

[23] See lonsea (http://www.lonsea.de/pub/person/977).

[24] See e.g. "Swedish businessmen will urge unrestricted world commerce," in: *Wall Street Journal*, 10.11.1944, p. 9.

[25] BISA 2/117, Union Internationale de Secours (Giovanni Ciraolo) to BIS Rome, 08.10.1941.

accounts in Paris, the Netherlands and Switzerland.[26] The BIS' careful documentation of the Union disclosed an organisation with global and diplomatic connections, including Latin American and Chinese diplomats, and Red Cross representatives around the globe. However, the density of information might be considered even more impressive than the connections themselves. While Germany sent a spy to Switzerland to knock on the doors of each international organisation to find out whether border-crossing entities were still working,[27] the international flow of money washed precise information ashore in Basel. The BIS knew remarkably well that the Union's practical work was limited, and that the organisation was trying to survive the war by fostering cooperation with international organisations located in Rome, while connections with the Red Cross stopped in 1941.

To a stronger degree, flows of information characterised the dense networks of Red Cross-related activities[28] in which the BIS participated. BIS literature mentions activities on behalf of the Red Cross[29] in a rather reluctant way without mentioning the multilayered networks involved. Indeed, the complex structure of the Red Cross, consisting of private national organisations and semi-official headquarters in Geneva that had difficulty paying for telegrams, food and money transfers to prisoners, seems difficult to connect with the BIS. Interestingly, the ICRC (International Committee of the Red Cross) and the BIS agreed to create a special structure, a "commission mixte de secours de la Croix-Rouge", which had BIS accounts for different purposes, from the payment of telegrams to relief goods, from money for landing sardines in Spain to the purchase of grain in Greece. In the BIS' own internal estimate, since the opening of a first account on behalf of the Red Cross, the Bank increased this service and opened the same kind of account at almost every central reserve bank worldwide. Even more important, its discreet service became well known. The money transfers on behalf of the ICRC were of special interest in occupied territories and carefully observed by exile governments,[30] but they also attracted the attention of the German Reichsbank. This institution, too, was interested in the benefits from the exchange of foreign currency, or in opportunities to

[26] BISA 2/117, Union Internationale de Secours to BIS, Geneva 07.09.1940.

[27] Herren 2002.

[28] During the War, the Union had an office in Rome, at 12 Via Toscana, an address still marked by an opulent red cross above the main entrance. BISA 2/117, Union Internationale de Secours, Paris 01.06.1940 – 31.07.1951.

[29] See Toniolo and Clement 2005, pp. 244 f.

[30] See memo 02/12/1941, mentioning the approach of the Polish Legation to BIS manager Marcel van Zeeland. In naming the BIS "banquier des organisations de la Croix-Rouge Internationale", the Polish representative was not only asking for support in the transfer of pharmaceuticals to Eastern Europe, but also for assistance in adventurous exchange processes, which included gold, Swiss Francs, Dollars, Escudos. In this highly sophisticated business, the ongoing deliberations give insight into the BIS's interests, since the BIS thought to propose to the Polish Bank a higher price than the American Treasury (see Commission mixte, Genève, Conversation téléphonique MM. Lalive – van Zeeland, BISA 2/118).

gain gold.[31] Again, as part of an institutional history, bilateral connections between single international organisations and the BIS are not exciting, not even as part of World War II history. The thrilling aspect unfolds in consideration of dense, border-crossing entanglements which grew in importance the more states closed their borders, and which gave the BIS a reflected global profile. On the rare occasions when this development became an issue in research, authors mentioned, besides their limited bilateral perspective, the technical character of these decisions. Indeed, all these highly political files about the connections between the BIS and international organisations of all kinds were represented as cases of technical cooperation – and quickly closed after World War II. The next section will show why.

## *Connections to International Governmental Organisations*

The examples already mentioned are limited to non-governmental organisations. The impression of a rather coincidental set of informal personal connections, however, is rectified with the actively supported relations between the BIS and the still largest international organisation, the Universal Postal Union (UPU). The doors to a closer relationship with international organisations were opened with an apparently technical decision made in Cairo by the delegates of the 10th Universal Postal Union congress. Out of fear of substantial financial losses, the delegates paved the way for the BIS to be included as a clearing institution for UPU-related transfers.[32] From this moment on, the BIS saved the membership fees from devaluation and later from blockade by war. The self-representation of the UPU in the League of Nations' Handbook of International Organisations helps us to understand the scope of this decision. In the late 1930s the UPU included "all the countries of the world", except the French mandate of Latakia, the Laccadive and Maldive Islands,[33] and provided the most global platform of the time. While the Telecommunications Union followed the model of the UPU, other international organisations used the BIS for other purposes, e.g. the preservation of their pensions. After the UPU decision, the International Labour Office (BIT) made an arrangement with the BIS.[34] In January 1936 BIS official J. Willem Beyen and Jan van Walré de Bordes from the League, being on cordial terms since the financial reconstruction of Austria,[35] resumed an older debate regarding the League of

[31] As an example, see the Reichsbank's interest in a BIS Red Cross account in occupied Greece of not less than 140 million drachmas. The Reichsbank proposed the conversion into a Red Cross account in Berlin at a fixed exchange rate. Reichsbankdirektorium to BIS, Berlin, 20.05.1942, BISA 2/118.

[32] Ministère des postes 1934, p. 112.

[33] League of Nations 1938, p. 383.

[34] BISA 2/92, International Labour Office to BIS, 24.04.1935.

[35] Concerning the close personal connections between League and BIS see Berger 2000.

Nations' accounts. The BIS now mentioned "no objection whatever on the part of the B.I.S. to receive deposits for the Staff Pension Fund of the League". In the meantime Basel informed the League that they had "several international institutions" as clients. The BIS, however, insisted on secrecy and suggested not disclosing the name of the League to the Bank holding the respective earmarked gold.[36] Bordes was not sure how to handle this question, but in the end the BIS held 7,632.146 ounces of fine gold at the League of Nations' disposal in London.[37]

Other organisations followed, including the Central Commission on the Navigation of the Rhine, and the corresponding organisation for the Danube. The European Commission of the Danube[38] provides a striking example of the political potential such activities had, even in cases where the amount of money involved seems rather small. The BIS became involved in the European Commission of the Danube in March 1940, shortly before Romania resigned from the League of Nations and the political situation escalated in German, Soviet and Hungarian claims. A letter addressed to Basel from Galatz, the seat of the Commission, discreetly and "à titre de pure information" inquired about the possibilities of transferring gold to the United States.[39] The BIS recommended the use of its own gold account in New York, and although we cannot say how this business developed, the BIS made transfers on behalf of the European Commission until June 1940. Again, the almost absurd simultaneity of business as usual on the one hand, and increasing political tensions on the other, is rather striking. In July 1941, the British Legation in Berne protested against the transfer of 50,000 Swiss Francs in gold from the European Commission's account to the Romanian Legation in Berne, which was at this point the representative of an Axis power. The BIS informed both parties, continued with business, and mentioned in a memorandum the countersignature of the British representative.[40] Almost the same happened at the end of 1944, when the German delegate to the European Commission, the diplomat Georg Martius, wrote a letter making it clear that financial transactions needed his approval.[41] This practice of conducting business between enemies within international organisations did not end until the Cold War started. When a new Danube commission with its seat in

---

[36] BISA 2/92, BIS (copy) to J. van Walré de Bordes, 29.01.1936.

[37] BISA 2/92, League of Nations, Treasurer, to BIS, Geneva 27.11.1936.

[38] The foundation of this organisation goes back to 1856. However, after World War I, international access to this important waterway and the guarantee of maintenance of the Danube mouth, preventing aggradation, was mentioned in special clauses of the treaties of Versailles and Trianon. Besides the UK, Italy, France and Romania, Germany held a crucial position up to 1938.

[39] BISA 2/106, vol. 1, Commission Européenne du Danube to BIS, Galatz 09.03.1940.

[40] BISA 2/106, vol. 1, Aktennotiz betreffend die in Schwebe stehende Überweisung von Gold D. Fr. 50.000.- an die rumänische Gesandtschaft in Bern für Rechnung der Europäischen Donaukommission, 30. Juli 1941 (Abschrift). Although without signature, the German notes in this case may have come from Paul Hechler, the German Assistant General Manager, who discussed the case in Berlin with Martius. See Aktennotiz 15.08.1941 sig. P. Hechler: Bericht über Besuch im Auswärtigen Amt in Berlin.

[41] BISA 2/106, Auswärtiges Amt to BIS, Berlin 28.12.1944.

Budapest was created in 1948, the British government insisted on resolving the question of the Commission's assets.

## *The BIS: Understanding Money as Information Carrier*

During the war, Basel remained a busy meeting point for financial experts, cosmopolitans and internationalists all around the discreet, apparently apolitical Bank for International Settlements. Although source material remains fragmented and incomplete, the BIS archives show both sides of a not yet fully investigated aspect of international organisations: economic crisis and war pressed these organisations, but the BIS supported financial transactions to an extent that gave an unexpected scope of action to some of these organisations. The money transfers on behalf of the Danube commission and the Red Cross organisations obviously found the support of very different actors, uniting neutrals and both parties at war in a way to bypass rigid national exchange control. During times of war the function of international organisations as border-crossing intermediaries overarched lacking (multi)national contacts and might serve as an explanation for why international organisations did not just disappear, even though business as usual, such as regular international conferences, stopped. Compared to the BIS' core business, reparations, the money involved in the transactions for international organisations remained small. This makes the BIS' disposition to be involved in complex decisions seem all the more remarkable. The invention of the "commission mixte" for the Red Cross presents a striking example of the difficulties of these transactions, but at the same time shows the unexpected scope of financial activities in times of war. In the case of the "commission mixte" a BIS memorandum listed five major problems in July 1942. According to the memorandum, the BIS struggled with the handling of national committees and their accounts.[42] The conversion of the overflowing Drachma account was mentioned, as well as the organisation of money transfers to France and the payment of telegraph connections for obtaining information about prisoners of war. But besides these complex transactions, some worth more than a million gold francs, small amounts fell within this scope as well. As the example of support for former Yugoslav officers' families shows, small transactions also needed complex forms of agreement. This case occupied the national banks of Italy, Hungary and Bulgaria.[43]

The "commission mixte", dissolved after World War II, brought in diplomatic connections, e.g. to Carl J. Burckardt, the former high commissioner and representative of the League of Nations in Danzig, and president of the International Red

---

[42] E.g. Belgian organisations, such as the Comité de coordination de ravitaillement de Belgique, an organisation based in Lisbon and directed by the former Belgian diplomat André Kerchove.

[43] BISA 2/118, Questions en suspens ou à l'examen avec la Croix-Rouge Internationale 03.07.1942.

Cross from 1944 on. The Red Cross, however, was just one among many highly powerful and important networks the BIS was involved in. Whilst hiding the League of Nations' account, the BIS disclosed cooperation between Basel and Geneva. Even during the war, the BIS' annual reports referred to results the League of Nations' experts published on the development of international loans, or assumed the world view the *Revue of Trade*, a League journal, had published.[44] It is important to mention the personal, rather than institutional contacts, and the fact that BIS officials still preferred face-to-face arrangements. The archival material shows memos written after phone calls and informal invitations, mostly connected to a great deal of travelling. F.W. Gray, the representative of the Chinese Bank in London, travelled to Basel, as did many other people whose mandate was not officially set. Pierre Vasseur, secretary general of the International Chamber of Commerce, thanked his hosts for a friendly reception in Basel with a dinner invitation to Paris, where BIS officials Fraser and Quesnay were to meet among others the ILO director-general Harold Butler.[45] Interestingly, travel did not stop during the war, and the BIS still acted in the legal limbo of semi-official and private connections.[46] Transfers conducted on behalf of the Jewish Agency provide a good example of the complexity involved and the methodological problems interpretations face when based on institutional histories. The BIS classified the Jewish Agency as an at least semi-official organisation, quoting Article 4 of the British Mandate for Palestine, where the Agency is mentioned.[47] However, in reality the complex structure of regional branches, the two main seats in Jerusalem, the private funds and banking institutions involved did not fit this official narrative; neither did the simple fact that the Jewish Agency was part of the World Zionist Organisation. Contacts took place via a private bank in Zurich, the Guyer-Zeller Bank, an institution authorised to accept Palestine pounds. The BIS official in charge was Paul Hechler and the BIS' legal advisor, Felix Weiser.[48] Both gained a detailed picture of the complex financial networks the Jewish Agency maintained.

The BIS never made a secret of doing business with international organisations, but the offensive mentioning of the international organisations' financial needs subsided during the war, when the BIS accentuated its neutrality. However, the multilayered semi-official contacts, the vertiginous juggling with different currencies on an immaterial, 'earmarked' basis did not stop until the political settings of the Cold War went back to a concept with which Fried would have been familiar with.

[44] Bank für Internationalen Zahlungsausgleich 1940, p. 44.

[45] BISA 6/19, Pierre Vasseur to Léon Fraser, Paris, 07.12.1933.

[46] The annual report, however, emphasised the connection with governmental organisations and described these activities as "natürliche Entwicklung der Tätigkeit der Bank"; Bank für Internationalen Zahlungsausgleich 1941, p. 205.

[47] BISA 2/116, Notiz, 20.08.1940.

[48] Toniolo and Clement 2005, p. 710.

## Conclusion

Returning to Fried's travelogue and his presentation of border-crossing networks awaiting discovery, the question is, do they exist? No, they don't; at least not in the imagined version of territorialised institutions, although many historians followed these imaginary lists in a way suggested by Fried. Instead of focusing on stable, well-delimited entities, transcultural history focuses its attention on the fragility of border-crossing processes. Transcultural history highlights what does not fit, but refuses to understand these processes as being an exceptional case. In fact, the awareness of the structural instability of international entities from a national point of view opens a window on their unexpected scope of action. Following this rationale, international organisations offer intermediary platforms and relational instead of territorial power. Their potential corresponds to the porosity of borders rather than the conjured narrowness of the nation state. This approach results in the detection of financing as a missing part in the history of international organisations. Money, the most fluid and global agent, seems to a remarkable extent to have been neglected in the history of international organisations. The Bank for International Settlements' archival material gives a promising first impression of how the border-crossing flow of money shaped the history of international organisations in the decisive years between 1930 and 1945. Instead of presuming death or at least hibernation, the BIS provides convincing insights into how international organisations solved their financial needs on one side, and how on the other, participating banking institutions and financial experts made use of these organisations as a way to bypass rigid exchange control. This finding might disillusion those who believe in Fried's peaceful international land. Indeed, the BIS maintained a balance between helping poor victims of war and hiding the illegal transactions of totalitarian states with the support of the same border-crossing networks. However, Fried is definitely right in one respect: the topic is worth analysing and describing, not as a well-organised map, but as a dynamic field of border-crossing exchange. Never stable, always ambivalent, this dynamic exchange comes with considerable costs involved and points to not-yet exploited opportunities to understand flows of foreign money as information carriers concerning the dynamics of international networks.

## Bibliography

"Abkommen über die Bank für Internationalen Zahlungsausgleich (20.01.1930)." Accessed 28.10.2011 (http://www.admin.ch/ch/d/sr/0_192_122_971/index.html).

Archer, Clive. 1992. *International Organizations*, 2nd ed. New York: Routledge.

*Archiv für das Recht der Internationalen Organisationen*, 1940–1943.

Baldwin, Simeon E. 1907. "International Congresses and Conferences of the Last Century as Forces Working Toward the Solidarity of the World." *The American Journal of International Law* 1, no. 3, 565–578, 808–829.

Bank for International Settlements Archive Basel (BISA): BISA 2/92, International Labour Office to BIS, 24.04.1935.
Bank for International Settlements Archive Basel (BISA): BISA 2/92, BIS (copy) to J. van Walré de Bordes, 29.01.1936.
Bank for International Settlements Archive Basel (BISA): BISA 2/92, League of Nations, Treasurer, to BIS, Geneva 27.11.1936.
Bank for International Settlements Archive Basel (BISA): BISA 2/104, Bank of China 1.6.1936 – 31.10.1936.
Bank for International Settlements Archive Basel (BISA): BISA 2/106 vol. 1, Commission Européenne du Danube to BIS, Galatz 09.03.1940.
Bank for International Settlements Archive Basel (BISA): BISA 2/106 vol. 1, Abschrift: Aktennotiz betreffend die in Schwebe stehende Überweisung von Gold D.Fr. 50.000.- an die rumänische Gesandtschaft in Bern für Rechnung der Europäischen Donaukommission, 30.07.1941.
Bank for International Settlements Archive Basel (BISA): BISA 2/106, Auswärtiges Amt an BIS, Berlin 28.12.1944.
Bank for International Settlements Archive Basel (BISA): BISA 2/117, Union Internationale de Secours (Giovanni Ciraolo) an BIS Rome, 08.10.1941.
Bank for International Settlements Archive Basel (BISA): BISA 2/117, Union Internationale de Secours to BIS, Geneva 07.09.1940.
Bank for International Settlements Archive Basel (BISA): BISA 2/117, Union Internationale de Secours, Paris 01.06.1940 – 31.07.1951.
Bank for International Settlements Archive Basel (BISA): BISA 2/118, Commission mixte, Genève, Conversation téléphonique MM. Lalive – van Zeeland.
Bank for International Settlements Archive Basel (BISA): BISA 2/118, Reichsbankdirektorium an BIS, Berlin, 20.05.1942.
Bank for International Settlements Archive Basel (BISA): BISA 2/118, Questions en suspens ou à l'examen avec la Croix-Rouge Internationale 03.07.1942.
Bank for International Settlements Archive Basel (BISA): BISA 6/19, Report on the International Chamber of Commerce: Relations with International Chamber of Commerce 01.08.1930 – 31.12.1974.
Bank for International Settlements Archive Basel (BISA): BISA 6/19, Pierre Vasseur to Léon Fraser, Paris, 07.12.1933.
Bank for International Settlements Archive Basel (BISA): BISA 6/48, International Payments under World Postal Conventions.
Bank für Internationalen Zahlungsausgleich. 1940. *Zehnter Jahresbericht, 1. April 1939 – 31. März*. Basel.
Bank für Internationalen Zahlungsausgleich. 1941. *Elfter Jahresbericht, 1. April 1940 – 31. März*. Basel.
Berger, Peter. 2000. *Im Schatten der Diktatur. Die Finanzdiplomatie des Vertreters des Völkerbundes in Österreich, Meinoud Marinus Rost van Tonningen 1931–1936*. Wien: Böhlau.
"BIS History – Overview." Accessed 28.10.2011 (http://www.bis.org/about/history.htm).
Boli, John & George M. Thomas. 1999. *Constructing World Culture: International Non-Governmental Organizations Since 1875*. Stanford: Stanford University Press.
Fried, Alfred H. 1908. *Das Internationale Leben der Gegenwart*. Leipzig: B.G. Teubner.
Fried, Alfred H. 1908. *Verzeichnis von 1000 Zeitungsartikeln A.H. Frieds zur Friedensbewegung*. Berlin.
Fried, Albert H. 1912. *Lehrbuch der Internationalen Hilfssprache "Esperanto"*. Stuttgart: Franckh'sche Verlagsh.
Fried, Albert H. 1913. "Wer ist's des Pazifismus (Who is Who? of the Peace Movement, Qui êtes-vous? Du Pacifisme)." *Handbuch der Friedensbewegung, Zweiter Teil*, 311–422. Berlin, Leipzig: Friedens-Warte.

Göhring, Walter. 2006. *Verdrängt und vergessen. Friedensnobelpreisträger Alfred Hermann Fried*, Wien: Kremayr & Scheriau.
Herren, Madeleine. 2002. "'Outwardly an Innocuous Conference Authority'. National Socialism and the Logistics of International Information Management." *German History* 20 (1) 67–92.
Herren, Madeleine, Christiane Sibille and Christof Meigen, "LONSEA: Searching the Globe through the Lenses of the League of Nations." Accessed: 28.10.2011 (http://www.lonsea.de).
Herren, Madeleine, Martin Rüesch & Christiane Sibille. Forthcoming. *Transcultural History*. Heidelberg: Springer.
League of Nations. 1938. *Handbook of International Organisations*. Geneva.
Ministère des postes, télégraphes et telephones. 1934. *Convention et Arrangements de l'Union Postale Universelle signés au Caire le 20 Mars 1934*. Paris.
Murphy, Craig. 1994. *International Organization and Industrial Change: Global Governance since 1850*. New York: Oxford University Press.
Poinsard, Léon. 1901. *Les unions et ententes internationals*. Berne: E. Baumgart.
Ridgeway, George L. 1938. *Merchants of Peace: Twenty Years of Business Diplomacy Through the International Chamber of Commerce, 1919–1938*. New York: Columbia University Press.
Schönemann-Behrens, Petra. 2004. *'Organisiert die Welt!': Leben und Werk des Friedens-Nobelpreisträgers Alfred Hermann Fried (1864–1921)*. Doctoral Thesis, Bremen.
Shavit, David. 1990. *The United States in Asia, A Historical Dictionary*. Westport CT: Greenwood Press.
"Swedish Businessmen Will Urge Unrestricted World Commerce." *Wall Street Journal*, 10.11.1944, 9.
Toniolo, Gianni and Piet Clement. 2005. *Central Bank Cooperation at the Bank for International Settlements, 1930–1973*. Cambridge: Cambridge University Press.
UEK, ed. 2002. *Die Schweiz und die Goldtransaktionen im Zweiten Weltkrieg*. Zürich: Chronos.
Walters, Francis P. 1960. *A History of the League of Nations*. London: Oxford University Press.
Weiss, Thomas G., Tatiana Carayannis and Richard Jolly. 2009. "The 'Third' United Nations." *Global Governance: A Review of Multilateralism and International Organizations* 15, no. 1, 23–142.

# Part II
# Technologies

# Chapter 4
# Institutionalised Co-operation on International Communication: The International Administrative Unions as a Means of Governing Globalisation Processes

**Norman Weiß**

**Abstract** The nineteenth century witnessed restoration and reformation, the heyday of the nation state in Europe and inter-state cooperation at the same time. Driven by technical progress, communication across borders became an everyday phenomenon demanding transnational cooperation and regulation. Whereas in the political field irregular conferences turned out to be an appropriate instrument for governing transnational cooperation, a more constant and institutionalised matter proved to be adequate for technical cooperation.

In 1865, the International Telegraph Convention set up a relevant administrative union which merged in 1932 with the International Radiotelegraph Union from 1906 to form the newly labelled International Telecommunication Union (ITU). The parties to the ITU met regularly in so-called plenipotentiary conferences every 3 years. Already in 1875 the International Telegraph Convention was completely redrafted and the organisation's structure changed. The contracting parties created an instrument that paved the way for a modern form of international standard setting. The new, simplified convention contained only general provisions of a policy nature that would remain in effect for an "indeterminate length of time" (Art. 20), detailed rules of a transitory and specific nature that might be subject to frequent changes with the progress of technology were put into the "Regulations for international service" (also known as the Telegraph Regulations). The newly established "administrative conferences" attended by technical experts from the member states were responsible for revising the regulations when necessary.

This was an early example of the transferral of power from sovereign nation states to an international organisation in order to govern transnational communication effectively. The administrative unions, as the first examples in modern history, show the ability of self-interested rational agents to overcome collective action dilemmas, i.e. situations where cooperation avoids sub-optimal outcomes for cooperators. The newly created institutions shaped a spirit of cooperation and the

N. Weiß (✉)
Human Rights Centre, University of Potsdam, Potsdam, Germany
e-mail: weiss@uni-potsdam.de

I. Löhr and R. Wenzlhuemer (eds.), *The Nation State and Beyond*, Transcultural Research – Heidelberg Studies on Asia and Europe in a Global Context,
DOI 10.1007/978-3-642-32934-0_4, © Springer-Verlag Berlin Heidelberg 2013

practice of standard setting proved that cooperation is effective. Furthermore, they show the spill-over effects of cooperation: increased cooperation in one area leads to increased cooperation in other areas.

## Introduction: The Need for Technical Co-operation

By the end of the Napoleonic Wars, European governments thoroughly reorganised the political order of Europe which had been overthrown by the French revolution and French imperialism.[1] While there was a strong tendency towards restoring the structures of societies and the foundations of government as they had been under the Ancien Régime, the consolidation of territories achieved in the meantime was in general disputed. The French Revolution had given a strong stimulus to the idea of the nation state and, during the following decades, especially the Austrian Empire and the Ottoman Empire were put under increasing pressure as their peoples struggled for self-determination, often being supported by the Russian government. In this situation, the idea of co-operation on the political level was outlined and implemented by the Austrian Chancellor of State, Metternich, and backed by the British government whose politics aimed at a balance of power in Europe.[2] The Holy Alliance and the subsequently concluded Quadruple-Alliance aimed at the "general Tranquillity of Europe". Thus, the "Concert of Europe" or the "Congress System" emerged and guaranteed peace in central Europe.[3]

This intergovernmental co-operation could either remain vague or become very concrete but, generally, happened to be established on an ad hoc basis. It was only in the German Confederation created by the Congress of Vienna in 1815 (and operating until 1866) that a continuous forum emerged with a very broad set of tasks.[4] At the same time, the newly established regimes of international rivers (Danube, Rhine) modelled an unprecedented type of technical co-operation by states sharing a common transnational interest. Co-operation was formalised and rules were standardised; national monitoring mechanisms were established that applied the same rules. These regimes, slightly modified, are still working today.[5]

The nineteenth century witnessed considerable developments in communication. Hitherto, mail had been transported by a private company, acting throughout Europe: the postal services of Thurn and Taxis. By the mid-century, the idea of the nation state had become popular all over Europe. Postal services were closely connected to the nation state and, therefore, co-operation between states in this

[1] For a general overview cf. Schulze 1998, pp. 185–250; with a focus on intergovernmental co-operation cf. Weiß 2009, pp. 13–90.

[2] Cf. Kissinger 1957.

[3] Baumgart 1987; Rosenne 1992.

[4] Gruner 1992, pp. 49–95; Rumpler 1990.

[5] Chamberlain 1923; Barberis 1995; Meißner 2000.

sector became essential. Finally, the Universal Postal Union was established in 1878, building on a previous initiative dating back to 1874.[6]

New technologies were developed that changed the face of Europe even more visibly and faster than had been the case in the seventeenth and eighteenth centuries.[7] A number of scientists and engineers in various European countries and in the United States of America tried to build an electrical telegraph, among them Carl Friedrich Gauss, the famous mathematician, who successfully co-developed a telegraph system in Germany. In 1837, Samuel Morse and Alfred Vail had developed an electrical telegraph with a special alphabet, the so-called Morse code. As a consequence, various technical systems existed which, however, lacked compatibility. Trans-border communication was complicated and time-intensive.

Postal services, electrical telegraphy and railway systems followed national standards – as was the case with currency, weights and measures. Each set of standards was closely linked to the sovereign state. This situation was even worse in Germany, as the German Confederation at one time consisted of 41 entities, decreasing to 37. Thus, a national or even particularistic approach contrasted with the emerging need for transnational co-operation and exchange.[8] As the realisation of economic development strove for trans-national efficiency, the political goal changed and governments made first steps to co-operate with each other. The German Customs Union (Zollverein), which was founded in 1837, was indispensable for progress in the economic sector.[9] The German Zollverein allowed a progressive economic modernisation whereas the German Confederation aimed at political stability by conserving the *status quo*. In the end, the dynamic element prevailed.[10]

The long nineteenth century (Hobsbawm) in Europe witnessed dramatic changes and far-reaching developments. At the same time, the European governments, after the experience of the French Revolution and the wars that followed, sought to maintain stability.[11] It was the political framework of the Concert of Europe on a large scale and the framework of the German Confederation at the regional level that allowed for stability and change to take place simultaneously. While governments defended their position and democratic reforms did not take place, there was progress and development within society, science and economy. Of course, governments dealt with economic questions and intervened in the economic sector, as the development of free trade policy shows. Thus, issues such as trade, traffic, tariffs and communication were of major importance for governments who clearly saw the need for international co-operation. But they

[6] Codding 1964; Weber 2000.

[7] Wiesner-Hanks 2006, pp. 402–437.

[8] Langewiesche 2004; Veit-Brause 1978.

[9] Lee 1991.

[10] Hamerow 1972, pp. 100ff.

[11] Schroeder 1996; Dülffer et al. 1990.

were not perceived as belonging to the same category as issues of foreign policy and military questions. Therefore, and because of the contemporary perception of sovereignty, international co-operation was organised in sectors: political co-operation was not mixed up with co-operation in technical matters. Thus, technical co-operation could go further than the political, as the example of the German Confederation and the German Zollverein shows. On the international level, technical co-operation was possible with partners from outside the Concert of Europe. Governments thus took a realistic approach to organising international co-operation in a given framework. Additionally, the pacifying and civilising force of trade was broadly acknowledged by European governments and societies.[12] In this way, an internationalist climate prevailed in the heyday of the nation state.

This framework was, of course, transformed in the course of time. Imperialism and globalisation posed a challenge as did unified Germany, especially after 1890.[13] The System of Vienna was finally abandoned by those governments who had the ability to create a new order.[14] The First World War brought this system and the internationalist climate to an end, although the administrative unions, which had been created as autonomous institutions, were able to survive the political framework from which they originated. After the war, a new internationalism emerged, which was sceptical about the capability of nation states to manage the challenges of the time and which expected a new impetus from the League of Nations.[15]

## The Creation and Development of the International Telecommunication Union (ITU)

### *Initial Phase, Founding and the First 10 Years of ITU*

Economic co-operation and free trade between European states and the US on the one hand, and the relations with the colonies on the other, increased the need for faster communication.[16] The electrical telegraph was the medium that met that need perfectly: on 24 May 1844, the Morse telegraph was publicly demonstrated for the first time by sending a message from Washington to Baltimore. The first transcontinental telegraph system was established in the US only 17 years later, on

[12] Howe 1997.

[13] Ullrich 1997, pp. 182ff.

[14] Langhorne 1981.

[15] Zimmern (1923) 1929; Trentmann 2007.

[16] Cf. Ewing, in this volume, pointing out both the disparities and similarities between European and dependent or less developed states with regard to ownership and use of cables and telegraphs as means of governing globalised or at least trans-regional processes or situations. Akami, in this volume, discusses the relation and governing processes between the metropolitan state and the colonies.

24 October 1861. By 27 July 1866, the first transatlantic telegraph cable had been successfully laid.[17]

To regulate the technical issues of trans-border communication, several bilateral and regional agreements were established between and among the states of Western Europe between 1849 and 1865. As telegraphic networks expanded rapidly, in 1865, the French government invited 19 European states to an International Telegraph Conference in Paris in order to develop a comprehensive agreement replacing these treaties and covering the relevant issues.[18] This international treaty was to establish the necessary framework that would allow further developments to be kept up with. As a foundation, the governments decided on common rules to standardise equipment to facilitate international interconnection, adopted uniform operating instructions which would apply to all countries, and laid down common international tariff and accounting rules.

On 17 May 1865, the International Telegraph Convention was signed in Paris.[19] The Regulations for International Service (also known as the Telegraph Regulations) were annexed to and supplemented the Convention. The Regulations covered matters of administrative details, such as operating procedures and settlement of accounts. The use of the Morse code as the international telegraph alphabet was adopted as was the protection of the secrecy of correspondence (Art. 5), and the right of everybody to use international telegraphy (Art. 4). Uniform charges (tariffs) for international telegram exchanges were established, whilst all terminal and transit charges were coded and published in a table annexed to the Convention.

These rules clearly show that the Convention respected strong economic and technical needs. But it was beyond doubt that in mainland Europe telegraphy was a state-run affair with both significant military implications and relevance for the control of public opinion (freedom of expression). Consequently, in the Convention, states reserved the right to stop any transmission they considered a danger to state security, or in violation of national laws, public order or morals (Art. 19).

The 1865 Conference also stipulated that in order to keep up with technical and administrative progress, the Convention should be periodically revised by international conferences held in the capitals of the contracting parties. This approach was very progressive for the time: the Convention for Rhine Navigation, as amended on 31 March 1831, could be amended only by a complicated procedure and the Convention's organ, the Central Commission for the Navigation on the Rhine, was expressly not permitted to alter any rules, not even in mere technical questions. Whilst this problem was solved in a pragmatic way among the small group of contracting parties, the larger number of signatories of the International Telegraph

[17] Cf. Müller-Pohl, in this volume, focusing on the specific trans-nationalism of "cable agents" on the one hand and the increasing nationalism since 1880 on the other.

[18] Cf. Codding 1952.

[19] A facsimile of this document can be accessed, "Convention télégraphique internationale de Paris (1865) et Règlement de service international (1865)," online: http://www.itu.int/dms_pub/itu-s/oth/02/01/S02010000014002PDFF.pdf, 20.04.2010. All the documents referred to in this section can be easily viewed via ITU's website (http://www.itu.int).

Convention established a simplified amending procedure with regard to technical details in Art. 54:

> Les dispositions de la présente Convention seront complétées, en ce qui concerne les règles de détail du service international, par un règlement commun qui sera arrêté de concert entre les administrations télégraphiques des États contractants.
>
> Les dispositions de ce règlement entreront en vigueur en même temps que la présente Convention; elles pourront être, à toute époque, modifiées d'un commun accord par lesdites administrations.

The setting of standards was thus delegated to the relevant bureaucracies acting on a common basis. Furthermore, the Convention itself was to be revised on a continuous basis (Art. 56). For this reason, the contracting parties were to meet every 3 years and these so-called plenipotentiary conferences proved to be an important element in keeping the Union up to date in its long history. In 1868, the plenipotentiary conference was held in Vienna. Here, a permanent secretariat, the "International Bureau of Telegraph Administrations", was established and entrusted with administrative duties: gathering and disseminating technical information, publishing rate (tariff) tables, collecting statistics and publishing a journal on telegraphy matters. The Bureau was located in Berne, Switzerland, and began its activities on 1 January 1869. The International Telegraph Union had become a true international organisation — the plenary organ, the plenipotentiary conference, was meeting every 3 years and the Bureau was acting permanently.

Already in 1875, 10 years after the first conference in Paris, the fourth plenipotentiary conference held in St. Petersburg completely re-drafted the International Telegraph Convention and changed the organisation's structure. The contracting parties created an instrument that paved the way for a modern form of international standard setting. The new, simplified convention contained only general provisions of a policy nature that would remain in effect for an "indeterminate length of time" (Art. 20). All the detailed rules of a transitory and specific nature that might be subject to frequent changes with the progress of technology were put into the "Regulations for international service" (also known as the Telegraph Regulations). The new convention contained only 21 articles.

The conference created a new organ, the so-called "administrative conferences", which would be responsible for revising the Regulations and the Table of Telegraphic Rates (Articles 15–16). Administrative conferences would be attended by technical experts from the member states who would not have the right to revise any of the provisions of the International Telegraph Convention itself. The convention could only be revised by a plenipotentiary conference.

## *Legal Assessment*

Sovereign states – which were at that time the only subjects of public international law –concluded a treaty and thereby created an international organisation, the ITU. States made basic rules for the conditions of transnational communication and, at the same time, regulated technical and financial details. They saw from the beginning that it was necessary to keep pace with technical development and thus did not conceptualise the 1865 convention as an "eternal" treaty, but opened it up for regular revision. This revision was a task for the states' delegates who had to meet periodically at plenipotentiary conferences for this purpose. These plenipotentiary conferences acted as the plenary organ of the ITU, bound by the object and purpose of the 1865 convention. Of course, states were always the "masters of the treaty" and could amend or even terminate the convention. But the institutionalised mechanism of the plenipotentiary conferences had a new quality and showed a higher level of integration. This was a conferral of power to the ITU.

States even went one step further and opened up the standard-setting procedure in technical matters. Article 54 of the 1865 convention empowered the relevant national bureaucracies to modify by consensus the technical regulations at any time. This implied regular meetings and continuous contact among these bureaucracies which again indicates a higher level of integration. Nevertheless, the nature of this interaction was still informal. This mode of integration did not restrict states' sovereignty legally, but was a clear political signal in favour of international co-operation.

With the revision of the 1865 convention in 1875, the ITU was re-conceptualised: the newly created organ, the administrative conferences, became the forum for the formalised and institutionalised co-operation of national bureaucracies. This meant a shift from earlier intergovernmental co-operation on the bureaucratic level to an ITU-internal organ with its own powers and competencies.

## *Further Development of the ITU*

After the conference in St. Petersburg (1875), the Union held a series of administrative conferences to revise the Telegraph Regulations, but the next plenipotentiary conference to revise the International Telegraph Convention, which had proved to be an adequate instrument, was not held until 1932.

The International Radiotelegraph Union was founded in 1906, based on the Radiotelegraph Convention. After broadcasting had become established in general usage in the 1920s, this sector needed regulation too. In 1932, the two unions held simultaneous conferences in Madrid, and decided to merge their organisations into a single entity, the International Telecommunication Union (ITU). The Telegraph Convention of 1875 and the (revised) Radiotelegraph Convention of 1927 were henceforth combined into a single convention. This instrument covered the three fields of telegraphy, telephony and radio. The new International Telecommunication Convention became effective on 1 January 1934. It served as the Union's charter and constitution, establishing its legal existence and setting forth its purposes, structure and functions.[20]

[20] Cf. Müller-Pohl in this volume, who discusses the role of private companies taking part in this governing process.

The technical regulations were treated separately in distinct sections of Telecommunication Regulations: Radio, Telephone and Telegraph Regulations. These regulations were annexed to and supplemented the Convention.

The convention defined the new term "telecommunication" as follows:

> [. . .] any telegraphic or telephonic communication of signs, signals, writing, facsimiles and sounds of any kind, by wire, wireless or other systems or processes of electric signalling or visual signalling (semaphores).

Following the break-down of several European empires after World War I, new states emerged by way of secession or dissolution; some former colonies were granted independence. Furthermore, the days of the absolute dominance of the European powers had ended. This led to the inclusion of a number of non-European countries, so that 80 states participated in the Madrid plenipotentiary conference. International communication had become truly worldwide.

This paper will not examine the further development of the ITU,[21] which became a specialised agency of the United Nations Organisation (UN) on 1 January 1949 after its charter had been revised in 1947.

## Governing Globalisation Processes by the ITU-Regime: Theoretical Approaches and Practical Results

As shown in the previous section, states had concluded a multilateral treaty in order to create an international organisation (primary level) and, in a second step, set out the legal foundation for technical co-operation on a day-to-day basis. Thus, an international regime was set up which allowed telecommunications to be standardised efficiently across borders (secondary level). This shows the linkage between public international law and international relations.

### *Theoretical Approaches*

In international relations theory,[22] rationalism portrays states as goal-orientated entities whose behaviour aims at the maximisation of their individual benefit. Therefore, they are assumed to act consequentially. According to rationalism, both foreign policies and international institutions are the products of calculations of advantage made by national decision units. As rationalism has deeply influenced the study of international regimes, regime theory[23] can be said to use rational

[21] Codding 1988; Magiera 1995; Noll 1995, 1999.

[22] Cf. Jackson and Sørensen 2007; Schieder and Spindler 2006.

[23] Hasenclever et al. 1997; Zangl 2010.

institutionalism as its main tenet. Its central thesis is that international regimes are created and maintained by rational and egoistic states because, and as long as, they are useful to them.[24] Regimes can be useful to states because they help them to achieve joint gains through co-operation. In many situations, states have common interests which they can only realise if they manage to co-operate effectively. Moreover, it can by no means be taken for granted that states with common interests will also co-operate. The existence of such interests is only a necessary, but not a sufficient condition for co-operation.[25]

The functionalist theory of integration assumes that international co-operation and economic interdependence lead to political integration and to peace among states.[26] Neo-functionalism pointed at the importance of political actors' commitment to co-operation and assumed that successful integration is a self-perpetuating process.[27]

Creating a regime is costly which in turn forms one basis for why regimes endure even if some or even all of their members are no longer satisfied with their performance.[28] As such, the expected utility of maintaining the present sub-optimal, albeit still beneficial, regime will be greater than that of abandoning or leaving it in order to re-build or re-organise it later, especially when this behaviour is likely to result in a situation where no regime exists at all, or only one which is very weak. The argument for the high costs of renegotiation, however, has been criticised and cannot be regarded as the only argument in favour of regime stability.[29] States' concern for their reputation – which might be tarnished by leaving a regime and thus being perceived as an unreliable partner – can be seen as a second argument. A more sociological approach to institutionalism assumes that states are significantly less free to ignore institutional commitments than rationalist approaches suggest. The behaviour of states, like any social behaviour, presupposes normative structures and fundamental institutions such as sovereignty, diplomacy and international law. This insight, then, is applied to international regimes. Both a regulatory and a constitutive dimension are found in principles and a shared understanding of desirable and acceptable forms of social behaviour.[30] Regimes, therefore, require states to behave in accordance with their norms and rules; in addition, they help to create a common social world for interpreting the meaning of behaviour. Furthermore, a self-stabilisation hypothesis of co-operation came into being:

[24] Keohane 1989, p. 167.

[25] Thiemeyer, in this volume, shows this using the example of the Latin Monetary Union.

[26] Mitrany 1933; Ibid. 1966.

[27] Haas 1958.

[28] Keohane 1984, p. 103.

[29] Mearsheimer 1995, p. 26.

[30] Kratochwil and Ruggie 1986, p. 764.

> Even if egoistic reasons were its starting point, the process of cooperating tends to redefine those reasons by reconstituting identities and interests in terms of new inter-subjective understandings and commitments.[31]

This constructivist approach points at the inter-relatedness of action and knowledge and underlines how co-operation may have the effect of causing states to develop a more collective identity. Of course, these identities are shaped domestically as well; at the very last, a readiness for co-operation must be found to exist. More recent contributions to regime analysis, therefore, have given more consideration to domestic factors.[32] In this light, liberal trading states with corporatist domestic structures are more likely to conduct regime-conducive foreign policies. The common practice of liberal states to transform international agreements into national law is likely to strengthen their commitment to these agreements.

The administrative unions, as the first examples in modern history, show the ability of self-interested rational agents to overcome collective action dilemmas, i.e. situations where co-operation avoids sub-optimal outcomes for co-operators. The newly created institutions shaped a spirit of co-operation and the practice of standard-setting proved that co-operation is effective. Furthermore, they show the spill-over effects of co-operation: increased co-operation in one area leads to increased co-operation in other areas. In this way, several administrative unions were created up until the First World War, and they were modelled after the ITU.

Spill-over effects were first described by neo-functionalism with regard to European integration in the European Economic Community.[33] They both symbolised the success of integration and served as a mechanism to explain the process of continuing integration. This explanatory mechanism has three dimensions, namely functional, political and cultivated.[34] Functional spill-over results from the growing interdependence of various sectors which need to be combined and 'harmonised' in order to optimise the effects of integration in each sector. Political spill-over strengthens the supra-national level from which greater influence meets changed expectations and awareness on the national level, both by governments and by societies. This leads to a new dynamic of co-operation which is, on the national level, now perceived as being in the self-interest of national societies. Cultivated spill-over results from the activities of the supra-national organs. They encourage and govern the integration process and, from a "neutral" position, mediate conflicts between national governments in the interest of stronger integration.

But spill-over effects are also relevant to the effects of international regimes. They reduce uncertainty and transaction costs, especially with regard to compliance on the one hand, and to continuing co-operation on the other.[35] Additionally,

---

[31] Wendt 1992, p. 417.

[32] Zürn 1993.

[33] Haas 1958; Schmitter 1970.

[34] For a systematic approach cf. Tranholm-Mikkelsen 1991.

[35] Keohane 1984, pp. 89–109.

a higher rate of interdependence makes the creation of regimes and the co-operation within regimes more attractive for states. This effect is greater the more states are involved. In this situation, a functioning regime is far more effective than the mechanisms provided for in the anarchical society of states.

## Practical Results

### *International Regimes and International Organisations*

In the decades following the foundation of the ITU in 1865, the spill-over effect was used to set up a growing variety of international administrative unions[36] in the various fields of technical and industrial progress each "regulating a revolutionary new communication technology"[37] or covering an issue with trans-border implications. Governments and business representatives had common interests and the pragmatic approach respected states' sovereignty while allowing smooth co-operation and the in-time creation of regulations according to technical progress.

It was a far greater leap to create international organisations which focus on issues that cut more strongly into states' sovereignty, such as peace, security and disarmament. The League of Nations (1919) and the United Nations (1945) are no mere administrative unions. They are modern international organisations, resulting from a still ongoing process of integration.[38] Therefore, this was not the step-by-step progress which is normally associated with the spill-over effect. Here, we can witness a true paradigm shift by facing a new category of integration. The League and the UN cover fields closely linked to state sovereignty which could only be approached after two World Wars showing the bitter results of inter-state anarchy. Thus, this was no development resulting logically out of the founding of the ITU in 1865.

However, the early administrative unions paved the way for these organisations which came into being in the course of the twentieth century. They set out the institutional structure – a plenary organ, a restricted organ, a secretariat – and, even more importantly, allowed the experience of continuous, peaceful co-operation. These administrative unions are an example of global governance *avant la lettre*: as they were linked to dynamically developing fields of technology, the administrative unions made progress themselves and, at the same time, governed these processes. Furthermore, they literally spread over the globe thereby giving evidence for the world-system of inter-connected states.[39]

---

[36] Wolfrum 1995.

[37] Murphy 1994, p. 7.

[38] Cf. Weiß 2009, pp. 96ff., pp. 132ff.

[39] Cf. Grewe 1984, pp. 535ff.

Interestingly, this happened during times when the state was perceived to be powerful and able to solve problems. Co-operation was not seen as a weakness resulting from the restricted or even diminishing power of the state, but as a means to create the future. (European) Civilisation was closely linked to progress and optimism.[40] By the end of the twentieth century, the world was facing a de-nationalisation of politics and thus discussing governance beyond or even without the state.[41] This led to sometimes irrational expectations of international organisations which, however, still depend strongly on the power of states.

## *ITU and Technical Progress*

The Union, already in its early days, was confronted with technical innovations. In the 1870s the telephone was invented and the first long-distance telephone line was installed (in California in 1877). At the plenipotentiary conference in Berlin, the innovation was successfully implemented and found its place in the International Service Regulations (Art. LXVII § 1, Berlin Revision (1885)):

> International telephonic communication may be established, as the want arises, by the Administrations of the contracting States, either by the construction of special wires, or the appropriation of already existing wires to that service.

The technical questions were delegated to the national administrations which were to act consensually.

Subsequently, new technologies, namely radio and television, satellite transmission and the internet were dealt with similarly. The ITU's competence was extended to these new media, which opened up the Union's mandate from individual communication to the new phenomenon of mass communication. By way of consequence, the political implication increased slightly over time, but has stayed closely linked to the basic technical question. From the point of view of the member states, this approach is adequate. The ITU is, as a result, more engaged in the debate about the internet than was the case with the New World Information and Communication Order (see below).

## *Challenges*

The first problem to be discussed results from new players entering into a well-established system as was the case after the process of decolonisation had reached

[40] Cf. the paradigmatic work of Buckle 1857–1861; Thiemeyer, in this volume, underlines the crucial effects of cultural driving forces.

[41] Zürn 1998; Teubner 1997; Risse 2003.

its end. Issues such as the possibility of altering rules and the question of in whose interests these rules were made shall be addressed here.

During the nineteenth century, the international system was set up by a small number of European and non-European states, and major parts of the world were under European control as colonies and dependant territories. The number of independent states which took part in the development of this international system increased very slowly.[42] The dissolution of the Austrian and the Ottoman Empires after World War I led to an increase in European states which were integrated into the international system without problem. The process of decolonisation began in India in 1947 and culminated in the mid 1960s. These new states became members of the UN,[43] but the UN charter and other multi-lateral treaties had been designed by the industrialised states of the North. International law and its forms of co-operation followed the concept of *ius publicum europaeum*, which had evolved since 1648. At this very moment, however, states from the South felt that there was a need for change. This was the case for public international law as a whole, but the debate[44] focused on the rules regulating the flow of information.

Here, the degree of disproprotionality between states was clearly reflected in the flow of news between nations, which was dominated by northern press agencies (including the Soviet TASS). The developing countries thus could not contribute any substantial input and had only restricted access to the radio spectrum. Because of the fact that information content was largely produced by the developed countries, the image of the developing countries was frequently false and biased. This incorrect image was presented to the developing countries themselves and had detrimental effects on their inner balance, a situation which resulted in a demand for a more balanced flow of information.

The debate about a New World Information and Communication Order (NWICO) was mainly conducted under the auspices of UNESCO. The 1980 "MacBride-Report" analysed the issue and made proposals to strengthen the situation of the countries from the South.[45] The United States, the United Kingdom and Singapore were strongly opposed to these ideas and all left UNESCO (USA: 1984–2003; UK: 1985–1997; Singapore: 1986–2007). The debate was clearly political and took place in a forum that was dominated by the developing countries, which were in the majority.

Whilst this debate did not lead to a new conception of the world information order and, thus, the structure and working methods of the ITU remained unchanged, the internet paved the way for a new and unprecedented openness of international communication.

[42] Grewe 1984; Verdross 1960.

[43] Henn 2010; Volger 2010.

[44] Österdahl 1992.

[45] International Commission for the Study of Communication Problems, Communication and Society Today and Tomorrow 1980.

Technical innovation had provided new answers to the question of limited resources and how to control them. Al Jazeera could not have come into existence 30 years earlier bearing in mind that access to the media had been limited technically. Today, the technical possibilities offered by the internet enable the fulfilment of many of the expectations which had been expressed in the course of the NWICO debate. Today, governments in developing countries can make information accessible to those in developed countries who have an interest in it. At the same time, they are confronted with the interests of their citizens to disseminate ideas and to gather information. This marks the second of today's challenges: what degree of freedom is desirable and how much regulation is possible in the age of the internet? Following this, discussions focus on regulation by the non-governmental agency ICANN[46] and the consequences of the so-called digital divide.[47] Another major issue touches upon the control of illegal content such as pornography or incitement to racial or religious hatred.

Whilst the debate concerning the NWICO took place chiefly within UNESCO, today's discussion about the regulation of the internet is a matter of concern for the ITU. The World Summit on Information Society (WSIS – held in Geneva in 2003 and in Tunis in 2005) and the plenipotentiary conference of 2006 entrusted the ITU with the task building confidence and security in the use of information and communication technologies.[48] The ITU Global Cybersecurity Agenda (GCA) is a framework for international co-operation aimed at enhancing confidence and security in information society. The CGA was launched in 2007, and one of its initiatives is Child Online Protection (COP) which is designed to tackle cybersecurity holistically. The COP initiative will address legal, technical, organisational and procedural issues as well as capacity building and international co-operation.

This new development shows that the ITU has broadened its activities over the decades as is apparent from the mission statement which can be found on the ITU website:

> Whether through developing the standards used to create infrastructure to deliver telecommunications services on a worldwide basis, through equitable management of the radio-frequency spectrum and satellite orbits to help bring wireless services to every corner of the world, or through providing support to countries as they pursue telecommunication development strategies, all the elements of ITU's work are centred around the goal of putting every human being within easy and affordable reach of information and communication and to contribute significantly towards economic and social development of all people.[49]

[46] Hartwig 2010.

[47] Norris 2001.

[48] Uerpmann-Wittzack 2009.

[49] Cf. "About ITU," online: http://www.itu.int/net/about/mission.aspx, 14.05.2010.

## Conclusion

The co-operation of states in international organisations was shaped during the nineteenth century by the administrative unions closely linked to technical innovation. These early international organisations offered a possibility for keeping up with technical development whilst respecting states' sovereignty and their role as primary subjects of public international law.

The ITU was and is characterised by its orientation towards technical co-operation and the readiness of states to find pragmatic solutions for governing globalisation processes. Therefore, mere political debates take place in other forums.

This concentration on technical issues thus allowed the degree of co-operation to keep pace or increase even in times of setbacks in other areas such as international arbitration[50] or disarmament.[51]

## Bibliography

"About ITU." Accessed 14.05.2010 (http://www.itu.int/net/about/mission.aspx).

Barberis, Julio A. 1995. "International Rivers." *Encyclopedia of Public International Law*. vol. 2, 1364–1386. Amsterdam: North-Holland.

Baumgart, Winfried. 1987. *Vom Europäischen Konzert zum Völkerbund – Friedensschlüsse und Friedenssicherung von Wien bis Versailles* (Erträge der Forschung 25), 2nd ed. Darmstadt: Wissenschaftliche Buchgesellschaft.

Buckle, Henry Thomas. 1857–1861. *History of Civilization in England*, 2 vols. London: J. W. Parker and son.

Chamberlain, Joseph Perkins. 1923. *The Regime of the International Rivers: Danube and Rhine, Studies in History, Economics and Public Law*, vol. XV no.1. New York: Columbia University.

Codding, George Arthur. 1952. *The International Telecommunication Union. An Experiment in International Cooperation*. New York: Arno Press.

Codding, George Arthur. 1964. *The Universal Postal Union. Coordinator of the International Mails*. New York: New York University Press.

Codding, George Arthur. 1988. "The International Telecommunication Union." In *International Institutions at Work*, edited by Paul Taylor and A.J.R. Groom, 167–183. London: Pinter.

"Convention télégraphique internationale de Paris (1865) et Règlement de service international (1865)," Accessed 20.04.2010 (http://www.itu.int/dms_pub/itu-s/oth/02/01/S02010000014002 PDFF.pdf).

Dülffer, Jost, Joseph Görres und Friedrich Gentz. 1990. "Modelle der Friedenssicherung in Deutschland seit der Französischen Revolution." In *Deutschland in Europa, Kontinuität und Bruch, Gedenkschrift für Andreas Hillgruber*, edited by Jost Dülffer et al., 52–72. Frankfurt/M., Berlin: Propyläen

Grewe, Wilhelm. 1984. *Epochen der Völkerrechtsgeschichte*. Baden-Baden: Nomos Verlagsgesellschaft.

[50] Cf. Weiß 2009, pp. 129f. with further references.

[51] For a good analysis cf. Steiner 2005.

Gruner, Wolf D. 1992. "Der Deutsche Bund als Band der deutschen Nation 1815–1866." In *Vom schwierigen Zusammenwachsen der Deutschen. Nationale Identität und Nationalismus im 19. und 20. Jahrhundert*, edited by Bernd Jürgen Wendt, 49–79. Frankfurt/M.: P. Lang.
Haas, Ernst B. 1958. *The Uniting of Europe: Political, Social and Economic Forces*. Stanford CA: Stanford University Press.
Hamerow, Theodore S. 1972. *The Social Foundations of German Unification 1858–1871, vol. 2: Struggles and Accomplishments*, Princeton: Princeton University Press.
Hasenclever, Andreas et al. 1997. *Theories of International Regimes*. Cambridge: Cambridge University Press.
Hartwig, Matthias. 2010. "ICANN: governance by technical necessity." In *The Exercise of Public Authority by International Institutions: Advancing International Institutional Law*, edited by Armin von Bogdandy et al., 575–605. Heidelberg: Springer.
Henn, Heike. 2010. "Decolonization," In *Concise Encyclopedia of the United Nations*, 2nd rev. ed., edited by Helmut Volger, 67–69 with an addendum by Sally Morphet, 69–71. Leiden: Martinus Nijhoff Publishers.
Howe, Anthony. 1997. *Free Trade and Liberal England 1846– 1946*. Oxford: Clarendon Press.
International Commission for the Study of Communication Problems, Communication and Society Today and Tomorrow, ed. 1980. *Many Voices, One World: Towards a New More Just and More Efficient World Information and Communication Order*. New York: Unipub.
Jackson, Robert and Georg Sørensen. 2007. *Introduction to International Relations. Theories and Approaches*, 3rd ed. Oxford: Oxford University Press.
Keohane, Robert O. 1984. *After Hegemony. Cooperation and Discord in the World Political Economy*. Princeton Princeton University Press.
Keohane, Robert O. 1989. "International Institutions. Two Approaches." *International Institutions and State Power, Essays in International Relations*, 158–179. Boulder: Westview Press.
Kissinger, Henry. 1957. *A World Restored: Metternich, Castlereagh and the Problems of Peace 1812–22*. Boston: Houghton Mifflin
Kratochwil, Friedrich V. and John Gerard Ruggie. 1986. "International Organization. A State of the Art on an Art of the State." *International Organization* 40, 753–775.
Langewiesche, Dieter. 2004. "Zentralstaat – Föderativstaat: Nationalstaatsmodelle in Europa im 19. und 20. Jahrhundert." *Zeitschrift für Staats- und Europawissenschaften* 2, 173–190.
Langhorne, Richard. 1981. *The Collapse of the Concert of Europe. International Politics 1890–1914*. New York: St. Martin's Press.
Lee, William R., ed. 1991. *German Industry and German Industrialization, Essays in German Economic and Business History in the Nineteenth and Twentieth Centuries*. London: Routledge.
Magiera, Siegfried. 1995. "ITU – International Telecommunication Union." In *United Nations: Law, Policies and Practice*, vol. 2, edited by Rüdiger Wolfrum and Christiane Philipp, 821–826. Munich: C.H. Beck.
Mearsheimer, John J. 1995. "The False Promise of International Institutions," *International Security* 19, 5–49.
Meißner, Friedrich. 2000. "Rhine River." *Encyclopedia of Public International Law*, vol. 4, 237–244. Amsterdam: Elsevier.
Mitrany, David. 1933. *The Progress of International Government*. New Haven: Yale University Press.
Mitrany, David (1943) 1966. *A Working Peace System*. Chicago: Quadrangle Books.
Murphy, Craig N. 1994. *International Organization and Industrial Change: Global Governance since 1850*. New York: Oxford University Press.
Noll, Alfons A.E. 1995. "International Telecommunication Union." *Encyclopedia of Public International Law*, vol. 2, 1379–1385. Amsterdam: Elsevier.
Noll, Alfons A.E. 1999. "The International Telecommunication Union (ITU). Its Inception, Evolution and Innate, Constant Reform Process." *Multimedia und Recht* 2, 465–469.

Norris, Pippa. 2001. *Digital Divide, Civic Engagement, Information Poverty, and the Internet Worldwide*. Cambridge: Cambridge University Press.

Österdahl, Inger. 1992. *Freedom of Information in Question. Freedom of Information in International Law and the Calls for a New World Information and Communication Order (NWICO)*. Uppsala: Iustus Förlag.

Risse, Thomas. 2003. "Law and Politics Beyond the Nation-State: Areas of Conversation and Common Ground." In *Linking Politics and Law*, edited by Christoph Engel, 81–105. Baden-Baden: Nomos.

Rosenne, Shabtai. 1992. "Conferences and Congresses, International." *Encyclopedia of Public International Law*, vol. 1, 739–746. Amsterdam: Elsevier.

Rumpler, Helmut, ed. 1990. *Deutscher Bund und Deutsche Frage 1815–1866*. Munich: R. Oldenbourg.

Schieder, Siegfried and Manuela Spindler, eds. 2006. *Theorien der Internationalen Beziehungen*, 2nd ed. Opladen: Budrich.

Schmitter, Philippe. 1970. "A Revised Theory of Regional Integration." *International Organization* 24, 836–868.

Schroeder, Paul W. 1996. "The Vienna System and Its Stability: The Problem of Stabilizing a State System in Transition." In *Das europäische Staatensystem im Wandel. Strukturelle Bedingungen und bewegende Kräfte seit der Frühen Neuzeit*, edited by Peter Krüger and Elisabeth Müller-Luckner, 107–122. Munich: Oldenbourg.

Schulze, Hagen. 1998. *Phoenix Europa. Die Moderne, Von 1740 bis heute. Siedler Geschichte Europas 5*. Berlin: Siedler

Steiner, Zara. 2005. *The Lights that Failed: European International History, 1919–1933*. Oxford: Oxford University Press.

Teubner, Gunther, ed. 1997. *Global Law without a State. Studies in Modern Law and Policy*. Aldershot: Brookfield, USA.

Tranholm-Mikkelsen, Jeppe. 1991. "Neo-Functionalism: Obstinate or Obsolete? A Reappraisal in the Light of the New Dynamics in the EC." *Millennium* 20, no. 1, 1–22.

Trentmann, Frank. 2007. "After the Nation-State: Citizenship, Empire and Global Coordination in the New Internationalism 1914–1930." In *Beyond Sovereignty. Britain, Empire and Transnationalism, c. 1880–1950* edited by Kevin Grant et al., 35–53. New York: Palgrave Macmillan.

Uerpmann-Wittzack, Robert. 2009. "Internetvölkerrecht." *Archiv des Völkerrechts* 47, 261–283.

Ullrich, Volker. 1997. *Die nervöse Großmacht. Aufstieg und Untergang des Deutschen Kaiserreichs 1871–1918*. Frankfurt am Main: S. Fischer.

Veit-Brause, Irmline. 1978. "Partikularismus." *Geschichtliche Grundbegriffe*, vol. 4, 735–766.

Verdross, Alfred. 1960. "Die Entwicklung des Völkerrechts." In *Propyläen Weltgeschichte, vol. 8: Das neunzehnte Jahrhundert*, edited by Golo Mann, 671–701. Berlin: Propyläen-Verlag.

Volger, Helmut. 2010. "History of the UN." *Concise Encyclopedia of the United Nations*, 2nd rev. ed., 231–246. Leiden: Martinus Nijhoff Publishers.

Weber, Ludwig. 2000. "Universal Postal Union." *Encyclopedia of Public International Law*, vol. 4, 1235–1240. Amsterdam: Elsevier.

Weiß, Norman. 2009. *Eine Kompetenzlehre internationaler Organisationen*. Heidelberg: Springer.

Wendt, Alexander. 1992. "Anarchy is What States Make of It. The Social Construction of Power Politics." *International Organization* 46, 391–425.

Wiesner-Hanks, Merry E. 2006. *Early Modern Europe 1450–1789*. Cambridge: Cambridge University Press.

Wolfrum, Rüdiger. 1995. "International Administrative Unions." *Encyclopedia of Public International Law*, vol. 2, 1041–1047. Amsterdam: Elsevier

Zangl, Bernhard. 2010. "Regimetheorie." In *Theorien der Internationalen Beziehungen*, edited by Siegfried Schieder & Manuela Spindler, 121–144. Opladen: Verlag Barbara Budrich.

Zimmern, Alfred. (1923) 1929. "International Organization – Its Prospects and Limitations." *America & Europe and Other Essays*, 138–156. New York: Oxford University Press.

Zürn, Michael. 1993. "Bringing the Second Image (Back) In. About the Domestic Sources of Regime Formation." In *Regime Theory and International Relations*, edited by Volker Rittberger, 282–311. Oxford:Oxford University Press.
Zürn, Michael. 1998. *Regieren jenseits des Nationalstaats. Globalisierung und Denationalisierung als Chance*. Frankfurt am Main: Suhrkamp.

# Chapter 5
# "A Most Powerful Instrument for a Despot": The Telegraph as a Trans-national Instrument of Imperial Control and Political Mobilization in the Middle East

**E. Thomas Ewing**

**Abstract** This chapter examines the Middle Eastern telegraph system in terms of globalisation processes related to imperialism, anticolonial resistance, and the establishment of new nation states. The history of technology is thus integrated into a social, cultural, political, and diplomatic history, in ways that emphasise the interactions between humans and wires, transmitters, relays, and codes. The telegraph served as an instrument and symbol of globalisation, yet the history of the telegraph at regional and local levels must always be understood in terms of the contours and contradictions of historical and immediate conditions. Most importantly, this chapter examines the telegraph as a web, connecting points into a broader network. These connections were determined by their location relative to major imperial powers by natural environmental conditions, such as proximity to a coastline or lower elevation passages, and local or regional political and cultural considerations. Topography and technology thus shaped adaptations to the environment, even as transnational flows of knowledge emerged as a form of imperial power. The telegraph also played a crucial role in the establishment of postcolonial relations across this region, as contesting the telegraph as a form of colonial power was transformed into controlling this means of political mobilisation.

## Introduction

This chapter examines the Middle Eastern telegraph system in terms of globalization processes related to imperialism, anti-colonial resistance, and the establishment of new nation states. The history of technology is thus integrated into a social, cultural, political, and diplomatic history, in ways that emphasize the interactions between humans and wires, transmitters, relays, and codes. The telegraph served as an instrument and symbol of globalization, yet the history of the telegraph at regional and local levels must always be understood in terms of the contours and

E.T. Ewing (✉)
Department of History, Virginia Tech, Blacksburg, VA, USA
e-mail: etewing@vt.edu

I. Löhr and R. Wenzlhuemer (eds.), *The Nation State and Beyond*, Transcultural Research – Heidelberg Studies on Asia and Europe in a Global Context,
DOI 10.1007/978-3-642-32934-0_5, 

contradictions of historical and immediate conditions. Most importantly, this chapter examines the telegraph as a web, connecting points into a broader network. These connections were determined by their location relative to major imperial powers, by the natural environmental conditions such as proximity to a coastline or lower elevation passages, and local or regional political and cultural considerations. Topography and technology thus shaped adaptations to the environment, even as trans-national flows of knowledge emerged as a form of imperial power. The telegraph also played a crucial role in the establishment of post-colonial relations across this region, as contesting the telegraph as a form of colonial power was transformed into controlling this means of political mobilization.

According to a British diplomat, Charles Eliot, in an era "when there were neither railroads nor telegraphs," the Ottoman Sultan might boast that regional governors "were his slaves, but as long as they were in their provinces they were necessarily independent in all matters concerning internal administration". With the spread of the telegraph throughout the empire, according to Eliot, the Ottoman Empire was approaching, for the first time in world history, "real autocracy—that is, a state where *everything* is directed by the pleasure of the ruler". The Ottoman Sultan thus embraced this new Western technology: "With the telegraph one can order [an official] about, find out what he is doing, reprimand him, recall him, instruct his subordinates to report against him, and generally deprive him of all real power." By facilitating the Sultan's power to issue orders to every regional and district office, the telegraph "is a most powerful instrument for a despot who wishes to control his own officials".[1] Even after accounting for the Orientalist perspective of an English observer determined to emphasize the arbitrary power of the Sultan, this statement illustrates how a Middle Eastern state adapted the new technologies to increase its power internally, even as it remained dependent externally on Western advisors and technology.

The spread of the telegraph established a network of trans-national connections between Europe and Asia during the nineteenth century. Although the initial motivation for the expansion of telegraph lines was to connect the British government to its colonies, particularly India, the telegraph was also adopted by local actors who recognized the advantages of communicating across extensive distances at a rapid speed. The telegraph spread throughout the Middle East along both submarine and overland routes. Submarine cables across the Mediterranean Sea reached land initially in Alexandria and Port Said, and then passed through the Red Sea to the Indian Ocean. Submarine cables were also laid along the Persian Gulf, connecting Fao at the northern end to the coastal city of Karachi in the Indian colony. Overland routes connected these international points of access, while also building internal networks available for use by governments, companies, and

[1] Eliot 1908, pp. 124, 149.

subjects.[2] Once the so-called Indo-European line had been completed, a striking transformation in trans-national communication had taken place. In 1870, the American George Sauer announced that a message of ten words could be sent from Berlin to Tehran, a distance of nearly 5,000 km, for less than three US dollars.[3]

This combination of distance, ease, and speed celebrated by Sauer illustrated the extent to which the Middle East was integrated into the expanding global system in the late nineteenth century. Existing globalization processes linking the Middle East to the rest of the world included shipping lanes, overland trade routes, migration patterns, and pilgrimage networks. The telegraph built upon these existing globalization processes, but in ways that extended and accelerated these connections. Yet the telegraph, in addition to furthering globalization processes, also exerted regional and local effects, as this means of communication served as a new instrument of control as well as a tool of resistance. By exploring these processes of projecting, appropriating, and contesting the power of communications, this chapter contributes to understanding how processes of globalization shaped relations, interactions, and identities in distinct historical contexts.

## The Telegraph in World History

The historiography on the telegraph primarily considers European and American perspectives, reflecting the availability of sources as well as the assumptions that technology can be best understood in terms of its inventors and developers, rather than its users. The first and still most visible accounts are the heroic narratives of the founders of the telegraph lines, with an emphasis on the Atlantic route, Anglo-American technical innovations, and the role of European corporations.[4] The telegraph also appears in studies of development, modernization, and Westernization, where the expansion of telegraph lines, along with the spread of railroads or the growth of factories, provides easy markers of economic and social transformation.[5] In histories of communication, the telegraph is described as part of a whole series of advances that bring people closer together, transform connections between countries, mark the spread of global corporations and capitalism, and anticipate the accelerated changes of the twentieth century.[6] Finally, more specialized studies of

---

[2] Bektas 2000, p. 677. Perhaps the most complicated overland route was the so-called Indo-European line, which went through London (submarine cable through the North Sea), Emden, Berlin, Warsaw, Odessa, Crimea (cable through the Black Sea), Tiflis, Tehran, Isfahan, Shiraz, and then to Bushir, Karachi, Bombay, and Calcutta. Fuchs 1990, p. 158.

[3] Sauer 1870, p. 88.

[4] The first such study was Bright 1908; this approach continues in Gordon 2003.

[5] Cole 1993, p. 112; Harcave 2004, pp. 54–55; Gelvin 2008, pp. 81, 83, 90, 92, 144.

[6] Winseck and Pike 2009, pp. 31–54; see also the chapter by Simone Müller-Pohe in this volume.

the agents, communities, and contexts have begun to incorporate the social dimension of this technological transformation.[7]

The Middle Eastern telegraph system has received increasing attention as part of a broader scholarship on political transformations. The laying of the first submarine wire through the Persian Gulf is often noted in histories of the telegraph, yet tends to be treated as derivative of the Atlantic cable, where most of the innovation occurred.[8] Extensive studies of the Persian telegraph by Michael Rubin and the Ottoman telegraph by Yakup Bektas and Soli Shahvar provide rich documentation of the diverse patterns, meanings, and experiences of the telegraph specifically in these neighboring states.[9] The Indo-European telegraph running across the Russian empire through Ukraine, Georgia, and Armenia has been the object of a couple of narrow studies and receives occasional mention in the telegraph histories, but with little elaboration.[10]

World historians have long seen the telegraph as an important step towards a new age of faster, longer, and more complex global connections. According to J.R. McNeill and William H. McNeill, the telegraph was an example of "the tightening of the web," which allowed the strong to get stronger, "because they oversaw the tightening of the web, they built and owned the infrastructure that did the tightening, and they benefited disproportionately from the faster and greater flows of information and goods".[11] As recognized by prominent world historian Patrick Manning, global history must address "the social impact and social sources of technological change," which can be done by viewing "technology as a web of interacting practices and ideas".[12] The telegraph is particularly well suited to this approach, not only because the network of telegraph lines, stations, and agents represented connections and nodes on an expanding web, but also because the very same advances in speed, distance, and accuracy advocated by their proponents were frequently seen as a further extension of imperial power and a threat to local cultures, regional powers, and established political hierarchies.

[7] For the importance of understanding how "local agents and local societies" sought to "transform and utilise new network technologies" for their own purposes, see Wenzlhuemer 2007b, "Development of Telegraphy," pp. 1722–1726.

[8] Bright 1911, pp. 90–95; Murray 1902, pp. 2299–2300; for the strategic dimensions of the telegraph to India, see Kennedy 1971, pp. 730–731.

[9] Rubin 1999; Bektas 2000, pp. 669–696; Shahvar 2007, pp. 23–42.

[10] Fuchs 1990, pp. 157–166; Karbellashvili 1991, pp. 277–281; in general, the telegraph in the Russian empire remains understudied, as historians have mostly emphasized first lines between major European cities, the construction of the trans-Siberian line, and the efforts to connect to North America across the Bering Straits; Mehlinger and Thompson 1972, pp. 86, 105.

[11] McNeill and McNeill 2003, p. 216.

[12] Manning 2003, pp. 219–223. See also the introduction to this volume for geographical proximity as a factor shaping global interactions and globalization processes.

The three states discussed in this chapter, Persia, Egypt, and the Ottoman Empire, had distinctive histories in the late nineteenth and early twentieth centuries, even as their regional location placed them in similar relationships to external powers.[13] The Ottoman Empire maintained jurisdiction over a large expanse of territory, including parts of the Caucasus, the eastern Levant, the northern section of the Arabian peninsula, Palestine, northern Africa, and territories in southeastern Europe. The empire was governed from Istanbul, through governors appointed by the Sultan, who also occupied the position of Caliph, the leader of Sunni Muslims. Despite claiming this vast territory, however, the nature of Ottoman control was increasingly challenged by external forces. Under pressure from the British, French, and Russian empires as well as movements for national self-determination, the Ottoman Empire yielded both territories and degrees of control. Although the term "sick man of Europe" primarily reflected the perceptions of European rulers and diplomats seeking to press their advantages over the Ottoman authority, it nevertheless offered a graphic image of the shifting balance of power in the Eastern Mediterranean region.[14] Despite the efforts of Sultan Abdulhamid II, who combined modernizing economic policies with determined opposition to constitutional reform, the Ottoman Empire occupied a position of increasing weakness relative to European powers. Military defeat as part of the Central Powers during World War One was followed by the dismembering of the Empire in post-war settlements, thus seemingly confirming the long-term decline of this once expansive political system. The history of Egypt in the nineteenth century was directly connected to the broader transformation of the Middle East, as the pursuit of greater autonomy from Ottoman control generated new forms of dependency on European powers, especially Britain. Even as Egyptian leaders, following the lead of Muhammad Ali, pursued policies intended to bring modernization, such as agricultural, financial, and educational reform, Egypt became the object of increasingly interventionist European imperial policies. This is symbolized by both the construction of the Suez Canal in 1869 and the British invasion in 1882 to overthrow the incipient nationalist movement led by Colonel Urabi. The gradual rise of an Egyptian nationalist movement, culminating in the 1919 uprising against British military occupation, thus pursued dual aims of expelling external power and promoting internal transformations. A similar dynamic characterized the nineteenth-century history of Persia, which remained beyond the control of the Ottoman Empire, yet also faced escalating pressure from European powers, especially the British and Russians. These regional pressures led a series of Qajar rulers to seek military reforms as a first step towards modernization, even as they allowed concessions to foreign companies and governments to encourage investment in economic growth. In Persia, the dual goals of anti-imperialism and political reform found expression in a series of protests, demonstrations, and oppositional activities, culminating in a revolution, constitutional government, and then reassertion of central power in the

[13] This background is drawn from Gelvin 2008, pp. 73–87, 92–96, 175–196.

[14] For this term, see Bellaigue 2001.

early twentieth century. The three states examined in this chapter thus shared common characteristics associated with processes of economic transformation and political change in a context of dependency relative to European imperial powers.

Exploring the telegraph as an instrument of imperial control, as well as political mobilization, focuses attention on how the use of technology transformed tangible objects, such as wires, poles, and transmitters, into instruments of political power. The Middle Eastern telegraph thus provides an excellent basis for engaging Roland Wenzlhuemer's thesis about the "dematerialization of telecommunication" in the late nineteenth century. According to this argument, the invention of telecommunication detached the flow of information from the movement of people, thus marking "a watershed in the history of globalization". By establishing communication links through a combination of land and sea routes, particularly between Europe and India, but also domestically within the Ottoman Empire and the Kingdom of Persia, the Middle Eastern telegraph served a similar purpose of facilitating the negotiation of long distances at the cost of relatively little time or energy.[15] Yet a history of the Middle Eastern telegraph also demonstrates additional dimensions of the complex relationship between the material and virtual realms of the telegraph.[16] As will be discussed below, the materiality of the telegraph – the poles, wires, and stations – became objects of political contestation, as did the political authority associated with this rapid means of communication. Through an exploration of the uses of the telegraph in the particular context of nineteenth-century Middle Eastern history, this analysis sets an agenda for future research on the significance of the telegraph in world history.[17]

## Projecting and Appropriating Power

The most obvious case of a European power using the telegraph to project authority into the Middle East involved the British government's decision to lay cables through Egypt, as a means to establish a direct communication link to India.

[15] Wenzlhuemer 2007a, "The dematerialization of telecommunication," pp. 346–350. According to Anthony Giddens, the first transmission of a telegraph message by Samuel Morse "initiated a new phase in world history. Never before could a message be sent without someone going somewhere to carry it." Giddens 2000, p. 28. See also the chapter by Norman Weiss in this volume.

[16] It is beyond the scope of this paper, but further research should examine the extent to which the Middle Eastern telegraph acquired a different kind of "virtual" reality to the extent that initial reactions to and deployments of the telegraph involved assertions and assumptions of certain kinds of mystical and religious power, some of which were specific to Muslim beliefs, authorities and political manipulations. For examples of Muslim responses to the telegraph in Persia and the Ottoman Empire, see Rubin 1999, pp. 379–384.

[17] For the importance of "use-oriented" study of the international telegraph, see Wenzlhuemer 2007b, p. 36.

According to a British publication in the early 1850s, the planned expansion of telegraph lines by both British and French powers demonstrated that "the necessity of the government becomes the opportunity of the people". From this perspective, the strategic necessity of connecting to colonies, extending communications with naval fleets, and accelerating diplomatic exchanges with allied governments were the imperatives that drove telegraphic expansion.[18] The stations at Alexandria, Cairo, and Suez connected the submarine lines from the Mediterranean to those in the Red Sea, which then continued to India. According to an anonymous article published in 1856, which endorsed William P. Andrew's proposal for railway and telegraphic connections across India, the goal was "an unbroken chain of electric communication, going straight from the head-quarters of Queen Victoria's government to every extremity of her eastern empire".[19] The Indian rebellion of 1857 demonstrated the urgent need for faster communication as a means to maintain military control of the colony.[20] Although problems with design, equipment, and maintenance led to a shift away from the Red Sea route, in favor of overseas routes and a submarine cable through the Persian Gulf, Egypt remained integrated into the British colonial telegraph network.[21]

The functioning and significance of the Egyptian telegraph remained tied to trans-national as well as domestic political considerations. In 1858 Said Pasha, who ruled Egypt prior to the Urabi revolt of 1882, initiated the construction of telegraph lines between major cities.[22] Within two decades, the Egyptian government administered more than 6,000 km of telegraph lines, thus reflecting the importance attached to this aspect of modernization. Yet the telegraph remained a potent instrument in the hands of powerful external actors. In the late summer of 1882, when British colonial forces participated in the suppression of the Urabi revolt, the telegraph guided the dispatch and movement of troops. In fact, when General Wolseley arrived in Cairo, he cabled to London: "The war is over. Send no more men from England." At the same time that Wolseley was using the telegraph to communicate that troops were no longer needed, the British also "intercepted" cables from regional officials urging that they "cut the canal and flood the country," with the goal of disrupting the movement of the colonial troops.[23] In this situation of intense political conflict, the telegraph remained an instrument used by European

[18] *Schaffner's Telegraph Companion* 1854.

[19] The original statement was made in an anonymous article: "The Euphrates Valley Railway and Indo-European Telegraph," in: *Bentley's Miscellany* 40 (1856), p. 275, and then reprinted in Andrew 1857, p. 143, as well as in Bektas 2000, p. 679.

[20] Preece 1879, p. 403; Bektas 2000, p. 676.

[21] Bright 1908, pp. 219–221.

[22] "Society of Telegraph Engineers and of Electricians," 1882, pp. 431–433. See also the interpretation of concessions offered by the Ottoman government to build telegraph lines, along with railways and other transportation projects, as an important aspect of "defensive developmentalism". Gelvin 2008, p. 81.

[23] "Arabi's Rebellion Ended," in: *The New York Times*, 16.09.1882, p. 1.

colonial authorities who combined superior military strength with precise knowledge of the technology involved in the networks.

The regional powers of the Middle East recognized the advantages of extending telegraph wires throughout their states, as a means to communicate with regional officials, acquire intelligence about activities beyond the capital, and extend their assertion of imperial power. While Ottoman leaders took advantage of imperial rivalries between the French and British to seek more advantageous concessions, they also expressed their determination, in the words of one English observer, to keep "the telegraph towards India in their own hands".[24] Although the Ottoman Sultan had personally observed demonstrations of the telegraph during the 1830s and 1840s, it was only as a result of the Crimean War in the 1850s that direct telegraphic connections were established between the European network and the Ottoman Empire. Under agreement with the British and French militaries, the Ottoman government provided labor and poles, while also guarding the new lines. At the same time, however, Ottoman engineers learned from their French and British counterparts about the workings of the telegraph. The Ottoman government soon began to construct its own lines, beginning with a line from Istanbul to the west, to the European city of Edirne (Adrianople), which was then connected to the European network. By 1861, Baghdad was connected to the European lines by way of Istanbul, Ankara, Diyarbekir, Kirkuk, and Mosul. As the British constructed a telegraph wire connecting inland cities with the coastal port of Karachi and then a submarine cable through the Persian Gulf, the combined Ottoman and British effort extended the telegraph lines to Fao, at the northern end of the Persian Gulf. In early 1865, the completion of these lines not only established a telegraphic connection between England and India, but also finalized the connections between the Porte in Istanbul and the more than 25 cities with stations along the nearly 5,000 km of this line.[25] Within two decades of the Crimean War, by the late 1870s, the Ottoman Empire had constructed the eighth largest telegraph network in the world, with more than 27,000 km of wires.[26] In 1882, early in the reign of Sultan Abdulhamid II, a submarine cable across the Red Sea connected two provinces of the Ottoman Empire, the Arabian peninsula and Egypt, even as both territories began their long struggle for greater autonomy, which in both cases would eventually involve the competing claims of British as well as Ottoman masters.[27]

A similar process occurred with the spread of the telegraph in Persia. The first line was established in 1859 between the capital, Tehran, and the city of Sultanieh, where the Shah was spending the summer, a distance of nearly 200 km. According to the Inspector General of Persian Telegraphs, A. Houtom Schindler, the telegraph

[24] Quoted in Bektas 2000, p. 679.

[25] Bektas 2000, pp. 674–687.

[26] "Society of Telegraph Engineers and of Electricians," 1877, p. 246; for the telegraph's influence on modernization efforts in the Ottoman Empire, including education, technology, and foreign language training, see Bektas 2000, pp. 688–690; Lewis 2002, pp. 186–187.

[27] Bektas 2000, p. 695.

line to this "place of little importance" was abandoned in the autumn, as soon as the Shah left. A year later, in 1860, a telegraph line was established from Tauris to Tehran, followed 3 years later by an extension of this line to the Russian frontier on the Arras River. At this same time, the British began construction of a telegraph line from Bushire to Tehran, and then to Khanegin, on the frontier of the Ottoman Empire, which then continued to Baghdad. Further construction in the 1860s involved the British and Persian governments as well as efforts by a German-led consortium involving Siemens, working in partnership with the Russian empire. By 1876, the Persian government operated nearly 5,000 km of lines, while the British government operated almost 4,000 km and the Indo-European Telegraph company operated nearly 2,000 km, reaching a total of more than 11,000 km of telegraph wires connecting the cities and regions of Persia.[28]

The telegraph thus represented an unusual convergence of imperial interests, as its spread through the Middle East actually enhanced the power of multiple political systems, including European empires, the British in particular, but also regional powers, such as the Ottoman and Persian governments.[29] The telegraph enhanced political power by reaching regions not yet accessible by railways, by transcending regional or local boundaries and making officials more directly accountable to the central government, and by accelerating the speed of communication within the bureaucracy. According to the eminent Orientalist Bernard Lewis, "the Turks were quick to realize the value of this new medium of communication".[30] Specific examples of the ways that the telegraph enhanced the power of the central government in the Ottoman Empire included the dispatches sent by internal networks of spies and agents, the dismissal or transfer of regional governors in response to petitions submitted by telegraph, and the suppression of revolts with the help of telegraphic communication.[31] In Iran, the spread of the telegraph during the reign of Nasir al-Din Shah had a "profound" effect, as the central government "took advantage of the new speed of communication to augment their domestic control," in the words of historian Michael Rubin, thus promoting the transfer of power "from the village to the province, and from the province to the central government".[32]

The British agents acknowledged this shift in the approach of the Persian government, as in this recollection by a visitor to the Persian telegraph offices in Tehran:

[28] Schindler 1876, pp. 262–264; Gelvin 2008, p. 83.

[29] According to Bektas, "the telegraph came to symbolize the sultan's authority and geographic reach, a socially constructed symbolic linkage that was skillfully exploited by the British promoters who marketed it as an imperial design associated with the sultan". In this situation, "the telegraph served two empires, British and Ottoman," by enhancing British commercial, political and military interests in the Middle East and Asia, while also facilitating Ottoman efforts "to consolidate control of their own empire". Bektas 2000, p. 670.

[30] Lewis 2002, p. 186.

[31] Bektas 2000, p. 695.

[32] Rubin 1999, pp. 349, 359, 365.

> The Shah is a frequent visitor at the Telegraph Office, which is close to the Palace, and exceedingly fond of conversing directly through the wires with the governors of the provinces through which they pass. As the day approaches for the payment of their annual tribute, the governors have an uneasy time of it, and often, no doubt, curse this invention of the "Christian Dogs"; for then his Majesty's visits are redoubled, and questions as to the amount of tribute and the time of its arrival become the burden of his messages.[33]

This report strikingly illustrates the use of the telegraph to enhance the central power of the Persian government in relation to provincial authorities, even as the observer used his recollections to assert the superiority of western technology.

According to another foreign observer, the initial efforts to introduce the telegraph into the Ottoman Empire attracted the attention and support of the sultan, but provoked resistance from high-ranking regional governors: "The pashas united against it. They wanted no such tell-tale to report their doings every day, while in the distant interior."[34] Implicit in their opposition was the feared loss of regional autonomy by means of an instrument that could concentrate more power in the central government by enhancing communication to and from the regional authorities.[35] As argued by historian Bektas, the telegraph official emerged as a local representative of the central Ottoman government and thus became involved in collecting taxes, acquiring other revenues, and recruiting military forces, all of which served to diminish the privileges and power of regional and local officials.[36]

In Persia, the telegraph system allowed the Shah to deploy state resources more efficiently, thus responding to possible uprisings in a timelier manner that forestalled greater crises.[37] Some provincial elites tried to obstruct the expansion of the telegraph, in some cases by instigating the destruction of lines almost as soon as they were constructed.[38] British officials suspected that much of the "mischief" done to the lines, in situations where "spans of exceptionally great length had been cut down," was done with the explicit, or at least implicit, approval of the regional "chief". Yet other elites were more receptive, according to this same British agent, as they demonstrated a "friendly feeling towards the telegraph, amounting to appreciation of its value, in the towns possessing stations".[39]

---

[33] Mounsey 1872, p. 184.

[34] Hamlin 1878, p. 194.

[35] See discussion of this political dynamic for the Ottoman and Persian states in Bektas 2000, pp. 671–673.

[36] Bektas 2000, p. 694.

[37] Rubin 1999, pp. 352–353.

[38] Dickson 1901, p. 215.

[39] Goldsmid 1874, pp. 83–84, 255–256.

## Contesting Power

Beyond these government actors, however, the telegraph also became an object for more irregular forms of contesting power. According to the historian Bektas, "[d] isrupting wires in the remote corners of the empire was often an effective way of attracting the attention of the government to social and economic problems".[40] Obviously, the vandalism of wires may have been just that, without additional political significance, yet recent historiography on everyday forms of resistance, on subaltern strategies, and on daily contestations of external authority calls attention to the potential political significance of these "local" responses to modern representations of imperial control. The telegraph is a particularly interesting way to approach these issues, because the lines had to be constructed across long distances that were far from centers of imperial control such as cities and military garrisons. In addition, simply cutting wires was a relatively easy and low-risk strategy that could have the effect of disrupting communication by the imperial powers. Finally, and probably most importantly, the extension of the telegraph brought unusual, and potentially valuable, objects into communities but without immediate mechanisms of surveillance and control. The wires themselves, as well as poles and insulators, were often seen as valuable on their own, even as the act of taking them served the indirect result of disrupting long-distance communication for imperial states.

Both the Ottoman and Persian governments imposed fines and strict punishments, including imprisonment, on those accused of harming telegraphic wires, stations, or transmission devices.[41] Reflecting the bias of both European and Ottoman imperialists, the populations of distant regions, such as the Arabs in the eastern provinces around Baghdad, were perceived as more wild, less obedient, and thus a particular threat to disrupt the communication networks spread throughout their territories. One British account predicted that the Ottoman government "would inevitably fail" in its efforts to complete the telegraph lines, "as the Arabs to the eastward of the Euphrates are badly disposed to the Turkish government".[42] In some cases, European agents in charge of expanding the network of telegraphs acknowledged that their fear of attack exceeded the actual threats posed by indigenous populations. According to the Inspector General of Persian Telegraphs, "great anxiety was felt on account of the Turcomans, who were expected to attack us every day" while the line was being constructed between Shahrud and Mazinan, "but not a single Turcoman was seen".[43]

---

[40] Bektas 2000, p. 696.

[41] Bektas 2000, p. 691.

[42] Quoted in Bektas 2000, p. 691; the most exaggerated claims about the inability of the Ottoman government to protect the lines were made by those advocating complete and direct English control of telegraph lines. Ibid., p. 692.

[43] Schindler 1876, p. 268.

British advisors and Ottoman officials often preferred to pursue more conciliatory and strategic responses. After the line from Mosul to Baghdad was disrupted in February 1861, just a month after it opened, the initial reaction by the regional governor was to create a cavalry force of 300 men for the dedicated purpose of guarding the line. According to a British advisor, however, deploying such a force might "render the telegraph a special object of attack," whereas a more successful strategy was to pay the local tribes to guard the lines themselves.[44] This local approach was deployed throughout the empire, as a less costly and more effective alternative to either building regularly spaced guardhouses or deploying special troops.[45] According to Colonel Goldsmid, who inspected the lines in early 1864, approximately 125 "inspectors" and "sub-inspectors" serviced the nearly 2,000 km of line from Baghdad to Izmid, just east of Istanbul.[46] According to an 1876 report, the Persian telegraphs employed 64 "line guards," who made up approximately one quarter of all staff.[47]

In Persia, even as the telegraph became an instrument for expanding and consolidating the power of the state, it also became an instrument for contesting the expansion and the application of this power. As pointed out by historian Rubin, the "telegraph wires, personnel, and stations became focal points for dissent" by many different opponents of the existing political apparatus, as telegraph wires became symbols of centralized state power: "A strike at the telegraph became a strike against the government in Tehran."[48] In Persia, telegraph offices also became sites for *bast*, the right to seek refuge, which initially applied to mosques and homes of religious figures, but in the nineteenth century began to encompass foreign embassies and eventually telegraph offices. According to the British diplomat Lord Curzon, Persians began to "invest the telegraph offices with the sanctity of a *bast*" based on "the underlying idea" that "the wire ran directly from the Shah's palace at Teheran, and that they could thus communicate at once with headquarters".[49]

Yet these attacks on telegraphs often had a more obviously political purpose. In the city of Shiraz in 1865, when protests began against the provincial governor, the telegraph emerged as both a means and an object of engaging in and responding to these protests. As crowds, including many women, gathered in the city center to protest against the rising prices, which they blamed on hoarding by the governor, they asked the British agents at the telegraph office to communicate to the Shah their dissatisfaction with the governor. When the police sought to suppress the

[44] Bektas 2000, pp. 692–693; see also the discussion of guards along the telegraph lines in Persia in Preece 1879, p. 416.

[45] Bektas 2000, p. 693.

[46] Goldsmid 1874, p. 106; Bektas 2000, p. 693.

[47] Schindler 1876, p. 266.

[48] Rubin 1999, pp. 349, 368.

[49] Curzon 1892, p. 175.

protests, the bazaars were closed. During the ensuing strike, the crowds directed their protests at the telegraph employees and the system itself, as they began to destroy the wires. Once Tehran had been informed by the telegraph of the scope and nature of the protests, a cable was sent dismissing the provincial governor. Not only did the telegraph accelerate the speed at which these events occurred, the technology itself became an object of contestation used by all participants.[50] More than 25 years later, a similar incident occurred, again in Shiraz, when "a procession of women, followed by an immense mob, all crying, shrieking, and beating their breasts," as described by a British intelligence officer, came to the telegraph office and demanded that "a message be sent to the Shah complaining about the price of bread" and requesting the removal of the provincial governor accused of fixing prices.[51] In this incident, however, efforts to subdue the protestors resulted in violence, as troops opened fire on protestors within the telegraph compound, causing numerous casualties. The contested space of the telegraph office was made even more evident in a confused report from *The Times*, which claimed that "[t]he soldiers who were sent to clear the telegraph compound sided with the mob," and fighting broke out among the different military units, although with uncertain casualty reports.[52]

Telegraph operators could also become personal targets of crowd protests. In Kashan in 1882, a British telegraph clerk cabled this alarmed statement to the main office in Tehran: "I am now in the hands of the mob and the Office is overrun and surrounded by thousand *[sic]*." As in the Shiraz protests cited above, the crowd focused their dissatisfaction on the local official, and they used the telegraph to communicate their demands that the regional governor appoint a new representative.[53]

As the political system in Persia entered new stages of crisis, the telegraph remained an instrument as well as an object of political control. During the revolutionary events associated with challenges to both foreign concessions and the Shah's power, beginning in 1905, the telegraph played a crucial role in communicating news during protests. Although the telegraph proved a valuable instrument for those challenging the established structures of power, it also enabled the government to dispatch security forces to quell disturbances.[54] When the Shah took strong measures to suppress the protests in 1908, his officials immediately seized all telegraph offices in Tehran, so the leaders of the constitutional movement no longer had access to this political instrument. Within a few weeks, expressing a new sense of confidence, the Shah sent a telegram to a Majlis deputy declaring, in no uncertain terms: "I have won."[55]

---

[50] This account is taken from Rubin 1999, p. 369.

[51] Cited in Rubin 1999, pp. 375–376.

[52] "Persia," in: *The Times*, 20.05.1893, p. 7.

[53] The text of the agent's telegraph is in Rubin 1999, p. 370.

[54] Ibid., pp. 494–502.

[55] Ibid., pp. 510–513.

The political contests over the telegraph in the Ottoman Empire acquired a different quality, as they became instruments for a new reform movement challenging the Sultan's power and authority. In the late nineteenth century, the spread of the telegraph was accompanied by changes in education, as telegraph operators received technical training in operating machines and encoding messages. By the early twentieth century, not only had the telegraph network spread across the empire, connecting all the disparate points back to the capital Istanbul, it had also changed the structure of officialdom in specific points, as described in this final statement by Lewis: "And in each station, however remote, there was an operator, usually young, with enough modern education to read his manual, and enough science to do his job – a natural recruit for the Young Turk committees."[56] In fact, Mehmet Talat Bey, one of the leaders of this movement who later became Minister of the Interior, began his career as a telegraph clerk in Salonika.[57] According to a foreign observer of this new political movement within the Ottoman Empire, it was no wonder that this group of former shopkeepers, schoolmasters, and "telegraph clerks" was "driving Turkey to ruin," for they lacked experience and real statesmanship.[58]

## The Power of a "Potent Instrument"

The rapid adoption of the telegraph has been cited by both contemporaries and historians who emphasize the power of Middle Eastern states such as the Ottoman Sultan and the Iranian Shah. According to Robert Murdoch Smith, a British superintendent involved in the Persian telegraph since its inception in the 1860s, the telegraph "greatly increased the power and control of the Shah and the Central government over the provinces".[59] Echoing this perception, Rubin describes the telegraph in Persia as allowing "a centralization of power and information" while Bektas argues that the "real value" of expanding telegraph networks for the Ottoman Empire was "demonstrated when it developed into an effective device for the centralization of power".[60] After citing, seemingly with approval, the statement by Eliot about the telegraph as "the most powerful instrument for a despot who wishes to control his own officials," Lewis concluded that for the

[56] Lewis 2002, p. 187.

[57] Howard 2001, p. 74.

[58] E.J. Dillon, "Young Turks Driving Turkey to Her Downfall," in: *The New York Times*, 19.11.1919, p. 5.

[59] Smith's 1885 telegram is quoted in Rubin 1999, p. 350.

[60] Rubin 1999, p. 404; Bektas 2000, p. 694.

Ottoman rulers, "the telegraph was a potent instrument of centralized and autocratic rule".[61]

As the examples described in this paper illustrate, however, the telegraph was also "a potent instrument" for those challenging the power of the state. To the extent that telegraph wires, stations, and operators were identified as representatives of the dominant political system, both disorganized protestors and organized movements found a convenient, vulnerable, and powerful symbol against which to express their dissatisfaction. While these protests often took the form of destructive vandalism, the telegraph could also be deployed for more constructive and productive purposes, particularly as a means to communicate dissatisfaction across distances, coordinate protests, and anticipate repressive responses. On July 22, 1908, the Committee of Union and Progress, soon to be known as the "Young Turks," seized the telegraph office in Salonika and began sending messages to other committees asking them to begin proclaiming the Constitution, which had been introduced in 1876 and then suspended within a few years. Two days later, on July 24, the Committee sent a cable directly to the Sultan, demanding that he implement the Constitution. According to a contemporary newspaper report, the telegram "landed like a thunderbolt" in the central government offices.[62] By the end of the day, convinced of the disloyalty of so many troops, the Sultan yielded and the Constitution was restored.[63] The telegraph lines constructed by the Ottoman state as a means to enforce centralized power had become a means by which that power could be challenged.

A decade later, the same dynamics that had strengthened the state – a fast network of far-reaching rapid communication – once again became targets of forces determined to challenge European imperialism. During the Egyptian popular uprising against the British in early 1919, which became known as the Wafd revolt, telegraph wires were often the deliberate target of urban as well as rural protestors. One of the signs of the rebellion that broke out immediately after Wafd leaders were arrested and deported in March 1919 was the effort to cut telegraphic communication, with the seeming intent of preventing the British from mobilizing their forces. In this situation, cutting telegraph wires was part of a broader indigenous campaign to bring to a halt all forms of colonial power, with the goal of forcing the British to compromise on their repression of nationalist leaders.[64] A *Times* correspondent reporting on the complete break in telegraphic communication between Upper and

[61] Lewis 2002, p. 187. Rubin judges Eliot's statement, even after setting aside its "cynicism and bias," to be called equally "valid" for the Ottoman Sultan, British government, and Iranian Shah: Rubin 1999, p. 350. See also the statement that the Ottoman reformer Sulan Abdulhamid II "linked the provinces to the center by means of a new invention, the telegraph," thus supporting "a vision of an efficient bureaucracy in control of the periphery". Hanioglu 2008, p. 125.

[62] "Sultan, in a Panic, Gives Constitution," in: *The New York Times*, 25.06.1908, p. 1.

[63] "Turkey-History," in: *The International Military Digest Annual* (1916), p. 578; Gottheil 1908, p. 526.

[64] For references to the disruption of telegraphic communication, see Richmond 1977, p. 180; Mansfield 1971, p. 224; Terry 1982, p. 98.

Lower Egypt, "except one line to Alexandria," warned that "an organization" had the objective of "destroying all communication, and thereby paralyzing the Government".[65] The British military responded with draconian warnings that anyone caught interfering with telegraphic communication would be shot on the spot, yet these threats did little to stop this form of protest.[66]

## Conclusion

The history of the telegraph in the Middle East thus encompassed a spectrum of practices and attitudes, ranging from state directed modernization to disorganized acts of disobedience. In these situations, the telegraph became a tangible instrument and polysemic object of political power. In the context of this powerful movement towards globalization, the telegraph served as a symbol of both the projection of external power and the expression of immediate dissatisfaction. As a communication device in the hands of a provincial governor, a space for organized protests, a means of directing troops to suppress an insurrection, or links in the web connecting a mass protest movement, the telegraph served an important role in shaping transnational responses to processes of globalization.

## Bibliography

Andrew, William P. 1857. *Memoir on the Euphrates Valley Route to India*. London: W.H. Allen.
"Arabi's Rebellion Ended." 1882. *The New York Times*, 16.09.
de Bellaigue, Christopher. 2001. "The Sick Man of Europe." *The New York Review of Books* 4811. Accessed 28.10.2011 (http://www.nybooks.com/articles/14331).
Bektas, Yakup. 2000. "The Sultan's Messenger: Cultural Constructions of Ottoman Telegraphy, 1847–1880." *Technology and Culture* 41, 669–696.
Bright, Charles. 1908. *The Life Story of Sir Charles Tilston Bright*. London: A. Constable.
Bright, Charles. 1911. *Imperial Telegraphic Communication*. London: P.S. King & Son.
Cole, Juan R.I. 1993. *Colonialism and Revolution in the Middle East. Social and Cultural Origins of Egypt's Urabi Movement*. Princeton: Princeton University Press.
Curzon, George N. 1892. *Persia and the Persian Question*. London: Longmans, Green, and Co.
Dickson, William Kirk. 1901. *The Life of Major General Sir Robert Murdoch Smith*. Edinburgh: Blackwood.
"Egyptian Nationalism." 1919. *The Independent*, 24.05.
Eliot, Charles. 1908. *Turkey in Europe*. London: E. Arnold.
"The Euphrates Valley Railway and Indo-European Telegraph." 1856. *Bentley's Miscellany* 40, 275.
Fuchs, Margot. 1990. "The Indo-European Telegraph System 1868–1931. Politics and Technical Change." *Berichte zur Wissenschaftsgeschichte* 13, 157–166.

[65] "Organized Disorder. Misleading the People," in: *The Times*, 24.03.1919, p. 12.
[66] "Egyptian Nationalism," in: *The Independent*, 24.05.1919, pp. 280–281.

Gelvin, James L. 2008. *The Modern Middle East. A History*. New York: Oxford University Press.
Giddens, Anthony. 2000. *Runaway World. How Globalization is Reshaping our Lives*. New York: Routledge.
Goldsmid, Frederic. 1874. *Telegraph and Travel*. London: Macmillan.
Gordon, John Steele. 2003. *A Thread Across the Ocean. The Heroic Story of the Transatlantic Cable*. New York: Perennial.
Gottheil, Richard. 1908. "The Young Turks and the Old Turkey," *The Forum*, 526.
Hamlin, Cyrus. 1878. *Among the Turks*. New York: R. Carter & Bros.
Hanioglu, M. Sukru. 2008. *A Brief History of the Late Ottoman Empire*. Princeton: Princeton University Press.
Harcave, Sidney. 2004. *Count Sergei Witte and the Twilight of Imperial Russia. A Biography*. Armonk: M.E. Sharpe.
Howard, Douglas A. 2001. *The History of Turkey*. Westport CT: Greenwood Press.
Karbellashvili, Andre. 1991. "Europe-India Telegraph 'Bridge' Via the Caucasus," *Indian Journal of the History of Science* 26, no. 3, 277–281.
Kennedy, Paul M. 1971."Imperial Cable Communications and Strategy, 1870–1914." *English Historical Review* 86, no. 341, 728–752.
Lewis, Bernard. 2002. *The Emergence of Modern Turkey*, 3rd ed. Oxford: Oxford University Press.
Manning, Patrick. 2003. *Navigating World History. Historians Create a Global Past*. New York: Palgrave Macmillan.
Mansfield, Peter. 1971. *The British in Egypt*. New York: Holt, Rinehart and Winston.
McNeill, John R. and William H. McNeill. 2003. *The Human Web: A Bird's Eye View of World History*. New York: W.W. Norton.
Mehlinger, Howard D. and John M. Thompson. 1972. *Count Witte and the Tsarist Government in the 1905 Revolution*. Bloomington: Indiana University Press.
Mounsey, Augustus H. 1872. *A Journey Through the Caucasus and the Interior of Persia*. London: Smith, Elder & Co.
Murray, Donald. 1902. "How Cable Unites the World." *The World's Work. A History of our Time* 4, 2299–2300.
"Organized Disorder. Misleading the People." 1919. *The Times*, 24.03.
"Persia." 1893. *The Times*, 20.05.
Preece, J.R. 1879 "Telegraphs in Persia." *Journal of the Society of Telegraph Engineers* 18, no. 29, 403–441.
Richmond, John C.B. 1977. *Egypt 1798–1952. Her Advance Towards a Modern Identity*, London: Methuen Co.
Rubin, Michael Allan. 1999. *The Formation of Modern Iran, 1858–1909: Communications, Telegraph and Society*. Ph.D. Dissertation, Yale University.
Sauer, George. 1870. *Overland Telegraph to Persia, Appendix 17: Postal Telegraph in the United States, House of Representatives, Report No. 114*. Washington DC, 88.
*Schaffner's Telegraph Companion*, vol. 1. 1854. New York: Pudney & Russell.
Schindler, A. Houtom. 1876. "The Persian Government Telegraphs." *Journal of the Society of Telegraph Engineers* 5, 262–268.
Shahvar, Soli. 2007. "Iron Poles, Wooden Poles: The Electric Telegraph and the Ottoman-Iranian Boundary Conflict, 1863–1865." *British Journal of Middle Eastern Studies* 34, no. 1, 23–42.
"The Society of Telegraph Engineers and of Electricians." 1877. *Electrical Review* October 15, 246–247.
"The Society of Telegraph Engineers and of Electricians." 1882. *Electrical Review* December 2, 431–433.
"Sultan, in a Panic, Gives Constitution." 1908. *The New York Times*, 25.06.
Terry, Janice J. 1982. *The Wafd, 1919–1952. Cornerstone of Egyptian Political Power*. London: Third World Centre for Research and Pub.
"Turkey-History." 1916. *The International Military Digest Annual*, 578.

Wenzlhuemer, Roland. 2007. "The Dematerialization of Telecommunication: Communication Centres and Peripheries in Europe and the World, 1850–1920." *Journal of Global History* 2, 346–350.

Wenzlhuemer, Roland. 2007. "The Development of Telegraphy, 1870–1900: A European Perspective on a World History Challenge." *History Compass* 5, no. 5, 1722–1726.

Winseck, Dwayne and Robert M. Pike. 2009. "The Global Media and the Empire of Liberal Internationalism, Circa 1910–30." *Media History* 15, no. 1, 31–54.

# Chapter 6
# *Working* the Nation State: Submarine Cable Actors, Cable Transnationalism and the Governance of the Global Media System, 1858–1914

**Simone Müller-Pohl**

**Abstract** The historiography of submarine telegraphy has been dominated by what David Edgerton defined as techno-nationalism, i.e. the assumption that the nation state is the key element of analysis. The most recent trend, to which also this essay contributes, stresses the interrelatedness of telecommunication and globalisation processes in the late nineteenth and early twentieth centuries. Following a global history approach, this paper focuses on the individual cable agents of nineteenth century submarine telegraphy and shows how for them the nation state was a category to work with, rarely one to be guided by. The cable agents' realm of action was based upon the concept of cable transnationalism, deduced from the border-transgressing character of telegraph science and technology. In its last part, this paper shows how discourses of mounting nationalism were met with strategic nationalism, i.e. the alleged adoption of a distinct nationality according to the relevant discourse.

Submarine cables inevitably expand beyond the nation state. Rivers, seas and oceans, as well as mountain ranges, had from the earliest times served as natural borders. Some of the most well known examples in European history are the Danube which separated 'barbarians' from the Roman Empire or the perennial Franco-German struggle for the Rhine.[1] Whilst in the nineteenth century borders – particularly in the United States and in Africa – were defined on the drawing board according to degrees of latitude, rivers and shorelines were still a popular means for defining territoriality and belonging. It was therefore only natural that telegraphy too should expand beyond national territoriality by going *sub-marine*. The first

[1] See for instance Demangeon and Febvre 1935; on the interdependence of mapping and nationalization see Winichakul 2009.

S. Müller-Pohl (✉)
John F. Kennedy Institute for North American Studies, FU Berlin, Berlin, Germany
e-mail: mueller@jfki.fu-berlin.de

I. Löhr and R. Wenzlhuemer (eds.), *The Nation State and Beyond*, Transcultural Research – Heidelberg Studies on Asia and Europe in a Global Context,
DOI 10.1007/978-3-642-32934-0_6, 

commercially used submarine lines were thus installed under the English Channel and the Irish Sea to connect Great Britain with mainland Europe in the early 1850s.[2] Conceptually speaking, submarine telegraphy is a transnational entity; in the nineteenth century it grew into a globe-spanning communications network as a small group of entrepreneurs and engineers developed a dense network of ocean cables to encircle the world.[3]

If this aspect of submarine telegraphy is essentially transboundary, the modern nation state is, according to Peer Vries, characterized as a fixed territory with defined subjects, enabling the distinction between *us* and *the other*.[4] Growing national identification further enhanced this distinction in the late nineteenth century and, according to Hobsbawm, in particular the period between 1880 and 1914 must be characterized as one of mounting nationalism promoted by the political right. National sovereignty was in this way defined by absolute national autonomy and incorporated aspects of language and ethnicity as constituents of national belonging.[5] Many a scholar has argued that terrestrial telegraph or telephone systems and the associated printing technology helped to create 'national' publics and were fundamental in the creation of a national neighbourhood in the form of the modern nation state.[6] Submarine telegraphy, by way of contrast transgressed these concepts and actually created a connection *between* us and the other. It enhanced the formation of new trans- and international spaces and classes, such as a distinct cable transnationalism, which were neither bound by a nation state's territory nor its nationalistic exclusiveness. This cable transnationalism was the basis for the individual cable actors' world-wide scheme of thinking and their sphere of action. They functioned as mediators between the macro and the micro level and so structured, constructed and governed the global communication system. Their analysis discloses to us the mechanisms of informal governance and the power of cultural notions, such as cable transnationalism, for the governance of globalization processes.

In the literature, the global media system is represented as a complex system with state and non-state actors, encompassing nation states, international organizations, the cable companies as well as prominent cable individuals. Even so, it is predominantly analyzed according to concepts of nation state or empire. Cables, cable manufacture and cable contractor companies are typically given a distinct nationality and thereby an implicit nationalistic agenda, as cables are read as an essential instrument for the economic and political benefits and security of the nation state. Consequently, the national framing is fundamental for works such as

[2] Marland 1962.

[3] The term 'transnational' only emerged in the early twentieth century. For its history see Tyrrell, "What is Transnational History?".

[4] Vries 2009.

[5] Hobsbawm 1990, pp. 183–184.

[6] See Hobsbawm and Ranger 2009; Pound 1926; Anderson makes a similar argument for the printing press. See Anderson 2006.

Arthur Kunert's *Telegraphen Seekabel*,[7] Kenneth R. Haigh and Edward Wilshaw's *Cableships and Submarine Cables*[8] or Lewis Coe's *The Telegraph*[9] to focus solely on the German, British and American telegraph networks. Themselves influenced in turn by contemporary terminology, scholars continue to use a national attribute when discussing the *French*, *British* or *German* ocean cable. Such techno-nationalist analysis in the form of methodological nationalism, which assumes the nation state to be the key unit of analysis is, however, problematic.[10] Not only does it underestimate the (financial) working structure of these ocean cable companies, some of which were the first multi-nationals, but it also invites the assumption that in particular the individual cable actors, such as the engineers or entrepreneurs, enjoyed little freedom of action within the macro-structures of nation states' world politics and world economy.[11]

Furthermore, in the literature the transnational nature of submarine telegraphy is expressed predominantly in the nations' "struggle for control of global communication"[12] as each nation sought to secure independent means of communication to secure imperial control and national security. Consequently and in particular during the era of new imperialism and mounting nationalism, the field of submarine telegraphy was, according to Pascal Griset and Daniel Headrick, one of the "great power rivalries".[13] Amongst the most eminent proponents of this 'imperial thesis' of great power rivalries are P.M. Kennedy and Daniel Headrick, who both argue from an imperial viewpoint, interpreting submarine telegraphs as "Imperial Strategy"[14] or *Tools of Empire*[15] and thus means to govern geographically distant parts of mainly British jurisdiction. Their argument, which highlights the interdependence of the imperial project and the emergence and structuring of global communication, has influenced an entire generation of history and media scholars. In a similar way to Robert Boyce, they posit the importance of submarine telegraphs for "Britain's ascendency as a world power".[16]

The most recent literature on the global media system largely deals with its interrelatedness with globalization processes and thereby challenges the imperial thesis. Works highlight the importance and entanglement of submarine telegraphy with regard to the course of globalization processes. Important publications in this

---

[7] Kunert 1962.

[8] Haigh and Wilshaw 1968.

[9] Coe 1993.

[10] On methodological nationalism see Wimmer and Glick-Schiller 2002; on techno-nationalism see Edgerton 2007.

[11] On the financial aspect Winseck and Pike for example highlight the financing argument. See Winseck and Pike 2007, p. 4.

[12] Hills 2002.

[13] Griset and Headrick 2001, p. 543.

[14] Kennedy 1971.

[15] Headrick 1981.

[16] Boyce 1995.

field are the collection of essays from 2010 edited by Roland Wenzlhuemer or the forthcoming edited volume on *Global Communication Electric* by Michaela Hampf and myself. Herein, the authors examine the interrelations between globalization processes and the history of telecommunication in the nineteenth century, looking at issues such as the impact of global submarine telegraphy on imperial control, the public sphere or the construction of transnational social networks.[17] Furthermore, authors like Dwayne Winseck and Robert Pike in *Communication and Empire* or Leonard Laborie in *L'Europe mise en résaux* question different nations' struggle for control and point to episodes of inter-imperial collaboration and international cooperation. In particular Winseck and Pike argue that "the notion of imperial rivalry has been overplayed". They highlight the companies' financial independence from national capital and governments, and the latter's willingness to rely on foreign firms to meet their international communication and military security needs. Moreover, they argue that the strong influence of the globalization of capitalism surpassed that of imperialism.[18]

My critique of the imperial thesis does not aim at doing away with it entirely. Daqing Yang has illustrated convincingly for the Japanese case that the politics and strategies of imperialistic logic did play an important role in the build-up of telegraphic connections.[19] Furthermore, we should not ignore the fact that the British Empire in particular was the enabling structure for the ocean cable business in its reliance upon colonial resources, such as gutta percha, or the laying of cables along international and colonial trading routes. Here Winseck and Pike underestimate the overlapping geographies of imperialism and global capitalism, although nevertheless they quite rightly observe that imperialism and nationalist rivalry may not be the only basis for the construction of the global media system.[20] This becomes even clearer when we look at the individual cable actors, who serve as links between the macro and the micro level. Their analysis allows us to uncover not only a range of perspectives on a global communication system, but also ways of adapting to the systemic changes brought about by the era of new imperialism without sacrificing the logic of their global ocean cable system. I am thus suggesting a more nuanced view, which not only accounts for the logic of imperial rivalry, but also for the logic of cable transnationalism, with which a nationalism based exclusively on the assumption of one's own nation's supremacy[21] was incompatible, but which still embraced nationalism as an instrument to uphold globality. The term *cable transnationalism* thus refers to the phenomenon of transboundary movements and conceptual systems as embodied by the actors of submarine telegraphy. They oriented themselves towards a global framework within which the nation state itself was merely an actor and for the sustenance of

[17] Wenzlhuemer 2010; Hampf and Müller-Pohl 2013 (forthcoming).

[18] Winseck and Pike 2007, p. xvii.

[19] Yang 2009.

[20] On the interrelation of a capitalist economy and imperialism see also Pomeranz 2000.

[21] Smith 1999.

which nationalist rhetoric was a strategy and not a goal.[22] In this vein, this paper focuses on the individual agents of cable-laying, such as the engineers, entrepreneurs, financiers, journalists, politicians and philanthropists involved in the various cable schemes and their transnational indebtedness. With this global-history approach the multidimensionality of historical processes in the nineteenth century becomes visible, marking the transnational in the century of the nation state.

To begin with, this essay introduces the concept of cable transnationalism, which is based upon the transnational character of submarine telegraphy's science and technology. This concept also represents the basis for the cable agents' sphere of action and the cable engineers' *raison d'être* as they emerged as a new class of transnationally oriented professionals. These findings challenge the dominant 'imperial thesis' of Headrick and Boyce or Hill's struggle for a control model to represent submarine telegraphy's historiography. The nation state, however, is not abolished, except as an analytical a priori. In a second step this paper deals with the agency of the nation state and the cable agents within the global media network and their relation to each other prior to 1898, the year of the Spanish-American War and the end of cable neutrality. It will demonstrate that for the cable agents the nation state was, on the national as well as the international level, a category to *handle* or to work with, rarely one to be guided by. The final section considers questions of increasing nationalism and the agents' counter-strategies in the decades of mounting cable nationalism preceding the First World War. As this essay will illustrate, during the heyday of an exclusive nationalistic ideology especially after 1898, the individual cable actors successfully applied their own strategic nationalism, which served as a disguise for the business's true internationalism. With regard to the relation between 'the global' and 'the national' in the history of telecommunication, this essay highlights their simultaneity as well as their complicated entanglements.

## The Concept of Cable Transnationalism

Although shorter submarine telegraphs had been around since the 1850s, it was the Great Atlantic Cable of 1866 that finally brought the breakthrough for submarine telegraphy and intercontinental long-distance communication. It connected the Old World and the New World and its success created a virtual "'run' upon companies for laying deep-sea cables".[23] After 1866, submarine cable technology advanced rapidly and construction began on a vast intercontinental network of telegraphic

[22] In its understanding of cable transnationalism, this study benefited from Scott Malcomson's concept of 'real existing cosmopolitanism' which is both located and embodied. In distinction, however, from contemporary notions of cosmopolitanism which acclaim universalism and the agents' use of nationalism as a strategy I found the term cable transnationalism more fitting. It avoids confusion with this universally acclaimed cosmopolitanism of the sources and on the other hand allows for the state to be an important structure, too. See Robbins 2008.

[23] *Leeds Mercury*, 6.9.1869.

communications. By the late 1870s, cables spanned the entire globe, stretching as far as India, South East Asia, Australia, South America and South Africa; about 64,000 nautical miles of cables were in operation[24] and the world's major land masses were "joined together" by a network of electric wires.[25] However, this was only the beginning. As with the Atlantic case, multiple cable routes were necessary for traffic and reliability and it proved profitable to connect even smaller units together; isolated islands with relatively few inhabitants "were suddenly thrust into immediate contact with the rest of the world".[26] Within three decades Shakespeare's dream had become true and "a girdle [was put] round the world in forty minutes".[27] By 1900, the world-wide network totalled about 190,000 miles and by 1923 about 366,000 miles of ocean cables.[28]

This global media system was based upon a complicated network consisting of state and non-state actors, all of them are important to consider in the analysis of its governance. For various reasons, which will become clear in the course of this paper, the system was overwhelmingly held in private hands until the 1930s. Nation states' responsibilities lay in granting financial and political support, as for example in the form of cable-landing concessions or, as with the early cables, providing cable-laying vessels and ocean soundings. The important cable companies, as non-state actors within the system, amounted to only a handful. Following a business strategy of "rampant cartelization" a very small number of companies, such as the Eastern and Associated Companies, controlled all of the global communication by means of a monopolistic system.[29] On the inter-national level, the International Telegraph Union (ITU) regulated transnational traffic. This international governing body was established in 1865 to codify European landline traffic; after 1871 and its Rome conference, it also took on the world-wide submarine network. As this paper will show, a number of individual cable agents were running the system: entrepreneurs such as John Pender (1815–1896), Cyrus W. Field (1819–1892) and William Siemens (1823–1883), the engineers Charles T. Bright (1832–1888) and Latimer Clark (1822–1898) and cable manager George von Chauvin (1846–192?) negotiated between the macro level of the nation states and global economy and the micro level of their daily work routine of providing global communication. They moved within the system outlined above according to their own rules of cable transnationalism.

The concept of cable transnationalism is predominantly based upon the transnationality of submarine telegraphy in terms of its science and technology. The term transnationalism thereby corresponds to border-transgressing relations and constellations, which may be even or asymmetric, but are always potentially

[24] Finn 1980.

[25] Coates and Finn 1979, p. 165.

[26] Ibid.

[27] *Trewman's Exeter Flying Post*, 1.8.1866.

[28] Headrick 1981, p. 162.

[29] Winseck and Pike 2007, pp. 5–6.

globe spanning and thus expand beyond being mere border traffic. This does not imply that the nation states were irrelevant, but questions their a priori and methodological nationalism.[30] *Cable* transnationalism was furthered by a cosmopolitan lifestyle, led and disseminated by the cable agents. This was expressed in the science as well as the technology of submarine telegraphy, and the means of global communication and transport facilitated the formation of a new transnational professional class. Lastly, it is essential to understand at base the cable agents' relation to the nation state and its nationalism as well as their governance of globalization processes.

Submarine telegraphy was already at the time of its formation, despite an indisputable preponderance of British science and scientists, "the work of many hands".[31] In many regards, it represents the prime example of transnational (natural) science. During the 1840s, various solutions for making telegraphy submarine were considered independently by Charles Wheatstone in England, James Bowman Lindsey in Scotland, Samuel Morse in America and others like a certain F.H. Basse from Hamel or a Mr. Erman from Berlin. Even though further developments were predominantly worked on in Great Britain, this was always done with reference to the work of others from 'abroad' and there was a constant exchange of letters, papers and knowledge.[32] Some of the main problems of early submarine attempts were eventually solved by Werner Siemens in Berlin. His invention of a gutta percha press for insulating the ocean cables and his *Legungstheorie* (theory of ocean cable-laying) were fundamental to the further development of submarine telegraphy from the banks of the Thames out into the world.[33] Although we are not dealing here with transnational research in its twentieth-century understanding of shared personnel, funding and equipment,[34] the ideas of telegraphic science were already at their inception not restricted to the boundaries of one nation state.

From the 1870s onwards, these transboundary habits were further institutionalized through the Society of Telegraph Engineers, International Electrical Exhibitions as well as the ITU's quintennial conferences. When in 1871 the Society of Telegraph Engineers was founded in London it emphasized its devotion to the trans-nationality of telegraph science. According to its first president William Siemens, the Society could be nothing else but a cosmopolitan institution. It had

---

[30] Conrad and Osterhammel 2006, pp. 13–15.

[31] Bright 1898, pp. x–xi.

[32] In support of this argument see Highton 1852, pp. v–vii. The author lists all the books he took into consideration for his work on the Electric Telegraph. Among many British authors, there are also other from Germany and France such as *Manuel de la Télégraphie Electrique* by L. Bregust, *Der Elektro-magnetische Telegraph* by Dr. H. Schellen or *Der Praktische Telegraphist, oder die Electro-magnetische Telegraphie nach dem Morse'schen System* by Clemens Gerke. An interesting monograph Highton consults is the work by Werner Siemens – albeit in French translation: *Rapport fait à l'Académie des Sciences sur les Appareils Télégraphiques de M. Siemens (de Berlin).*

[33] Burns 2004, p. 129; Scott 1958, p. 24.

[34] Crawford et al. 1993, p. 1.

to pay tribute to the vast extent of the ocean cable system "to every portion of the civilised and semi-civilised world" and the various systems of knowledge thereby created. In order to combine "the knowledge of these diverse circumstances, and of the diverse practice resulting therefrom," the Society was installed as the "focus into which the thoughts and observations of all countries flow, in order to be again radiated in every direction for the general advancement of this important branch of applied science".[35] In order to bring about these goals, the Society created the class of 'foreign members' and in subsequent years several foreign branches were established right across the globe to coordinate the exchange of knowledge on a global basis.[36] International Electrical Exhibitions as well as the ITU conferences, at which telegraph engineers and scientists played leading roles, were additional venues for the coordination and codification of scientific processes and apparatuses, but also for defining electrical standards, such as the ohm, volt and ampere for global usage.[37] In effect, the science of submarine telegraphy headed a process of growing scientific transnationalism, which took off especially after the 1880s when science per se "expanded into the international arena as never before".[38] In a similar manner to the transnational academic networks between German and British universities, as described in the chapter in this volume by Heather Ellis, in its scientific substance, the business of submarine telegraphy essentially drew from the earlier concept of the republic of letters and a transboundary exchange of knowledge.

However, it was not only the science of submarine telegraphy, but also technology as such which induced transnational thinking and acting. With the growing extension and development of a world-spanning ocean cable network, the engineers' and entrepreneurs' sphere of action too expanded as they followed their cable projects and routes around the globe. The prominent American entrepreneur Cyrus W. Field crossed the Atlantic 64 times in pursuit of the Great Atlantic Cable enterprise of 1854–1866.[39] For the cable engineers, the seas and oceans of the world – untouched by national territoriality – were their workplaces as they laid cables right around the earth. Consequently, telegraph expert Charles Bright emphasized that "[t]here is probably no branch of engineering which lends itself so readily to a full sight of the world as that of telegraphy".[40] Outstanding and yet thoroughly representative examples amongst such a transnationally active workforce include the consulting engineers Charles T. Bright, father of the above Charles Bright, and Latimer Clark as well as the Anglo-German cable engineer and manager George von Chauvin.

The biographies of Latimer Clark and Charles Bright vividly illustrate how their work itinerary took them all over the globe. Bright, who was distinguished with a knighthood for the part he played in the 1858 Atlantic cable, began his telegraph

[35] Siemens 1872/73, p. 22.

[36] A complete run of membership lists and forms can be found at the IET Archives in London.

[37] Hunt 1994, p. 57.

[38] Crawford et al. 1993, p. 13.

[39] Bright 1898, p. 80.

[40] Ibid., p. xiii.

career with submarine cables in the Irish Sea in 1853, followed by others in the Mediterranean, the Red Sea and eventually the Atlantic. Clark had taken up submarine engineering in 1850 and later laid several of the early cables in the English Channel, the Irish Sea and the Mediterranean.[41] After the breakthrough of the Atlantic cable, both men expanded the geographic range of their work even further. In 1860, they entered into partnership and laid cables in the Persian Gulf and the West Indies and even pursued plans to go as far as the Cape of Good Hope.[42] After the partnership was dissolved in the late nineteenth century, Charles T. Bright turned to mining, partly for health reasons, whilst Clark continued with the ocean cables. During the remainder of the nineteenth century, some 50,000 miles of ocean telegraphs were laid just under Clark's supervision.[43] In their movements and the choice of their cable projects, neither Bright nor Clark were bound to the British government or thus the realm of its Empire with regards to where they went. Indiscriminately they laid cables for the English, Spanish, French and Danish governments both contracted and as contractees. When the nature of a cable project's region demanded it, as in the case of the West Indies, they sometimes even worked for several governments at once and created one 'international' network of ocean cables between the various islands.[44] Up until the 1890s, governments employed cable companies and engineers regardless of their nationality and the companies' headquarters' location as a handful of chiefly British engineers laid almost the entire globe's cable network.

It was not only the cable engineers and hence the process of cable-laying, but also the cable companies' managers and staff and thus the procedures of cable operating and managing which followed a transnational pattern of working. In the same time as multi-national firms such as Siemens Brothers or the Eastern and Associated Companies moved with their submarine cable projects around the globe, they also relocated their engineers and personnel. Analysis of staff records and diaries from different cable stations thereby illustrates that the transnational sphere of action encompassed managers as well as operators and that it was common to work at two or three different stations throughout one's career.[45] The example of George von Chauvin must therefore be seen as representative: having probably started out as a Prussian military telegrapher, he can first be traced as a cable man with the Anglo-German cable manufacturer Siemens Brothers in London in 1866. F Throughout his life he followed his telegraph profession across the entire western hemisphere, moving between states as if borders were non-existent. He often changed employers, positions and projects. Despite this, in all of his projects he always remained closely associated with the Siemens Brothers and it seems as if he was actually placed there by them. George von Chauvin worked on the Siemens

[41] Pollard 2004.

[42] Bright 1908, pp. ix–xi.

[43] Pollard 2004.

[44] Bright 1908, pp. 202, 308.

[45] de Cogan 2005.

Brothers' Indo-European Telegraph line of 1868–1870, in the 1870s he was managing director of the Direct United States Telegraph Company, the Compagnie Française du Télégraphe de Paris à New York, representative of Western Union in London and crowned his telegraph career from 1900 on as managing director of Siemens Brothers, where he remained until his retirement in 1925.[46] By then, he had lived and worked in Berlin, London, New York and Paris in addition to the various places where he had laid ocean cables.

As this brief section shows, the science and technology of submarine telegraphy allowed its engineers and electricians, such as Charles T. Bright and Latimer Clark, but also entrepreneurs and managers like Cyrus W. Field and George von Chauvin to live, work and think transnationally. Moreover, from the mere geographical perspective of submarine telegraphy, transnationalism seems to be a dominant pre-requisite as its actors made the globe's seas and oceans their working place and the location between states from which they acted. The Society of Telegraph Engineers and institutions such as the International Electrical Exhibitions and the ITU thereby defined and codified their sphere of action on a global scale. As one consequence, this cable transnationalism furthered the development of a new transnational class that formed its identity across national borders and ultimately created new transnational spaces. The cable actors can thus be characterized according to Isin and Wood's concept of a professional citizenship, which centres upon the importance of an emerging professionalism that is removed from the nation state. Accordingly, the cable agents gained their wealth, status and power through their telegraph profession; their rights and obligations were not necessarily dependent upon their citizenship but rather their professional occupation and practices. Ultimately, they represented a distinct transnational class of professionals that identified, as the final section of this paper will show, more with their profession than with their own nation state.[47]

Lastly, we should not forget the conceptual restrictions of this cable transnationalism and its class of professionals. The aforementioned Bright, Clark and von Chauvin represented a unique sort of transnational labourers benefitting from the imperial power constellations of the time. Having made a name for themselves as pioneers in the cable industry and in the case of Bright and Clark as members of the class of 1866 that launched the Great Atlantic Cable, they could work as independent advisors, consulting engineers and general managers "to the various companies that were constantly being floated for carrying out new submarine telegraphic schemes".[48] Essentially, they were in the position to pick and choose. Their transnational labour had little in common with the more dominant

[46] Scott 1958, p. 73.

[47] Isin and Wood 1999, pp. 91, 103.

[48] Bright 1898, p. 155; the wiring of the Atlantic was fundamental to the development of a distinct and elite group of cable agents, who came to dominate the business of submarine telegraphy until the twentieth century. The concept of the 'Class of 1866' is more thoroughly elaborated in Müller 2010.

phenomenon of (forced and voluntary) labour migration during the nineteenth century. Nevertheless, the two men were typical representatives of their profession. In addition, however, we must also consider that cable transnationalism had a distinct western, imperial and gendered colouring. The science and technology, the cable companies and its actors were primarily based in London and New York and could be clearly distinguished as Euro-Americans. In contrast to the terrestrial systems, it was hardly ever the case that 'natives,' let alone women, were employed to work on the 'complicated' ocean lines. Apart from the case of Japan[49] and its collaboration with the Great Northern Telegraph Company, little is known about submarine telegraph engineers from outside the western hemisphere. Throughout the nineteenth and early twentieth century, ocean telegraphy remained a western technology from which principally the industrialized nations benefited.[50] The cable actors, and with them cable transnationalism, represented a distinct western and elitist phenomenon.

## Working the Nation State: Cable Agents and the Governance of Globalization Processes

Where the foregoing has described the structure of cable transnationalism as the basis of its actors' thoughts and action, the following will focus on how this elitist group of cable professionals 'governed' the global media system and hence globalization processes prior to 1898 and the end of cable neutrality. It will analyze the relation between the national and the transnational, the role of the nation states within this system and the actors' engagement therewith. Despite the outline given above of the transnational character of submarine telegraphy which almost suggests a certain obliviousness to national boundaries, the nation state cannot be reduced to a mere passive framework. As already indicated, the various nation states have to be identified as agents themselves within the system of international ocean telegraphy and not the analytical frame; their influence, however, was less dominant than the historiography argues and changed over the course of the nineteenth century. Indeed, as will be demonstrated, the individual cable agents found ways to influence the relevant state institutions and structures on the national and international level through unofficial channels and their excellent personal relations with state officials and state institutions.

Generally speaking, the laying and operation of international submarine cables was free from immediate government involvement. This was mainly because of unresolved questions concerning landing rights, territorial belonging and national jurisdiction at the extending end of the cable. In the case of state ownership, governments would need to obtain authorization for the landing, their cable stations

[49] Yang 2009.

[50] Ahvenainen 1995, p. 80.

as well as their cable staff on foreign territory and hence ask for territorial status within another nation state's territoriality and jurisdiction. As this was quite difficult, the ocean cables were usually run by private companies on the principle of 'cable neutrality' assuming that the 'nationality' of the provider did not matter and that in case of war ocean cables might remain neutral.[51] As a consequence, in 1898, out of the total mileage of submarine cables almost 90 %, thereby including the majority of long-distance lines, had been provided by private enterprise.[52] Even during this period of cable neutrality though, the various nation states still fulfilled several functions in which they were essential for the cable industry and appeared to determine the system's governance: they played an important part in giving material and financial support and granted landing rights. In particular, before the coming of age of submarine telegraphy in 1 , its business was considered to be a risky investment. Oftentimes, nation states were sought out for support and cable promoters relied upon state subsidies or guarantees in order to be able to carry out their undertakings.[53] Another important means of imposing influence were the monopolistic landing rights, which the various governments frequently connected to exclusive concessions. Cable companies were obliged to give government messages priority and often at reduced rates or even free transmission.[54] Finally, the nation states provided the necessary legal, economic and political framing of ocean telegraphy by means of the ITU, their trading routes and the politics of imperialism.[55] It would therefore be wrong to assume that nation states did not play an important role. As the following will show, however, when it came to aspects of governance, in particular the cable entrepreneurs found ways to 'work' the nation states and have them govern the global media system according to their liking.

## Working *the Nation State: The National Realm*

Most of all it was the individual entrepreneurs of the various ocean cable companies who maintained outstanding personal connections with the relevant government

[51] Ahvenainen 2009, p. 65.

[52] Bright 1898, p. 154.

[53] Ibid., p. 167.

[54] In turn, when seeking landing rights, the cable companies asked for exclusive rights. As the cable's manufacture and laying equipment was exorbitantly expensive, it was vital that they could depend upon a certain amount of business, without competition: Ahvenainen 2009, p. 67.

[55] The attitude of the various nation states towards submarine telegraphy as well as their engagement with it changed during the course of the nineteenth century. Although there are different models of state involvement, government support generally became less important and less common after 1866 as cable companies managed to find ample private investors and had their own cable ships and personnel. Haigh and Wilshaw 1968, pp. 317–319; a noted difference may be discerned in the case of the French government, which continually, but rather unsuccessfully, attempted to install a French cable company as a state enterprise, see Griset 1996.

officials and institutions and thereby influenced the nation states' decisions from within. Each company's board of directors generally retained a "remarkable combination of influential aristocrats, businessmen, politicians, and talented engineers," and many of its members were recruited from and closely associated with the imperial power elites.[56] Through such human resource management, the cable companies assured their say in political debates since they always had a political spokesman within their midst. Additionally, they maintained close relations with the various administrative offices of importance for them. A key example is Sir John Pender, the 'cable king', who controlled through his Eastern and Associated Companies the world's most important submarine lines and by 1900 about 4/5 of the world's ocean cable traffic. His wife's correspondence relates how her husband, almost on a weekly basis, would go "to see [. . .] Herbert [. . .] on cable business".[57] Here she is referring to nobody less significant than Sir Robert George Wyndham Herbert (1831–1903), the Under-Secretary of the Colonial Office. At a banquet celebrating the opening of the second cable line to Australia in 1876, Herbert was further reported to have offered "to attend personally to any business that Pender might have with the Colonial Office about cables".[58]

Little is known about how far Herbert extended his offer and what he actually did for John Pender, although the history of cable-laying, does reveal that Pender's unofficial relationship with the imperial administration was indeed fruitful. The example of the Pacific cable, which was promoted in vain from the late 1870s until 1902 primarily by the Canadian colonial government, illustrates that British government officials banned or impeded such a project simply because it was not in John Pender's business interest. With his Eastern and Associated Companies, Pender controlled all communication to India and South East Asia; a Pacific cable would have meant an alternative route and hence a rival on this line. As a consequence, Pender actively opposed such a cable project and did all he could to counter any schemes. Robert Boyce argues that the reasons for the 30 years' delay in this particular cable project (it was finally laid in 1902) were not because the British government saw no economic or political benefits in it, but because it considered such a cable connection to be detrimental to leading British commercial, that is John Pender's interests.[59] A common example of British official criticism of the Pacific project throughout the three decades of the project's promotion was that of John Lamb. The British Secretary of the Post Office argued that while the Pacific cable would "cause a perfect revolution in communication [. . .] it would be a matter of great difficulty, [. . .] for the English government itself to [. . .] constitute itself a competitor with an existing commercial enterprise carried on by Citizens of the British Empire".[60] It was clear that this particular citizen was John Pender who had managed to convince the relevant government officials that his business interests

---

[56] Winseck and Pike 2007, p. 165.

[57] Pender, September 14, 1877, Cable and Wireless Archive.

[58] Hills 2002, p. 60.

[59] Boyce 2000, p. 40.

[60] Winseck and Pike 2007, p. 106.

were *more* national than those of inter-imperial communication between Canada and Australia and hence had to be dearer to them. Like John Lamb, the British Royal Navy refused for decades to undertake the necessary ocean soundings for such a Pacific project: in 1881/1882 the British Admiralty refused to undertake hydrographic surveys firstly on account of costs. When the Canadian government declared it would pay half the expenses and a group of gentlemen offered to pay the other half, the Admiralty claimed that there were no ships available. Even after the main promoter, the Canadian engineer Sandford Fleming, had located a suitable Canadian vessel, the Admiralty still refused to undertake the survey.[61] Only after John Pender's death in 1896 and with the rise of cable nationalism, did the Pacific cable project finally became a reality as a British government undertaking in 1902.

## Working *the Nation State: The International Realm*

With similar success, the cable agents worked their way through the *inter*-national realm, which provided the legal basis for their doings. Relatively early on, the various governments had become convinced of the power of communications "to move markets, affect foreign policy, and shape public opinion". They therefore attempted to subject them to greater control, "as instruments of imperial politics" through international agencies such as the International Telegraph Union (ITU).[62] Transnational telegraph traffic, in the form of technological standards, rates, the distribution of revenues, citizens' rights to privacy or the prerogative of states to censor messages, was thus from 1865 onwards regulated by the ITU. The International Telegraph Union, which was the merger of two European agencies, namely the Austro-German Telegraph Union and the West European Telegraph Union, is seen as the first multi-lateral organization of the nineteenth century and an important milestone in the world's internationalization.[63] At the same time, however, it represented an institution of nation states and their government officials. Even though the private cable companies had been able since the convention of Rome in 1871 to join the Union, they could not decide upon matters that concerned them. They enjoyed the right to attend and to speak during sessions, but in the decision-making process their interests were represented by their governments.[64]

Despite this obvious shortcoming in the organization of the ITU, the cable actors still managed to influence the conferences and their outcomes. A good example is the International Telegraph Conference of 1879 in London to which 24 countries

[61] Boyce 2000, pp. 44–45.

[62] Winseck and Pike 2007, p. 2; for internationalism in the nineteenth century cf. Lyons 1963; Geyer and Paulmann 2008; Herren 2009.

[63] Laborie 2010.

[64] Ahvenainen 2009, p. 70.

and as many as 16 telegraph companies sent their representatives. As the conference was held in London it was chaired by C.H.B. Patey, the director-general of the Department of Posts and Telegraphs o Great Britain.[65] In spring 1879, before the conference, several meetings too place between Patey and the representatives of the British-based ocean cable companies, fine-tuning *their* propositions for the conference with regard to extra-European tariffs, code and languages, repeated messages and press rates.[66] Prior to this, the British Post Office had distributed its own proposal among the cable companies.[67] Patey's original intention was to introduce a proposition at the conference for lower tariffs in order to allow the usage of global communication beyond its then elitist clientele. He was quite stern about the fact that he could not have "the dividends of submarine companies [...] stand in the way of a reduction of tariff".[68]

Such a move, however, was in stark contrast to the business philosophy of the cable companies which believed that less traffic and higher tariffs were preferable to lower tariffs and higher traffic. In his response to Patey, James Anderson, former captain of the famous *Great Eastern* cable ship and now managing director of the Eastern Telegraph Company, reminded him that it was his "duty" to protect these companies' interests "that [were] an essential part of the telegraph system of the Empire".[69] Anderson's letter was backed by the signatures of several other general managers of other cable companies located in London. Their concerted action and their claim to represent "20 millions of British capital" demonstrated such power that Patey and with him the General Post Office as an emerging power eventually had to yield.[70] During the next meeting between the Post Office and the submarine cable companies, Patey not only refrained from his initial proposition, but informed the gentlemen present that he would now even support an increase in tariffs on extra-European routes, hence the ocean cable lines.[71] The London conference itself was another demonstration of the cable companies' power. Their representatives had no voting rights, but the sheer presence of the cable representatives at the Conference was almost oppressive and illustrated how fervently they attempted to steer ITU decisions. Of the 68 delegates, 35 were government officials, 3 came directly from the ITU and 30 from the cable companies. One of the results of the conference was that the tariffs on the extra-European connections, i.e. the ocean cables, remained untouched.[72]

---

[65] Bureau International des Administrations Télégraphique 1880, pp. 253–256, 261, 291–293, 419, BT Archives.

[66] General Post Office 1879, BT Archives.

[67] Ibid.

[68] C.H.B. Patey cited in James Anderson 1879, POST 30/361, BT Archives.

[69] Ibid.

[70] Ibid.

[71] General Post Office, "Telegraph Conference 1879", BT Archives.

[72] "International Telegraph Conference," in: *The Times*, 23.06.1879.

As we have seen, from a systemic point of view, governmental institutions such as the Colonial Office, the British Navy, the General Post Office or the ITU officially regulated and structured the workings of the global media system on the national as well as the international level. The actors' perspective, however, shows that by means of unofficial channels, the employment of social capital in the form of personal relations and through their economic presence, the cable actors found ways to influence the decisions of these state institutions. The most forceful argument they could bring forward in these 'negotiations' was certainly their economic presence and their representation of British capital, which turned their business interests into 'national' interests.

## Countering Nationalism: Professional Citizenship and Strategic Nationalism

In representing submarine telegraphy as a transnational entity by highlighting its border-transgressing character, it has to be emphasized that the importance and nature of these borders, in particular when they were political boundaries, changed over time. Beginning in the 1880s and in parallel to the development of an exclusive nationalism,[73] a "non-British cable industry" started to take form as the industrialized western nations understood that a national capability to manufacture, lay and repair cables was essential if dependence on Great Britain was to be avoided.[74] However, only after the Spanish-American war, which came to be known as the "war of coals and cables", did it become relevant which nationality the cable company, the provider of global communication, belonged to.[75] Henceforth, ocean cables became an object of military security and imperial control, landing rights were distributed more and more restrictively and state involvement in the area of cable manufacture and cable operating grew. In this way, in 1891 the French government invited tenders for a cable from Marseille to Oran and Tunis and thereby for the first time in ocean cable history excluding British contractors altogether.[76] Simultaneously to these developments we can also find an increasing national "territorialization" of the ocean space as midway islands or formerly insignificant rocks become important as cable-landing places.[77] Sandford Fleming, the Pacific cable promoter, caused a diplomatic *faux-pas* when in 1894 he attempted to claim the Hawaiian territory of Necker Island for the British as a cable relay station. Spurred on by jealousies over the future of Hawaii and influence in the

[73] Hobsbawm 1990, pp. 181–185.

[74] Coates and Finn 1979, p. 171; this is congruent with a nationalist understanding that national sovereignty is based upon absolute national autonomy: Hobsbawm 1990, p. 184.

[75] Scholz 1904, p. 1.

[76] Bright 1898, pp. 137–140.

[77] On territorialization as the key concept of the nineteenth and early twentieth centuries, see Maier 2000.

Pacific, the U.S. government became set on its own Pacific cable. When in the mid-1890s John Pender finally warmed to laying a cable across the Pacific his American friend Abrahm Hewitt warned him that U.S. Congress "appear[ed] committed to Cable as a National Necessity". This implied that the legislation proposed state ownership and manufacture, which made it impossible for the Briton Pender and his London-based cable empire to take on the project.[78] In 1914 this process of increasing cable nationalism peaked when the allegedly *German* Atlantic cables, which were actually operated by an American-based company, were cut almost immediately after the start of the First World War.[79]

As this last example shows, the cable agents not only had to negotiate with or between nation states, but particularly after the 1880s also had to deal with increasingly nationalistic interpretations of their work. Returning to the case of the Pacific cable: in the context of mounting nationalism and imperial rivalry preceding the First World War, the American government's concern was that – considering that the telegraph lines in Asia were controlled by the British-based Eastern and Associated Companies and the Danish-based Great Northern Telegraph Company – access to Asia could be gained only at the expense of relinquishing control to such foreign interests. As a cable from the west coast of the United States to its new territorial possessions in the Pacific and onwards to Asia turned into a "national necessity",[80] it became essential that its manufacture, laying and operating was "wholly under the control of the United States".[81] The two American-based competitors for the Pacific cable contract thus "sought to outdo the other by wrapping themselves in the American flag and extolling their corporate virtues and national purity". In the end, the American John W. Mackay and his Pacific Commercial Cable Company laid the trans-Pacific cable.

This was, however, only one side of the story following the logic of imperialism and heightened nationalism; another story following the logic of cable transnationalism and the rules of the global media system lies underneath. This relates how, in fact, purely national ocean cable enterprises were simply not feasible. This was mainly because of the restrictiveness of landing monopolies securing the individual cable companies exclusive rights for decades. The early Atlantic cable landing right in Newfoundland, for instance, only expired in 1904, 50 years after the Newfoundland government had issued it.[82] As a result, behind closed doors the ocean cable companies made business arrangements across national boundaries and irrespective of national sentiments, while in public they employed nationalist rhetoric as a strategy to soothe national sentiments. It was only in 1921 that the American government finally learned that 75 % of its allegedly *American* company providing

[78] Hewitt, February 11, 1895, Cooper Union Archives.

[79] *New York Times*, 6.8.1914.

[80] Hewitt, February 11, 1895.

[81] *New York Times*, 11.2.1899.

[82] Griset and Headrick 2001, pp. 566–567.

for communication across the Pacific was foreign-owned by John Pender's Eastern and Associated Companies and the Danish-based Great Northern Telegraph Company, which both owned the landing rights along the coasts of Japan and China.[83] Such business arrangements were not uncommon during the two decades preceding the First World War, as can be shown by the examples of cooperation between German and Dutch entrepreneurs, in the form of the Deutsch-Niederländische Telegraphengesellschaft (German-Dutch Cable Company), to lay cables in the East Indies or between German and French entrepreneurs to lay a cable across the South Atlantic.[84] The logic of cable transnationalism and the governance of the global media system was therefore entirely different from that of nationalist exclusion. Winseck and Pike even argue that "it seems questionable that the nationality of corporate actors was easy to establish or highly relevant".[85] Nationalism, however, still played a major role in the construction of the global media system prior to the First World War. It was though a strategy to uphold the transnational workings of a global system and not a status to achieve.

On a personal level too, the cable agents applied nationalism as a strategic means. They changed citizenships whenever it was appropriate for their work. Throughout the nineteenth century, London was the capital of the world's submarine telegraph business and thus also attracted many engineers of non-British background. Because of the Siemens Brothers' presence in London, many German telegraph engineers and entrepreneurs came to the city. Most of them, such as William Siemens, eventually renounced their German and took on British citizenship. In some cases this was done for mere personal reasons as the agents had come to stay in Great Britain for good.[86] In other cases, changing citizenship was – similar to the example above of the Pacific Commercial Cable Company – an act of strategic nationalism. George von Chauvin, who had, as this essay has shown earlier, lived and worked all over the Western hemisphere, had never bothered about his legal status until the start of the First World War. Being a *German* telegraph engineer in London was now hindering his career. He benefited, however, from the fact that Britain showed a relatively liberal policy towards wartime naturalization. Although trade with Germany was outlawed immediately upon the start of the War in July 1914, Chauvin only renounced his German citizenship in November by dropping the particle from his name. Undisturbed, he continued to serve the London-based Siemens Brothers until his retirement in 1925.[87]

---

[83] Winseck and Pike 2007, p. 170.

[84] Griset and Headrick 2001, pp. 566–567.

[85] Winseck and Pike 2007, p. 5.

[86] An example of this is Carl Ludwig Loeffler. He was the pervious incumbent as managing director at Siemens Brothers before the aforementioned George von Chauvin and renounced his German citizenship in 1890. Carl Ludwig Loeffler, Letter to the Home Office, June 14 1890, National Archives Kew.

[87] Owen 1991, p. 184; for further case studies concerning the "National Identities of Engineers" see the special edition of *History and Technology* 23 (2007), no. 3.

The period of new imperialism and mounting nationalism prior to the First World War and with it the end of the principle of 'cable neutrality' created, as the examples have illustrated, an impediment to the logic of cable transnationalism. It made the boundaries to be crossed less permeable and seemed to restructure the governance of the global communication system. For the cable actors, these developments were not only detrimental to their concept of cable transnationalism, but also to their companies' financial and working structure. Their shareholders were recruited from the entire Euro-American money elite and, as the Pacific cable case shows, certain agreements between the companies had to be made for reasons of market strategy.[88] The cable agents evaded the problem by acting according to strategic nationalism, taking on the nationality required as well as entering the necessary discourse while at the same time disguising their true working and financing structure.[89] In this manner, the cable companies and their actors successfully managed to uphold their working structures and professional networks beyond the Great War. By seemingly subordinating themselves to the nationalistic ideology they actually upheld a *global* system.

The governance of globalization processes, as exemplified in the global media system, was a complicated undertaking which involved state and non-state actors. As the individual cable actors' perspective of the entrepreneurs, engineers and operators revealed, much of it involved the use of unofficial channels or secret agreements. The basis for the global business of submarine telegraphy, and one could almost say the actors' *raison d'être*, was cable transnationalism, the concept of which, as detailed at the beginning of this paper, is embodied in the creation of new spaces and identities that developed beyond the nation state. This furthered the formation of a distinct transnational professionalism to which the agents' allegiance was greater than to any nation state. The nation state was identified as an entity to handle and collaborate with; and not to be guided by. Above all, the cable agents' excellent personal relations with important state institutions, such as John Pender's friendship with Robert George Wyndham Herbert helped them in their attempts to arrange the national and international arena to benefit their business. One of the actors' prime arguments in this regard was certainly their economic presence and capitalist power. Contrary to what Winseck and Pike originally proclaimed, the actors' strategy revives the thesis of the importance of global capitalism.

---

[88] This can be seen in the shareholder lists of various companies. One of the best examples because of its archival continuity is the Direct United States Cable Company. Shareholder lists exist from its foundation in 1873 well into the twentieth century; among the most important shareholders were various members of the Siemens family, the Anglo-Austrian Bank, the Deutsche Bank, the Banque Centrale Anversoise as well as various merchants from Germany, Belgium, France and England. Direct United States Cable Company, Ltd; BT 31/14576/11597, National Archives Kew.

[89] Interesting in this context is Edgerton's interpretation of Ernest Gellner's account of nationalism, whereby he understands modern nationalism as being vital to (industrial) modernity "not as a way of escaping from a globalized cosmopolitan world, but a means of participating in it while retaining one's dignity, and indeed creating one's capacity to participate". Edgerton 2007, p. 2.

As the last part of this essay showed, the boundaries to be crossed and the role of the nation states within the governance of the global media system changed over time. In the two decades preceding the First World War, the national category grew in importance and challenged by its understanding of national exclusiveness the very transnational structures of submarine cable business and lifestyle. The cable actors met this challenge, on the company as well as on the individual actors' level, with the application of strategic nationalism, i.e. the tactical pretension of a distinct nationality which fitted the relevant nationalistic discourse and ultimately benefited the cable agents and their business. The example of the American Pacific cable here demonstrated that there were two stories to be told, one following the logic of nationalism, the other the logic of cable transnationalism. Consequently, national identity, if not patriotism, had become a category to toy with in various strategic ways just as the nation state had from the beginning of submarine cable business been an actor to collaborate with. Thus, the concepts of cable transnationalism and strategic nationalism, as they could be identified in the cable actors' actions, are important for understanding the nature of submarine cable business in the late nineteenth and early twentieth century in particular in its relatedness to the simultaneity of globalizing and nationalizing processes in later decades. For the cable agents both were realities to deal with.

## Bibliography


Ahvenainen, Jorma. 1995. "The Role of Telegraphs in the 19th Century Revolution of Communication." In *Kommunikationsrevolutionen*, edited by Michael North, 73–80. Cologne: Böhlau.

Ahvenainen, Jorma. 2009. "The International Telegraph Union: The Cable Companies and the Governments." In *Communications Under the Seas*, edited by Bernard S. Finn and Daqing Yang, 61–80. Cambridge, Mass.: MIT.

Anderson, Benedict. 2006. *Imagined Communities: Reflections on the Origin and Spread of Nationalism*, revised ed. London: Verso.

Anderson, James. 1879. POST 30/361, BT Archives.

Boyce, Robert. 1995. "Submarine Cables as a Factor in Britain's Ascendency as a World Power." In *Kommunikationsrevolutionen*, edited by Michael North, 35–50. Cologne: Böhlau.

Boyce, Robert. 2000. "Imperial Dreams and National Realities: Britain, Canada and the Struggle for a Pacific Telegraph Cable, 1879–1902." *English Historical Review* 115, no. 460, 39–70.

Bright, Charles. 1898 *Submarine Telegraphs: Their History, Construction and Working*. London: Crosby Lockwood.

Bright, Charles. 1908. *The Life Story of Sir Charles Tilston Bright Civil Engineer: With Which is Incorporated the Story of the Atlantic Cable, and the First Telegraph to India and the Colonies*. London: A. Constable.

Bureau International des Administrations Télégraphiques 1880, BT Archives.

Burns, Russell W. 2004. *Communications: An International History of the Formative Years*. London: Institution of Electrical Engineers.

Coates, Vary T. and Bernard S. Finn. 1979. *A Retrospective Technology Assessment: Submarine Telegraphy – The Transatlantic Cable of 1866. (Studies in Science and Technology)*. San Francisco: San Francisco Press.

Coe, Lewis. 1993. *The Telegraph: A History of Morse' Invention and its Predecessors in the United States*. Jefferson: McFarland.

de Cogan, Donard, ed. 2005. *The Autobiography of James Graves*, transcribed from the manuscript.
Conrad, Sebastian and Jürgen Osterhammel. 2006. *Das Kaiserreich transnational. Deutschland in der Welt 1871–1914*. Göttingen: Vandenhoeck & Ruprecht.
Crawford, Elisabeth, ed. 1993. *Denationalizing Science: The Contexts of International Scientific Practice*. Dordrecht: Kluwer Academic Publishers.
Crawford, Elisabeth et al. "Introductory Essay." In *Denationalizing Science*, edited by Elisabeth Crawford, 1–41.
Demangeon, Alberg and Lucien Febvre. 1935. *Le Rhin: Problèmes d'Histoire et d'Économie*. Paris: A. Colin.
Direct United States Cable Company. Ltd; BT 31/14576/11597. National Archives Kew.
Edgerton, David. 2007. "The Contradictions of Techno-Nationalism and Techno-Globalism: A Historical Perspective." *New Global Studies* 1, 1–32.
Finn, Bernard S. 1980. "Introduction." *Development of Submarine Cable Communications*, unpaginated. New York Arno Press.
Finn, Bernard S. and Daqing Yang, eds. 2009. *Communications Under the Seas: The Evolving Cable Network and Its Implications. Dibner Institute Studies in the History of Science and Technology*. Cambridge: MIT Press.
General Post Office 1879. BT Archives.
General Post Office. 1879. "Telegraph Conference 1879. Meeting of Representatives of Telegraph Companies in Mr. Patey's Room." February 10. BT Archives.
Geyer, Martin H. and Johannes Paulmann. 2008. *The Mechanics of Internationalism: Culture, Society, and Politics from the 1840s to the First World War*. Oxford: Oxford University Press.
Griset, Pascal. 1996. *Entreprise, Technologie et Souveraineté. Les Télécommunications Transatlantiques de la France, XIXe-XXe siècles*. Paris Editions Rive droite.
Griset, Pascal & Daniel Headrick. 2001. "Submarine Telegraph Cables: Business and Politics, 1838–1939." *Business History Review* 75, no. 3, 543–578.
Haigh, Kenneth and Edward Wilshaw. *Cableships and Submarine Cables*. London: Adlard Coles.
Hampf, Michaela and Simone Müller-Pohl. Forthcoming. *Global Communication Electric*. Frankfurt am Main: Campus Verlag.
Headrick, Daniel. 1981. *The Tools of Empire: Technology and European Imperialism in the Nineteenth Century*. New York: Oxford University Press.
Hennig, Richard. 1909. "Die historische Entwicklung der deutschen Seekabelunternehmungen." *Beiträge zur Geschichte der Technik und Industrie: Jahrbuch des Vereines Deutscher Ingenieure* 1, 241–250.
Herren, Madeleine. 2009 *Internationale Organisationen seit 1865: Eine Globalgeschichte der internationalen Ordnung*. Darmstadt: Wissenschaftliche Buchgesellschaft.
Hewitt. 1895. February 11. Cooper Union Archives.
Highton, Edward. 1852. *The Electric Telegraph: Its History and Progress*. London: J. Weale.
Hills, Jill. 2002. *The Struggle for Control of Global Communication: The Formative Century. The History of Communication*. Urbana: University of Illinois Press.
*History and Technology* 23. 2007, no. 3.
Hobsbawm, Eric. 1990. *Nations and Nationalism since 1780*. Cambridge: Cambridge University Press.
Hobsbawm, Eric & Terrence Ranger, eds. 2009. *The Invention of Tradition*, 13th ed. Cambridge: Cambridge Univ. Press.
Hunt, Bruce J. 1994. "The Ohm is Where the Art is: British Telegraph Engineers and the Development of Electrical Standards." *Osiris* 2, no. 9, 48–63.
"International Telegraph Conference." 1879. *The Times*, 23.6.
Isin, Engin F. and Patricia K. Wood. 1999. *Citizenship and Identity*. London: Thousand Oaks.
John, Richard R. "Cyrus W. Field." *American National Biographies*. Accessed 18.09.2008 (http://www.anb.org/articles/10/10-00542.html).
Kennedy, Paul M. 1971. "Imperial Cable Communications and Strategy, 1870–1914." *English Historical Review* 86, no. 341, 728–752.

Kroes, Rob. 2000. *Them and Us: Questions of Citizenship in a Globalizing World*. Urbana: University of Illinois Press.
Kunert, Arthur. 1962. *Telegraphen-Seekabel. Geschichte der deutschen Fernmeldekabel 2*. Cologne: Glitscher.
Laborie, Léonard. 2006. *La France, l'Europe et l'ordre international des communications (1865–1959)*. Ph.D. Dissertation, University of Paris IV – Sorbonne.
Laborie, Léonard. 2010. *L'Europe mise en réseaux: La France et la coopération internationale dans les postes et les télécommunications (années 1850–années 1950)*. Brussels: Peter Lang.
Lebow, Irwin. 1995. *Information Highways and Byways. From the Telegraph to the 21st Century*. New York: IEEE Press.
*Leeds Mercury*. 6.9.1869.
Loeffler, Carl Ludwig. "Letter to the Home Office, June 14 1890." National Archives Kew.
Lyons, Francis S.L. 1963. *Internationalism in Europe, 1815–1914*. Leyden: A.W. Sythoff.
Maier, Charles. 2000. "Consigning the Twentieth Century to History: Alternative Narratives for the Modern Era." *American Historical Review* 105, no. 3, 807–831.
Marland, Edward A. 1962. "British and American Contributions to Electrical Communication." *The British Journal for the History of Science* 1, no. 1, 31–48.
Müller, Simone. 2010. "The Transatlantic Telegraphs and the Class of 1866: The Formative Years of Transnational Networks in Maritime Space, 1858–1884/89." *Historical Social Research* 35, no. 1, 237–259.
*New York Times*. 11.2.1899.
*New York Times*. 6.8.1914.
North, Michael. ed. 1995. *Kommunikationsrevolutionen: Die neuen Medien des 16. und 19. Jahrhunderts. Wirtschafts- und sozialhistorische Studien 3*. Cologne: Böhlau.
Owen, Thomas C. 1991. *The Corporation Under Russian Law, 1800–1917: A Study in Tsarist Economic Policy*. Cambridge: Cambridge University Press.
Pender. September 14, 1877. Cable and Wireless Archive.
Pike, Robert M. and Dwayne R. Winseck. 2004. "The Politics of Global Media Reform, 1907–1923." *Media, Culture & Society* 26, 643–675.
Pollard, Albert F. 2004. "Clark, (Josiah) Latimer (1822–1898)." *Oxford Dictionary of National Biography*. Oxford: Oxford University Press. Accessed 15.09.2008 (http://www.oxforddnb.com/view/article/5469).
Pomeranz, Kenneth. 2000. *The Great Divergence. China, Europe, and the Making of the Modern World Economy*. Princeton: Princeton University Press.
Pound, Arthur. 1926. *The Telephone Idea: Fifty Years After*. New York: Greenberg.
Robbins, Bruce. 2008. "Introduction Part I: Actually Existing Cosmopolitanism." In *Cosmopolitics: Thinking and Feeling Beyond the Nation*, edited by Pheng Cheah, 1–19. Minneapolis: University of Minnesota Press.
Scholz, Franz. 1904. *Krieg und Seekabel: Eine völkerrechtliche Studie*. Berlin: F. Vahlen.
Scott, John D. 1958. *Siemens Brothers 1858–1958: An Essay in the History of Industry*. London: Weidenfeld and Nicolson.
Siemens, William. 1872/73. "The Society of Telegraph Engineers: Inaugural Address." *Journal of the Society of Telegraph Engineers: Including Original Communications on Telegraphy and Electrical Science* 1, 19–33.
Smith, Anthony D. 1999. *Nationalism and Modernism: A Critical Survey of Recent Theories of Nations and Nationalism*. London: Routledge.
Spear, W.F. 2004. "Canning, Sir Samuel (1823–1908)." *Oxford Dictionary of National Biography*. Oxford: Oxford University Press. Accessed 15.09.2008 (http://www.oxforddnb.com/view/article/32279).
La Société des ingénieurs civils. 1889. *Réception des Ingénieurs Américains par la Société des ingénieurs civils de France, du 20 au 26 Juin 1889, Extraits des mémoirs de la société des ingénieurs civils*. Paris.
*Trewman's Exeter Flying Post*. 01.08.1866.
Tyrrell, Ian R. "What is Transnational History?" Accessed 28.08.2011 (http://iantyrrell.wordpress.com/what-is-transnational-history/).

Vries, Peer. 2009. "Concluding Remarks. The Nation State and Beyond: Governing Globalization Processes in the Nineteenth and Early Twentieth Century." Paper presented at the workshop on "The Nation State and Beyond. Governing Globalization Processes in the 19th and Early 20th Century", Cluster of Excellence, Heidelberg University, 3–5 December.

Wenzlhuemer, Roland, ed. 2010. *Global Communication. Telecommunication and Global Flows of Information in the Late 19th and Early 20th Century.* Special Issue of Historical Social Research 35, no. 1.

Wimmer, Andreas and Nina Glick-Schiller. 2002. "Methodological Nationalism and Beyond. Nation-State Building, Migration and the Social Sciences." *Global Networks* 2, no. 4, 301–334.

Winichakul, Thongchai. 2009. *Siam Mapped. A History of the Geo-Body of a Nation.* Honolulu: University of Hawaii Press.

Winseck, Dwayne R. and Robert M. Pike. 2007. *Communication and Empire. Media, Markets, and Globalization, 1860–1930.* Durham, N.C.: Duke University Press.

Yang, Daqing. 2009. "Submarine Cables and the Two Japanese Empires." In *Communications Under the Seas*, edited by Bernard S. Finn and Daqing Yang, 227–256. Cambridge: MIT Press.

# Part III
# Education

# Chapter 7
# National and Transnational Spaces: Academic Networks and Scholarly Transfer Between Britain and Germany in the Nineteenth Century

**Heather Ellis**

**Abstract** Traditionally seen as the epoch of the nation state, historians have recently begun to question the dominance of this category for those living, working, and travelling in nineteenth-century Europe. Frequently, transnational movement of people, money, and ideas had a greater impact than movement within national boundaries and under the supervision of individual states. As such, the nineteenth century is perhaps better understood as an era of increasing globalisation. While scholars have recently done much to emphasise the importance of supranational contexts in the area of economic transactions, the history of universities and knowledge transfer is still dominated by the category of the nation state. This essay attempts to challenge this tendency by pointing to the creation and growing importance of transnational university networks over the course of the nineteenth century. It focuses in particular on the development of a wide range of contacts between universities based in Britain and Germany including student migration and exchanges, collaborative projects, and joint publications. In particular, it argues that intellectual and cultural links which flourished under older political formations, in particular the eighteenth-century constitutional union between England and the Electorate of Hanover, survived to determine the nature of cultural contact between Britain and Germany in the following century. In the wider context of continental Europe, the essay also points to the longevity of an early-modern paradigm of intellectual relations—the "republic of letters" in which transnational collaboration and exchange played a normal and important part.

The history of universities and of higher education in general has tended to be written from a national perspective. Developments within particular countries have been concentrated on at the expense of important cross-border connections and transfers. This is particularly the case with the history of higher education in the

H. Ellis (✉)
Centre for British Studies, HU Berlin, Berlin, Germany
e-mail: heather.ellis@staff.hu-berlin.de

I. Löhr and R. Wenzlhuemer (eds.), *The Nation State and Beyond*, Transcultural Research – Heidelberg Studies on Asia and Europe in a Global Context,
DOI 10.1007/978-3-642-32934-0_7, © Springer-Verlag Berlin Heidelberg 2013

nineteenth century when historians have frequently linked the modernization of universities with the emergence of the nation state. Typical here are studies such as John E. Craig's *Scholarship and Nation Building: The Universities of Strasbourg and Alsatian Society, 1870–1939*.[1] In the words of Konrad Jarausch, the reform of higher education has too often been treated as "a dependent variable of the wider process" of nineteenth-century nation building.[2]

There is no doubt that higher education institutions did play an important role in the construction of emerging nations in the nineteenth century. Many universities were founded explicitly to represent, embody and promote national identities. Such cases are particularly obvious where institutions focused on research and teaching in national languages, many of which, particularly in Eastern Europe, were new. Their potential value to governments seeking to create a sense of national identity is obvious – perhaps more than any other institution, they possessed the means of 'discovering', conserving and disseminating the cultural and linguistic heritage of the nation. In so doing they were crucial in the very act of nation- building itself.

It needs to be recognized, however, that this tendency to see the modern university as a by-product of the rise of the nation state in the nineteenth century has led to a misunderstanding of the relationship between the field of higher education today and contemporary processes of globalization. In particular, it has encouraged the production of unduly pessimistic assessments of the university's future as a relevant institution in a rapidly globalizing world. Thus, Bill Readings is able to speak of "the university in ruins": no longer required to act as "the ideological arm of the nation state",[3] it is depicted as foundering amid the uncertainties of a "post-historical" world in which key processes take place on a global, rather than a national level.[4]

Reconceptualizing the nineteenth century as an era of growing globalization, in which transnational[5] contacts played an increasingly important role, allows a significantly different picture of the university to emerge. Just as it is possible to trace the expansion of transnational networks in the spheres of trade, finance and law, so one can see the development of numerous cross-border scholarly connections between individual academics, experts, students and higher education

[1] Craig 1984; for a more recent endorsement of this view, see Välimaa 2004, pp. 31–36; in the importance it has traditionally conferred upon the nation state, the history of higher education in nineteenth-century Europe fits in well with the wider historiographical tendency to unduly privilege the analytical category of the nation state set out by the editors in the Introduction.

[2] Jarausch 1983, p. 9.

[3] Readings 1996, p. 40.

[4] Ibid., pp. 119–134.

[5] In this article, the term 'transnational' is generally used to refer to contacts and movements across national-state borders; in line with this definition, the term 'cross-border' is sometimes used as a synonym for 'transnational'. However, when referring to scholarly transfer as producing a genuinely 'transnational' space, the term should be understood to carry the additional meaning of 'supranational' or a discursive space in which the nation state as category is of only limited or secondary importance.

institutions in nineteenth-century Europe.[6] Nor were such connections in themselves new. The formation of such scholarly networks should be understood within the context of the survival of the early-modern ideal of the 'republic of letters' in which, under the influence of eighteenth-century Enlightenment thought, scientific endeavor came to be seen as a common pursuit across national borders for the betterment of humanity as a whole.[7]

Recovering the importance of such cross-border networks and challenging the dominance of the paradigm of the nation state is one of the particular theoretical advantages of transnational history as a scholarly approach. We must be careful, however, to avoid falling into the opposite extreme and underplaying the ongoing significance of national differences.[8] Recent research on transnational university networks in the late twentieth and early twenty-first centuries has highlighted precisely this point. As Ravinder Sidhu has argued in a study of the 'transnational' dimension in contemporary Australian higher education, we must pay attention to "real actors embedded in real places" and avoid describing what he terms an "abstract", "dematerialized", "virtual" globalization.[9] Studies of globalization can often reproduce precisely the same kind of reductive grand narratives which transnational history and other post-modern approaches have sought to deconstruct. In such cases, globalization too often appears as a monolithic, almost inevitable process, comprising abstract 'flows' and 'networks' which leave the crucial question of agency unaddressed. Here, it is wise to heed the caution of Simon Marginson and Erlenawati Sawir in their study of the concept of "global flows" in contemporary higher education, that "all technologies are inscribed in social and economic life", that "they enable cultural practices" and "are deployed by identifiable interests".[10] Above all, discussions of globalization must be embedded "in agency and history" and "global connectedness" must be explored "in terms of situated cases".[11]

In order to pursue such an approach, this essay investigates the development of academic networks between individual scholars and universities in two specific

[6] Those interested in pursuing further the relationship between cross-border transfers of knowledge and expertise and the governing of globalization processes should also see the chapters in this collection by Klaus Dittrich and James Casteel.

[7] For a useful discussion of the 'Republic of Letters' as an Enlightenment ideal, see Goodman 1994, pp. 1–11.

[8] For a more detailed discussion of the nature and theoretical opportunities which global history, as an approach, offers, as well as the need to integrate the role of the nation state as both actor and subject within globalization processes, see the editors' Introduction. For the continuing need to pay attention to the nation state within globalization processes, see also the chapter in this volume by Madeleine Herren.

[9] Sidhu 2004, p. 53; for additional analyses of the ways in which a wide range of differing interests may be operating in cross-border connections, see also the chapters in this volume by Guido Thiemeyer and Simone Müller-Pohl.

[10] Marginson and Sawir 2005, p. 282.

[11] Ibid., p. 281.

countries, Britain and Germany, over the course of the nineteenth century. The first section considers the historiographical approach which has most commonly been adopted when examining higher education in nineteenth-century Britain and Germany and points out the ways in which a transnational perspective has the potential to shed new light. It will then go on to examine the evidence for growing cross-border relations between individual academics and higher educational institutions in Britain and Germany over the course of the nineteenth century. In particular, it will suggest that when we focus on intellectual and scholarly transfer, the key actors, in both countries, were not motivated, in the first instance, by national or nationalistic concerns, but rather by a shared sense of academic (and, we might say, professional) identity which transcended the traditional political boundaries of the nation state.[12]

In the final section, the ways in which such cross-border transfers were conceptualized by the British and German governments is examined. As both the British and German political elites were more closely concerned with the national and imperial interests of their respective countries, it will be suggested that both groups tended to view the development of transnational academic networks with a degree of suspicion. Many within British government circles feared that the English universities might be infiltrated by what they considered the dangerous culture of political radicalism in the German universities, visible, in particular, in the enthusiastic participation of students and professors in the revolutions of 1848. The German government, by contrast, increasingly keen to project an image of national unity and imperial power in the years after 1870, came to view the growing contact with universities in Britain (and other countries) as a threat to its own control over higher education at home. Indeed, throughout the second half of the nineteenth century, we see parallel moves on the part of both governments to increase control over their own universities and to attach them more closely to an ideal of nation and empire.

## The Historiography of Higher Education in Nineteenth-Century Britain and Germany

In the case of Britain and Germany, a focus on transnational connections in the field of higher education has the potential to alter substantially our perception of the relations between these two countries over the course of the nineteenth century. In what comparative studies there have been, they have generally been portrayed as

[12] A useful comparison presents itself here with the group of cable agents working on submarine transatlantic cables between 1858 and 1914, as examined in the chapter in this volume by Simone Müller-Pohl; here we see another group of individuals who developed a comparable sense of professional identity which transcended (and, at times, superseded) loyalty to national (and imperial) interests.

rivals with fundamentally dissimilar university systems shaped by differing national priorities.[13] This, in turn, has formed part of a long-standing and highly influential historiography highlighting rising tensions generally between Britain and Germany in the years leading up to the outbreak of World War I.[14] When comparing systems of higher education in the two countries, historians usually point to the dominance in Britain of the so-called 'association-autonomy model', characterized by a high degree of independence from political influence, and in Germany, to the 'state-education model' in which state governments exercised a high degree of control over the functioning of higher education.[15] While there undoubtedly were important differences, the use of such models obscures the considerable level of intellectual and scholarly transfer taking place between individual academics and universities in nineteenth-century Britain and Germany.

It is indeed one of the most notable flaws in the comparative approach that it is often underpinned by a reliance on a binary distinction of similarity/difference which tends to reduce analytical complexity. Instead of analyzing two self-contained systems side by side, the decision to focus on the formation and developments of cross-border networks has the potential to overcome many of the limitations of the traditional comparative approach. In particular, the transnational network, as unit of study, has the distinct advantage of being, in the words of Manuel Castells, "an open structure, able to expand without limits"[16] which allows the relationship between systems of higher education in two countries – in this case, Britain and Germany – to be placed in a much broader context. It also allows varying degrees of similarity and difference to be incorporated within a single analytical model.

It should, however, be pointed out that, despite its advantages, using the concept of the transnational network is not in itself a guarantee against the reductionism of binary models. Too often the flexibility of the 'transnational' as category is compromised by a tendency to set it up unnecessarily as part of a binary with the 'national'. Too often research agendas are framed around the question: 'national' or 'transnational'? – instead of the more interesting task of considering how these categories may overlap and interact with each other, and indeed, with other spatial frames of reference such as the 'local', 'regional' and the 'global'. Despite the tendency of the scholarly literature dealing with British and German higher education in the nineteenth century to separate the 'national' and the 'transnational' as categories of analysis, all the evidence points to their co-existence, and even interdependence. Just as transnational networks have the potential to incorporate

---

[13] See, for example, Jarausch 1983, pp. 9–36; Charle 2004, pp. 33–80; Anderson 2004, pp. 191–208; Brockliss 1997. For a study which allows for a greater degree of similarity between university cultures in Britain and Germany before World War I, cf. Levsen 2008.

[14] Cf., for example, Padfield 1974; Kennedy 1980; Fremdling 1995; van't Padje 2001; for a recent summary of the impact of this historiographical trend, see Weber 2008a *Our Friend*, p. 3.

[15] See, for example, Jarausch 1983, p. 35, fn. 39.

[16] Rizvi 2009, p. 55.

both similarity and difference, they also allow for the combination of national and transnational perspectives. This is precisely the point made by Thomas Weber in his recent examination of German and British elite higher education on the eve of the First World War. Weber's study seeks to challenge the notion, promoted, he argues, by traditional comparative studies, that it was the existence of fundamental and long-standing ideological and cultural differences between Britain and Germany which led ultimately to the outbreak of war in 1914. In his introductory chapter, he asks,

> Were national and transnational identities mutually exclusive concepts? Did nationalizing tendencies run opposite to transnational tendencies? Or was a marriage of transnational and national identities before 1914 more common than we have hitherto thought?[17]

In his study of elite students at Oxford and Heidelberg in the early years of the twentieth century, Weber concludes that many of them "shared a strong sense of cultural proximity, of a transnational identity, that bound them together but that did not run contrary to their strong nationalism."[18] Indeed, he is able to speak of a "fusion of a nationalist and a transnational European identity" among both student communities, whose members are perhaps best described, he suggests, as "cosmopolitan nationalists."[19]

It should, however, be possible to go further than this and look not only at the combination of national and transnational perspectives, but also at the particular conditions under which one has been rendered more prominent than the other. Thus, it will be contended here that an investigation of cross-border transfers involving intellectuals and academics has the potential to reveal a greater concern with a genuinely 'transnational' (or 'supranational') space than transfers more directly connected, for instance, with economics or politics, spheres more closely entangled with the priorities and concerns of the nation state. Another reason why intellectual transfers are likely to be particularly productive of a transnational space is the survival into the nineteenth century of pre-existing early-modern formations of scholarly relations, most importantly, the ideal of the inter- or transnational republic of letters. Too often, the republic of letters has been written off as an out-of-date paradigm after the end of the seventeenth, or, at the very latest, the eighteenth century.[20] Generally, historians have tended to postulate an almost inevitable and relatively trouble-free transition from an early-modern model of scholarly relations based on the transnational migration of students and scholars to a modern paradigm comprising self-contained systems of higher education governed and controlled by the nation state.[21] In such a view, the transnational character of the republic of letters is not viewed as a positive characteristic, but is rather seen as reflecting the

---

[17] Weber 2008a *Our Friend*, p. 9.

[18] Ibid., 234.

[19] Idem

[20] For a fairly recent discussion of the relationship between the Enlightenment and the republic of letters, see Brockliss 2002, pp. 1–20.

[21] See, for example, the argument put forward in Jarausch 1983.

absence of strong nation states which would not appear until the 'modern' era of the nineteenth century. However, as Benedikt Stuchtey and Peter Wende point out in their study of British and German historiography between 1750 and 1950:

> The great European *res publica litteraria* still existed, that international community which, in the Middle Ages, had been attached to the church of Christ, and which, since the Renaissance and especially during the Enlightenment, had become a transnational congregation of men of letters. Out of this tradition, still vigorous in nineteenth century Europe, grew numerous contacts, mutual perceptions, and transfers which contributed to the formation of modern university education in the age of nationalism.[22]

In the particular case of Britain and Germany, the dynastic union of the crowns of England and Hanover in 1714 added an extra dimension to scholarly relations between the two countries whose impact continued well into the nineteenth century despite the official severance of the link with the accession of a female monarch, Queen Victoria, in 1837. The eighteenth and early nineteenth century witnessed a dramatic rise in the number of British students studying at German universities, particularly within the Electorate of Hanover following the foundation of Göttingen in 1734 by George II.[23] Although less significant by comparison, the number of German students continuing their education at British universities as well as the number of German academics seeking employment in Britain and the British Empire, also increased.[24] While most scholars who have examined these links argue that such exchanges ceased with the French Revolution and Napoleonic Wars, the matriculation registers at Göttingen, for example, show that British students continued to enrol throughout the nineteenth century.[25]

## Scholarly Exchange Between Britain and Germany in the Nineteenth Century

Despite the fact that investigation of cross-border scholarly connections between Britain and Germany in the nineteenth century may do much to revise the traditional picture of growing rivalry and tension between the two countries, it must be stressed that we are not normally dealing with a process of equal exchange. The importance of highlighting stratification and power differentials within

[22] Stuchtey and Wende 2000, p. 3.

[23] For British students at German universities in the eighteenth and early nineteenth centuries, see Stewart 1979; Biskup 2007.

[24] See Weber 2008b "Cosmopolitan Nationalists"; Davis 2007; for German scholars in the British Empire, see Kirchberger 2000, 2001.

[25] For the continuing appeal of Göttingen and other German universities for British (especially Scottish) students, cf. Wallace 2006.

transnational and global networks has recently become a focus of scholarly attention[26] and is particularly important here. Although German scholars showed an interest in the research activities of British academics and considerable numbers of German students spent time at British universities, in almost all fields of scholarship, it was German academia which functioned as the model and inspiration for those working at British universities. This had much to do with the unprecedented investment made by many of the German states in the field of higher education and scientific research in the years following the French Revolution. Looking back on these developments in 1885, the British jurist and historian, James Bryce, gave the following assessment of Germany's contribution to higher education reform. "It would be superfluous", he wrote,

> to dwell on the value for other countries of the example of Germany. There is no people which has given so much thought and pains to the development of its university system as the Germans have done – none which has profited so much by the services universities render – none where they play so large a part in the national life.[27]

It is particularly noteworthy that when outlining his reasons for his admiration of the German achievement in higher education, he spoke on both a national and transnational level – the German university system,[28] in his eyes, was both a particular treasure of the German people, but also an invaluable contribution to the progress of mankind as a whole, from which Britain and many other countries had much to learn. From little more than glorified high schools a century or so earlier, the German universities had become prestigious centers in virtually all areas of scholarly enquiry. In many respects, they were increasingly seen from the perspective of Britain and other countries as *the* model of how to establish a successful university system. Germany had a much greater proportion of young people in higher education (in 1882–1883 some 24,187 out of a population of 45.25 million compared with under 5,500 out of 26 million in Britain);[29] the proportion of university teachers to students was similarly higher in Germany (with a ratio of 1 professor for every 10 pupils compared with 1–50 or 60 in the Scottish universities).[30] A university education was moreover considerably cheaper in Germany than in Britain with the state providing a much greater financial

---

[26] See, for example, Marginson and Sawir 2005, pp. 287f.; on the importance of asymmetrical political and economic power relations in globalization processes, see also the chapter in this volume by Tomoko Akami.

[27] Bryce 1885, p. xiii.

[28] The term 'German university system' is used here in the sense employed by nineteenth-century British commentators – not to denote a centrally-controlled system of higher education (which did not exist in any sense prior to German unification in 1870) but rather to point to the fact that most (if not all) universities located within the German states shared certain characteristics which distinguished them from higher education institutions in other countries. For this sense, cf., for example, Perry 1845, p. iv.

[29] Ibid., p. xvii.

[30] Ibid., p. xxiii.

investment,[31] while students in Germany tended also to require little if any additional (and expensive) professional training after completing a university course.[32] "No student of contemporary history", declared Bryce in his preface to the 1885 English edition of Johannes Conrad's study *The German Universities for the Last Fifty Years*, "can fail to enjoy and profit by the light which Dr. Conrad throws on the circumstances and tendencies of Germany itself, the central country of Europe, the state which dominates Continental politics, the nation which does the largest part of the intellectual work of the world".[33]

There is no doubt that state investment in higher education institutions in Prussia and the other German states formed part of a nation-building project; it is my contention, however, that when engaged in international scholarly exchange, the particular actors involved, both students and academics, more often pursued aims which had little to do with the nation state and its welfare but rather concerned their own intellectual development, their institutions, or the progress of their particular discipline. Such aims, I would argue, of necessity generated a genuinely 'transnational' perspective, in the sense of being beyond (or above) the 'national'. The creation of such a discursive space in relation to academic transfer has been remarked upon elsewhere, perhaps most notably with regard to transnational cooperative projects in the history of science, in particular, of medicine, in the nineteenth century. Here we frequently encounter references to what has appropriately been termed "the gospel of internationalism in science".[34]

We see a similar concern with intellectual and scholarly priorities among British academics in their interactions with the German university system. On few occasions do we see national borders or national identity acting as an obstacle or stumbling block in the cultivation of such relationships. This is especially clear in the case of historical scholarship, in the early decades of the nineteenth century, when the work of German historians, most notably Barthold Niebuhr and Leopold von Ranke, gained particular prominence in Britain. Hugely significant in promoting the researches of Niebuhr on ancient Rome was the German scholar and diplomat, Christian Karl Josias von Bunsen, who spent some 12 years in Britain as the Prussian ambassador to London between 1842 and 1854. Here, we see an interesting example of the way in which diplomatic and political relations between the two countries could actually facilitate and reinforce scholarly contacts. Bunsen had served for a number of years in Berlin as Niebuhr's private secretary, and introduced his work to a diverse range of English scholars including Thomas Arnold at Oxford and Connop Thirlwall and Julius Hare at Cambridge.[35] Some were so inspired through their contact with Bunsen that they entered on their own historical researches employing Niebuhr's techniques and methodology. Thus, in

[31] Ibid., pp. xviii, xxii.

[32] Ibid., p. xx.

[33] Bryce 1885, p. xxix.

[34] Bynam 1994, p. 96.

[35] For the influence of Bunsen, cf., for example, Stark 1999, pp. 24–27.

the preface to his *History of Rome*, only partially published before his death in 1842, Thomas Arnold referred to his "intense admiration" for Niebuhr, whom he had taken as the "example and model" for his own *History*.[36] He embarked on the project, he declared, "not with the foolish notion of rivalling so great a man", but in order that his "discoveries and remarkable wisdom might best be made known to English readers by putting them into a form more adapted to our common taste".[37] Nor was Arnold alone in owing such a significant intellectual debt to Niebuhr. English historians no less prominent than Thomas Babington Macaulay and Thomas Carlyle acknowledged Niebuhr's influence upon their own work in the 1830s and 1840s.[38]

As the century progressed, it was not merely individual British scholars who were influenced by German historical scholarship. From the 1860s onwards, precisely the period in which many historians have detected the beginnings of Anglo-German rivalry, we see efforts to institutionalize the German historicist approach, made famous by Ranke, at a number of British universities. As Regius Professor of Modern History at Oxford, from 1866, William Stubbs worked hard to popularize Ranke's work among his colleagues and pupils. He was responsible for initiating an English translation of Ranke's *Englische Geschichte*, carried out by no less than six of his colleagues at Oxford. In a lecture entitled "On the Present State and Prospects of Historical Study" given before an Oxford audience on 20 May 1876, Stubbs declared Ranke to be "not only beyond all comparison the greatest historical scholar alive, but one of the very greatest historians who has ever lived". With his "unrivalled stores of knowledge, depth of research, intimate acquaintance with the most recondite sources", he embodied the best characteristics of the "German School of History" which he had founded.[39] Similar enthusiasm for Ranke's work was shown by two successive Regius Professors at Cambridge, Sir John Robert Seeley and Lord Acton, in the final decades of the nineteenth century. With the founding of the *English Historical Review* in 1886, inspired once again by a German model, the *Historische Zeitschrift*, which first appeared in 1859, scholarly exchange between English and German historians became, in an important sense, institutionalized. In the final decade and a half of the nineteenth century, new publications in one country were noticed and reviewed in the other and a permanent space was thereby created for an ongoing transnational scholarly dialogue. This development also had the effect of rendering intellectual transfer less unidirectional by stimulating a greater degree of interest in English historical scholarship among German academics. The final years of the century thus witnessed a dramatic rise in the number of English historical works translated into German[40]

[36] Arnold 1868, p. vi.

[37] Ibid., p. vi.

[38] Fitzsimons et al. 1954, p. 193.

[39] Stubbs 1887, p. 65.

[40] Stuchtey and Wende 2000, pp. 14, 18, 20.

although the overall number remained relatively small in comparison with English versions of German works.

Such a situation presents a sharp contrast with the increasing tension and rivalry usually seen as developing in this period between Britain and Germany in the sphere of political and military relations. Indeed, those scholars who have examined historical study in both England and Germany have tended to reinforce this interpretation. Their works have been almost exclusively comparative in nature, treating scholarly traditions within the two countries as separate and self-contained, tending, in both cases, to underpin a government-driven nation-building project. As Stuchtey and Wende have noted, a transnational, cross-border approach has been almost entirely lacking: "Relations between British and German historical scholarship", they write, "have not been extensively explored. Nor have the modes of mutual perception, or the ways and means of academic transfers between the two academic communities in the field of history been studied."[41] This, they have pointed out, has largely been due to the particular association which historians have identified between the rise of modern history as a scholarly discipline and the growing popularity of nationalism and nation-building among governments in nineteenth-century Europe.[42]

Arguably even greater enthusiasm for cross-border contact with Germany can be seen in the field of natural science. Here, however, far more so than with historical scholarship, we are dealing not merely with the transfer of ideas, knowledge and scholarly techniques, but of people as well. From the 1830s onwards, many British students and academics were drawn to undertake primary or further scientific study at a number of specialist research institutes which had emerged in Germany in the first decades of the nineteenth century. Most important among these was Justus von Liebig's Chemistry Institute at the University of Giessen. The popularity of Liebig's institute in Britain seems to have developed primarily as a result of a number of high-profile visits Liebig made to Britain in the 1830s and early 1840s when he was repeatedly celebrated as a pioneer and hero of modern science. During the several months which Liebig spent in Britain, he was invited to address the Liverpool meeting of the newly founded British Association for the Advancement of Science where he spoke about the latest results of his research at Giessen.[43] In addition, he met with prominent academic chemists in Britain such as Thomas Andrews, based at the Royal Belfast Academical Institution, Thomas Graham at Glasgow University and William Gregory at Edinburgh.[44] The latter had himself spent a semester studying at Giessen under Liebig.

Both sides, however, recognized the inequality of the relationship. British periodicals raved about Liebig's visit and the potential for advancing British science which further contact with Germany might bring. Writing in 1845,

---

[41] Ibid., p. 2.

[42] Ibid., p. 3.

[43] Fruton 1990, p. 51.

[44] Idem

Walter Copland Perry, a writer and jurist who had himself gained a Ph.D. from Göttingen, summed up the impact of Liebig's visits in the following terms: "Even the Yorkshire farmer thinks of the German Liebig as he manures his fields, and many a Lancashire manufacturer has found his way to Giessen, to sit for a while at the feet of the same distinguished Chemist."[45] Indeed, he related the warm reception of Liebig, and of German chemistry as a whole, to a more general, over-arching enthusiasm for German science among Britons, who in recent years had been particularly "industrious ... in endeavouring to divert, for our own use, a portion of the abundant streams of knowledge which flow from the 'Fatherland'".[46] Liebig, for his part, described his 1837 visit in the following terms to his friend Jens Jakob Berzelius:

> I have spent some months in England, have seen an awful lot and learned little. England is not a land of science, there is only a widely practiced dilettantism, the chemists are ashamed to call themselves chemists because the pharmacists, who are despised, have assumed this name.[47]

Before Liebig's initial trip in 1837, there had only been three British students enrolled at his laboratory;[48] by mid-century this number had increased dramatically and it would not be incorrect to say that Liebig's Institute became a veritable training ground for British chemistry professors. In February 1847, one of Liebig's former British assistants tried to explain the popularity of Giessen with British students and its importance for the further development of British chemistry. "A great portion of the Students of the University are Englishmen", he declared, "which circumstance is to be attributed to the cheapness of medical education, and to the brilliant reputation of professors Liebig, Balser, and others, who have rendered it one of the finest schools in the world for the study of medicine and chymistry [*sic*]."[49] By 1850, it had produced professors for institutions as diverse as Oxford, University College, London, Edinburgh, Glasgow, Nottingham and Owen's College, Manchester, and a total of 84 British students had spent time as his pupils.[50] Once back in Britain, many of Liebig's former pupils set themselves to translating his most important scholarly works into English thus perpetuating his influence still further. Lyon Playfair, for example, one of Liebig's most favored pupils and who went on to become one of Britain's leading chemists, produced an English translation of his most famous work, *Die organische Chemie in ihrer Anwendung auf Agricultur und Physiologie* in 1840.[51] Similarly, John Gardner, who was made an M.D. at Giessen in 1847 and was to play a fundamental role in establishing the Royal College of Chemistry in Britain, produced an English edition

[45] Perry 1845, pp. 3f.

[46] Ibid., p. 4.

[47] Ibid., p. 52.

[48] Ibid., p. 53.

[49] *The Times*, 22.02.1847, p. 3.

[50] Morrell 1972, p. 19.

[51] Gooday 2008.

of Liebig's *Die Chemischen Briefe* which appeared in several volumes between 1843 and 1854.[52]

Although his is perhaps the most prominent example, Liebig was not alone among German professors in attracting large numbers of British science students. Friedrich Wöhler, Professor of Chemistry at Göttingen for much of the nineteenth century, counted numerous Britons among his students as did Liebig's successor at Munich, Adolf von Baeyer, in the late 1870s and 1880s. Thus, William Henry Perkin, for example, who went on to become Professor of Chemistry at Owen's College, Manchester, studied for 4 years between 1882 and 1886 under Baeyer at Munich. Baeyer and his research group acted as an important model for Perkin's subsequent development of an internationally respected organic chemistry school at Manchester.[53] Another successful former pupil of Baeyer's was Frederick Stanley Kipping, who entered Baeyer's laboratory in 1886 and went on to become Professor of Chemistry at University College, Nottingham and one of the most prominent British chemists of the early twentieth century.[54] The ability of the interests of a scientific discipline to overcome national boundaries in a period of supposed intense and growing rivalry between Britain and Germany is clear in the regret shown when Reinhard Hofmann, another of Liebig's pupils, resigned as head of the Royal College of Chemistry in London (a post he had held since 1843) to take up the chair at Berlin in 1865. In the words of William Henry Perkin:

> Hofmann's departure was not only a cause of regret to those who had worked under him and to all his friends; it was a heavy loss also to the country at large, as no one had ever done so much for the cause of chemical science in the kingdom as Hofmann did, nor had any one exercised to such an extent that wonderful power he had of stimulating the enthusiasm of his students and of inciting in them a love of chemistry and of scientific research.[55]

While it may be impossible to find British equivalents of Liebig and Baeyer, there is no doubt that both individual German scholars and universities showed an increasing interest in, and willingness to acknowledge the importance of, English language scholarship. Particularly in the final third of the nineteenth century, a significant number of new chairs in English Language and Literature were established at leading German universities.[56] A growing enthusiasm for British scholarship may also be traced in the foundation of a number of societies and organizations set up with the deliberate intention of fostering scholarly relations between Germany and other countries in the late nineteenth and early twentieth centuries. In 1909, the Heidelberg Academy of Science and Arts was founded. Linked officially to the University of Heidelberg, which had a particularly high number of British students and alumni, its self-professed mission was "to support scientific and scholarly work and cooperation with the joint academies of Europe".

---

[52] Mendes da Costa 2004.

[53] Morrell 2004.

[54] Challenger 2004.

[55] Perkin 1896, p. 620.

[56] Weber *Our Friend* 2008a, p. 58.

As Thomas Weber has shown, connections with universities in Britain and the British Empire were to be particularly prominent in the Academy's activities.[57]

In addition, many German students spent time at British universities, most notably, at Oxford and Cambridge. That the greatest numbers arrived during the final decades of the nineteenth and the first years of the twentieth century provides further evidence to suggest that academic and scholarly relations between Britain and Germany did not follow the same pattern of increasing rivalry as seems to have been the case in the political and military spheres. Indeed, as late as 1907, the municipality of Heidelberg was hosting events designed to celebrate the historic links between the university town and Britain. A British journalist reporting on one such event cited the views of Henry Lunn, the founder of the travel agents, Lunn Poly, on the importance of student exchanges for the maintenance of peaceful relations between Britain and Germany. "Oxford has been home to many German scholars", he is reported as saying, "and many of Germany's best sons have come to Oxford on Rhodes scholarships, while England has for her part sent many of her sons to German universities, especially Heidelberg. Nothing ... is more conducive to promoting international friendship."[58]

The growing number of German students traveling to Britain for academic study may possibly be related to the fact that the ancient English universities had undergone substantial modernizing reforms by the early years of the twentieth century which rendered their curricula and teaching methods far more compatible with continental systems of higher education. This was in itself a direct result of the significant influence which the German model of the research university, represented, above all, by the University of Berlin, had exercised upon reform discourses at Oxford and Cambridge in the second half of the nineteenth century.[59] As Thomas Weber and others have pointed out, however, the evidence suggests that it was mainly on account of the social prestige attached to an Oxbridge education among the German elite and the valuable connections which might be formed there that so many young men were sent to the English universities. The relatively narrow cross-section of society from which the German students were drawn supports this view; nearly all came from noble families or from those with close connections to the economic and political elite of the various German states.[60] It is also significant that very few went to other universities within Britain, such as the Scottish universities, which, although less socially prestigious, were considered by many at the time to be intellectually superior to Oxford and Cambridge. By contrast, the social mix of British students who studied in German universities was much more diverse and far more widely distributed geographically. They seem, in most cases,

[57] Ibid., 62.

[58] Cited in ibid., p. 64.

[59] For the influence of the 'Humboldtian model' on university reform in Britain, cf. Schalenberg 2002.

[60] Weber 2008a *Our Friend*, p. 86.

to have been clearly drawn by the reputation of a particular professor or institute and desired to progress intellectually and professionally, rather than socially.[61]

## Nationalization as a Political Response to Growing Cross-Border Contact

One of the major challenges for scholars adopting a transnational approach is how best to relate the conceptual and analytical categories of the 'national' and 'transnational' which have too often been artificially separated within the secondary literature. A key aspect of this discussion is to what extent it may be said that the 'national', as a category, precedes, or develops out of, the 'transnational'. So far I have argued that as far as scholarly relations between nineteenth-century Britain and Germany are concerned, the most relevant category is the transnational – the early-modern 'republic of letters' paradigm which stressed the importance of cross-border scholarly contacts retaining significant importance long after the close of the eighteenth century when its influence has generally been thought to have ended. Here, I would like to take this argument a stage further by suggesting that attempts by both the British and German governments to tie higher education in their respective countries far more closely to an ideal of nation and empire in the second half of the nineteenth century may be explained, at least in part, as a reaction to the growth of cross-border contact between individual scholars and universities in Britain and Germany. In other words, a 'nationalizing' discourse, in so far as it was used with reference to higher education in nineteenth-century Britain and Germany, was employed primarily by those in government circles, rather than those within academia itself, and developed only after extensive transnational networks between individual scholars and universities had already been established.

In the case of the British government's policy towards the universities, it is almost impossible to find them referred to as 'national', let alone 'imperial', institutions until the unprecedented reforms of the 1850s, when, following the recommendations of two detailed parliamentary commissions which had visited Oxford and Cambridge, the government intervened directly in the affairs of the ancient English universities for the first time. Along with suggesting radical changes to their curricula, teaching practices and examination systems, the reports of the two commissions, which formed the basis for the Oxford and Cambridge University Acts of 1854 and 1856 respectively, suggested for the first time that the English universities had a duty to serve national (and imperial) interests. As such, the legislature also had the right to intervene to ensure that this duty was being fulfilled. This new position was outlined by the Oxford commissioners in 1852. "Such an institution", they declared of the university,

[61] Idem

> cannot be regarded as a mere aggregation of private interests; it is eminently national. It would seem therefore to be a matter of public policy that inquiry should be made, from time to time, in order to ascertain whether the purposes of its existence are fulfilled, and that such measures should be taken as may serve to raise its efficiency, to the highest point, and to diffuse its benefits most widely.[62]

In the reports of both commissions, Oxford and Cambridge were referred to as "great National Institutions,"[63] with an important responsibility to contribute not only to "national progress"[64] and "well-being"[65] but also to the "education of the youth of the Empire".[66] Over the next 40 or 50 years, moreover, government intervention in the affairs of Oxford and Cambridge (as well as, albeit to a lesser extent, in those of the Scottish universities) became a regular event with the appointment of further parliamentary commissions and the passing of further legislative reform.[67] In particular, the ancient English universities were transformed into nurseries for the burgeoning imperial civil service by the end of the century, with a majority of successful candidates for the prestigious Indian Civil Service entrance examinations having previously attended Oxford and Cambridge.[68]

There is, moreover, considerable evidence to suggest that we ought to link this growing government interest in 'nationalizing' the universities with the increasingly popular perception within political circles that growing contact between British and German universities was likely to spread dangerous political ideas among the student body within Britain. In the minds of many MPs, German universities had the reputation of being hotbeds of anti-establishment revolutionary fervor since the assassination of the German playwright August von Kotzebue by Karl Ludwig Sand, a German student and member of a radical undergraduate fraternity in 1819. Shortly after the assassination, the prominent civil servant and future Under-Secretary of State for the Colonies, Robert William Hay, warned starkly of the dangers posed by German universities in the periodical, *The Quarterly Review*. "The great cause of the irregularities which prevail at the German universities", he wrote, "is – the want of power to enforce discipline."[69] Worse still, he claimed, German professors were often to be found "at the head of the malcontents", fomenting rebellion and revolution.[70] He was likewise deeply

---

[62] *Report of Her Majesty's Commissioners* 1852, p. 3.

[63] Ibid., pp. 22, 44.

[64] Ibid., p. 105.

[65] Ibid., p. 454.

[66] Idem

[67] For a detailed account of government intervention in higher education in Britain in the period between 1850 and the outbreak of the Second World War, see Vernon 2004.

[68] Dewey 1973, pp. 274–276; Ellis 2012.

[69] Hay 1820, p. 446; for a comparable condemnation of the German universities at this time, cf. "German Universities," in: *The Literary Panorama and National Register* (1819), no. 56, pp. 590–595; "Memoir of Charles Louis Sand," in: *Edinburgh Monthly Review* 3 (1820), no. 4, pp. 575–591; Dodd 1821.

[70] Hay 1820, p. 447.

suspicious of what he saw as the moral implications of the "extremely extensive" syllabus which prevailed at most German universities, with its "lectures psychological, philological, pathological". "[T]he course is not", he complained, "merely confined to the safer round of wholesome learning which forms the staple of our college education."[71] Here, he was clearly referring to the traditional classical curriculum of Oxford, which "st[ood] forth", in Hay's words, "like the lofty Greek tragedians, as a teacher of moral prudence, high actions and high passions". By contrast, he wrote,

> German students are all speculative to a degree far surpassing even the highest flights of those in our northern capital [Edinburgh]; and all are puffed up with the most absurd notions of their own superiority to the rest of the world, – with their perfect fitness to introduce a new order of things and to become the regenerators of Europe.[72]

It was, however, to be the widely reported involvement of German students and professors in the 1848 revolutions in Berlin and Vienna which acted as an important spur for government-initiated reform of the universities in Britain. Typical of the way in which the role of the students was reported in the British press is the following account of the revolution in Vienna by the historian and lawyer, Archibald Alison, which appeared in *Blackwood's Edinburgh Magazine* in January 1849:

> The emperor was weak, the citizens of Vienna infatuated; and an insurrection, headed by the boys at the university ... overturned the imperial government ... All Germany caught the flame: the dreams of a few hot-headed enthusiasts and professors seemed to prevail alike over the dictates of wisdom and the lessons of experience.[73]

Equally clear was the fear of similar events taking place in Britain. "The balance of power in Europe appeared irrevocably destroyed", the article continued,

> by the breaking up of its central powers, – and England, in the midst of the general ruin, seemed rocking to its foundations. The Chartists were in raptures, the Irish rebels were in ecstasy: threatening meetings were held in every town in Great Britain ... revolution was openly talked of.[74]

In the years after German unification in 1870 and victory in the Franco-Prussian War the following year, it is possible to detect a comparable move to bring the German university system much more closely under central state control and to tie it firmly to a narrative of national and imperial greatness. This policy was to be particularly pronounced under Kaiser Wilhelm II. In a speech to mark the opening of the Higher Education Conference in November 1890, he outlined his attitude towards Germany's school and university system very clearly. "We must found our gymnasiums on a German basis", he is reported as stating. "We want to train young

---

[71] Ibid., p. 446.

[72] Ibid., p. 447.

[73] [Alison] 1849, p. 2.

[74] Idem

national Germans, not young Greeks and Romans."[75] These comments highlight one of the central reforms introduced during his reign – a clear move away from the traditional classical syllabus of the universities towards a modern, technical curriculum which he felt would be of more service to Germany's prowess as a military and technological power. The universities, he declared, were "his instrument" and he was determined to promote "the development of the exact sciences as a means of raising our nation".[76] Gone was Humboldt's early nineteenth-century ideal of raising both the culture of the German nation and of humanity as a whole through his new university. In the project of university reform, carried through in the 1880s and 1890s, there is no longer a gospel of scientific internationalism. Indeed, one British commentator, the prominent ideologue Laurie Magnus writing in November 1898, described the German universities as having undergone "an Imperial sea-change" in the years since 1870.[77] Now the emphasis was on the potential of university education to further German trade and industrial prowess, to help her to advance ahead of her national (and imperial) rivals. Magnus condemned this as nothing less than "a contraction of the old *Lehrfreiheit*".[78]

In addition to changes in the curriculum, there were significant moves taken to further tighten state control over university teaching. This seems to have been done with the deliberate intention of combating the spread of socialist ideas among professors and students, the devastating consequences of which the revolutions of 1848 had made all too clear. In a number of cases, professors who stepped out of line were publicly rebuked with future appointments being made with a careful view to the political opinions of the candidates. More controversially, in 1898 the government proposed a bill which would have subjected the majority of university teachers, the *Privatdozenten*, to unprecedented levels of state control over the content of their teaching. The measure proposed to give the Minister of Education the right to remove the *venia legendi* or right of lecturing no longer simply on the grounds of intellectual inefficiency but also if teachers were found to have articulated unsafe or dangerous opinions whether inside or outside the lecture hall. Writing at the time, Laurie Magnus explained the significance of the change in the following terms. *Privatdozenten* "may no longer express a republican or anti-monarchical sentiment", he declared, "even in a place or at a time quite alien to his duties to the university. His political heresies are to rank as disqualifications, and will render him liable to dismissal by the State."[79] "The men are there", he stated bluntly of the professors and *Privatdozenten*, "to teach what the State requires should be learned as to the blessings and obligations of citizenship in the German Empire of today."[80]

---

[75] Magnus 1898, p. 820.

[76] Ibid., p. 832.

[77] Ibid., p. 822.

[78] Ibid., p. 821.

[79] Ibid., p. 827.

[80] Ibid., p. 826.

## Conclusion

In what has necessarily been a brief examination of a few aspects of cross-border scholarly connections between Britain and Germany I hope to have given some indication of the peculiar characteristics of academic transfers in the nineteenth century. In particular, I wanted to show that actors involved in cross-border scholarly exchange, both academics and students, frequently pursued aims not connected, in the first instance, with the nation state and its interests; indeed, that such individuals cultivated transnational relations according to a very different set of priorities, involving the welfare of their own particular institutions, their own intellectual development, and the progress of their discipline as a whole. A number of scholars have recently indicated their concern to relate the categories of the 'national' and 'transnational' in a more complex way than has hitherto been the case. As I suggested earlier, they have too often been treated as a straightforward pair of opposites within a simple binary framework. While historians like Thomas Weber have taken the first step in showing how the two categories have often co-existed in the past, a notion well captured in his use of the phrase, 'cosmopolitan nationalists', I wanted to take this line of argument a stage further by attempting to discover under which historical conditions, and for which historical actors, the 'transnational' emerges as a particularly relevant category of experience. As such, I have argued that academic transfer in the nineteenth century (at least in the case of connections established between British and German scholars and universities) deserves to be seen as having created a distinctly transnational discursive space in which the interests and concerns of the nation state played only a secondary role.

In the final section, I attempted to show how the language of 'nation' and 'empire' was most often used in connection with higher education in both Britain and Germany by those in government circles keen to regain control over scholarship and the development of the university system. Indeed, I suggested that the ideal of the university as a national and imperial institution developed in both Britain and Germany only after growing cross-border contact between higher education institutions in the two countries and in response to a fear that such contact might lead to a loss of control by the state. A key question in recent work in the field of transnational history has been to what extent the 'national' as a category preceded or developed out of the 'transnational' (or indeed *vice versa*). With regard to the development of higher education in nineteenth-century Britain and Germany, I have argued here that the 'national' (and indeed a 'nationalizing' discourse) was the product of an earlier pattern of growing transnational exchange and cross-border transfer.

## Bibliography

[Alison, Archibald]. 1849. "The Year of Revolutions." *Blackwood's Edinburgh Magazine* 65, no. 399, 2–19.

Anderson, Robert D. 2004. *European Universities from the Enlightenment to 1914*. Oxford: University Press.

Arnold, Thomas. 1868. *The History of Rome*. New York: Appleton.
Biskup, Thomas. 2007. "The University of Göttingen and the Personal Union, 1737–1837." In *The Hanoverian Dimension in British History, 1714–1837*, edited by Brendan Simms and Torsten Riotte, 128–160. Cambridge: Cambridge University Press.
Brockliss, Laurence W.B. 1997. "The European University in the Age of Revolution, 1789–1850." In *The History of the University of Oxford, vol. VI: Nineteenth-Century Oxford Part I*, edited by Michael G. Brock and Mark C. Curthoys, 77–133. Oxford: Clarendon Press.
Brockliss, Laurence W.B. 2002. *Calvet's Web: Enlightenment and the Republic of Letters in Eighteenth-Century France*. Oxford: Oxford University Press.
Bryce, J. 1885. "Preface." In *The German Universities for the Last Fifty Years*, Johannes Conrad. Glasgow: David Bryce.
Bynam, William F. 1994. *Science and the Practice of Medicine in the Nineteenth Century*. Cambridge: Cambridge University Press.
Challenger, Frederick. 2004. "'Kipping, Frederic Stanley (1863–1949)', rev. John Shorter." *Oxford Dictionary of National Biography*. Oxford: Oxford University Press. Accessed 21.02.2010 (http://www.oxforddnb.com/view/article/34335).
Charle, Christophe. 2004. "Patterns." In *A History of the University in Europe, vol. III: Universities in the Nineteenth and Early Twentieth Centuries (1800–1945)*, edited by Walter Rüegg, 33–80. Cambridge: Cambridge University Press.
Craig, John E. 1984. *Scholarship and Nation-Building: The Universities of Strasbourg and Alsatian Society, 1870–1939*. Chicago: University of Chicago Press.
Davis, John R. 2007. "Friedrich Max Müller and the Migration of German Academics to Britain in the Nineteenth Century." In: Stefan Manz et al. (eds) *Migration and Transfer from Britain to Germany, 1660–1914*, 93–106. Munich: Saur.
Dewey, Clive. 1973. "The Education of a Ruling Caste: the Indian Civil Service in the Era of Competitive Examination." *English Historical Review* 88, no. 347, 274–276.
Dodd, Charles E.. 1821. *An Autumn Near the Rhine*, 371–387. London: J. Murray.
Ellis, Heather. Forthcoming 2012. "Efficiency and Counter-Revolution: Connecting University and Civil Service Reform in the 1850s." *History of Education*.
Fitzsimons, Matthew A. et al.,eds. 1954. *The Development of Historiography*. Harrisburg PA: Stackpole Co.
Fremdling, Rainer. 1995. *Anglo-German Rivalry on Coal Markets in France, the Netherlands and Germany, 1850–1913*. Groningen: University of Groningen.
Fruton, Joseph S. 1990. *Contrasts in Scientific Style: Research Groups in the Chemical and Biochemical Sciences*, Philadelphia: American Philosophical Society.
"German Universities." 1819. *The Literary Panorama and National Register* 9, no. 56, 590–595.
Gooday, Graeme J.N. 2008. "Playfair, Lyon, first Baron Playfair (1818–1898)." *Oxford Dictionary of National Biography*. Oxford: Oxford University Press. Accessed 21.02.2010 (http://www.oxforddnb.com/view/article/22368).
Goodman, Dena. 1994. *The Republic of Letters: A Cultural History of the French Enlightenment*. London: Cornell University Press.
Hay, Robert William. 1820. "State of Society, &c. in Germany." *Quarterly Review* 23, no. 46, 434–454.
Jarausch, Konrad H. 1983. "Higher Education and Social Change: Some Comparative Perspectives." *The Transformation of Higher Learning, 1860–1930: Expansion, Diversification, Social Opening, and Professionalization in England, Germany, Russia, and the United States*, 9–36. Chicago: University of Chicago Press.
Kennedy, Paul. 1980. *The Rise of the Anglo-German Antagonism, 1860–1914*. London: Allen & Unwin.
Kirchberger, Ulrike. 2000. "Deutsche Naturwissenschaftler im britischen Empire: Die Erforschung der außereuropäischen Welt im Spannungsfeld zwischen deutschem und britischem Imperialismus." *Historische Zeitschrift* 271, 621–660.
Kirchberger, Ulrike. 2001. "German Scientists in the Indian Forest Service: A German Contribution to the Raj?." *Journal of Imperial and Commonwealth History* 29, no. 2, 1–26.

Levsen, Sonja. 2008. "Constructing Elite Identities: University Students, Military Masculinity and the Consequences of the Great War in Britain and Germany." *Past and Present* 198, no. 1, 147–183.

Magnus, Laurie. 1898. "Recent Progress in German Universities." *Nineteenth Century* 44, no. 261, 819–834.

Marginson, Simon & Erlenawati Sawir. 2005. "Interrogating Global Flows in Higher Education." *Globalization, Societies and Education* 3, no. 3, 281–309.

"Memoir of Charles Louis Sand." 1820. *Edinburgh Monthly Review* 3, no. 4, 575–591.

Mendes da Costa, Charlotte. 2004. "Gardner, John (1804–1880)." *Oxford Dictionary of National Biography*. Oxford: Oxford University Press. Accessed 21.02.2010 (http://www.oxforddnb.com/view/article/10374).

Morrell, Jack B. 1972. "The Chemistry Breeders: The Research Schools of Liebig and Thomas Thomson." *Ambix* 19, no. 1, 19–40.

Morrell, Jack B. 2004. "Perkin, William Henry (1860–1929)." *Oxford Dictionary of National Biography*. Oxford: Oxford University Press. Accessed 21.02.2010 (http://www.oxforddnb.com/view/article/35478).

Padfield, Peter. 1974. *The Great Naval Race: Anglo-German Naval Rivalry, 1900–1914*. London: Hart-Davis, MacGibbon.

Perkin, William H. 1896. "The Origin of the Coal-Tar Colour Industry, and the Contributions of Hofmann and his Pupils." *Journal of the Chemistry Society* 69, 596–637.

Perry, Walter C. 1845. *German University Education; Or, the Professors and Students of Germany*. London: Longman, Brown, Green, and Longmans.

Readings, Bill. 1996. *The University in Ruins*. London: Harvard University Press.

*Report of Her Majesty's Commissioners Appointed to Inquire into the State, Discipline, Studies and Revenues of the University and Colleges of Oxford: Together with the Evidence and an Appendix*. 1852. London.

Rizvi, Fazal. 2009. "Internationalization and the Assessment of Research Quality in Education." In *Assessing the Quality of Educational Research in Higher Education: International Perspectives*, edited by Tina Besley, 49–58. Rotterdam: Sense Publishers.

Schalenberg, Marc. 2002. *Humboldt auf Reisen?: Die Rezeption des 'Deutschen Universitätsmodells' in den Französischen und Britischen Reformdiskursen, 1810–1870*. Basel: Schwabe & Co. AG Verlag.

Sidhu, Ravinder. 2004. "Governing International Education in Australia." *Globalization Societies and Education* 2, no. 1, 47–66.

Stark, Susanne. 1999. *Behind Inverted Commas: Translation and Anglo-German Cultural Relations in the Nineteenth Century*. Cleveland: Multilingual Matters.

Stewart, Gordon M. 1979. "British Students at the University of Göttingen in the Eighteenth Century," *German Life and Letters* 33, no. 1, 24–41.

Stubbs, William. 1887. *Seventeen Lectures on the Study of Mediaeval and Modern History and Kindred Subjects: Delivered at Oxford under Statutory Obligation in the Years 1867–1884*. Oxford: The Clarendon Press.

Stuchtey, Benedikt and Peter Wende, eds. 2000. *British and German Historiography, 1750–1950: Traditions, Perceptions and Transfers*. Oxford: Oxford University Press.

*The Times*. 22.02.1847.

Välimaa, Jussi. 2004. "Nationalization, Localization and Globalization in Finnish Higher Education." *Higher Education* 48, 27–54.

van't Padje, Willem-Alexander. 2001. *At the Heart of the Growing Anglo-German Imperialist Rivalry: Two British Ambassadors in Berlin, 1884–1908*. Ph.D. Dissertation, University of Oxford.

Vernon, Keith. 2004. *Universities and the State in England*. London: Routledge.

Wallace, Stuart. 2006. "National Identity and the Idea of the University in Nineteenth-Century Scotland." *Higher Education Perspectives*, Special Issue, 124–146.

Weber, Thomas. 2008. *Our Friend, 'The Enemy': Elite Education in Britain and Germany before World War I*. Stanford CA: Stanford University Press.

Weber, Thomas. 2008. "'Cosmopolitan Nationalists': German Students in Britain – British Students in Germany." In *Wilhelmine Germany and Edwardian Britain: Essays on Cultural Affinity*, edited by Dominik Geppert and Robert Gerwath, 249–270. Oxford: Oxford University Press.

# Chapter 8
# Appropriation, Representation and Cooperation as Transnational Practices: The Example of Ferdinand Buisson

**Klaus Dittrich**

**Abstract** This contribution focuses on the transnational activities of the French intellectual and education expert Ferdinand Buisson (1841–1932). The liberal Protestant Buisson played a crucial role in implementing republican educational reforms during the last decades of the nineteenth century. Investigating his motivations for crossing borders and contacting his peers in foreign countries, this contribution distinguishes three transnational practices. Firstly, Buisson "went transnational" in order to learn from abroad. Secondly, once his institutionalisation efforts showed a certain maturity, he proudly presented his achievements neatly packaged in a nationalist discourse. Thirdly, Buisson called for common international effort projects. It is suggested that these practices of appropriation, representation, and cooperation provide a general tool for analysing the activities of expert actors on the international scene in the late nineteenth and early twentieth centuries.

## Introduction

Transnational history has seen a considerable boom during the last few years with numerous publications, workshops and research programmes having adopted the notion of "transnational" in their titles.[1] However, scholars charge this notion with a variety of different meanings. Sometimes "transnational" refers to phenomena that potentially concerned the entire globe, sometimes more emphasis is put on the circulation of ideas and practices between different parts of the world.

[1] Cf. recently Iriye and Saunier 2009.

K. Dittrich (✉)
Department of Korean History, Korea University, Seoul, South Korea
e-mail: ragazzodelleuropa@hotmail.com

I. Löhr and R. Wenzlhuemer (eds.), *The Nation State and Beyond*, Transcultural Research – Heidelberg Studies on Asia and Europe in a Global Context,
DOI 10.1007/978-3-642-32934-0_8, © Springer-Verlag Berlin Heidelberg 2013

The question of what "transnational" actually meant with regard to the experiences of individuals – the concrete historical actors – has mostly been absent from debates.[2] I am convinced that the solution for a more precise understanding and use of the notion "transnational" is to be found in a more empirical and methodologically sophisticated observation of the actors. For Marc Bloch, history was the science of human beings in time.[3] Bloch wrote that "the good historian is like the giant of the fairy tale. He knows that wherever he catches the scent of human flesh, there his quarry lies."[4] I do not want to overstrain this metaphor, but one could argue that in every archive where he catches the scent of a foreigner (or other forms of foreign interaction), a scholar of transnational history finds his quarry. Social history which has liberated itself from its former quantitative orientation on aggregate social groups provides the tools for an innovative actor-centred perspective.[5] It provides the scholar of global phenomena with sober but insightful empiricism.[6] Prosopographic approaches can inform us "who the guys were".[7] In consequence, this paper does not start from theoretical or philosophical assumptions on the nature of "the transnational" in order to set out to search for its actors; instead it begins with the human beings and their empirically traceable activities. From these observations, this chapter suggests, historians can generalise activity patterns and proceed to an original understanding and definition of notions such as "transnational" and "globalisation".

From the perspective of late nineteenth-century education experts, there were no abstract and anonymous globalisation processes that needed to be governed. It was rather the case that these actors themselves brought globalisation forward, pursuing specific goals through specific practices. This paper argues that individuals affiliated to national ministries and administrations actively advanced globalisation processes. In consequence, rather than governing globalisation processes – as the title of this volume suggests – the leitmotiv of governing nationalisation and processes of international cooperation through transnational practices would be most appropriate for my purposes.

This chapter is concerned with the biographies and activities of experts. In various fields of specialisation experts were one of the groups with pronounced transnational contacts during the nineteenth century. The study of experts provides elements for a socio-cultural history of an intellectual and administrative elite. As recent research shows, the status of experts was characterised, on the one hand, by the mastery of specialised skills and on the other hand by the recognition and

[2] Hausberger 2006.

[3] Bloch 1949, p. 4.

[4] Translated as in Bloch 1992, p. 22.

[5] Charle 1993.

[6] Kocka 2006, p. 316.

[7] Pyenson 1977; cf. also Stone 1972 and the works on microstoria, such as Levi 1995.

esteem in which they were held by the public, their peers and the state.[8] The second half of the nineteenth century saw the professionalistion of expert activities.[9]

Education experts constitute an excellent sample for analysing the transnational activities of a group of expert actors. The establishment of state education systems engendered the rise of a group of education administrators and thinkers, whilst the nineteenth century saw the progressive establishment of systems of modern primary education. The schooling of youths from 6 to 14 years of age became compulsory and free of charge in selected European, American and East Asian countries. Public authorities took over the control of education from religious organisations. Primary education not only transmitted elementary skills, it also assumed a crucial role in the socialisation of future citizens or subjects and defined the relationship between the government and the governed as well as between the citizens themselves. This chapter is a contribution to the transnational dimension of the establishment of modern education systems in the nineteenth century.[10]

The creation of education systems was part of nation-building processes. It took place in a period of nationalisation, a category which definitely applies to the nineteenth century.[11] Education systems were established in spaces separated from one another, mostly nation-states. Even in federally organised nation-states where the administration of education was organised on a state or local level, such as Germany and the United States, the nation became a central reference. However, we should not only concentrate on isomorphic developments, but also on what happened between the nation-states that actors were institutionalising. Nation-building, as well as attempts to overcome nation-centredness, were intimately linked to transnational activities.

Even though the role of the nation-state was paramount, each historical actor, as Jacques Revel has argued, operated at various spatial levels, ranging from the local to the global.[12] Charles S. Maier distinguished between identity space and decision space, arguing that identity and decision space became identical during the second half of the nineteenth century.[13] Paul-André Rosental's notion of an invested space (*espace investi*) which he suggested for the study of migration can also be made useful for the study of experts.[14] The invested space of an education expert was therefore flexible and multiple. The nation-state as an invested space of an education expert is a historical category.

Research has already figured out different vehicles for transnational communication in the nineteenth and early twentieth centuries. Experts contacted their

[8] On the role of experts cf. Raphael 1996; Engstrom 2005; Kesper-Biermann 2012.

[9] Siegrist 1988.

[10] Cf. recently for France: Matasci 2010.

[11] Maier 2000.

[12] Revel 1996.

[13] Maier 2000, p. 816.

[14] Rosental 1990.

colleagues from other countries through networks,[15] and print materials, such as books, academic journals, their translation and transnational circulation, played a foremost role. Experts were dispatched to foreign countries in order to investigate education systems for possible emulation in their home context.[16] The role of world exhibitions for transnational communication was also fundamental, and although their function to entertain grew steadily, world exhibitions attracted specialists in all fields of knowledge.[17] As meta-media they brought together various means of communication and developed into one of the few specifically global events of the period.[18] World exhibitions aimed at classifying and representing the entirety of human knowledge, and since the London exhibition of 1862 they comprised educational sections which became larger and gained importance in the following years. International congresses, which in the nineteenth century took place mostly in the framework of the exhibitions, provided an additional occasion for exchange between experts from different countries.[19] Later on, especially after the First World War, international organisations replaced the exhibitions as arenas for transnational exchange and provided a more permanent form of cooperation.[20] All these media provided opportunities for education experts to get in touch with foreign experiences.

Transnational history designates such circumstances when actors surpassed the boundaries of their usual institutional context.[21] Why did actors surpass the boundaries of their institutional context? Why did they go transnational? Which methodologies can historians use in order to analyse these phenomena in a theoretical way? I want to argue that actors pursued conscious strategies when going transnational. Three reasons are prominent: first, they wanted to appropriate foreign features for their own institutions, to learn from abroad. The approach of cultural transfers is the best tool for analysing these practices. Second, they wanted to represent their own institutions and achievements on an international stage. Christophe Charle's interpretation of European society around 1900 as a set of imperial societies is especially helpful for understanding competition as a distinctive feature of this period. Third, actors wanted to cooperate on an international level, transcending the boundaries of their own nation-state. For this kind of practice I draw especially upon Madeleine Herren's concept of governmental internationalism.

[15] Fuchs 2007 "Networks".

[16] Gonon 2004.

[17] Fuchs 2007 "Gouvernementaler Internationalismus".

[18] On world exhibitions as meta-media cf. Geppert 2004, p. 13.

[19] Fuchs 2004.

[20] Fuchs 2007 "The Creation".

[21] Middell and Naumann 2010, p. 160.

I will outline these three transnational practices by focusing on one personality, the French educator Ferdinand Buisson. It is not my intention to draw a complete biography of Buisson, however, most scholarship about him has taken a national perspective and neglected contextualisations other than French.[22] This chapter puts the transnational dimension of Buisson's professional activities as an education expert as the central point of interest.[23]

The Protestant Buisson was born in Paris in 1841. He studied at the Faculté de lettres in Paris, receiving his *licence* in 1863. Having refused the oath of allegiance to the Emperor Napoléon III, Buisson could not start a professional or academic career in the France of the Second Empire. Consequently, he spent several years in the Swiss university town of Neuchâtel as a professor of philosophy. There he developed his ideas and his personality as a liberal protestant, free thinker and radical socialist. After the end of the Second Empire, Buisson came back to the French capital. He joined the Ministry of Public Instruction where he occupied different positions from a modest primary inspector to the Director of Primary Instruction, a crucial position he filled from 1879 to 1896. Afterwards he became professor of educational sciences at the Sorbonne. From 1902 he was a radical deputy who was also active in numerous organisations, such as the Ligue des droits de l'homme et du citoyen. Nevertheless he continued to deal with education and exercised influence on educational decision-making. Buisson received the Nobel Peace Prize together with the German pacifist Ludwig Quidde in 1927. When he died in 1932 he was a national hero of the Third Republic.[24]

In the following I will analyse the different transnational stages of Buisson's career. This chapter consists of three parts, each standing for one of the transnational practices – appropriation, self-representation and cooperation. Within each part I will suggest theoretical conceptualisations and present biographical data on Buisson and some of his close collaborators. I will also compare these data to activities of similar actors from other countries during the same period. This chapter aims at proposing empirically proofed theoretical conceptualisations for further research in transnational history.

## Appropriation: Ferdinand Buisson as an Actor of Cultural Transfers

The first reason why Ferdinand Buisson passed beyond the boundaries of the hexagon was to build up a system of free, compulsory and secular primary education in France. He wanted to learn from foreign experiences and Buisson thus

[22] Chase 1977; Denis and Kahn 2003; Hayat 1999; Toméi 2004.

[23] Some recent studies have dealt similarly with other French personalities: see Bantman 2009.

[24] Pierre Nora elevated one of Buisson's key projects, the publication of the *Dictionnaire de pédagogie*, to a French realm of memory (lieu de mémoire): Nora 1984.

became an actor of cultural transfers. The concept of cultural transfers permits an analysis of the appropriation efforts of actors or groups of actors who tried to develop their own institutional context.[25] According to Matthias Middell, cultural transfers can be divided into four phases. First, actors identify deficits. Second, they choose the context for the rhetorical and material appropriation. Third, they engage in efforts of transposition and translation. Fourth, they localise the elements they want to appropriate.[26] As this model makes clear, the agency of the actors in the receiving context was decisive for appropriation processes. Cultural transfers often achieve the subversion of prevailing models: reference to foreign models was a way to criticise institutions.

When Buisson joined the Ministry of Public Instruction in the early 1870s, he was confronted with a specific situation: the nineteenth century, in France and elsewhere, was witnessing the transfer of authority over education from private to state actors. First efforts to establish a public system of primary education in France had been made during the first decades of the nineteenth century. In the 1830s the Guizot Law organised a legal framework for public instruction on the elementary level in France. In the subsequent decades, decision-makers tended more to neglect rather than expand the education system, so that, for example, Victor Duruy, the modernising Minister of Public Instruction of the Second Empire, failed in making primary instruction free of charge and compulsory. In contrast to the German states and parts of the United States, elementary education in France was not made compulsory and remained the responsibility of the *pater familias* up to the 1870s. In France, the Catholic Church had traditionally been the foremost provider of elementary instruction and Catholic congregations continued to tutor a large percentage of children in primary instruction. Indeed, control of primary education became one of the fields of confrontation between progressive and conservative forces at the beginning of the Third Republic. The conservative faction of the political elite successfully discouraged the further development of the public education system in qualitative and quantitative terms.[27]

A group of Republican reformers headed by Buisson laboured to change this situation. In January 1872 Buisson was appointed primary inspector in Paris by the moderate republican Jules Simon, the first Minister of Public Instruction of the Third Republic. However, strenuous attacks from the right urged Simon to put Buisson on leave, an illustration of the political situation in France during the early 1870s. The first years of the Third Republic are generally referred to as the regime of moral order. It was a period of conservatism; a monarchical restoration still seemed possible.[28] The government was not inclined to introduce changes in the organisation of primary instruction.

[25] Espagne and Werner 1988.

[26] Middell 2007; for a discussion of similar approaches in the history of education see Fuchs and Lüth 2008.

[27] Mayeur 2004.

[28] Mayeur 1984.

But reformers succeeded in taking over the French participation in world exhibitions. The experiences of countries that had already introduced compulsory schooling or reached a near-total scholarisation of youths evoked the curiosity of French reformers and this interest materialised in numerous publications on foreign education systems, such as those by Célestin Hippeau who had travelled to several European and American countries.[29] In 1873, after Buisson's dismissal as primary inspector, Simon, a promoter of public instruction, charged him with a mission to the world exhibition in Vienna. On the one hand, Buisson had to represent French education in the Austrian capital; on the other hand, and far more importantly, he was to study the exhibits of the participating nations and write up a report on his observations. Buisson himself had actually proposed this kind of investigation.[30] In Vienna, he met colleagues from other countries, amongst them key administrators from Austria, Germany, Italy and the United States.[31] After the exhibition was over, Buisson then toured Germany too in order to acquaint himself with its educational state systems. The outcome of the mission to Vienna was a report which described the state of the art in elementary education in all participating countries in a detailed and scientific way.[32] Buisson discussed all aspects of primary schooling, ranging from school houses and desks through the pedagogical and administrative organisation of education to particular subjects taught in elementary schools.

Three years later Buisson once again travelled to a world exhibition. This time he headed a commission to visit the Centennial Exhibition which took place in Philadelphia in 1876. There was no French educational exhibit in Philadelphia, rather the mission had the exclusive purpose of investigating into the organisation of primary education in the United States. Indeed, American education was highly likely to evoke the interest of the French Protestant – public school systems, embedded in a republican, capitalist and Protestant ideology, had been flourishing in the north-eastern and mid-western states of the American Union since the 1830s.[33] In the United States, education was administered on the state and city level, the most advanced states having introduced compulsive attendance and abolished tuition fees. While in America Buisson did not keep just to the exhibition grounds but toured the United States and Canada and participated in educational conventions. He made the acquaintance of school administrators who belonged to the generation of American "common school crusaders".[34] After his return to

[29] Camara Bastos 2002.

[30] ANF, F17, 2343 C, Records of Buisson's mission to the Vienna Exhibition.

[31] A list with the addressees of Buisson's report provides a detailed list of his contacts, see ANF, F17, 9386, Letter of the Deuxième bureau.

[32] Buisson 1875.

[33] On American primary education in the nineteenth century cf. Kaestle 1983.

[34] The historians of education Tyack and Hansot used this formulation to designate the American educators who built up a system of free public schools from the 1830s onwards; Tyack and Hansot 1982.

France, Buisson published a monumental report on his observations:[35] it was an enthusiastic evaluation of the American free school system.[36] Buisson admired its Republican impetus and its public service character and commented favourably, for example, on history instruction in American schools which, as he argued, was closely related to civic instruction and provided a common basis for American society, notably in assimilating immigrants. He also admired the non-sectarian character of American schooling, although this concept differed from the French notion of *laïcité*.

Despite this fascination and approval, Buisson rejected certain American features. Although he became a supporter of the suffragette movement in later years, Buisson criticised the coeducational character of American schools and the, in his opinion, excessive use of women teachers. Even more, he did not question the national organisation of education in France. Theoretically, he could have encouraged local supervision of schools according to the American model in order to bypass the conservative policies of the central Ministry. As Katherine Auspitz has shown for France, local decision-makers tried to counteract conservative policies on the local level.[37] As an official of a national ministry, however, Buisson adopted a national perspective and refrained from handing additional powers to the municipalities.

In 1878, Buisson was one of the most active organisers of the educational section of the *Exposition universelle* taking place in the French capital. The experts he had met in the United States were now received in Paris, and Buisson himself housed John D. Philbrick, Superintendent of Public Instruction in Boston and head of the United States educational exhibit, in his own apartment on the Boulevard Montparnasse.[38] The American exhibit fulfilled the expectations of the French Republicans – quotations on the importance of primary instruction from the French philosopher Charles Montesquieu as well as the former president of the United States George Washington decorated the exhibit's entrance and provided a link to French debates.[39] Buisson was commissioned to prepare the opening of an educational museum as an educational think-tank in Paris and negotiated with the commissioners of the exhibiting foreign nations to leave their exhibits to the new museum.[40] Additionally he edited the monumental *Dictionnaire de pédagogie* in 1887.[41] This was an attempt to collect the accumulated knowledge and present it so that it could be applied for administrational purposes, with those Buisson had got to know during his trips abroad writing the entries on foreign education systems.[42]

---

[35] Buisson 1878.

[36] Cf. also Portes 1990, pp. 205–226 and Tomći 2004, pp. 286–293.

[37] Auspitz 1982.

[38] Dunton 1887, p. 180.

[39] Emile Levasseur published a favourable article on the American exhibit: Levasseur 1878.

[40] Majault 1959.

[41] Dubois 2002 *Le dictionnaire de Ferdinand Buisson.*

[42] Dubois 2002 *Le 'dictionnaire de pédagogie…'.*

Buisson established contacts with peers from various countries and found his place in network structures. His transnational experience, in a slightly subversive way, furthered his pedagogical competence and advanced his standing on the national scene.[43]

Ferdinand Buisson was not an isolated case. The idea of profiting from foreign institutionalisations goes back to the French Marc Antoine Jullien, generally considered the father of comparative education, who published his *Esquisse et vues préliminaires d'un ouvrage sur l'éducation comparée* in 1817. In several countries, education experts were engaged in similar efforts of appropriation during the second half of the nineteenth century, especially in the decade of Buisson's activities. Exactly as Buisson, Japanese commissioners used the world exhibitions of the 1870s in order to meet with American pedagogues. Young former samurai who had become officials of the new Department of Education after the Meiji restoration developed the Japanese system of primary education. For them, missions to world exhibitions played an important role.[44] Simultaneously, American educators turned to European experiences in order to build up institutions of technical learning and universities.[45]

In all these cases the appropriation of foreign knowledge and institutional models played a crucial role for institution building and reforms in national contexts. Contemporaries were well aware of the importance of foreign models. In the conclusion of his report from the Centennial Exhibition Buisson wrote:

> Ç'a été notre ambition et ce sera notre plus chère récompense d'apporter notre contingent de renseignements utiles à ceux qui veulent que l'instruction primaire en France, sans se modeler sur autrui, s'inspire assez de ce que produisent de meilleur tous les autres pays pour n'avoir à redouter la comparaison avec d'eux.[46]

Similarly, Andrew S. Draper, New York State Commissioner of Education, expressed in 1889:

> It is obligatory upon everyone engaged in this work to have full knowledge of all that is being done the wide-world over to diffuse public education, and it is their duty to seize hold of those methods, *and put them to use here*.[47]

These quotations are representative of many others that underline the central role which knowledge circulation played for contemporary decision-makers. They show that actors, when going transnational, were not primarily occupied with a vague sense of international harmony, but cared about developing their own institutional context.

One German scholar provided an intellectual framework for these kind of appropriations. Karl Lamprecht, historian at the University of Leipzig, was himself

[43] Dittrich 2008.

[44] Dittrich 2011; more generally see Duke 2009.

[45] Cremin 1961.

[46] Buisson 1878, p. 677.

[47] Cited in Tyack 1974, p. 40; emphasis is mine.

a traveller to the Louisiana Purchase Exposition where he participated in the Congress of Arts and Sciences in September 1904.[48] In a series of lectures at Columbia University in New York 1 month later, Lamprecht reflected on conceptual questions of historiography, and stressed the importance of interactions between different societies. Lamprecht saw the ability to appropriate innovations made elsewhere as a central force in global history.[49]

Education experts who had crossed the Atlantic together in 1904 referred directly to Lamprecht. Franz Kuypers, director of the municipal continuation school in Düsseldorf, participated in a commission sent to the Louisiana Purchase Exposition by the Prussian Ministry of Commerce in order to investigate technical education in the United States. Kuypers quoted Lamprecht's *Americana* as an epigram in the report on his trip to the United States:

> "Noch immer sind Lebensaustausche verwandter und doch nicht zu nahe verschwisterter Völker die fruchtbarsten der Weltgeschichte gewesen."[50]

This approach allowed Kuypers to understand the establishment of up-to-date school systems in remote areas such as Salt Lake City. It also justified his own practice as an actor of cultural transfers from the United States to Germany.[51] Some decades later French and German scholars built on Lamprecht and formulated the approach of cultural transfers.

## Representation: Staging the Educational Achievements of the Third Republic

Ferdinand Buisson and his collaborators went transnational, in a second instance, in order to communicate to the world the success and assumed superiority of the French institutionalisation of primary education. While historians in recent years have developed sophisticated models for the conceptualisation of cultural transfers, the scholarly community still lacks adequate models to describe more arrogant behaviour on the transnational scene. How do actors from an intellectual and administrative elite behave during a period of confidence in their achievements? The empirical data on Buisson suggests a chronological sequence from appropriation to self-representation. There was a logic in this sequence in which the proud self-representation was the final phase of successful institutionalisations through cultural transfers, whereby foreign references were not always made explicit and

[48] Lamprecht 1906; on Lamprecht cf. Chickering 1993.

[49] Lamprecht 1905, pp. 103–130; see also Middell 2005, pp. 277 f.

[50] Kuypers 1907, p. iv; the quote is taken from: Lamprecht 1906, p. 85.

[51] Heinrich Leobner, an Austrian commissioner to the St. Louis Exposition, also referred to Lamprecht's *Americana*: Leobner 1907, p. 137.

often remained hidden.[52] The plurality of institutional solutions in different spaces entailed that these spaces entered into competition.[53]

Christophe Charle saw European society around the turn of the century as a set of *sociétés impériales*.[54] This notion offers a useful conceptualisation. Charle saw France, Germany and Britain as the countries that best fitted the definition of imperial societies, but suggested that outside Europe the United States and Japan also showed similar characteristics. The notion of *sociétés impériales* implies competition – Charle even speaks of an obsession for competition – between the major nation-states.[55] Actors had an extreme desire to outperform the competitors, with prestige being at stake, something which also found expression in linguistic imperialism. Historical actors saw their own nation as a cultural model for others whilst competition also implied constant explicit or implicit reference to competitors, neighbouring nations and institutions. This was related to the elaboration of a proper tradition and an emphasis on identity.

Sophisticated tools for cultural diplomacy were used in order to achieve these goals.[56] The founding of research institutes and technical schools abroad were further enterprises in cultural diplomacy which occurred in the fierce competition between France and Germany.[57] Scientific missions sent out by the French Ministry of Public Instruction aimed at marking the territory of national excellence[58] while the Alliance française, founded in 1883 in order to promote the French language in the colonies and abroad, was a similar attempt.[59]

Returning to the case of Ferdinand Buisson, his accumulated knowledge certainly helped him to make a decisive contribution to French institution-building in the sector of primary education. At the end of the 1870s the political situation in France changed in favour of the Republicans. With the Republican electoral successes in the parliamentary and presidential elections of 1877 and 1879, the regime was henceforth secured,[60] as situation which was also well reflected in educational decision-making. After a period of knowledge accumulation and subversion of existing models, the time had now come for institutional changes. Buisson was promoted to *inspecteur général de l'instruction publique* on 31 August 1878, the very day he made a presentation at the World Exhibition in front of

[52] Middell 2004.

[53] The concept of multiple modernities proposed by Shmuel Eisenstadt also suggests that specific forms of modernity started to compete with one another: Eisenstadt 2000.

[54] Charle 2001.

[55] Charle 2003, p. 10.

[56] Von Brocke 1981.

[57] Düwell 1981; Pyenson 1985, 1993.

[58] Bourquin 2004.

[59] Bruezière 1983.

[60] Mayeur 1984.

primary instructors from the entire nation.[61] In February 1879, Buisson became Director of Primary Education (*directeur de l'enseignement primaire*). This was one of the highest positions in the Ministry of Public Instruction and one he held under changing ministers until 1896. It was a crucial position for supervising the implementation of republican reforms. In the early 1880s the French Republic introduced a system of primary education that was a milestone in the history of French education.[62] The legislation was mostly put in place by the Minister of Public Instruction Jules Ferry, after whom three laws of particular importance are referred to as the Ferry laws. A law passed in 1881 made primary instruction free of charge, with the laws on compulsory attendance and schools being secular institutions being passed a year later. As some American educationalists suggested in their comments, Buisson had now put into practice what he had learned before with them.[63]

However, there were some elements Buisson had observed and liked in the United States he was not able to implement in France. For this reason he did not feel fully satisfied with the situation of primary instruction in France, even after the reforms, since two effectively separate education systems continued to exist. On the one hand primary schools received the large number of children of the workers and peasants, whilst on the other hand the bourgeois elite continued to send their children to the secondary schools (*lycées* or *collèges*) and their preparatory classes which charged for tuition. Almost no link existed between the two systems. This contrasted with the American model where the high school provided continuing free education for all who had graduated from primary schools.[64] Buisson had heard his American colleagues saying that providing every child with the same chances in education was the "American idea".[65] Buisson argued that this was also the "French idea" and struggled for the implementation of the idea of an *école unique* with varying intensity during the following decades.[66]

Even so, Buisson and his collaborators could be proud of their achievements. Ferdinand's brother, Benjamin Buisson, subsequently played an important role in representing France at international exhibitions. For several years he had lived in London as a professor of French language and a newspaper correspondent and was thus well acquainted with developments in the Anglo Saxon countries. He served as commissioner of the Ministry of Public Instruction to the first international exhibitions after the adoption of the Ferry laws, the International Health and

[61] *Conférences pédagogiques faites aux instituteurs primaires venues à Paris pour l'Exposition universelle de* 1878; Paris 1878.

[62] Mayeur 2004, pp. 582–601.

[63] The mission of Ferdinand Buisson to the Centennial Exhibition and the subsequent publication of the report found an extensive echo in specialised and general journals in the United States. See for example: "Editorial Notice," in: *Pennsylvania School Journal* 28 (1879), p. 385.

[64] Reese 1995.

[65] Coste 1873.

[66] Dubois 2007, pp. 18–19; a comprehensive school was only established in the inter-war period.

Education Exhibition in London in 1884 and the World's Industrial and Cotton Centennial Exposition a year later in New Orleans. In a speech he gave at the annual meeting of the National Education Association (NEA) of the United States being convened at the same time he boasted of the reforms made by his government in front of the American public, showing that the French Republicans were the "true friends of the school-master and the school-boy".[67]

Four years later, the educational section of the Exposition universelle of 1889 was the largest put together thus far, although foreign participation was weak. Within the exhibition grounds, the French Ministry of Public Instruction presented its achievements to the world. In the 1870s the most important publications from the educational sections were retrospective reports which had the goal of inspiring reforms; now, in 1889, the most complete publication appeared even before the exhibition had opened and showed the accomplishment of these same reforms. The Musée pédagogique prepared 60 monographs bound in six volumes, covering all aspects of French primary education.[68] They constituted a first official evaluation and competitive staging of the new Republican primary school. Buisson saw these papers as a chance to eradicate the stereotypes foreigners held concerning French education: "Les étrangers corrigeront l'idée un peu trop sommaire qu'ils se font de l'uniformité de nos méthodes et de la rigidité de nos cadres."[69] He wrote this comment in order to counter German criticism that mocked French educational administration as being oppressive centralisation – French institutionalisations in the field of elementary education were now compared to German ones. The exhibition vitrines of the Ministry of Public Instruction displayed the *Dictionnaire de pédagogie* which was no longer restricted to the mere cataloguing of practical knowledge, but had now become an emanation of French pedagogical thought.[70]

If we want to study how Republican French educators presented their institutional achievements to the world, the exhibit at the following Parisian exhibition of 1900 was even more revealing. Buisson's name appears as a member of numerous preparatory committees and as an organiser of and participant in several congresses. His colleagues were also active in promoting the French vision of elementary schooling that had developed during the past two decades. Charles Bayet, Buisson's successor as Director of Primary Education, published a volume similar to that of 1889 where he gave "un coup d'œil sur le chemin parcouru".[71] The *exposition rétrospective* put the development of education in a distinctively French tradition.[72]

[67] Buisson 1886, p. 114.

[68] *Recueil des monographies pédagogiques publiées à l'occasion de l'Exposition universelle de* 1889, Paris 1889.

[69] Ibid., vol. 1, p. ix.

[70] Dubois 2000.

[71] *Rapport sur l'organisation et la situation de l'enseignement primaire public en France*, Paris 1900.

[72] *Musée rétrospectif du groupe 1, éducation et enseignement, à l'exposition universelle internationale de* 1900, *à Paris. Rapport du comité d'installation*, Saint-Cloud [ca. 1900].

Gabriel Compayré, rector of the Academy of Lyon and with many transatlantic contacts, spoke at the closing session of the congress on primary education which took place within the framework of the Exhibition. Immediately after everyone had joined in singing the *Marseillaise* Compayré stated how free, compulsory and secular primary education had become an integral part of French nationalism:

> Il y a vingt ans seulement que, faisant une véritable révolution scolaire, nous avons fondé l'école gratuite, obligatoire et laïque: et déjà nous y sommes habitués au point qu'elle fait maintenant partie intégrante de notre patrimoine, au même titre que les conquêtes de la Révolution; et il ne serait plus au pouvoir de personne de nous le prendre. [...] Et ne voit-on pas déjà qu'au delà des frontières françaises l'école primaire publique, telle que nous l'imaginons, telle que nous la maintenons, est l'objet de l'attention générale? Car telle est la force de la vérité! Notre conception de l'école entrera un jour dans tous les esprits, parce que c'est la conception vraie. Nous ne savons si ce temps est proche, mais le temps viendra [...] où [...] l'école publique française, l'école de neutralité, de tolérance, de paix et de justice, sera l'école universelle.[73]

Within just three decades Republican primary education turned from being an idea of leftist trouble-makers something being claimed as a universal model. French Republican educators no longer perceived the Exhibitions as a means to learn from foreign experiences. Instead, they promoted their own institutional achievements as a universalist truth, thinking of them as arrangements that would eventually be adopted across the entire globe.

The world exhibitions were an optimal stage for educational administrators from all over the world to represent their institutional achievements. The German Empire used the American exhibitions of Chicago and St. Louis in order to stage its education system, the Prussian Ministry of Education preparing the German educational exhibits which were to transmit the essence of German scholarship. The exhibits were intended to visualise the effective administration of elementary schools and the excellence of higher education. Organisers represented science and research in Germany as part of a German tradition, creating the myth of the Humboldtian university, with scientific exhibits, as for example in chemistry, testifying to the scientific excellence and related economic power of the country. A monumental statue of the Emperor unambiguously showed the display as part of a nationalist discourse.[74]

Americans represented how education integrated more and more practical elements, reflecting the growth of the progressive education movement. After participation in the Paris exhibition of 1900 Americans were convinced of their superiority. F. Louis Soldan, an educational administrator from St. Louis, saw global developments as being an imitation of the situation in the United States. He saw "the growing tendency in Europe and thruout the civilized world to imitate the United States in spreading the benefits of education among the masses."[75]

---

[73] Ibid.

[74] Fuchs 2007 "Gouvernementaler Internationalismus".

[75] Unsigned note on "F. Louis Soldan and the Paris Exposition" in: *The School Journal*, LXI (1900), p. 299.

The Japanese were amongst the most eager participators in world exhibitions at the turn of the century, and the Japanese Ministry of Education showed how education had consequently legitimated a "uniformly loyal nation of subjects" with an "unbroken line of illustrious sovereigns" for 2,000 years.[76] Publications proudly stated that the establishment of an education system had now been achieved, but the exhibit also stressed the scientific excellence the University of Tokyo had begun to acquire. In seismology, one publication argued, Europe and America were already "using inventions which had their origin in Japan".[77] It is not so much of interest if these statements are true or not, but they serve well to express the struggle for superiority, the ambition to be the first, of being emulated and in general a desire to outperform competitors.

These examples show that world exhibitions were not only, as Buisson once said, "grandes enquêtes internationales" or "object lessons in all the world's industry",[78] but also, as other contemporaries argued, "battlefields"[79] where rival nation-states staged their achievements. This was more than true in the field of education.

## Cooperation: From Patriotism to Inter-patriotism

Should arrogant national self-representation shape the fortune of the world for good? Competition with colleagues from neighbouring nation-states was not the only option for education experts in the late nineteenth and early twentieth century. Ferdinand Buisson did not lack the intelligence to imagine collaborative efforts – he went transnational, taking a third option, in order to consciously promote the transnational level as a space of cooperation, standardisation and regulation, thus imagining a global community in its infancy.

In order to conceptualise these practices, Madeleine Herren has convincingly introduced the notion of governmental internationalism.[80] This designates a multilateralism which set out to continue and coordinate the modernisation projects begun by nation-states. Governmental internationalism was related to the standardisation of disparate national norms, and actors tended to facilitate the international flow of information and to guarantee access to this information. The control and administration of networks became crucial as power became increasingly wielded. Herren insists that transnational cooperation cannot be disconnected from national ambitions; internationalism was sometimes a strategy of foreign policy and thus

---

[76] *History of the Empire of Japan* 1895, pp. 16, 18.

[77] *Catalogue of Objects* 1893, pp. 57–58; see also Clancey 2006, pp. 160 ff.

[78] Harris 1898, p. 131.

[79] See for example: *Reports to the General Assembly of Illinois at Its Thirty-First Regular Session Convened January 8, vol. 4*, 1879, Springfield 1879, p. 6.

[80] Herren 2000.

related to the imperial competition described in the previous section. Herren has recently also shown how international organisations – apart from international conferences the main vehicles of governmental internationalism – developed over the last two centuries.[81] Beyond state interests, these forums provided a platform for sincere internationalism and pacifism. Akira Iriye in his history of international organisations focused on the role these organisations played for the constitution of "another world" beyond nation-states which he called "global community", highlighting the cultural aspect.[82]

Buisson without doubt belonged to the faction of internationalists discussed by Herren. As early as the 1860s, during his exile in Neuchâtel, Buisson had participated in the international peace congresses. In addition, as an education official and expert Buisson cared about bringing together different national experiences. By 1875, on his return from the Vienna Exhibition, he had proposed an international statistical bureau on education. He recommended that all governments learn from their experiences at the exhibition and apply the knowledge to their own institutions. But, he added, this was not sufficient. A more regular regime than the exhibitions had to be established which would permit institutional comparison and the exchange of information. Isolation and mutual ignorance was hindering educational progress in Europe, Buisson argued; an international bureau modelled after the United States Bureau of Education in Washington, he suggested, could improve this situation. In the United States, the federal states were responsible for educational affairs; the Bureau in the national capital served only to collect statistics and contributed to the circulation of information through the publication of its reports. Buisson called for a special commission that could be in charge of current educational questions in Europe and which should publish international statistics on a regular basis.[83] He was thus concerned about institutionalising the international level. Emile Levasseur, a geographer and educational administrator who worked closely with Buisson and had accompanied him to Vienna, urged the preparation of a set of international educational statistics in time for the next world exhibition of 1876, which, however, did not come about.[84] Buisson and Levasseur proposed to establish the international bureau in Paris; besides investing in international exchanges, this proposition also included the idea of strengthening France's position on the international scene.

Buisson took an active part in the organisation of international education congresses in France. He held leading positions in the organising committees for the international conferences which took place as part of the 1889 Exhibition and he was vice-president of the organising committee of the International Congress on Primary Education. This congress aimed at providing a platform for transnational

---

[81] Herren 2009; cf. also Reinalda 2009.
[82] Iriye 2002, pp. 6–8.
[83] Buisson 1875, pp. 343 ff.
[84] Levasseur 1875, pp. 506 ff.

exchange, even though its agenda reflected contemporary French debates.[85] The same was true for the conferences held in conjunction with the Paris world exhibition of 1900.

Buisson also participated in various international conferences abroad. He was a delegate to the first international congress on education in Brussels in 1880, and in 1915, during the First World War, he attended the International Congress on Education in Oakland. At the Panama-Pacific International Exposition in San Francisco in 1915 and its related congresses, issues of international understanding and cooperation were discussed in a large framework. Commenting on the opening speech of David Starr Jordan, president of Stanford University, Buisson approved of his idealism; however, it might come as quite a surprise that he did not completely approve of the pacifist rhetoric of the congress. At a time when France, and concomitantly all its diligently established and symbolically charged institutions, were under attack one could not only talk of peace, he argued. The hopes of tomorrow should not distract from the duties of the present which in this case was the defence of one's country with arms.[86]

In the long run, however, the First World War did not shake Buisson's belief in international understanding. In 1919, he used a trip to the annual meeting of the NEA of the United States to investigate the possibility of establishing an international bureau of education. This time Buisson spoke in English for the first time in a public meeting, "a maiden speech in the 78th year of my age", as he remarked.[87] He raised three points in his speech and had the backing of the French Minister of Public Instruction for his initiatives. First, he fully supported the idea of the NEA to establish an International Bureau of Education. This would not only serve to promote the professional exchange of information, but also ideological purposes, as it should "promote the full development of the democratic ideal amongst free nations". Second, the French educator suggested bringing together French and American teachers. Third, Buisson spoke as a fervent supporter of the League of Nations and urged American cooperation: "You Americans have once delivered the world from the tyranny of militarism. Now we ask you to help to deliver the world from the tyranny of ignorance."[88] Buisson also became a promoter of Franco-German cooperation after the First World War for which he was rewarded with the Nobel Peace Prize. His urgings of cooperation corresponded to a critical evaluation and an international contextualisation of his efforts in nation-building. But they were also a logical continuation of his efforts.

Buisson also offered theoretical perspectives on internationalism. In 1900, in his function as a member of the Ligue française des droits de l'homme et du citoyen, he

---

[85] *Congrès international de l'enseignement primaire* 1889.

[86] Buisson 1916, pp. 11–12; on education at the international exposition in San Francisco more generally see: Sobe 2007.

[87] *National Educational Association of the United States* 1919, p. 93.

[88] Ibid., p. 94.

gave a speech entitled "Pourquoi nous sommes patriotes et ne sommes pas nationalistes" – why we are patriots and not nationalists. In this speech Buisson is concerned with current French politics and does not present the problem of the transnational. According to his categorisation, patriots are the political left with their tradition going back to the French Revolution, the nationalists are the right, representing conservatism, reaction and clericalism. The speech in itself is not so interesting for our purposes, but does at least inform us that patriotism and nationalism are not necessarily similar. It states that patriots are not necessarily nationalists; and that nationalists are not necessarily patriots.[89]

Patriotism being a leftist force for Buisson, for him it meant opening up from parochial, provincial, social and religious groups to the larger entity of the nation. This implied that the state was not only the affair of a dominant religious group or social class, but belonged to everyone. Seen from the perspective of an individual, the national level already meant opening up to a certain degree. Why then stop the loyalties of patriotism at the arbitrary boundaries of nation-states? Exactly as he wanted to bring together working-class and middle-class youths in the *école unique*, Buisson wanted to bring together people of different nations.

Buisson developed this idea in a speech on "International Instruction and International Education" delivered at the Congrès de la paix in Lille in April 1905 and subsequently published in the *Grande revue*.[90] International education sought to instruct young people in how to become conscious cosmopolitans. It was an emerging field of educational thought and curricular content at the beginning of the twentieth century. Buisson maintained that the principle of internationality was continuously replacing the principle of nationality; for him this was a fact, a clear moment in the history of human societies. In the first part of his speech Buisson argued that it was necessary to teach children that science and industry, the dominant forces in contemporary civilisation, were international by definition. For example, students should get to know that many processes of everyday life would be impossible without contributions from distant parts of the world – post, telegraph and railway services were unthinkable without international cooperation. Buisson proposed to teach that the *lutte pour la vie* should henceforth be replaced by the *union pour la vie*. In the future, the rule for living should be international solidarity. Pupils should develop an internationalist vision. In the meantime, however, they should remain prepared to defend their nations with arms, because – as Buisson recalled – the United States of Europe had not yet been founded.[91]

---

[89] Buisson 1902.

[90] Buisson 1905; when I had my first contact with this text, I consulted an offprint at the Thüringische Universitäts- und Landesbibliothek in Jena; it contains a trace of transnational communication in the form of a manuscript dedication from Buisson to Wilhelm Rein, professor of pedagogy at the University of Jena: "Mon cher ami, le professeur Rein."

[91] At a congress of the Fédération internationale de la libre pensée in Paris in 1905 Buisson supported a pacifist resolution, but also made clear that being a free-thinker did not authorise desertion. See Laqua 2009, p. 266.

In the second part of his speech Buisson developed the moral foundations of international cooperation. The notion of patriotism was central to his interests and he began by explaining it as the human characteristic of altruism as opposed to egotism, as an expression of social interest as opposed to individual interest. It was the expression of an individual's integration into a larger social aggregate, and this was a voluntary, though necessary process. Buisson's starting point was thus the individual and not the state. Patriotism meant the constant opening-up of the individual to larger contexts in concentric circles: family, clan and tribe level, province, nation. The idea of the fatherland (*patrie*) constitutes the human being as a conscious social being, an idea which also expresses the consciousness of what the individual owes to the social collectivity. Each time the circles expand there is a crisis of patriotism. When speaking in 1905, Buisson urged that the nationalistic limitations of patriotism be overcome. The future of patriotism would be an interpatriotism: "Le patriotisme d'hier, c'était la haine des autres patries, celui de demain ce sera presque un *interpatriotisme*."[92] Buisson's understanding of patriotism was open-minded and was related to the idea of solidarity promoted by Léon Bourgeois which was one of the central themes of the World Exposition of 1900. This was based on voluntary association in order to harmonise individual and social interests.[93] In some respects, Buisson appears in his speech as a precursor of contemporary historical methodologies. His definition of patriotism as the integration of an individual into larger societal entities organised in concentric circles recalls the *jeux d'échelles* as Jacques Revel described them.

Various international conferences and associations dealt with international regulation and cooperation in the field of education, with many individuals from different backgrounds being involved in these activities. Pen friends (*correspondances internationales entre écoliers*) were encouraged to bring students from different countries together.[94] The Czech educator Heřman Alferi published a book on international education in 1906, the Hungarian educator Franz Kemény doing likewise.[95] In the United States, William T. Harris estimated that as long as war was necessary, the individual must submit to the will of the social whole. But the time would come, according to Harris, and education would hasten the day, when each people would so participate in the thought of other nations that war would be obsolete.[96] In Japan as well, internationalist educators questioned the state's role in fostering nationalist and confrontational policies.[97] With the creation of the League of Nations and its educational activities educational internationalism was strongly reinforced in the interwar period.[98]

[92] Buisson 1905, p. 15; italics in the original.

[93] Blais 2007.

[94] Deniker et al. 1901.

[95] Marek 1907.

[96] Harris 1898.

[97] Lincicome 1999.

[98] Fuchs 2007 "The Creation".

## Conclusion

In this chapter I have asked why education experts as representatives of an administrative and intellectual elite went transnational in the late nineteenth and early twentieth centuries. "Transnational" refers to such moments when individuals crossed the boundaries of their home context or invested space. The study of Ferdinand Buisson demonstrates that actors, such as education experts, went beyond their own institutional context for three reasons. First, they went abroad in order to learn on behalf of their own institutions. Second, they staged their own institutions on a competitive international scene. Third, they tried to overcome national fragmentation and envisioned international cooperation. The model of appropriation, self-representation and cooperation applies for experts affiliated to national or municipal bureaucracies as well as academics. It applies less for other individuals and groups that went transnational during the same period, such as migrant workers or businessmen. In order to analyse the transnational practices of those individuals other analytical frameworks might be more appropriate.

What do the transnational practices of education experts tell us about globalisation? Globalisation means that actors increasingly transgress the boundaries of their own institutional context, for various reasons. We can speak of a period of globalisation whenever individuals crossing borders are not isolated cases, but are part of practices which can be observed on a larger scale. In this sense the half century before the First World War undoubtedly was a period of globalisation. We can then distinguish phases of globalisation according to which of the three patterns was dominant. Pierre-Yves Saunier has suggested calling these patterns circulatory regimes (*régimes circulatoires*).[99] The evidence gathered from Buisson's case suggests that a period of mutual appropriations with a peak in the 1870s was followed by a period of more nationalistic practices which arrogantly tended to show the institutionalised models as universalist ones.[100] At the same time, however, a limited faction of experts saw the need to unite the divergent national developments and deliberately promoted cooperation on the international level.

This conceptualisation has implications for history in general. It proves the close relationship between the establishment of modern institutions and globalisation. Modernity in Europe and elsewhere developed in competing centres that were being consolidated into nation-states. This implementation and consolidation implied mutual learning processes and ultimately led to the competitive confrontation of institutional models. Simultaneously actors were taking part in searches for for cooperation. The boundary was the "civilised world" or the "*Kulturländer*" as contemporaries used to say. Actors from other parts of the world, notably the colonies, were excluded from this scheme.

---

[99] Saunier 2008.

[100] Pierre-Yves Saunier observed a similar learning-curve for the participation of the city of Lyon in international exhibitions: Saunier 1999.

Was Buisson a national or a transnational actor? To use Marc Bloch's words, Buisson is definitely a quarry for a scholar of transnational history, but I would argue that this is not the best question since it is impossible to answer and – maybe – there is no need to qualify every actor as either national or transnational. If we first agree with Jacques Revel that individuals participate in various spatial frameworks and then consider that they pursue specific goals when going transnational, we gain a clearer view. Buisson went transnational for purposes of nation-building, for national self-representation and international cooperation. He was an educational globaliser of the nineteenth century, and made effective use of the possibilities offered by his time. As a promoter of liberal ideas, Buisson was one of the foremost representatives of a major stream of thought of the Third Republic. After establishing the French institutions of primary instruction and legitimising them to the world at large, he became one of the few who seriously engaged in activities to promote cooperation. We should not underestimate his uprightness in a period of nationalism.

## Bibliography


Archives nationales de France, F17, 2343 C, Records of Buisson's Mission to the Vienna Exhibition.

Archives nationales de France, F17, 9386, Letter of the Deuxième Bureau de la direction de l'enseignement primaire of the Ministry of Public Instruction to the Ministry of Foreign Affairs, 14 March 1876.

Auspitz, Katherine. 1982. *The Radical Bourgeoisie, la Ligue de l'enseignement and the Origins of the Third Republic, 1866–1885*. London: Cambridge University Press.

Bantman, Constance. 2009. "The Militant Go-between: Emile Pouget's Transnational Propaganda (1880–1914)." *Labour History Review* 74, no. 3, 274–287.

Blais, Marie-Claude. 2007. *La solidarité: histoire d'une idée*. Paris: Gallimard.

Bloch, Marc. 1949. *Apologie pour l'histoire ou le métier d'historien*. Paris: A. Colin.

Bloch, Marc. 1992. *The Historian's Craft. Translated from the French by Peter Putnam.* Manchester Manchester University Press.

Bourquin, Jean-Christophe. 2004. "National Influence on International Scientific Activity: The Case of the French Missions Littéraires in Europe, 1842–1914." In *Transnational Intellectual Networks: Forms of Academic Knowledge and the Search for Cultural Identities*, edited by Christophe Charle et al., 451–471. Frankfurt am Main: Campus.

Brueziere, Maurice. 1983. *L'Alliance française. Histoire d'une institution.* Paris: Hachette.

Buisson, Benjamin. 1886. "The Recent Reforms in Public Instruction, and Especially in Primary Instruction, in France." *Special Report by the Bureau of Education: Educational Exhibits and Conventions at the World's Industrial and Cotton Centennial Exposition. New Orleans 1884–85, vol. 2: Proceedings of the international congress of educators,* 111–119. Washington: Gov. Print. Off.

Buisson, Ferdinand. 1875. *Rapport sur l'instruction primaire à l'exposition universelle de Vienne en 1873*. Paris: Imprimerie nationale.

Buisson, Ferdinand. 1878. *Rapport sur l'instruction primaire à l'exposition universelle de Philadelphie en 1876*, Paris: Imprimerie nationale.

Buisson, Ferdinand. 1902. "Pourquoi nous sommes patriotes et ne sommes pas nationalists." Paris: Ligue française pour la défense des droits de l'homme et du citoyen.

Buisson, Ferdinand. 1905. "L'instruction et l'éducation international." *Grande revue* 9, 5–19.

Buisson, Ferdinand. 1916. "Le congrès international d'éducation." *Revue pédagogique* LXVIII, 1–40.

Buisson, Ferdinand. 1919. "Le congrès international d'éducation," *Revue pédagogique* LXVIII, no. 1, 1–40.

Camara Bastos, Maria Helena. 2002. "Leituras da Ilustração Brasileira: Célestin Hippeau (1803–1883)." *Revista brasileira de história da educação* 3, no. 1, 67–112.

*Catalogue of Objects Exhibited at the World's Columbian Exposition*. 1893. Tokyo: Department of Education.

Charle, Christophe, ed. 1993. *Histoire sociale, histoire globale? Actes du colloque des 27–28 janvier 1989, organisé par l'Institut d'histoire moderne et contemporaine*. Paris: Éd. de la Maison des Sciences de l'Homme.

Charle, Christophe. 2001. *La Crise des sociétés impériales: Allemagne, France, Grande-Bretagne, 1900–1940. Essai d'histoire sociale compare*. Paris: Éditions du Seuil.

Charle, Christophe. 2003. "Les références étrangères des universitaires: Essai de comparaison entre la France et l'Allemagne, 1870–1970." *Actes de la recherche en sciences sociales* 148, 8–19.

Chase, George W. 1977. "Ferdinand Buisson: A Study in Laicité in the Third Republic 1870–1914." Ph.D. Dissertation, University of Toronto.

Chickering, Roger. 1993. *Karl Lamprecht: A German Academic Life (1856–1915)*. Atlantic Highlands: Humanities Press.

Clancey, Gregory. 2006. *Earthquake Nation. The Cultural Politics of Japanese Seismicity, 1868–1930*. Berkeley: University of California Press.

*Conférences pédagogiques faites aux instituteurs primaires venues à Paris pour l'Exposition universelle de 1878*. Paris: Hachette, 1878.

*Congrès international de l'enseignement primaire. Analyse des mémoires*, Paris: Delagrave/ Hachette, 1889.

Coste, Felix. 1873. "Report of the President." *Eighteenth Annual Report of the Board of Directors of the St. Louis Public Schools, for the Year Ending August 1, 1872*, 9. St. Louis: Democrat Litho. and Printing Co.

Cremin, Lawrence Arthur. 1961. *The Transformation of the School: Progressivism in American Education, 1876–1957*. New York: Knopf.

Deniker, Joseph et al. 1901. *Congrès international de l'enseignement des langues vivantes, tenu à Paris du 24 au 28 juillet 1900. Procès-verbaux sommaires*. Paris: Société pour la propagation des langues étrangères en France.

Denis, Daniel & Pierre Kahn, eds. 2003. *L'Ecole républicaine et la question des savoirs: Enquête au cœur du 'Dictionnaire de pédagogie' de Ferdinand Buisson*. Paris: CNRS Editions.

Dittrich, Klaus. 2008. "Die amerikanische Referenz der republikanischen Grundschule Frankreichs: Kulturtransfer auf Weltausstellungen im 19. Jahrhundert." In *Transkulturalität. Gender- und bildungshistorische Perspektiven*, edited by Wolfgang Gippert et al., 161–179. Bielefeld: Transcript-Verlag.

Dittrich, Klaus. 2011. "La modernisation du système éducatif à travers les Expositions universelles, 1873–1904." *Japon pluriel 8*, 347–356. Arles: Picquier.

Dubois, Patrick. 2000. "Le Dictionnaire de F. Buisson et ses auteurs (1878–1887)." *Histoire de l'éducation* 85, 25–45.

Dubois, Patrick. 2002. *Le dictionnaire de Ferdinand Buisson: Aux fondations de l'école républicaine (1878–1911)*. Bern: Lang.

Dubois, Patrick. 2002. *Le 'dictionnaire de pédagogie et d'instruction primaire' de Ferdinand Buisson: Répertoire biographique des auteurs*. Paris: INRP.

Dubois, Patrick. 2007. "Figures de l'école juste et politique scolaire dans les années fondatrices de la Troisième République." *Revue française de pédagogie* 159, 13–21.

Duke, Benjamin C. 2009. *The History of Modern Japanese Education: Constructing the National School System, 1872–1890*. New Brunswick: Rutgers University Press.

Dunton, Larkin. 1887. *A Memorial of the Life and Services of John D. Philbrick*. Boston: New England Pub. Co.

Düwell, Kurt. 1981. "Der Einfluss des deutschen technischen Schul- und Hochschulwesens auf das Ausland (1870–1930)." *Zeitschrift für Kulturaustausch* 31, no. 1, 80–95.
"Editorial Notice." 1879. *Pennsylvania School Journal* 28, 385.
Eisenstadt, Shmuel N. 2000. "Multiple Modernities." *Daedalus* 129, no. 1, 1–29.
Engstrom, Eric J. 2005. *Figurationen des Experten: Ambivalenzen der wissenschaftlichen Expertise im ausgehenden 18. und frühen 19. Jahrhundert.* Frankfurt am Main: Lang.
Espagne, Michel & Michael Werner, eds. 1988. *Transferts. Les relations interculturelles dans l'espace franco-allemand (XVIIIe et XIXe siècles)*, Paris: Editions Recherche sur les civilisations.
"F. Louis Soldan and the Paris Exposition." 1900. *The School Journal* LXI, 299.
Fuchs, Eckhardt. 2004. "Educational Sciences, Morality and Politics: International Educational Congresses in the Early Twentieth Century." *Paedagogica Historica* 40, no. 5, 757–784.
Fuchs, Eckhardt. 2007. "The Creation of New International Networks in Education: The League of Nations and Educational Organisations in the 1920s." *Paedagogica Historica* 43, no. 2, 199–209.
Fuchs, Eckhardt. 2007. "Gouvernementaler Internationalismus und Bildung: Deutschland und die USA am Anfang des 20. Jahrhunderts." In *Weltkultur und kulturelle Bedeutungswelten: Zur Globalisierung von Bildungsdiskursen*, edited by Jürgen Schriewer, 45–73. Frankfurt am Main: Campus.
Fuchs, Eckhardt. 2007. "Networks and the History of Education." *Paedagogica Historica* 43, 185–197.
Fuchs, Eckhardt and Christoph Lüth. 2008. "Transnationale Bildungsbemühungen und die Konstruktion des Raumes in historischer Perspektive. Einleitung zu diesem Heft." *Bildung und Erziehung* 61, no. 1, 1–10.
Geppert, Alexander C.T. 2004. "Città brevi: Storia, storiografia e teoria delle pratiche espositive europee, 1851–2000." *Memoria e Ricerca* 17, 7–18.
Gonon, Philipp. 2004. "Travel and Reform: Impulses Towards Internationalisation in the Nineteenth-Century Discourse on Education." In *Educational Policy Borrowing: Historical Perspectives*, edited by David Phillips and Kimberley Ochs, 125–143. Oxford: Symposium Books.
Harris, William T. 1898. "Our Educational Exhibit at the International Exposition in Paris in 1900." *National Educational Association. Journal of Proceedings and Addresses of the Thirty-Seventh Annual Meeting held at Washington, D.C., July 7–12, 1898*, 122–131. Chicago: University of Chicago Press.
Hausberger, Bernd, ed. 2006. *Globale Lebensläufe: Menschen als Akteure des weltgeschichtlichen Geschehens.* Vienna: Mandelbaum-Verlag.
Hayat, Pierre. 1999. *La passion laïque de Ferdinand Buisson.* Paris: Éd. Kimé.
Herren, Madeleine, *Hintertüren zur Macht: Internationalismus und modernisierungsorientierte Außenpolitik in Belgien, der Schweiz und den USA 1865–1914*, Munich 2000.
Herren, Madeleine. 2009. *Internationale Organisationen seit 1865. Eine Globalgeschichte der internationalen Ordnung.* Darmstadt: Wiss. Buchgesellschaft.
*History of the Empire of Japan, Compiled and Translated for the Imperial Japanese Commission of the World's Columbian Exposition*, Chicago 1893, 2nd ed. 1895. Tokyo: Dai Nippon Tosho Kabushiki Kwaisha.
Iriye, Akira. 2002. *Global Community. The Role of International Organizations in the Making of the Contemporary World.* Berkeley: University of California Press.
Iriye, Akira and Pierre-Yves Saunier. 2009. *The Palgrave Dictionary of Transnational History*, New York: Palgrave Macmillan.
Kaestle, Carl F. 1983. *Pillars of the Republic: Common Schools and American Society, 1780–1860.* New York: Hill and Wang.
Kesper-Biermann, Sylvia. Forthcoming 2012. "Kommunikation, Austausch, Transfer. Bildungsräume im 19. Jahrhundert." In *Transnationale Bildungsräume. Wissenstransfers im*

*Schul- und Hochschulsektor in der Moderne*, edited by Sylvia Kesper-Biermann and Johannes Wischmeyer. Göttingen: Vandenhoeck & Ruprecht.

Kocka, Jürgen. 2006. "Sozialgeschichte im Zeitalter der Globalisierung," *Merkur. Deutsche Zeitschrift für europäisches Denken* 60, 305–316.

Kuypers, Franz. 1907. *Volksschule und Lehrerbildung der Vereinigten Staaten in ihren hervortretenden Zügen*. Leipzig: B.G. Teubner.

Lamprecht, Karl. 1905. *Moderne Geschichtswissenschaft: 5 Vorträge*. Freiburg im Breisgau: Heyfelder.

Lamprecht, Karl. 1906. *Americana: Reiseeindrücke, Betrachtungen, geschichtliche Gesamtansicht*. Freiburg im Breisgau: Heyfelder.

Laqua, Daniel. 2009. "'Laïque, démocratique et sociale'? Socialism and the Freethinkers' International." *Labour History Review* 74, no. 3, 257–273.

Leobner, Heinrich. 1907. *Die Grundzüge des Unterrichts- und Erziehungswesens in den Vereinigten Staaten von Nordamerika: Eine pädagogisch-didaktische Studie*. Vienna: F. Deuticke.

Levasseur, Emile. 1875. "Instruction primaire et secondaire," *Exposition universelle de Vienne en 1873. Rapports, vol. IV*, 351–529. Paris: Imprimerie nationale.

Levasseur, Emile. 1878. "L'Exposition scolaire des Etats-Unis." *Revue pédagogique* II, 219–231.

Levi, Giovanni. 1995. "On Microhistory." In *New Perspectives on Historical Writing*, edited by Peter Burke, 93–113. University Park: Pa.: Pennsylvania State Univ. Press.

Lincicome, Mark Elwood. 1999. "Nationalism, Imperialism, and the International Education Movement in Early Twentieth-Century Japan." *Journal of Asian Studies* 58, no. 2, 338–360.

Maier, Charles S. 2000. "Consigning the Twentieth Century to History: Alternative Narratives for the Modern Era." *The American Historical Review* 105, no. 3, 807–831.

Majault, Joseph. 1959. *Les origines de l'I.P.N.: Le Musée pédagogique (1872–1879)*. Paris: Institut pédagogique national.

Marek, J. 1907. Review of "Herman Alferi, Mezinárodní výchova a vyučování," in: *Čechische Revue* 1, 571.

Matasci, Damiano. 2010. "Le système scolaire français et ses miroirs. Les missions pédagogiques entre comparaison internationale et circulation des savoirs (1842–1914)." *Histoire de l'éducation* 125, 5–26.

Mayeur, Françoise. 2004. *Histoire générale de l'enseignement et de l'éducation en France, vol. III: De la Révolution à l'École républicaine, 1789–1930*. Paris: Perrin, impr.

Mayeur, Jean-Marie. 1984. *La vie politique sous la Troisième République. 1870–1940*. Paris: Seuil.

Middell, Matthias. 2004. "Das 'Spiel mit den Maßstäben' gestern und heute. Kompatibilität oder Diversität europäischer Wissenschaftssysteme – ein Blick auf die Transferprozesse im 19. Jahrhundert." In *'... immer im Forschen bleiben': Rüdiger vom Bruch zum 60. Geburtstag*, edited by Marc Schalenberg and Peter T. Walther, 199–212. Stuttgart: F. Steiner

Middell, Matthias. 2005. "Weltgeschichte um 1900." In *Europa und die Europäer. Quellen und Essays zur modernen europäischen Geschichte*, edited by Rüdiger Hohls et al., 277–282. Stuttgart: Steiner.

Middell, Matthias. 2007. "Kulturtransfer und transnationale Geschichte." *Dimensionen der Kultur- und Gesellschaftsgeschichte: Festschrift für Hannes Siegrist zum 60. Geburtstag*, 49–72. Leipzig: Leipziger Univ.-Verlag.

Middell, Matthias and Katja Naumann. 2010. "Global History and the Spatial Turn: From the Impact of Area Studies to the Study of Critical Junctures of Globalization." *Journal of Global History* 5, no. 1, 49–170.

*Musée rétrospectif du groupe 1, éducation et enseignement, à l'exposition universelle internationale de 1900, à Paris. Rapport du comité d'installation*, Saint-Cloud [ca.1900].

*National Educational Association of the United States. Addresses and Proceedings of the Fifty-Seventh Annual Meeting Held at Milwaukee, Wisconsin, June 28–July 5, 1919*, Washington: NEA, 1919.

Nora, Pierre. 1984. "Le Dictionnaire de pédagogie de Ferdinand Buisson. Cathédrale de l'école primaire." *Les lieux de mémoire. I, La République*, 353–378. Paris: Gallimard.

Portes, Jacques. 1990. *Une fascination réticente: Les Etats-Unis dans l'opinion française*. Nancy: Presses Universitaires de Nancy.

Pyenson, Lewis. 1977. "'Who the Guys Were': Prosopography in the History of Science." *History of Science* 15, 103–108.

Pyenson, Lewis. 1985. *Cultural Imperialism and Exact Sciences: German Expansion Overseas 1900–1930*. New York: P. Lang.

Pyenson, Lewis. 1993. *Civilizing Mission: Exact Sciences and French Overseas Expansion (1830–1940)*. Baltimore: Johns Hopkins University Press.

Raphael, Lutz. 1996. "Die Verwissenschaftlichung des Sozialen als methodische und konzeptionelle Herausforderung für eine Sozialgeschichte des 20. Jahrhunderts." *Geschichte und Gesellschaft* 22, 165–193.

*Rapport sur l'organisation et la situation de l'enseignement primaire public en France*. 1900. Paris: Imprimerie Nationale.

*Recueil des monographies pédagogiques publiées à l'occasion de l'Exposition universelle de 1889*. 1889. Paris: Imprimerie nationale.

Reese, William J. 1995. *The Origins of the American High School*. New Haven: Yale University Press.

Reinalda, Bob. 2009. *Routledge History of International Organizations: From 1815 to the Present Day*. London: Routledge.

*Reports to the General Assembly of Illinois at Its Thirty-First Regular Session Convened January 8, 1879*. 1879. Springfield: Weber & Co.

Revel, Jacques. 1996. "Micro-analyse et construction du social." *Jeux d'échelles. La micro-analyse de l'expérience*, 15–36. Paris: Gallimard.

Rosental, Paul-André. 1990. "Maintien/rupture: Un nouveau couple pour l'analyse des migrations." *Annales ESC* 6, 1403–1431.

Saunier, Pierre-Yves. 1999. "Changing the City: Urban International Information and the Lyon Municipality, 1900–1940." *Planning Perspectives* 14, 19–48.

Saunier, Pierre-Yves. 2008. "Les régimes circulatoires du domaine social 1800–1940: Projets et ingénierie de la convergence et de la difference." *Genèses* 71, 4–25.

Siegrist, Hannes, ed. 1988. *Bürgerliche Berufe: zur Sozialgeschichte der freien und akademischen Berufe im internationalen Vergleich*. Göttingen: Vandenhoeck & Ruprecht.

Sobe, Noah. 2007. "Attention and Spectatorship: Educational Exhibits at the Panama-Pacific International Exposition, San Francisco 1915." In *Innovation and Education in Expos/ Innovation et Education dans les Expos. 75th anniversary of the BIE/75ème anniversaire du BIE*, edited by Volker Barth, 97–115. Paris: BIE.

Stone, Laurence. 1972. "Prosopography." In *Historical Studies Today*, edited by Felix Gilbert and Stephen R. Graubard, 107–140. New York: Norton.

Toméi, Samuel. 2004. *Ferdinand Buisson (1841–1932): Protestantisme libéral, foi laïque et radical-socialisme, sous la direction de Serge Berstein*. Ph.D. Dissertation, Paris.

Tyack, David Bruce. 1974. *The One Best System: A History of American Urban Education*. Cambridge, MA: Harvard University Press.

Tyack, David Bruce and Elisabeth Hansot. 1982. *Managers of Virtue: Public School Leadership in America, 1820–1980*. New York: Basic Books.

Von Brocke, Bernhard. 1981. "Der deutsch-amerikanische Professorenaustausch. Preußische Wissenschaftspolitik, Internationale Wirtschaftsbeziehungen und die Anfänge einer deutschen auswärtigen Kulturpolitik vor dem Ersten Weltkrieg." *Zeitschrift für Kulturaustausch* 31, 128–182.

# Part IV
# Borders

# Chapter 9
# The Nation-State/Empire as a Unit of Analysis in the History of International Relations: A Case Study in Northeast Asia, 1868–1933

**Tomoko Akami**

**Abstract** In this chapter I propose the notion of the "nation state/empire" as a new way of conceptualising an actor in international politics, and as a basic unit in an analysis of international politics for the period between the late nineteenth century and 1945. The period is exemplary for two reasons. First, in the late nineteenth century, the nation state that was based on popular or national principles of legitimacy became prominent: at the same time, many nation states were competing for new colonial acquisitions. Second, as elaborated below, many empires retained formal colonies throughout the interwar period.

In the first section of the chapter I will demonstrate how this notion of the nation state/empire can be located in debates on the state system. Acknowledging a recent move to incorporate empire both as an idea and as an actor in analyses of international relations, the chapter nonetheless questions a still widely assumed dichotomy between the nation state and empire in these works, and suggests the need to see them as an integral unit. This also means the need to see the European state system and the extra European system as an integral whole. It argues that the international society of the time may be best understood not as a society of relatively equal national states, but as one composed of nation states/empires with diverse power. In the second section of this chapter I apply this notion whilst examining the international politics of Northeast Asia between the late nineteenth century and 1933. I see Japan as an empire in which the problem of the international society of nation states/empires was manifested.

---

This chapter is based on a paper presented at a seminar of the Cluster of Excellence"Asia and Europe"/History Department of the University of Heidelberg, 3 December 2009. I would like to thank Madeleine Herren and the Cluster Excellence for providing me with a research fellowship at the University of Heidelberg in October-December 2009. My thanks as well to Isabella Löhr and Roland Wenzlhuemer for this opportunity, and for their comments, so too my thanks to Urs Matthias Zachmann and Shogo Suzuki for their comments.

T. Akami (✉)
College of Asia and the Pacific
Australian National University, Canberra, Australia
e-mail: Tomoko.Akami@anu.edu.au

I. Löhr and R. Wenzlhuemer (eds.), *The Nation State and Beyond*, Transcultural Research – Heidelberg Studies on Asia and Europe in a Global Context,
DOI 10.1007/978-3-642-32934-0_9, © Springer-Verlag Berlin Heidelberg 2013

## Introduction

In this chapter I propose the notion of the 'nation-state/empire' as a new way of conceptualizing an actor in international politics, and as a basic unit in an analysis of international politics for the period between the late nineteenth century and 1945.[1] The period is exemplary for two reasons. First, in the late nineteenth century, the nation-state that was based on popular or national principles of legitimacy became prominent: at the same time, many nation-states were competing for new colonial acquisitions. Second, as elaborated below, many empires retained formal colonies throughout the inter-war period.

In the first section of the chapter I will demonstrate how this notion of the nation-state/empire can be located in debates on the state system. Acknowledging a recent move to incorporate empire both as an idea and as an actor in analyses of International Relations, the chapter nonetheless questions a still widely assumed dichotomy between the nation-state and empire in these works, and suggests the need to see them as an integral unit.[2] It argues that the international society of the time may be best to be understood not as a society of relatively equal national states, but as one composed of the nation-states/empires with diverse power. In the second section of this chapter I apply this notion whilst examining international politics of Northeast Asia between the late nineteenth century and 1933. I see Japan an empire in which the problem of the international society of nation-states/empires was manifested.

By using the notion of the nation-state/empire, the chapter pinpoints the two major themes of this book, 'beyond the nation-state' and 'the process of governing globalization'. First, the notion draws attention to the fact that many modern nation-states were empires, which contemporaries called "Great Powers", and whose boundaries went beyond the metropolitan nation (the nation where the imperial metropolitan centre was located). Their 'national' state was the imperial state which governed the territories beyond the metropolitan nation. These metropolitan national "centres" did not exist independently or separately from their colonial "peripheries", and the "peripheries" also shaped metropolitan national ideas and institutions, which in turn became the bases for global governance.

Second, this notion of the nation-state/empire emphasizes the role of not only the nation-states, but also empires in managing and governing what we now call the globalization process. Empire-building was a part of the development of the infrastructures for governing various trans-national movements of people, goods and money. Making and enacting on the international codes and norms for

---

[1] I have already used the notion of the nation-state/empire elsewhere. In 2002, I used the term in my analysis of Wilsonian internationalism in the Asia-Pacific region. In 2007, I further articulated the idea in the context of the debate on informal empire. See Akami 2002, 2007.

[2] On some important recent attempt, see Cox et al. (2001) and Jones (2006). They are mainly concerned with the relationship between empires and the Third World. This perspective probably also explains why these works still largely assume the dual systems of the "West" and "non-West".

managing these issues was, therefore, not only an inter-national exercise (among independent nation-states), but also intra-empire (imperial/colonial matters) or inter-empire exercise (among empires). This meant that the making of global norms involved both the concern of empires' colonial governance and inter-empire politics.

While this nexus of the nation-state and empire has been largely neglected in mainstream works on globalization, the Introduction and following chapters of this book demonstrate how empires have been present at various levels of inter-"national" and trans-"national" actions. Mueller-Pohl and Ellis discuss the convergence of national and imperial interests respectively in the areas of cable networks and educational networks. The other authors suggest that "inter-national" or "trans-national" projects were indeed "imperial", "inter-empire", or "trans-empire". Thiemeyer, for example, shows how the development of an international monetary union in Europe could be understood as a French empire project. Casteel argues that a German project in Siberia was "transnational" and "imperial", whilst Ewing also discusses "inter-empire" alliances against cable radicalism in the Middle East.

As the Introduction and each of the chapters make clear, this book reflects a shift in historical studies from compartmentalization and essentialization to multi-layered inter-connectivity. The notion of the nation-state/empire epitomizes this very point, focusing in particular on the mutually constitutive relationship between metropolitan centres and the colonial peripheries. The idea is mainly inspired by recent scholarship on empire and post-colonialism. Unlike Hannah Arendt, who in 1951 argued that European empires' colonial activities little affected their metropolitan structures of politics and law,[3] Ronald Robinson suggested in 1986 an asymmetrical, yet still two-way relationship between the metropolitan state and colonial collaborators.[4] While Robinson called such a view "eccentric" in 1986, by 2002 Catherine Hall summarized a recent trend in post-colonial literature as:

> The idea that colonies and their peoples were made by the colonizers was of course nothing new: what was new was the argument that this relationship went both ways, even if in unequal relations of power.[5]

I am, however, not proposing the notion of the nation-state/empire in order to examine cultural and social aspects of these entanglements between the metropolitan centres and the colonial peripheries. Excellent works have already done in this area, as discussed in the Introduction. Instead of this, by using this concept of the nation-state/empire in a historical case study, I want to suggest that the idea that the European system and the extra-European system existed in parallel is historically inaccurate. Furthermore, the notion of the nation-state/empire questions the assumption that the International Society was comprised of "liberal" and "democratic" nation-states. More specifically, it questions an assumption that "liberal"

---

[3] Arendt noted: "It is characteristic of imperialism that national institutions remain separate from the colonial administration"; Arendt 1951, p. 131.

[4] Robinson 1986, pp. 267–89.

[5] Hall 2002, p. 2.

ideas and institutions, which became the basis of the global governance system, were formed within the metropolitan centres internally, *and then* applied to the rest of the world. In contrast, the notion (nation-state/empire) put forward here allows us to see that colonial peripheries were constitutive elements of metropolitan "liberal" ideas and institutions, that metropolitan actors had complex motivations, and that the global norms derived from these metropolitan/colonial ideas had ambivalent impacts on the people beyond the metropolitan nations.[6]

In this chapter, the nation-state/empire is treated as an actor and a basic unit in international politics during the historically specified period, and is to be distinguished from imperialism. The chapter's focus is the state. It suggests that the modern state was often not only the national state that governed the nation, but also the imperial state that governed its formal colonies. This national/imperial state had a physically defined territory, an entity that I am calling the nation-state/empire. By empire, therefore, I do not mean certain kinds of power relations in which the centre of power is unclear, as Negri and Hardt have suggested,[7] but a formal empire with a formal colony or colonies that the imperial state gained by treaties and/or military conquests.[8] Imperialism here is understood as the specific nature and/or idea of the policy of a certain political regime. This was based on asymmetrical economic and political power relations, and was backed by the use of force or at least the threat of using force.[9]

Accordingly, the political regime, which conducted an imperialistic policy, as this chapter will elaborate, further, might not have had a formal colony. In other words, a non-formal empire, like the Japanese state before 1894, conducted an imperialistic policy. Furthermore, even metropolitan states, which possessed formal colonies, condemned other states' imperialistic nature and/or policies. Examples include the Allied powers' criticism of the Central Powers during the First World War, and the U.S.'s criticism of Japanese aggression in Northeast China (then called Manchuria) in 1931–1932.

Lastly, the terminology, nation-state/empire, suggests that analysis is made from the perspective of the colonizer, not the colonized. This concept is, however, relational in the sense that empires could not exist without their less powerful counterparts.[10] I use this concept, therefore, in order to present a critical view of, not to accept and justify, the power hierarchy among the nation-states.

---

[6] Semmel, for example, examined the connection between ideas of radical metropolitan social reform and its imperialist foreign and military policy. Semmel 1960.

[7] Hardt and Negri 2000.

[8] For a definition of formal and informal empires, see Gallagher and Robinson 1953. For further debates on formal and informal empires and the use of the terminology beyond 1945, see the essays in Mommsen and Osterhammel 1986.

[9] The term 'imperialism' is often used for 'new imperialism' of European Empires after the 1880s, while others understand it more broadly. See Mommsen 1981; Chilcote 2000.

[10] Akami 2007, pp. 34 f.

## Empire Versus the Nation-State in the Discourse of International Relations

Hitherto the nexus of the nation-state and empire has been largely neglected in the discourse of international relations. This is even more pronounced when we analyse international politics between the late nineteenth century and 1945, the crucial transitional stage to decolonization in our human history. Here instead, empire has often been understood in opposition to the nation-state. Arendt, for example, regarded imperialism as the ideology of an empire that was inherently expansionist, and argued that "this expansionist movement ... could only destroy the political body of the nation-state".[11] Such a view has been dominant in critical scholarship, which regarded empires as oppressors and exploiters of weaker actors. Indeed, lesser political entities and nations resisted imperial rule, and many national states were created when they became independent from the empires in Europe after the First World War, and in Asia, Africa and the Pacific after the end of the Second World War.

Orthodox scholarship of international relations has also accepted such a dichotomy. Stanley Hoffmann, for example, noted that

> all theorists of international relations have taken for granted the notion of a 'system of states' ... The dichotomy in their minds has been: systems of several states versus imperial systems.[12]

As a result, analyses of the state system had to a large extent not incorporated empires.[13] Hedley Bull's 'International Society' is one such example. He defined international society as follows:

> [A] group of states, conscious of certain common interests and common values, [that] form a society in the sense that they conceive themselves to be bound by a common set of rules in their relations with one another, and share in the working of common institutions.[14]

For Bull, the state "possesses a government and asserts sovereignty in relation to a particular portion of the earth's surface and a particular segment of the human population".[15]

Although he does not exclude empires as a variation of the state,[16] empires disappear from his discussion on the historical development of an international

[11] Arendt 1951, p. 125.

[12] Hoffmann 2002, p. xxviii.

[13] This is not to say that a hierarchical aspect of international politics has been ignored: cf. Clark 1989; here, hierarchy is understood as a structural mechanism for reform, and its focus was the hierarchy among independent states.

[14] Bull 2002, p. 13.

[15] Ibid., p. 8.

[16] Bull's states included not only city-states, dynastic absolutist states, and nation-states based on "popular or national principles of legitimacy", but also empires – "multinational states, such as European empires of the nineteenth century" and "the oceanic imperial states of Western Europe". Bull 2002, pp. 8 f.

society in the nineteenth century. In this development, he suggests, the ideas and realities of the international society emerged in Europe as a Christian International Society, and developed into European International Society.[17] He argues:

> By the nineteenth century the orthodox doctrine of the positivist international lawyers was that international society was a European association, to which non-European states could be admitted only if and when they met a standard of civilization laid down by the Europeans.[18]

To an extent Bull regrets a receding universalistic element, but accepts this development as the reality of the time. The premise was then set as: the European International Society of states "existed out there" by the time of the nineteenth century.[19] Accordingly, subsequent works on the International Society (the English School) were concerned with the two main questions: "when was each extra-European state drawn and accepted into the *expanding* European society, and how?" (emphasis added).[20]

This premise was based on three related assumptions in which the 'empire' aspect of the European states has been largely neglected. First, the International Society was composed of European nation-states. Second, this Society existed *independently* from the outside world: it had emerged first in Europe, and *then expanded* into the rest of the world. Third, these nation-states developed advanced civilizations internally within Europe, and independently from the rest of the world.

By the late nineteenth century, however, many of the European metropolitan states were already global. They had formal and informal colonies beyond Europe, and in the late nineteenth century they went into a new phase of colonization. Meanwhile, Europe had been defining itself not internally, but in relation to "new worlds".[21] Furthermore, its metropolitan life-styles, infrastructures, economic and social developments had long been funded and even shaped by exploitive interactions with its formal and informal colonies. As Stuart Hall reminds us, what we think most essentially English, the 'English' cup of tea, was a product not of the British nation, but its colonies.[22]

The idea of the expansion of the International Society, therefore, neglects these elements of empire, as well as the fact that this European international society was the society of the nation-states/empires. Instead, European (and American) empires

---

[17] Ibid., pp. 26–36.

[18] Ibid., p. 32.

[19] Although Onuma is generally critical of Bull's idea, he agrees on this point. Onuma 2000, pp. 63 f.

[20] Zhang 1991, p. 3. The most significant works in this tradition are Bull and Watson 1984 and Gong 1984.

[21] Hall 1992, pp. 289 ff.

[22] Hall 1991, pp. 48 f. The British merchants smuggled opium to China via India to pay off their debts for tea leaves, the production of which was then taken over by the plantations in the British colonies of India and Sri Lanka. Sugar had been produced in the Caribbean islands by slave labour, and the British (as well as the Swedish, French and Dutch) ended this system only in the mid-nineteenth century, when it was then taken over by cheap 'local' labour.

were often termed collectively the 'West', which was viewed not as an oppressor, but as a positive agent of political and economic modernization and liberalization of the 'extra-European' world.[23]

Criticism of this orthodox view is not absent in the literature of International Relations. Stephen Krasner argues that "the idea that states ought to be autonomous, free from external intervention, was only developed as an explicit principle" in the late eighteenth century, and that breaches of this sovereignty state model have been more a norm than an exception.[24] By examining major treaties made between 1648 and 2001,[25] he has demonstrated how this model has been violated in four ways: conventions, contract, coercion and imposition.

Although Krasner does not refer to empire here, by doing so, one can explain two of these types of violation. First, Krasner defines 'convention' as the following:

> During the nineteenth century, the domestic autonomy of all of the successor states to the Ottoman Empire as well as many Latin American countries was compromised through contractual arrangements involving international loans.[26]

European nation-states/empires made these contractual arrangements, and they did so in the areas trade as well as finance. Historians understood such unequal trade treaties as the basis of the British "informal empire of free trade",[27] while others applied this notion of informal empire to the other empires.

Second, Krasner defines violation by means of coercion and imposition, as follows:

> Coercion occurs when rulers in one state threaten to impose sanctions unless their counterparts in another compromise their domestic autonomy ... Imposition occurs when the rulers or would-be rulers of a target state have no choice: they are so weak that they must accept domestic structures, policies, or personnel preferred by more powerful actors or else be eliminated. When applied against states, coercion and imposition are violations of international legal as well as the Vattelian sovereignty. When applied against the would-be rulers of not yet created states, coercion and imposition are violations of the sovereignty state model ... *but not violations of international legal sovereignty* ... (emphasis added).[28]

The above pattern fits well the relationships between Euro-American empires and weaker states or with their formal colonies (would-be states) in the late nineteenth and first two decades of the twentieth century. The empires legitimized colonization of these "weak states" or "non-states" after the use of force through

[23] On the historical process of positive values being associated with the idea of the 'West', see Roberts 1985. Cynics might suspect that the term had been invented in order to cover up unsavoury aspects of the empires' extra-European doings. On the ideas of the West in the discourse of International Relations, see O'Hagan 2002.

[24] Krasner 2001, p. 17. This state sovereignty model was developed by the Swiss international lawyer Emmerich de Vattel, and in his view the model has been "a cognitive script: its basic rules are widely understood but also frequently violated".

[25] Treaties selected are: Westphalia, Utrecht, Vienna, Versailles, Helsinki, and Dayton.

[26] Krasner 2001, pp. 26, 28.

[27] Gallagher and Robinson 1953, pp. 11 f.

[28] Krasner 2001, pp. 30 f.

internationally accepted (among empires) legal documents that assumed "limited sovereignty" of weaker counterparts.[29]

One can even argue that a similar violation of sovereignty could have happened within the nation-state, and see the making of the nation-state as a process of internal colonization. Nation-state creation was often the process of making a dominant nation *the* nation among many nations within the territorial boundary of a certain state. As a result, lesser nations within this territory became 'minority groups'.

The 'pure' nation-state with no history of possessing formal colonies, or of being colonized, has rarely existed in international history. Most nation-states experienced some degree of internal colonization in their making. The pure nation-state is, therefore, an ideal prototype, rather than representative of a majority. Most nation-states contained imperial/colonial constituents within their territorial boundaries.

Other criticism of the idea of the International Society has come from scholars of International Relations, who reflect recent debates on empire and postcolonialism. Edward Keene, for example, stressed that imperial/colonial relationship as a critical factor in the idea of Grotius's international law. He argued that Bull's notion of the International Society had focused on the European state-system, and neglected "the other pattern of order, which developed roughly simultaneously in the colonial and imperial systems that were established beyond Europe".[30] Scholars of international law, such as Antony Anghie and Wilhelm Grewe, also argue for the centrality of empire, not the nation-state, in the development of international law.[31] Their works also indicate that colonialism was a crucial and integral part of the development of ideas and institutions for global governance.

[29] One of the most influential works of international law in the late nineteenth century noted, "Some States are completely sovereign and independent ... The sovereignty of other States is limited and qualified in various degrees"; Wheaton (as 1936), p. 44. Wheaton's book was first published in 1836, and in 1936, the book was described as "a classic in the literature of International Law" by James Brown Scott. Scott ("Preface", in ibid., p. 6a). The same phrase was also included in the 1904 version (Wheaton 1904, p. 51). For the case of Africa, a leading British international law expert noted in 1894 that it was unthinkable to bestow "uncivilized natives" with sovereignty, as cited in Koskenniemi 2002, p. 127.

[30] Keene 2002, p. xi. For a critical assessment of the problem of post-colonialism in International Relations, see Bain 2003.

[31] Grewe argued this point in 1944, and 1984 (second edition) in his German publication, which was translated into English in 2000; Grewe 2000, pp. 23–29. Part Two, Chap. 8 discussed in particular the Spanish-Portuguese negotiations and Vitoria, while later chapters dealt with the French and British empires and international law; ibid., pp. 240 ff. I would like to thank Zachmann for his insight into Grewe's works. While Grewe's argument was more to legitimize the anticipated German phase of international law, recent critical works on international law were influenced by post-colonialism. Anghie argued that although the idea of international law as a tool of colonialism had been well established by 2005, his new point was that colonialism was central in the development of international law. Anghie 2005, pp. 2 f. In addition to politics of dominant empires, Clark pointed out the other critical factor which contributed to norm changes, the role of the "public conscience" of World Society; Clark 2007, pp. 1–9.

To argue that empire was a crucial factor in the making of international codes and norms for global governance, however, is not the same as to understand empire as an integral component of the nation-state. Despite recent critical work, it is still common to see the European system and the extra-European system being portrayed separate, not integral. It is also common to find neglected the complex roles and impacts of empires in international politics between the late nineteenth century and 1945. Krasner, for example, does not refer to Euro-American empires of this period when he discusses the violation of state sovereignty. Instead, he draws attention to how these "great powers" acted for a progressive cause, such as "[securing] minority rights in eastern and central Europe" in 1832, 1878 and 1919.[32]

Let us now apply the notion of the nation-state/empire to Northeast Asia in this rather neglected period.

## The International Society of the Nation-States/Empires in Northeast Asia

### *Before 1919: The Making of the Meiji Nation-State/Empire*

It is not difficult to incorporate empire in an analysis of international politics between the mid-nineteenth century and 1919. What is difficult is to understand the metropolitan state's formal colonization process as an integral part of the nation-state-making in metropolitan centres, which included the development of greater popular political participation.

In the context of Northeast Asia, most scholars do agree that imperialism was the defining factor for international politics during this period. They regard European powers not as democratic nation-states, but as exploitive empires, and saw that Japan "imitated Western imperialism", although its imperialism was "different from Western imperialism".[33] In contrast, scholars of the English School have understood the period as one of the "expansion of the European International Society" into Northeast Asia, and of the "socialization" of the states in the region

[32] Krasner 2001, pp. 32 f. Krasner concluded with three reasons why this "organized hypocrisy" of violating state sovereignty has been characteristic of international relations. First, actors, by which he distinguished state from empire, "have different levels of power". Second, "rulers ... will be responsible to different domestic norms", to which they are more bound than they are to international obligations. Third, when more than one rule exists in an international context, "there is no authority structure" to decide which rule is to be applied; ibid., p. 42. Clark notes the role of the Great Powers, and uses the notion of hegemony as an institution to understand the power hierarchy of the International Society; Clark 2011, pp. 203–28.

[33] Beasley 1991, p. 6; Peattie 1984, pp. 6–15; Peattie 1988, p. 217. Peattie's point, however, was made in reference to European maritime empires, and he noted that this distinction could not be made between the imperialism of Japan and that of other continental European empires; Peattie 1984, p. 14.

to this Society. The European nation-states that constituted this Society, as they see it, were agents of modernization and civilization, not oppressors of the regional states.[34] One of the most recent works from this school by Suzuki Shogo, however, acknowledges that the English School had neglected the empire element. He argues that socialization meant learning "imperialistic behaviour as well as the 'standard of [European] civilization'".[35]

The point I would like to stress is that this idea of the "standard of civilization" was not contradictory to "imperialistic behaviour", but they were integral parts of colonization. Here it is useful to understand history of international law as the development of the law for nation-states/empires. In the nineteenth century, so-called international law experts recognized military conquest as an accepted state action,[36] and international law not only regulated these actions, but also legitimized the result of the use of force in post-conflict settlements. The rhetoric of civilization was a crucial factor in this process. As one of the most influential works of international law of the time, Henry Wheaton's *Elements of International Law* (first published in 1836), made clear, only "civilized" nations shared the ideas of reason and justice on which international law was based.[37]

To be sure, certain international law experts tried to promote humanitarianism inspired by natural-law on behalf of the "uncivilized". They did not, however, regard "uncivilized" nations as being equal to "civilized" nations. Civilized nations, which were recognized only in the presence of uncivilized nations, were imperial nations (the nation-states/empires). These metropolitan international law experts tried to regulate and manage their empires' colonial activities. In this process, while they maintained humanitarian concerns with "uncivilized natives", they ultimately legitimized their states' colonial activities either reluctantly or unwittingly.[38] Koskenniemi points out the irony: these experts advocated the establishment of creating a formal colonial administration as a means of protecting "natives" against uncontrolled private colonial activities in the 1880s.[39] A comment by a leading British international law expert, John Westlake, summarized this point in 1894:

> International law has to treat natives as uncivilized. It regulates, for the mutual benefit of the civilized states, the claims that they make to sovereignty over the region and leaves the treatment of the natives to the conscience of the state to which sovereignty is awarded.[40]

---

[34] Watson 1984, pp. 27, 29, 30. Such a view was also common in works which applied modernization theory to the case of Japan. Reischauer and Craig 1989.

[35] Suzuki 2009, pp. 20–25, 27.

[36] Wheaton (1866) 1936, p. 33. The point was also included in the 1904 edition; Wheaton 1904, p. 38.

[37] Wheaton (1866) 1936, p. 20. The point was also included in the 1904 edition; Wheaton 1904, p. 24.

[38] On this ambivalence among international law experts between being an advocate for universal humanitarianism and a legitimizer of colonialism, see Koskenniemi 2002, chap. 1 and 2.

[39] Ibid., pp. 143 ff.

[40] Cited in ibid., p. 127.

The "uncivilized" nature of "natives" justified empires in dictating the their lives for them. The consequences of the actions of metropolitan liberal legal experts, therefore, might not have been so much the empowerment of the "natives", as the preservation of the interests of empires.

The Meiji state (the Japanese state in the Meiji period, 1868–1912) emerged into this international politics governed by the international law of the nation-states/empires. It was a 'weaker state' located to the far east of Europe and the East Coast of the U.S.

When the Meiji state took power from the Shogunate in 1868,[41] it was not an empire yet in the sense that it did not have a formal colony. In January 1868, the Meiji state declared itself to the other empires which already had diplomatic relations with the previous Shogunate state: the new Meiji state restored the emperor (*Tennō*) as the political head of the state (*Ōsei fukko*).[42] In 1868, however, the emperor had no empire. The diplomatic documents of the first two decades of the Meiji period indeed referred to the Meiji state not as the Japanese empire, but either as the Japanese state (*Nihon koku*), the Japanese government (*Nihon seifu*) or occasionally Great Japan (*Dai Nihon*).[43]

The Japanese state started to call itself an empire before it had a formal colony, in order to be treated equally in international law, which was defined by the nation-states/empires. The first diplomatic document that used the term 'the Japanese Empire' (*Nihon teikoku*) appeared in June 1886, still almost a decade before the Meiji state gained its first formal colony. The use of this new term reflected the Meiji state's conscious quest to be treated equally with Euro-American nation-states/empires in international law. This 1886 document was concerned with treaty reform with the relevant empires,[44] marking a new phase of treaty reform negotiations that had begun a month earlier.[45] Three years later, in 1889, *Nihon teikoku* became the official term for the Japanese state, when the Meiji Constitution (*Nihon teikoku kenpô* or the constitution of the Japanese empire) was proclaimed. The Meiji state, however, still had no formal colony at this time.

Despite the use of the term 'empire' in legal documents, one could argue that the Meiji state was an informal colony of free trade with the treaty empires. The previous Shogunate government (1603–1868) had entered into bilateral treaties with other empires (the U.S., Britain, France, the Netherlands and Russia) in 1854–1855. These treaties were followed by the Treaty of Amity and Commerce:

---

[41] This was the same period as the national integration of Italy in 1870, and Germany in 1871.

[42] "Kaikoku washin no hōshin o tsuguru chokugo" 1 January 1868, "Taisei fukko o rekkoku ni hōzuru kokusho" 10 January 1868, in: Kodama et al. 1991, pp. 118f.

[43] A survey of the 50 main diplomatic documents between 1854 and 1886 shows that *Kōtei*, a generic term for an emperor, was used, and not the specific Japanese term, *Tennō*. Gaimushō 1955, pp. 1–106.

[44] "Eidoku gōan jōyakusho" (an agreement between Britain and Germany on the reform of the [unequal] treaty), 15 June 1886, reprinted in Gaimushô 1955, pp. 107–111.

[45] On 1 May 1886, Foreign Minister Inoue Kaoru held the first conference for treaty reform with the heads of the missions of the treaty powers in Tokyo.

it was formed with each of these empires in 1858, and inherited by the Meiji government in 1868. Each treaty included two major unequal clauses: Japan had no tariff right over the goods of the treaty empires; and their residents came under their consulate jurisdiction).

Gallagher and Robinson regarded such unequal trade clauses as the basis of the British informal empire.[46] These treaties complied with an international legal framework that was accepted among the nation-states/empires of the time. The Meiji state had no choice but to enter this framework as a lesser partner.[47]

For the Meiji state, a repeal of these unequal clauses meant becoming an equal nation-state/empire (Great Powers: *Rekkyō*). Shortly after notifying the establishment of the new state to the treaty empires, it issued a chartered statement on foreign policy to the domestic public in January 1868.[48] Its foreign policy principle was "to open a country and cooperate [with other powers]" (*Kaikoku washin*).[49] Here, repealing the unequal treaty clauses was clearly the new state's most significant foreign policy objective, and it recognized that to achieve this military might have to be accompanied by knowledge and skill in international law.[50] It is symbolic that after the Meiji state annexed Korea (1910) it repealed all these unequal clauses (1911).[51] A civilized state, therefore, meant a mighty state and an empire, and this combination made a newcomer state legally accepted as equal to the other nation-states/empires.

In 1868, the Meiji state fully understood the dual nature of the international law of nation-states/empires. Henry Wheaton's *Elements of International Law* had been translated into Japanese and was read among the Meiji elite. On one hand, the Meiji elite realized that international law was a significant and necessary tool for enhancing the status of a lesser country, such as Japan.[52] On the other hand, they understood that international law was created by and worked for Euro-American empires.[53] In late 1868, therefore, a leading member of the Meiji oligarchy noted

---

[46] Gallagher and Robinson 1953, pp. 11 f.

[47] Auslin 2004, p. 148. Auslin indicates that the new treaty which the Meiji state concluded with the Austro-Hungarian Empire in 1869 further clarified Japan's status as an informal colony of free trade to the 14 treaty powers; ibid., p. 162.

[48] This was 2 months earlier than the famous Chartered Oath on the principle of domestic governance (14 March 1868).

[49] "Kaikoku washin no hōshin o tsuguru chokugo", 1 January 1868, reprinted and compiled in Kodama 1991, pp. 118 f.

[50] Its three stated goals were: first, it would reform the unequal treaties; second, it would build up military capacity and increase national prestige; and third, it would comply with international law; idem.

[51] All the consulate jurisdiction clauses were repealed in 1899, and the tariff right was restored to Japan in 1911.

[52] Yamamuro 2002, p. 598.

[53] It was first translated in China, and then introduced to Japan and Korea; in Japan, it became a textbook on international law in schools in various places after 1865, and after the Meiji Restoration, it was studied in schools and universities. Yamamuro 2002, pp. 222 ff.

that "international law (*Bankoku kōhō*) was a tool to exploit the weak".[54] The Meiji state was soon to use this tool in its colonization process.

As the Meiji state did not have a formal empire, it was also not a nation-state in the sense that it was not governed by the principle of popular legitimacy until 1889. Since it sought to be modern and civilized, it began drastic domestic reforms in its first few years. It soon achieved this goal, and emerged with modern economic, financial and education systems, a standing military, and transportation and telecommunication networks.[55] Yet the Meiji state was still dominated by the new oligarchy (*Hanbatsu*) that led the fall of the Shogunate government. They soon, however, took a path to constitutional monarchy and parliamentary democracy.

They desired to be equal with the other powers, but domestic factors also contributed to the oligarchy's decision to move to parliamentary democracy. The oligarchy was concerned with the survival of the state. In the first two decades of its rule, the Meiji state faced fierce opposition. There were *samurai* rebellions and numerous riots against land tax and conscription, many of which were violent.[56] Former *samurai*s who missed out on becoming a part of the oligarchy also mobilized broader anti-oligarchy government forces. In the mid-1870s they pressured the government to open the political process to a "popular" election. As a result, the government promised to create a constitution, and began to prepare drafting it in 1876. The oligarchy understood bourgeois revolutions as a dominant and irreversible world trend. It was inevitable, they concluded, that all regimes throughout the world sooner or later had to abandon absolutism and "share political power with the people (*jinmin to seiji no ken o wakatsu*)".[57] In 1881, the oligarchic government promised the establishment of a national representative assembly (and a general election) in 10 years' time.

As a result, by 1890 the Meiji state had become a modern nation-state, with a political regime as democratic and as authoritarian as many contemporary European constitutional monarchies. The Meiji oligarchic government tried to

[54] Kido Takayoshi's diary entry of 8 November 1868, cited in Yamamuro 2002, p. 598. In 1874, a textbook in what became the Tokyo Imperial University even called international law "Rekkoku kôsaihô" (law of intercourse among the powers). Ibid., p. 224.

[55] The Meiji state abolished the old status system (1868–1872), introduced the new currency (1871), established the national banking system (1872), reformed the land tax (1873, 1877) and promoted industries; it began the new school system (1872, then reformed this in 1879 and 1886) and towards the end of the Meiji era (1912) it achieved a 98 % school attendance rate (for boys, 99 % and for girls, 97 %). The Meiji state also established conscription (1873), whilst the central government structure was reformed in 1873. The Home Ministry that supervised the police force and local governments was founded later that year. It also began to build modern national transportation and communication networks (telegraph, from 1869, postal service, from 1871, railway, from 1872) while also developing shipping services.

[56] More than a 100 such riots were listed in the official records, both in 1869 (110) and 1884 (167); Aoki 1994, p. 335.

[57] Itō Hirobumi's note on constitutional government of 19 March 1880 in Kaneko 1943, p. 194.

preserve its power against elective bodies,[58] and modelled its constitution on that of Prussia to achieve this goal. It declared the Meiji Constitution in 1889. While the constitution limited the power of the Diet[59] and the Cabinet, it nonetheless established a constitutional monarchy, and parliamentary democracy had begun.[60] In 1890, the first general election took place, in which 1.1 % of the whole population was able to vote.[61]

Could this Meiji nation-state have become just a nation-state without becoming an empire? Meiji policy-makers conceived the idea of a buffer zone to protect the sovereignty of the Japanese state from other empires' advances. This could be formed either by the internal colonization of these areas to become a part of the nation-state, or external colonization as a part of the formal empire.

According to Yamamuro Shin'ichi, such an idea of a buffer zone had emerged already in 1786. This was almost 70 years before Commodore Perry's arrival in Tokyo Bay, and a century earlier than the Meiji Restoration. At this time of the late eighteenth century, the Shogunate government and certain regional domain (*Han*) governments in Japan were aware of foreign threats: Russian advancement in the North, and French and British colonial expansion into Asia. As a result, books on defence policy began to emerge, and in 1786, one of these pioneering experts, Hayashi Shihei, wrote *Sangoku tsūran zusetsu* (Illustrated survey of the three poles [of the West, China and Japan]). In this book, he argued that Japan needed to annex the northern island (*Ezo*), the southern islands (the Ryūkyū Kingdom), and Korea as a buffer zone in case these other empires tried to invade Japan by allying with China.[62]

Hayashi's idea that Japan needed outposts nearby to secure its independence was a piece of geopolitical wisdom, something military strategists did not have to "learn from the West", but "saw". A similar idea was apparent among Meiji politicians. In 1890, Yamagata Aritomo, the so-called father of Japan's modern army and one of the most prominent members of the oligarchy, became Prime Minister after the first general election. In his speech at the first Imperial Diet, Prime Minister Yamagata justified the defence budget, and argued that in order to defend the independence of the state against mighty powers (*Rekkoku*), it needed to secure not only its

[58] It issued the order to create the peers (1884) as a preparation for establishing the (non-elective) House of Peers, and set up the Cabinet system (1885) and the (non-elective) Privy Council (1888).

[59] The Meiji Imperial Diet had two houses, the House of Peers and the House of Representatives.

[60] All political actors, including the emperor, were now bound to the constitutional process and to his ministers' counsel; Mitani argues that the Emperor's prerogative was meant to act as an integrating force for these multiple power centres, but in reality it was entrusted to, and shared among these power centres; Mitani 1988, p. 60. The Constitution became the centrepiece of Japan's modern legal system, which included the Criminal Codes (1880) and the Civil Codes (1899).

[61] The percentage increased as the electorate was expanded; in 1900, it was 2.2 %, 1919, 5.5 %, 1925, 20.8 %, and finally it reached 50.4 % in 1945 when the universal (male and female) franchise was realized.

[62] Yamamuro 2002, pp. 581 f.

sovereignty border (*Shuken sen*) but also its interest border (*Rieki sen*), which was "closely connected to the security (*Anpi*) of the sovereignty border".[63] For Yamagata, this interest border meant Korea.

In order to secure such a buffer/interest zone, the Japanese state needed to take control of the area. This, however, did not necessarily have to take the form of external colonization. The state could colonize an area and integrate it into the nation-state (internal colonization). By 1890 when Yamagata made the above speech, this was what the Meiji state had done on the northern front (Ezo) and the southern front (Ryūkyū Kingdom). The internal colonization in the south, however, challenged China's suzerainty over the Ryūkyū Kingdom. Only after Japan's military victory over China in 1895, therefore, did Okinawa (a new prefecture name for the former Ryūkyū Kingdom) become 'internationally' recognized as a part of the Meiji 'nation-state'.[64] By 1890, the only missing buffer zone for the Meiji state was Korea.

Korea, however, could not become a part of the Japanese nation-state. Here, the Meiji state first had to eliminate China's suzerain right to control Korea, and it was the victory in this war with China, which made the Meiji state a formal empire, because Taiwan (not Korea) became Japan's first formal colony (1895).[65]

[63] Yamagata Aritomo's speech, 6 December 1890, reprinted in Dai-Nihon Teikoku Gikaishi Kankōkai 1926, p. 469. This point has been well discussed among scholars. See, for example, Jansen 1984, p. 67.

[64] Immediately after declaring the change of regime to the treaty empires, the Meiji state began formalizing its territorial border with Russia in the north (1869) and in the south (1871); it renamed Ezo 'Hokkaido', and sent settlers from the mainland to claim this land against Russian advancement. Being concerned about the intervention of other powers, especially the U.S., it also asserted its authority over Ryūkyū, which had been under both the Satsuma domain of Japan and the Qing dynasty in the Shogunate days; against the opposition of the Qing dynasty and the Ryūkyū Kingdom, Ryūkyū was formally integrated into the Meiji nation-state as Okinawa Prefecture in 1879. In similar fashion, Hokkaido became a part of the Meiji nation-state in 1886; Qing China, however, continued to claim its suzerain power over what was now Okinawa, and it was only after 1895 that the Meiji state took full legal control there. On making people in Ryūkyū and Ezo Japanese nationals, see Morris-Suzuki 1998, pp. 23–28.

[65] In 1895, the Meiji state failed to take possession of the Liaodong Peninsula in China because of the Triple Intervention of Russia, France and Germany. The Meiji state's first 'external' military expedition was to Taiwan in 1874 (still under the suzerainty of the Qing dynasty). According to McWilliams, then Foreign Minister Soejima Taneomi did indeed have colonial ambition towards Taiwan as well as to Korea in 1873–1874, although his vision was not realized as he was defeated politically beforehand. McWilliams 1975, pp. 238, 274 f. Significantly, in 1873, Soejima argued that the lack of China's control over indigenous tribes in Taiwan meant that China's suzerainty did not extend to a certain part of Taiwan, and he justified Japan's military expedition to Taiwan in 1874 as 'punishing' their violence against people in Ryūkyū. The expedition was intended to establish the Meiji state's claim over Ryūkyū. Suzuki has also stressed Japan's colonial intentions, not only with regard to military conquests over Taiwan, but to demonstrate Japan's prestige as a civilizing empire; Suzuki 2009, pp. 147–52.

The Japanese 'empire' now added substance to its name,[66] and became a nation-state/empire.

Colonization of Korea was not an absolute necessity in order to maintain the independence of the Meiji nation-state, at least in the minds of some of the Meiji elite. The first alternative was an alliance among the three independent states (Japan, Korea and China) against other empires, an idea already conceived in 1862.[67] Soon after the Meiji Restoration, the Meiji state concluded a treaty with the Qing dynasty (1871) with both parties being seen as equal and independent states. The treaty was, however, not a military alliance, nor did it indicate both states' commitment to the state sovereignty system.[68] The idea of an East Asian alliance remained the hope of a minority, and by the turn of the century Meiji officials even dismissed the idea as 'damaging' for its treaty reform negotiation with other empires.[69]

The second alternative was to control Korea under joint management with the Russian empire. According to Zachmann, the idea that the Meiji state should have a military alliance with another empire emerged after Japan's victory over China (1895), although there was no consensus on which empire this partner should be.[70] In late 1901, Itō Hirobumi (recently Prime Minister for a fourth term in October 1900–June 1901) was exploring the possibility of such an alliance with Russia as a way of avoiding either party's formal colonization of Korea and coordinating both empires' interests in the peninsula. The then Prime Minister, Katsura Tarō, however, saw the Japanese empire's interests in Korea as being incompatible with those of the Russian empire, and argued for Japan's alliance with Britain.[71] Katsura's view prevailed, and the Anglo-Japanese alliance, which regarded Russia as a common enemy, was concluded in 1902.

All these options were different means to take control of Korea, which Meiji foreign policy-makers as vital for the security of state, nation and then empire. In order to secure this vital national/imperial interest and legitimize its control over Korea, the Meiji state not only used force, but also international law, the rhetoric of the state sovereignty system, and metropolitan public opinions. Initially in 1873, a majority of the Meiji elite overruled the use of force (a military invasion of Korea)

---

[66] Even after it formalized possession legally, however, the Meiji state still had to use force to suppress local resistance.

[67] In 1862, Katsu Kaishū, Navy Minister of the Shogunate government, argued for such an East Asian alliance. Yamamuro 2002, p. 586.

[68] Yamamuro argues that both states saw it as a means towards their other strategic agenda: China wanted to prevent Japan from allying with European empires, while Japan wanted to challenge China's suzerain status over Korea; ibid. p. 601.

[69] In 1885, Fukuzawa Yukichi had already argued that Japan should be included in a league of Euro-American empires. On the views of the officials at the Ministry of Foreign Affairs in this period, see Zachmann 2009, p. 72.

[70] Ibid., pp. 43 f.

[71] Itō to Katsura, 6 December 1901 and *Katsura Tarō jiden*, both compiled in Kodama 1991, pp. 133 f., 135 f. Nish 2001, "Itō Hirobumi", pp. 87 f.

because they judged that the Meiji state was not ready and lacked a great cause (*taigi*).[72] Three years later, the Meiji state imposed an unequal treaty on Korea (1876). Then in 1895, it eliminated China's suzerain right over Korea by defeating China. The Meiji state justified this war against China as a "great cause" – "securing the independence of the Korean state" from China's suzerain rule.[73] It utilized, therefore, the rhetoric of the state sovereignty and international legal conventions for nation-states/empires. The military victory resulted in the peace treaty of 1895, the first article of which noted that "the Qing state (*Shin koku*) would recognize the Korean state (*Chōsen koku*) as a completely independent state". The second article then violated China's sovereignty, detailing various interests that China was obliged to hand over to Japan.[74]

After 1895, the Meiji state further eroded Korea's sovereignty with a similar combination of force and modern codes and norms of international relations of the time. In 1905, it eliminated the other remaining empire in Korea, Russia, by force. It then made Korea Japan's protectorate in 1905, and finally a formal colony in 1910. For the years 1905–1910, as Alexis Dudden demonstrates, the Meiji state used a combination of force, the international legal framework, and the argument that Korea was not 'civilized enough' and needed guidance in order to legitimize the process of occupation. While other nation-states/empires were concerned with Japan's aggressive imperial policies, they nonetheless saw the annexation as legal, and Japan's prestige increased.[75]

Kant argued that republics were unlikely to go to war with each other,[76] and this argument was often used to support the idea that popularly elected regimes (whether a republic or constitutional monarchy) were less likely to engage in military aggression. Historical cases, however, did not always endorse this point. Already in 1874, Itagaki Taisuke, a leading advocate of parliamentary democracy and anti-oligarchy, used the term 'empire' (*Teikoku*) for Japan, much earlier than the official documents did. He argued for the equality and liberty of the people in Japan, as well as the prestige (*Son'ei*) of the emperor. If the people had the right to govern themselves, he argued, it would foster independent spirit, and increase the

[72] In October 1873, Ōkubo Toshimichi argued that this invasion was too early, first, because of drastic reforms the Meiji state had begun, the foundations of the state were yet to be established, and widespread discontent was still evident; second, the cost would be enormous and the Meiji state would need to levy higher taxes or seek foreign loans, either of which would further burden the domestic economy; third, much more preparations and planning would be required for such military action; fourth, this military expedition might provide an opportunity for Britain to intervene in Japanese domestic matters; fifth, he could not find a great cause for this invasion; Ōkubo 1928, pp. 53–64. The government was also still negotiating the northern borders with Russia at this time (resolved in 1875).

[73] Mutsu Munemitsu's account, compiled in Kodama 2002, pp. 125 f.

[74] "Nisshin kōwa jōyaku," signed on 17 April 1895, in Kodama 2002, p. 128.

[75] Dudden 2005, pp. 60–73, 109–111.

[76] Kant 1957.

prosperity (*Shōsei*) of the empire.[77] In the 1880s–1900s, the anti-oligarchy and parliamentary democracy advocates were often supporters of Japan's colonial expansion.[78] Matsuo Takayoshi and Andrew Gordon also demonstrate a similar tendency among advocates for the universal male franchise movement in Japan in the following decades.[79]

Was this a sign of the "immature" or "under-developed" democracy of Japan? It might rather be understood as a problem inherent in the system based on the nation-state/empire. Indeed in the 1880s, "advanced" nation-states in Europe, which were furthering greater political participation in metropolitan centres, were formally colonizing Africa and Asia by using military forces and international law. Formal colonization was at times thought to be a means for providing social welfare in the metropolitan centres, or even the means to protect "natives".[80]

For Western European powers that were largely maritime empires, colonized territories were mostly located far away (except for cases such as Ireland). It was easier for them to argue their metropolitan "national" policies were detached from their colonial doings. Such separation was, however, harder for other continental/congruent empires that colonized neighbouring nations. Arendt recognized that the dichotomy between the nation-state and empire could only be applied to maritime Western European empires, not to the continental empires in Central and Eastern Europe (the Austro-Hungarian Empire, the Ottoman Empire and the Russian Empire).[81]

The Meiji nation-state/empire was emerging more like these contiguous empires. It made a crucial strategic decision in the mid-late 1900s, and it is clear how its rhetoric shifted from pushing for the creation of a buffer/interest zone for the independence of the nation-state to the expansion of an empire (the nation-state/empire).[82] Japan's victory over Russia in 1905 moved its empire's front line to the central part of Northeast China (Manchuria). This was a new buffer zone against Russia, which was also seen as resource-rich. Kitaoka Shin'ichi argues that Japan's imperial/national defence guideline (*Nihon teikoku kokubō hōshin*) of 1907 marked "a shift from the Navy-led defensive policy of an island empire to the Army-led offensive defence policy of the continental empire". This 1907 document noted:

---

[77] [Itagaki Taisuke], "Risshisha setsuritsu no shuisho," April 1874, compiled in Kodama 2002, pp. 63 f.

[78] Norman 1940, pp. 201–204; Miyaji 1973. Sakeda argued that a hard-line foreign policy was a standard feature of anti-oligarchy and pro-constitutional democracy groups in the 1890s and 1900s. Sakeda 1978, p. 3.

[79] Matsuo 1998; Gordon 1991.

[80] Semmel 1960, pp. 23–8; Koskenniemi 2002, pp. 143–5.

[81] Arendt 1951, pp. 223–5. The point is clarified more in the 1968 version; Arendt 2003, p. 161. The terms used by Arendt were continental imperialism and overseas imperialism.

[82] At the same time, one can also see that the line between internal and external colonization was less clear for contiguous empires than for maritime empires.

> The Japanese empire should now seek an active expansion, not only defending the already established interests in Manchuria and Korea. It should now promote non-official expansion to the southern part of Asia and the other Pacific shore across the ocean.[83]

This continental empire remained integral to the metropolitan nation-state. In the Meiji era (1868–1912), the Japanese state created formal and informal colonies,[84] according to the international norms and conducts of nation-states/empires. While it developed metropolitan parliamentary democracy and sought to modernize and industrialize the country, it subjugated and governed the people in the formal and informal colonies, suppressing their rights and exploiting their resources for metropolitan needs. While maritime empires also treated colonial subjects and metropolitan subjects differently, continental empires were confronted by the problem more intensely because they subjugated neighbouring nations.

## *After 1919: The Nation-State/Empire in the Time of the League of Nations of the 1920s*

Towards the end of the First World War and in its aftermath between autumn 1918 and spring 1919, a new norm was emerging in international politics. Erez Manela argued that Woodrow Wilson then "became for millions worldwide the ... most prominent exponent of the vision ... of a just international society based on the principle of self-determination". Examining this transnational momentum, Manela demonstrated that a new norm, self-determination, entered into international politics.[85] Can we then still apply the notion of the nation-state/empire as a basic unit of international politics in the period after 1919?

Wilson did not cause anti-colonial movements, as the movements already existed. He did, however, give legitimacy to the term self-determination, which also consolidated various existing anti-colonial movements. As Manela demonstrated, Wilson did not invent this empowering term, but took it from the Bolsheviks. The expression he used in the 14 Points was "the consent of the governed", a sort of uninspiring managerial terminology.[86] This change in

[83] Kitaoka 1985, p. 12. In 1905, as a result of the military victory over Russia, the Meiji nation-state/empire gained not only the territory of the south of Sakhalin, but more importantly, significant rights in the southern part of Manchuria. These rights were: leasing of the main railway lines in the southern part of Manchuria; mining and other interests along the railway line; the right to protect these railway lines and associated interests and the territory of the tip of the Liaodong Peninsula, where there were significant trading and strategic ports. The Meiji nation-state/empire established the legitimacy of these rights internationally in 1909–1912; ibid., p. 32.

[84] Through military might and treaty negotiations (imposed under duress), the Japanese state became a part of the collective of these nation-states/empires which made China their informal colony; Duus 1989, pp. xi–xxix.

[85] Manela 2007, pp. 6, 218–9, 220, 221.

[86] Ibid., p. 41.

terminology in early 1918 proved to be crucial: now anti-colonial activists, not colonial administrators, could own the term, which captured the desires of millions beyond Europe. Combined with Bolshevik influences, anti-colonial movements were given momentum.

As a result, self-determination became a new norm after 1918. Wilson condemned 'new' colonial acquisition as being morally wrong at the Paris Peace Conference. Then, in Europe, the principle of self-determination came to be applied, and the new nation-states were created in the aftermath of the disintegration of the Austro-Hungarian and Ottoman Empires.

Although Hobsbawm ended his age of empire in 1914,[87] empires continued to rule in the aftermath of the First World War. The victorious British, French, Dutch, American and Japanese Empires not only retained their formal colonies, but some even gained new territories or new mandates.[88]

Beyond Europe, the basic unit of international politics did not shift from empires to the nation-state.[89] As Akira Iriye argued, "[u]ntil after World War II, the Far East had been a land of empires, not nation-states".[90] Yet these empires were also nation-states in the metropolitan centres. The nation-states/empires, therefore, remained the main actors in international politics after 1919.

Accordingly, the League of Nations' new world (not European) order was not the order of just the nation-states. There were the 'pure' nation-states (the nation-state without an empire) that had existed before 1919, such as Switzerland, and those that were newly created in Europe in 1919, such as Poland. There were the nation-states which used to be empires, but had lost their colonies, and joined the League, such as Germany, Austria, Hungary and Turkey. There were also the former allied empires which remained nation-states/empires, and as well the colonies of these empires, which remained as colonies even after 1919. Among them, new nation-states/dominions, such as Australia, had self-government and a greater autonomy in domestic affairs. Along with former allied nation-states/empires, some of these dominions (such as Australia and New Zealand) became mandate powers. Then there were former colonies of defeated empires, which became mandates.

The nation-states/empires (so-called great powers) were the most influential actors in the League of Nations and League-related international organizations. These great powers were the League's permanent Council members and they were central in the League's implementing bodies of technical (expert) committees. When colonies were invited to attend the League's official international forum or

[87] Hobsbawm 1994, p. 338.

[88] In the case of Japan, new territories were gained in Shandong, a former German territory in China during the war, which Japan made other powers accept at the Paris Peace Conference. The territory was "returned" to China at the Washington Conference of 1921–1922.

[89] Manela did not argue that this shift occurred either, but suggested that the failure of Wilsonian anti-colonialism in 1919 to deliver what it had promised led its supporters to alternative, and more radical anti-colonialism, and to the "revolt against the West"; Manela 2007, pp. 212, 224.

[90] Iriye 1965, p. 4.

other unofficial ones, colonial officers or bureaucrats from metropolitan centres represented the colonies' interests.[91]

At the same time, smaller powers (nation-states without an empire, or with dominion status) were to play a greater role after 1919. The League discussed and decided important matters at the General Assembly, at which each country, whether it was an empire or not, had an equal vote. These smaller powers, such as Australia and China (especially Nationalist China after 1928), actively used the League as a stage to enhance and assert a greater sovereignty.[92] Furthermore, as Giddens suggested, the League of Nations co-opted experts and their organizations into their operations. These experts became influential within the League's technical committees and other international organizations. They had greater input into decision-making, voicing views not necessarily as state representatives.[93] Reflecting the rapid technological development of telecommunication and greater popular political participation, the League was also conscious of the "moral force of public opinion".[94] As a result, the League became a site where these various actors negotiated new norms of international conduct. The League also disseminated these new norms to experts and policy-makers, and propagated and educated the public about them.[95]

It was, however, not only the nation-states, but also the nation-states/empires that negotiated and formed these new norms for what we now call global governance at the League and League-related organizations. While the process also was intended to integrate other voices, the managerial concerns of empires remained an important factor, and negotiation entailed cooperation and conflicts among empires. Members of the League's mandate committee, for example, represented major nation-states/empires and new mandate powers. They were not eager to let their mandates (let alone their own colonies) go independent too soon. Pedersen argues that the League's mandate committee did not advance the new radical idea of self-determination, but rather showcased to the world public that mandate powers were 'discussing' this new norm.[96]

As a result, a new rhetoric of legitimization of the colonial rule of nation-states/empires became prevalent at the League. New colonization by military conquest was now condemned as morally wrong. On the other hand, the League's nation-states/empires members stressed the inability of a given mandate (or a colony) in

[91] Akami 2002, pp. 98 ff., 142 ff., 200 f.

[92] Herren 2009. I owe this reference to Frank Beyersdorf.

[93] Giddens 1985, pp. 261 f.; Dubin 1983, p. 491.

[94] Akami 2008, p. 12. Carr thought there was too much expectation of the moral power of public opinion at the League; Carr 1939, pp. 31–38.

[95] Pedersen 2007, pp. 1–33. On these normative works of the League's Health Organization, see Borowy 2009, pp. 143–60.

[96] Pedersen 2006, pp. 560–582. Anghie argues that the mandate system demonstrates how central colonialism continued to be for international organizations after 1919; Anghie 2005, p. 117.

apolitical areas (public health or labour management), and used this argument to justify their continued rule.[97]

While the League's order could be understood as the order of various types of the nation-state, including the nation-state/empire, the international order in Northeast Asia in the 1920s was defined by factors other than the League. Japan and China joined the League, but among the major nation-states/empires that were either located in Northeast Asia, or had a big stake in the region, the U.S. and Russia did not become members. The region's order after 1919 was, therefore, defined more by the Washington Treaties (1922), which embodied the American-led new regional order of the Pacific region.[98] This still excluded Russia, but complemented the League's order. Consequently, scholars have called the regional order of the inter-war period the Versailles-Washington system.[99]

The Washington Treaties were in essence agreements among the nation-states/empires. These treaties, led by the U.S., checked Japanese expansion, secured the Anglo-American regional naval supremacy, and reaffirmed the existing interests of those nation-states/empires in China and the Pacific. In 1921–1922, the U.S. nonetheless initiated a modification of the imperialistic behaviours practised by the various states and an adaptation of a multilateral and cooperative framework.[100] Its most important initiatives were to respect China's sovereignty, and to restore its tariff right and abolish the extraterritoriality of the empires.[101]

Another international agreement, the Pact of Paris (or Kellogg-Briand Pact), defined states' conduct in Northeast Asia and elsewhere in the world in the 1920s. Fifteen countries, including the U.S., Britain, France, Italy and Japan, signed it in August 1928.[102] Its formal name was the "General Treaty for Renunciation of War as an Instrument of National Policy", and it aimed to abandon war as a means of solving inter-state disputes. The treaty was the beginning of outlawing war.[103] At the same time, however, it was also a pact for the nation-states/empires. Its initial signatory members were mostly the nation-states/empires, and it protected their existing formal and informal colonies against new aggression.[104]

[97] Akami 2010.

[98] Iriye 1965, p. 16.

[99] Hosoya 1993, p. 11; Hattori 2001, pp. 4–12. Hata regarded the system as "protect[ing] the interests of the two major victorious powers, Great Britain and the United States"; Hata 1988, p. 282.

[100] Iriye understood this as a U.S. attempt to "demolish the existing system of imperialist diplomacy". Iriye 1965, p. 14. On Iriye's definition of the diplomacy of imperialism, distinguished from an empire's diplomacy, see ibid., p. 5.

[101] Ibid., pp. 18, 20 f.

[102] 63 further countries would join later on, including the USSR.

[103] The wording of Clause 1 of Article 9 of the Japanese Constitution of 1946 came from the first article of this Pact of Paris, and is still in place today.

[104] While this prevented an attack on their existing territories and spheres of influence, the governments of the U.S., Japan and Britain interpreted the pact in the light of their own Monroe Doctrine. Accordingly, the British government reserved an exception of its applicability to the

These treaties, concluded largely among the nation-states/empires, constituted a legal framework for their international actions in the 1920s and 1930s. Accordingly, the defining spirit of Japan's cooperative diplomacy of the 1920s (*kyōchō gaikō*) could be described not only as inter-nationalism, but also inter-empire-ism. It pursued Japan's national/imperial interests through economic means and multilateral cooperation with other nation-states/empires, while respecting China's sovereignty outside Northeast China (Manchuria).

How do we then understand Japanese aggression in Manchuria in 1931, and the relationship between Japan and the League in 1931–1933 through the notion of the nation-state/empire?

## *1931–1933: Japan's Policy Towards China and the League*

An orthodox historiography has tended to see the Japanese aggression in Manchuria in 1931–1933 as a watershed for Japanese external policy shift from internationalism to nationalism. Scholars especially stressed the rise of nationalism among military officers in Japan to explain this alteration. Internationalism declined, as often argued or assumed, in the 1930s, while the Japanese government stopped complying with international law. Ian Nish, for example, understands the period of 1932–1936 as that of Japan's foreign policy's "departure from internationalism", and argues that internationalists lost to stronger advocates of nationalist objectives.[105]

A framework of nationalism versus internationalism, however, does not work for an analysis of Nationalist China's foreign policy in the same period. Nationalist China used the League's multilateral framework in its attempt to restore and assert its sovereignty in 1928–1937. Already in mid-1929, it had appealed to the League against Russian aggression in Manchuria: although the League did not react then, China continued to use the League. Kawashima Shin argues that this was a conscious decision by Nationalist China to improve its international status. It pursued a League Council seat and it also initiated cooperation with the League to build up the state's capability in public health (from 1929) and expanded the scope of this cooperation into other technical, economic and cultural cooperations (from 1931).[106] By doing so, Nationalist China tried to restore its sovereignty, and to refute imperialistic arguments that China was an "incompetent" state and needed guidance from outside. In 1931, before Japan's Guandong Army began its

regions of the world where it thought special and vital interests existed for its own peace and security, while the Japanese government informally communicated its wish to preserve a special right in Manchuria; Yanagihara 1996, pp. 154 f. I owe this reference to Urs Matthias Zachmann.

[105] Nish 2002, pp. 85–101; it was a period of struggle for Japanese internationalists against anti-Leaguers; these anti-Leaguers included army officers whose "pursuit of the nationalist objective was stronger than any pressure to conform to world public opinion"; Nish 1993, pp. 8–16.

[106] Kawashima 2006, pp. 30 f.; Osterhammel 1979, pp. 661–80.

aggression in Manchuria, the League had been involved in major flood relief in China. On 14 September, only a few days before the aggression began, China also became a League Council member. After the Japanese army garrison opened hostilities on 18 September, Nationalist China quickly appealed to the League. The League's inter-national framework then supported China's efforts to assert its sovereignty against empires.

A rather artificial opposition between nationalism and internationalism was indeed a projection of contemporary "liberal [non-communist/socialist/anarchist] internationalists, as much as later scholars".[107] As these internationalists made clear, internationalism meant the pursuit of the national interests in cooperation with other nation-states.[108] Nitobe Inazō, a leading internationalist in the 1920s who became the League's Under-Secretary, noted that in order to be an internationalist, one had to be a nationalist. His fellow Wilsonian internationalists in other countries shared the view.[109]

The second common understanding of the 'Manchurian Incident' is to see the League as an advocate of a new norm based on the principle of self-determination of the nation-state. Japan tried to comply with this new norm in the 1920s, but reverted back to the old nineteenth century norm of imperialism in the 1930s. As such, the Japanese aggression in Manchuria in 1931 was understood as a challenge made by Japan's old norm of the empire to the League's new norm of the nation-state. Here, an 'insufficient' level of modernization and democratization in Japan was also assumed to be a factor which hindered its political, economic and social system from stopping imperial aggression in 1931–1932.[110]

Japan had, however, been a nation-state/empire since 1895. In this context, nationalism in Japan was not merely an inward-looking ideology to integrate the nation, nor an ideology for defending its sovereignty against other empires. As was the case for other empires, nationalism was also an external ideology for asserting national/imperial interests and prestige. E.H. Norman and Maruyama Masao used the terms "radical nationalism/statism" (*Kagekina kokkashugi*) or "ultra-nationalism/statism" (*Chō kokkashugi*), to denote the ideological source of Japan's imperialism.[111] Here, the nexus between the nation-state and an empire was indicated.[112]

The notion of the nation-state/empire can take our analysis of international power dynamics in Northeast Asia in 1931–1933 beyond an artificial dichotomy of internationalism versus nationalism or internationalism versus imperialism.

As pointed out earlier, inter-nationalism in the 1920s could be understood as inter-empire-ism which meant a pursuit of imperial interests in cooperation with

[107] Nish 2001 "The Uncertainties", p. 301.

[108] Akami 2002, pp. 8 ff.; Burkman 2008, pp. 216 ff.

[109] Akami 2002, p. 146.

[110] Norman 1943, pp. 56 f.

[111] Norman 1941, pp. 261 ff.; Maruyama 1968, pp. 11–28. Such a view became a conventional understanding. See, for example, Hanneman 2001, pp. 42 ff.

[112] Titus 1983, pp. 184 ff.

other empires. Many Wilsonian internationalists of the 1920s, including Nitobe, did not challenge their countries' empire status, nor did they condemn their colonial possessions. The Versailles-Washington system in Northeast Asia meant to secure the existing national/imperial interests of the major nation-states/empires, which had high stakes in the region.

The Japanese Guandong Army's aggression in Manchuria in 1931–1933, and the subsequent metropolitan state's acceptance of the *fait accompli* of Japan's military occupation after December 1931, meant that the Japanese state now pursued its national/imperial interests by force, not just by economic or diplomatic means. The initial decision to use force was made by the Guandong Army, not the metropolitan state, which was still exploring other options for securing and expanding its interests in the region. The army garrison became increasingly agitated by the movements of Nationalist China, the U.S.S.R. and the League, planned its attack carefully, and waited for a chance to execute it.[113] The metropolitan state was unable to restrain the garrison from acting, and soon accepted the resulting military occupation and adopted it as its policy.

The Guandong Army and the metropolitan state therefore did not agree on the means, but shared the ultimate goal of securing Japan's national/imperial interests in Manchuria. In consequence, the Japanese state broke one crucial accepted norm after 1919: nation-states/empires would not change the pre-existing borders of their sphere of influence by force. This did not, however, mean that the Japanese state abandoned all the post-1919 norms of international conduct defined by the nation-states/empires and other new factors.

First, the Japanese metropolitan state attempted to manipulate post-1919 hierarchical power dynamics at the League of Nations to its own advantage. As noted, while the nation-states/empires held a dominant position at the League, smaller powers (the nation-states without an empire) and expert groups were increasing their influence. For Nationalist China, the General Assembly and the League's Health Organization, where the influence of experts was strong, were helpful in Nationalist China's effort to restore and assert greater sovereignty. By way of contrast, the Japanese tactics in 1931–1932 focused on the nation-states/empires in the League: it tried to exploit an anxiety among the nation-states/empires which had been caused by Nationalist China's greater assertion of its sovereignty and relinquishment of certain imperial interests in North China in 1926–1928.[114] The Japanese metropolitan state wanted these nation-states/empires to sympathize with Japan's anxiety over its interests in Manchuria.[115]

The Japanese state assumed that other nation-states/empires, especially Britain, were sympathetic to its claim for "internationally and legally acknowledged rights in China" and its argument that law and order needed to be restored to secure its

[113] Peattie 1975, pp. 107–118.

[114] Duus 1989, p. xxv.

[115] Yoshizawa Kenkichi, the Foreign Minister, wanted the League's inquiry commission to be composed of the nation-states/empires (great powers) in November 1931; Usui 1995, p. 13.

imperial interests in China.[116] This was evident in the report of October 1932 of the League's Inquiry Commission on the Japanese aggression in Manchuria, which was headed by the British Lord Lytton. As Nish argues, while the report condemned Japan's two major arguments (that the military acted in self-defence and that Manzhouguo was a genuine nation), it argued for protecting Japan's original, pre-September 1931 interests in Manchuria.[117]

Second, both the Japanese metropolitan state and Guandong Army used the post-1919 norm of self-determination to secure Japan's imperial interests in the region. The Guandong Army established not a new formal colony in its militarily occupied area, but a puppet regime, Manzhouguo, in March 1932. The garrison's intelligence unit had been manipulating local Chinese collaborators to establish new political bodies that were more cooperative with the Guandong Army than the now pro-Nationalist northern warlord, Zhang Xueliang. Less than a week after the initial military attack on 18 September, the Guandong Army's headquarters decided that it would establish an autonomous local government, which would consolidate these collaborators' political units in the military-occupied areas.[118] The Japanese metropolitan state tacitly agreed this means of controlling the military occupation by establishing a puppet regime, and formally recognized the regime by concluding a diplomatic treaty in September 1932.

Third, while this puppet regime did not adopt the principle of popular legitimacy, the Japanese imperial authorities (the metropolitan government, the Guandong Army and other Japanese official missions in Manchuria) wanted it to demonstrate its competence in governing to the world. The founding documents of various key official institutions thus included the department of public health, as well as the "law to secure [social and economic] human rights" (*Jinken hoshō hō*).[119] These documents stressed that the regime could look after social and economic rights and the welfare of the local population.

Fourth, the Guandong Army's headquarters at Shenyang (Mukden), as well as the Japanese metropolitan state, recognized the power of international public opinion and were concerned with the League's movements. In December 1931 the garrison decided to found a news agency in order to manage international public opinion in relations to the League. The Manzhouguo News Agency was then established almost a year later.[120] It was a propaganda and intelligence gathering machine, which sought to legitimize Japan's military occupation, its puppet regime and its 'guiding' role for the regime.

---

[116] Nihon kokusai seiji gakkai Taiheiyō sensō gennin kenkyūbu 1988, pp. 353, 359 f.

[117] Nish 1993, pp. 175 ff.

[118] [Kantōgun Sanbō honbu], "Manmō mondai kaiketsusaku an, 22 September 1931", in Inaba et al. 1964, p. 328.

[119] "Seifu soshiki hō narabini shokansei", [March 1932], in Kobayashi and Shimada 1964, pp. 410, 418, 426.

[120] Akami (forthcoming).

Fifth, Japanese experts sought to justify the military aggression within the framework of the international law of the time. China, the U.S. and the League condemned the aggression as a violation of the Nine Powers Treaty on China (one of the Washington Treaties) and the Pact of Paris. Except for a very few, such as Yokota Kisaburō, Japanese international law specialists, who had earlier supported the League, sought to justify the aggression within these legal frameworks.[121] Some went even further. Using Carl Schmitt's then-current geopolitical theory, Rōyama Masamichi, a prominent political scientist, argued for the need for a new category of international law, "regional international law", to deal with the Manchurian case.[122] This could be understood as an effort to "adjust" international law closer to the reality of the nation-states/empires.

The Japanese decision to withdraw from the League of Nations in March 1933 has been argued as the beginning of Japan's diplomatic isolationism.[123] The rise of nationalism and/or imperialism has often been cited as a major reason for this policy shift. This did not, however, mean the end of Japanese engagement with the rest of the world, the beginning of an inward-looking nationalism, or a reversion to the 'old' imperialist norm. Japan continued to appeal its case in Manchuria especially to the other nation-states/empires, which had similar imperial interests in China. It also did not dismiss the post-1919 factors of international politics, either. After 1933, Japanese foreign policy shifted the targets of its overseas propaganda from Geneva to New York. Just as many other countries did in the same period, it also began to develop a systematic policy for international propaganda.[124] This move reflected policy-makers' recognition of the new norms and conducts of international politics of the day – mass-based politics, new techniques of advertisement and propaganda, and new technological developments in telecommunication. These new norms and conducts, however, were not alternative to the use of force for the nation-states/empires. The world was moving into a new era of bloc economy in which the nation-states/empires were to tie their spheres of influence more closely together. The Japanese state used force to expand its yen bloc. Nor did greater transnational/empire networks guarantee or reinforce peace, as the Herren chapter here demonstrates.

The International Society of the nation-states/empires was a global system made of actors of different levels of power. It advocated 'liberal' and 'democratic' norms, but within the framework of empire. It reinforced the order, but often at the expense of weaker states and other political units. In other words, the system inherently contained grievance of weaker members. On one hand, the new norm

[121] Yokota based his criticism of the Japanese aggression on the theory of Hans Kelsen; Mitani 1974, pp. 233 f. On the movements of international law specialists after 1931, see Matsui 1979, pp. 361–405.

[122] Mitrani 1974, pp. 236–239. On the introduction of Carl Schmitt to Japan, see also Matsui 2004, pp. 1–22. I owe this reference to Urs Matthias Zachmann.

[123] Nish 2002, p. 90; Crowley 1966, p. 186.

[124] Carr 1939, pp. 137 f.; Akami 2008, pp. 22–29.

of self-determination encouraged anti-imperial revolts, which enhanced greater justice in the system. On the other hand, the existence of such systemic grievance gave a room for a weaker empire, such as Japan, to exploit it for strengthening its power in the system. It was this power hierarchy among the national/imperial states, not the power balance among relatively equal national states, which defined international politics in Northeast Asia in the inter-war period.

## Conclusion

This chapter has demonstrated the need to examine the nexus between a nation-state and an empire, and understand developments at the imperial metropolis and colonial peripheries in a more integrated manner. For such an analysis the notion of the nation-state/empire was proposed, and this was then used in an analysis of international politics in Northeast Asia for the period 1868–1933.

The chapter suggested that the problem of the modern Japanese state could be understood not only as Japan's adjustment and then challenge to the International Society of the liberal, democratic and civilized national states. Rather it could also be understood as a problem inherent in the development of the nation-state/empire system. It was firstly demonstrated how nation-state building meant the making of the nation-state/empire, which involved internal and external colonization, and how the Meiji state used international law and the rhetoric of state sovereignty to legitimize its colonial expansion. Second, the chapter argued that the nation-state/empire remained a significant actor in international politics even after self-determination became a dominant norm after 1919. It demonstrated how this notion might interpret the new framework of international conduct in the 1920s, as well as Japanese aggression in Manchuria and Japan's response to the League in 1931–1933.

I hope that this paper will contribute to further discussion of the empire aspects of orthodox understandings of international politics, within and beyond the context with which this chapter has dealt. I also hope it has demonstrated that the issues of 'beyond the nation-state' and 'the process of governing trans-national issues' cannot be discussed without examining the role of empires as integral factors of many nation-states.

## Bibliography

Akami, Tomoko. 2002. *Internationalizing the Pacific: The United States, Japan and the Institute of Pacific Relations in War and Peace, 1919–45*. London: Routledge.

Akami, Tomoko. 2007. "The Nexus of the Nation-State and the Empire: Reconsidering the League's Order and Japan in the Inter-War Period." In *Japan and the UN in International Politics: Historical Perspectives*, edited by Hanzawa Asahiko, 33–84. Sapporo: Hokkaidō Daigaku Daigakuin Hōgaku Kenkyūka Fuzoku Kōtō Hōsei Kyōiku Kenkyū Sentā

Akami, Tomoko. 2008. "The Emergence of International Public Opinion and the Origin of Public Diplomacy in Japan in the Inter-War Period." *The Hague Journal of Diplomacy* 3, 1–30.
Akami, Tomoko. 2010. "Public Health Experts at the League of Nations: Agents of Health for a Nation, Empire, Colony or the Globe?" Paper presented at the workshop on "Lives Beyond the Borders", Cluster of Excellence, Heidelberg University, 12 February.
Akami, Tomoko. Forthcoming. "Between a Fiction of the Nation-State and the Empire: The Manzhouguo News Agency and Japan's News Imperialism in Military Occupied Manchuria, 1932–1945." In *Global Challenge and Regional Response — Early 20th Century Northeast China: Their Social, Cultural, Economic and Political Encounters with the World,* edited by Ines Prodöhl, Frank Grüner and Dan Ben-Canaan. Heidelberg, New York: Springer.
Anghie, Antony. 2005. *Imperialism, Sovereignty, and the Making of International Law.* Cambridge: Cambridge University Press.
Aoki, Kōji. 1994. "Meiji nōmin sōjō no nenjiteki kenkyū." In: *Shōsetsu Nihonshi kenkyū,* edited by Kasahara Kazuo et al.., 335. Tokyo: Yamakawa Shuppansha.
Arendt, Hannah. 1951. *The Origins of Totalitarianism.* New York: Harcourt, Brace.
Arendt, Hannah. 2003. Ōshima Michiyoshi & Ōshima Kaori. *Zentaishugi no kigen,* vol. 2 (The Origins of Totalitarianism). Tokyo: Misuzu Shobô.
Auslin, Michael R. 2004. *Negotiating with Imperialism: The Unequal Treaties and the Culture of Japanese Diplomacy.* Cambridge MA: Harvard University Press.
Bain, William. 2003. *Between Anarchy and Society: Trusteeship and the Obligations of Power.* Oxford: Oxford University Press.
Beasley, William G. 1991. *Japanese Imperialism, 1894–1945,* Oxford: Clarendon Press.
Borowy, Iris. 2009. *Coming to Terms with World Health: The League of Nations Health Organization, 1921–1946,* Berlin: Lang.
Bull, Hedley, ed. 2002. *The Anarchical Society: A Study of Order in World Politics,* 3rd ed. Basingstoke, Hampshire: Palgrave.
Bull, Hedley and Adam Watson, eds. 1984. *The Expansion of International Society.* Oxford: Oxford University Press.
Burkman, Thomas. 2008. *Japan and the League of Nations: Empire and World Order, 1914–1938.* Honolulu: University of Hawai'i Press.
Carr, Edward Hallett. 1939. *The Twenty Years' Crisis, 1919–1939: An Introduction to the Study of International Relations.* London: Mac Millan.
Chilcote, Ronald H., ed. 2000. *Imperialism: Theoretical Directions.* Amherst NY: Humanity Books.
Clark, Ian. 2007. *International Legitimacy and World Politics.* Oxford: Oxford University Press.
Clark, Ian. 1989. *The Hierarchy of States: Reform and Resistance in the International Order.* Cambridge: Cambridge University Press.
Clark, Ian. 2011. "Towards an English School Theory of Hegemony." *European Journal of International Relations* 15, no. 2, 203–28.
Crowley, James B. 1966. *Japan's Quest for Autonomy: National Security and Foreign Policy, 1930–1938.* Princeton: Princeton University Press.
Dubin, Martin David. 1983. "Transgovernmental Processes in the League of Nations." *International Organization* 37, no. 3, 469–493.
Dudden, Alexis. 2005. *Japan's Colonization of Korea: Discourse and Power.* Honolulu: University of Hawai'i Press.
Duus, Peter. 1989. "Introduction: Japan's Informal Empire in China, 1895–1937: An Overview." *The Japanese Informal Empire in China, 1895–1937,* edited by Peter Duus and Banno Junji, xi–xxix. Princeton: Princeton University Press.
Cox, Michael et al, eds. 2001. "Empires, Systems and States: Great Transformation in International Politics." *Review of International Studies* 27 (special edition).
Gaimushō, ed. 1955. *Nihon gaikō nempyō narabini shuyō monjo,* vol. 1: 1840–1945. Tokyo: Nihon Kokusai Rengō Kyōkai, Shōwa 30.

Gallagher, John and Ronald Robinson. 1953. "The Imperialism of Free Trade." *Economic History Review* 6, ser. 2, 1–15.
Giddens, Anthony. 1985. *The Nation-State and Violence*. Cambridge: Polity Press.
Gong, Gerrit W. 1984. *The Standard of 'Civilization' in International Society*. Oxford: Clarendon Press.
Gordon, Andrew. 1991. *Labor and Imperial Democracy in Prewar Japan*. Berkeley: University of California Press.
Grewe, Wilhelm G. 2000. *The Epochs of International Law*. Berlin: Walter de Gruyter.
Hall, Catherine. 2002. *Civilizing Subjects: Metropole and Colony in the English Imagination, 1830–1867*. Oxford: Blackwell Publishers.
Hall, Stuart. 1991. "Old and New Identities, Old and New Ethnicities." In *Culture, Globalization and the World System*, edited by Anthony D. King, 41–68. London: MacMillan.
Hall, Stuart. 1992. "The West and the Rest: Discourse and Power." In *Formations of Modernity*, edited by Stuart Hall and Bram Gieben, 275–320. Oxford: Polity in Association with Open University.
Hanneman, Mary L. 2001. *Japan Faces the World, 1925–1952*. Harlow: Longman.
Hardt, Michael and Antonio Negri. 2000. *Empire*. Cambridge MA: Harvard University Press.
Hata, Ikuhiko. 1988. "Continental Expansion, 1905–1941." In *The Cambridge History of Japan*, vol. 6, edited by Peter Duus, 271–314. Cambridge: Cambridge University Press.
Hattori, Ryūji. 2001. *Higashi Ajia kokusai kankyō no hendō to Nihon gaikō, 1918–1931*. Tokyo: Yūhikaku.
Herren, Madeleine. 2009. *Internationale Organisationen seit 1865: Eine Globalgeschichte der Internationalen Ordnung*. Darmstadt: Wissenschaftliche Buchgesellschaft.
Hobsbawm, Eric. 1994. *The Age of Empire, 1875–1914*. London: Abacus.
Hoffmann, Stanley. 2002. "Foreword to the Second Edition: Revisiting The Anarchical Society." In *The Anarchical Society: A Study of Order in World Politics*, 3rd ed., edited by Hedley Bull. Basingstoke, Hampshire: Palgrave.
Hosoya, Chihiro. 1993. "Kokusai shakai no naka deno Nichibei kankei." In *Nichibei kankeishi*, edited by Chihiro Hosoya and Honma Nagayo, 11. Tokyo: Yûhikaku.
Iriye, Akira. 1965. *After Imperialism: The Search for a New Order in the Far East, 1921–1931*. Cambridge MA: Harvard University Press.
Jansen, Marius B. 1984. "Japanese Imperialism: Late Meiji Perspective." In *Japan's Colonial Empire, 1895–1945*, edited by Ramon H. Myers and Mark R. Peattie, 61–79. Princeton: Princeton University Press.
Jones, Branwen Gruffydd. 2006. *Decolonizing International Relations*. Lanham: Rowman & Littlefield.
"'Kaikoku washin no hōshin o tsuguru chokugo', 1 January 1868" and "'Taisei fukko o rekkoku ni hōzuru kokusho', 10 January 1868". (1961) 1991. In *Shiryō niyoru Nihon no ayumi, Kindai hen*, edited by Kodama Kōta et al., 118–119. Tokyo: Kikkawa kôbunkan.
Kaneko, Kentarō. 1943. *Ito Hirobumi den*, vol. 2. Tokyo: Tôshôsha.
Kant, Immanuel. 1957. *Perpetual Peace*, edited by Lewis White Beck. New York: Liberal Arts Press.
[Kantōgun Sanbō honbu], "Manmō mondai kaiketsusaku an, 22 September 1931," compiled in Sanbō honbu, "Manshū jihen ni okeru gun no tōsui (an)," reprinted in: Inaba Masao et al. (eds.), *Gendaishi shiryō*, vol. 11, Tokyo: Misuzu Shobō 1964.
Kawashima, Shin. 2006. "Chūgoku gaikō ni okeru shōchō to shiteno kokusaiteki chii." *Kokusai seiji* 145, 17–35.
Keene, Edward. 2002. *Beyond the Anarchical Society: Grotius, Colonialism and Order in World Politics*. Cambridge: Cambridge University Press.
Kitaoka, Shin'ichi. (1978) 1985. *Nihon rikugun to tairiku seisaku*. Tokyo: Tokyo Daigaku Shuppankai.
Kodama, Kōta et al., eds. (1961) 1991. *Shiryō niyoru Nihon no ayumi, Kindai hen*. Tokyo: Kikkawa kôbunkan.

Koskenniemi, Martti. 2002. *The Gentle Civilizer of Nations: The Rise and Fall of International Law 1870–1960*. Cambridge: Cambridge University Press.
Krasner, Stephen D. 2001. "Rethinking the Sovereignty State Model." *Review of International Studies* 27, 17–42.
McWilliams, Wayne C. 1975. "East Meets East: The Soejima Mission to China, 1873." *Monumenta Nipponica* 30, no. 3, 237–275.
Manela, Erez. 2007. *The Wilsonian Moment: Self-Determination and the International Origins of Anticolonial Nationalism*. Oxford: Oxford University Press.
Maruyama, Masao. 1968. *Gendai seiji no shisō to kōdō*. Tokyo: Miraisha.
Matsui, Yoshirō. 1979. "Nihon gunkoku shugi no kokusai hōron: Manshū jihen ni okeru sono keisei." In *Senji Nihon no hōtaisei*, edited by Tokyo daigaku shakai kagaku kenkyūjo, 361–405. Tokyo: Tokyo daigaku shuppanka.
Matsui, Yoshirō. 2004. "Gurōbaruka suru sekai ni okeru fuhen to chiiki: Daitōa kyōeiken ron ni okeru fuhen shugi no hihanteki kentō." *Kokusaihō gaikō zasshi* 102, no. 4, 1–22.
Matsuo, Takayoshi. 1998. *Minpon shugi to teikoku shugi*. Tokyo: Misuzu Shobō.
Mitani, Taichirō. 1974. *Taishō demokurashi ron*. Tokyo: Chūō kōronsha.
Mitani, Taichirō. 1988. "The Ambiguity of the Meiji Constitution." In *The Cambridge History of Japan*, vol. 6, edited by Peter Duus, 59–65. Cambridge: Cambridge University Press.
Miyaji, Masato. 1973. *Nichirosengo seijishikenkyū*. Tokyo: Tokyo Daigaku shuppankai.
Mommsen, Wolfgang J. 1981. *Theories of Imperialism*. London: Weidenfeld and Nicolson.
Mommsen, Wolfgang J. and Jürgen Osterhammel, eds. 1986. *Imperialism and After: Continuities and Discontinuities*. London: Allen & Unwin.
Morris-Suzuki, Tessa. 1998. *Re-inventing Japan: Time, Space, Nation*. Armonk NY: M.E. Sharpe.
Nihon kokusai seiji gakkai Taiheiyō sensō gen'in kenkyūbu. 1988. *Taiheiyō sensō eno michi*, vol. 2. Tokyo: Asahi shimbunsha.
Nish, Ian. 2002. *Japanese Foreign Policy in the Interwar Period*. Westport, Conn: Praeger.
Nish, Ian. 2001. "Itō Hirobumi in St Petersburg, 1901." *Collected Writings of Ian Nish*, Part 1, 85–91. Richmond, Surrey: Japan Library.
Nish, Ian. 2001. "The Uncertainties of Isolation: Japan between the Wars." *Collected Writings of Ian Nish*, Part 1, 295–309. Richmond, Surrey: Japan Library.
Nish, Ian. 1993. *Japan's Struggle with Internationalism, Japan, China, and the League of Nations, 1931–1933*. New York: K. Paul International.
Norman, E. Herbert. 1941. "The Genyosha: A Study in the Origins of Japanese Imperialism." *Pacific Affairs* 17, no. 3, 261–284.
Norman, E. Herbert. 1940. *Japan's Emergence as a Modern State: Political and Economic Problems of the Meiji Period*. New York: International Secretariat, Institute of Pacific Relations.
Norman, E. Herbert. 1943. *Soldier and Peasant in Japan: The Origins of Conscription*. New York: International Secretariat, Institute of Pacific Relations.
O'Hagan, Jacinta. 2002. *Conceptualizing the West in International Relations: From Spengler to Said*. New York: Palgrave.
Ōkubo, Toshimichi. 1928. "Seikanron ni kansuru ikensho, October 1873." *Ōkubo Toshimichi monjo*, vol. 5, 53–64. Tokyo: Nihon Shiseki Kyōkai.
Onuma, Yasuaki. 2000. "When Was the Law of International Society Born?: An Inquiry for the History of International Law from an Intercivilizational Perspective." *Journal of the History of International Law* 2, 1–66.
Osterhammel, Jürgen. 1979. "'Technical Co-Operation' between the League of Nations and China." *Modern Asian Studies* 13, no. 4, 661–680.
Peattie, Mark R. 1975. *Ishiwara Kanji and Japan's Confrontation with the West*. Princeton: Princeton University Press.
Peattie, Mark R. 1984. "Introduction." In *The Japanese Colonial Empire, 1895–1945*, edited by Ramon H. Myers and Mark R. Peattie, 6–15. Princeton: Princeton University Press.

Peattie, Mark R. 1988. "The Japanese Colonial Empire, 1895–1945." In *The Cambridge History of Japan*, vol. 6, edited by Peter Duus, 217–270. Cambridge: Cambridge University Press.

Pedersen, Susan. 2006. "The Meaning of the Mandates System: An Argument." *Geschichte und Gesellschaft* 32, no. 4, 560–582.

Pedersen, Susan. 2007. "Back to the League of Nations." *The American Historical Review* 112, no. 4, 1–33.

Reischauer, Edwin O. and Albert M. Craig. 1989. *Japan: Tradition & Transformation*. Sydney: Allen & Unwin.

Roberts, John M. 1985. *The Triumph of the West*. London: British Broadcasting Corporation.

Robinson, Ronald. 1986. "The Eccentric Idea of Imperialism, with or without Empire." In *Imperialism and After*, edited by Wolfgang J. Mommsen and Jürgen Osterhammel, 267–289. London: Allen & Unwin.

Sakeda, Masatoshi. 1978. *Kindai Nihon ni okeru taigaikō undō no kenkyū*. Tokyo: Tokyo Daigaku Shuppankai.

"Seifu soshiki hō narabini shokansei," [March 1932], included in Katakura Tadashi, "Manshū jihen kimitsu seiryaku nisshi, sono 5," (1 February—9 March 1932), reprinted in Kobayashi Tatsuo & Shimada Toshihiko (eds.), *Gendaishi shiryō*, vol. 7, Tokyo 1964.

Semmel, Bernard. 1960. *Imperialism and Social Reform: English Social-Imperial Thought 1895–1914*. London: George Allen & Unwin Ltd.

Suzuki, Shogo. 2009. *Civilization and Empire: China and Japan's Encounter with European International Society*. London: Routledge.

Titus, David A. 1983. "Political Parties and Nonissues in Taisho Democracy." In *Japan Examined: Perspectives on Modern Japanese History*, edited by Harry Wray and Hilary Conroy, 181–190. Honolulu: University of Hawaii Press.

Usui, Katsumi. 1995. *Manshūkoku to kokusai renmei*. Tokyo: Yoshikawa Kōbunkan, Heisei 7.

Watson, Adam. 1984. "European International Society and its Expansion." In *The Expansion of International Society*, edited by Hedley Bull and Adam Watson, 13–32. Oxford: Clarendon Press.

Wheaton, Henry. (1866) 1936. *Elements of International Law*. Reprinted in *The Classics of International Law*, no 19, edited by James Brown Scott. Oxford: Clarendon Press.

Wheaton, Henry. 1904. *Elements of International Law*, 4th ed. London: Stevens.

Yamagata, Aritomo. 1926. "[Speech], 6 December 1890." Reprinted in *Dai Nihon teikoku gikaishi*, vol. 1, edited by Dai-Nihon Teikoku Gikaishi Kankōkai, 469. Tokyo.

Yamamuro, Shin'ichi. 2002. *Shisō kadai to shiteno Ajia*. Tokyo: Iwanami shoten.

Yanagihara, Masaharu, ed. 1996. *Kokusaihō senrei shiryōshū I: Fusen jōyaku*. Tokyo: Shinzansha.

Zachmann, Urs Matthias. 2009. *China and Japan in the Late Meiji Period: China Policy and the Japanese Discourse on National Identity, 1895–1904*. London: Routledge.

Zhang, Yongjin. 1991. "China's Entry Into International Society: Beyond the Standard of 'Civilization'". *Review of International Studies* 17, 3–16.

# Chapter 10
# On the Civilizing Mission of the Global Economy: German Observers of the Colonization and Development of Siberia, 1900–1918

**James Casteel**

**Abstract** This paper examines a group of German social scientists and economists who observed the Russian Empire's efforts to colonise and develop Siberia in the two decades before World War I. In writing about Siberia, these observers exhibited a fascination with the vastness of the territory and the benefits of possessing a continental empire. For many commentators, Siberia was viewed as Russia's America – one in which individualistic settlers were able to rapidly increase productivity and bring their goods to the global market. These developments contrasted with the peasants in European Russia, who German observers considered to be both culturally and economically backward. In writing and commenting on Russia's development of Siberia, Germans observers were contributors to a transnational discourse on imperial governance. They also fantasised about the ways in which Germans might develop and order the territory if they were to possess the land and resources of a continental empire.

## Introduction

In 1902 Otto Auhagen, an agricultural expert on Russian Asia for the German consulate in St. Petersburg, published a study on the Russian Empire's policies to settle and develop Siberia and their impact on the territory. For Auhagen, the construction of the Trans-Siberian Railway and the growing population of Russian settlers were transforming Siberia's status within the Empire and the territory's

I would like to thank the participants of the Nation-State and Beyond workshop, especially Isabella Löhr, Roland Wenzelhuemer and Katja Naumann, for their insightful comments and suggestions for revision. The research for this paper was supported by the German Academic Exchange Service (DAAD), the Rutgers Centre for Historical Analysis, and the Faculty of Arts and Social Sciences at Carleton University.

J. Casteel (✉)
Institute of European, Russian and Eurasian Studies, Carleton University, Ottawa, Canada
e-mail: james_casteel@carleton.ca

I. Löhr and R. Wenzlhuemer (eds.), *The Nation State and Beyond*, Transcultural Research – Heidelberg Studies on Asia and Europe in a Global Context,
DOI 10.1007/978-3-642-32934-0_10, 

relationship to the global economy. Auhagen noted that before the railway, Siberia had been only of academic interest to ethnographers, geographers and linguists, since the harsh conditions of the territory ruled out any consideration of Siberia as a space of settlement for a "civilized nation" (*Kulturnation*). However, the Russian state's effort to develop and populate the territory was changing that perception, a shift Auhagen saw as being reflected in the optimistic mood among business people and administrators in Siberia about the region's future. Emblematic of the potential in Siberia for developing its agricultural and productive resources was the rapid expansion of the Siberian butter trade. Auhagen viewed the growth of butter production in Siberia as being "all the more important since the bearer of this development was not an American farmer, but rather the Siberian peasant, whom one would have thought to have been much less progressive than the peasants of the black earth region in central Russia".[1] While Auhagen was somewhat surprised by these developments, which went against his own cultural assumptions about the limited capability of the Russian peasantry, he and later commentators would soon come to see a connection between the relative freedom of the frontier space of Siberia and the ability of peasants to be transformed into independent and productive smallholding farmers.

Auhagen was not alone in his engagement with Siberia at the turn of the century. The two decades before the First World War saw a heightened German interest in Siberia that was no longer viewed as a territory of exile and backwardness, but rather as a land rich in resources awaiting development. This increased attention toward Siberia is a compelling example of what Michael Geyer has termed "the transnational horizon of the nation," a concept that points to the ways in which the nation is inevitably shaped by interactions with the world outside its boundaries.[2] This chapter explores one aspect of this transnational horizon by analyzing German accounts of Russia's attempts to colonize and develop Siberia in the early twentieth century. During this period, German observers viewed Siberia as entering the global economy for the first time, and reports about the development of Siberia were widely publicized in the press. In particular, the construction of the Trans-Siberian Railway was perceived as opening up vast new markets for the export of German industrial goods, capital and expertise, while also providing new sources of raw materials, resources and foodstuffs for the German economy. Since Germany was Russia's largest trading partner, many German observers believed that Germany was well placed to take advantage of the development of Siberia, expanding the scope for and the space of German action in the world.

This chapter will examine these changing perceptions of Siberia by focusing on a group of early twentieth-century social scientists and economists who observed and commented on the development of Siberia. In writing about Siberia, these observers exhibited a fascination with the vastness of its territory and the benefits of possessing a continental empire. For many commentators, Siberia was viewed as

[1] Auhagen 1902, p. 6.
[2] Geyer 2006, pp. 31–32.

Russia's America – a territory in which individualistic settlers could rapidly increase productivity and bring their goods to the global market. Siberia's settlers were contrasted with the peasants in European Russia, whom German observers considered to be both culturally and economically backward. In commenting on Russian efforts to settle and develop Siberia, German observers were participants in a broader transnational discourse concerning the spread of modern forms of imperial governance and their application in different parts of an increasingly interconnected world. In the process, German observers also fantasized about the ways in which Germans might develop and order the territory if they were to possess the land and resources of a continental empire. While many of these figures were sympathetic to the Russian desire to modernize its empire, with the outbreak of World War I, most would put their knowledge to new use in support of the German occupation of western Russia and the planning of a German sphere of influence in eastern Europe. German observers' interest in Siberia was indicative of broader trends concerning the changing conceptions of the relationship between territories, peoples and cultural development in the pre-war years. It also reflects some of the tensions between the global horizon of German *Weltpolitik* and the limited abilities of German citizens or state officials to act beyond the borders of the German Empire.

## Changing Perceptions of Russian Asia at the Turn of the Century

There has been a growing interest among historians of modern Germany in German views of "the East" in general and of Russia in particular.[3] Drawing inspiration from Edward Said's *Orientalism*, some scholars have suggested that there emerged a strong image of the Russian enemy before the First World War, an image that represented a clear divide between the western, European subject and a barbarous, Asiatic, and backward Russia.[4] To be sure, Russophobic voices shaped the academic fields and public perceptions of Russia from the turn of the century to the First World War. These are most clearly represented in the figure of Theodor Schiemann, a Baltic German émigré and Director of the Seminar für osteuropäische Geschichte und Landeskunde at the University of Berlin, who had close connections to the military and the monarchy and whose regular contributions to the conservative *Kreuzzeitung* had a strong influence on public perceptions of Russia.[5] However, such an interpretation tends to overlook the more ambiguous position of Russia in Germans' imaginings of the world in the late Kaiserreich.[6] In particular, the turn of the century witnessed a growing interest from a number of

[3] Jenkins 2004, pp. 97–100; Kontje 2004; Thum 2006; Liulevicius 2009.

[4] Paddock 2006, pp. 214–243; Liulevicius 2009, pp. 125–129.

[5] Voigt 1994, pp. 89–92; Meyer 1956.

[6] Koenen 2005, pp. 7–10, 21–36.

German intellectuals in the humanities and social sciences in Russia's attempts to reform and modernize its empire.[7] German observers viewed Russia in a contradictory manner as a European imperial power in Asia and as an object of European domination. This ambiguous position was characteristic of European perceptions of eastern Europe since the Enlightenment which, as Larry Wolff has argued, constructed eastern Europe as an "intermediary cultural space" separating "civilized" Europe from "barbarous" Asia, modernity from backwardness.[8] Russia's location on these geographical and civilizational axes was not absolute, but relative and very much dependent on the positioning of the observer and context in which such claims were articulated.

For most German observers of Russia at the turn of the century, these boundaries between modernity and backwardness were not fixed but rather in a state of flux. In the nineteenth century, the European civilizing mission had been structured in part based on a conception that the "white race" was superior to other races, thereby legitimizing European dominance. However, as Andrew Zimmerman has argued, there was a shift in this European (and global) racial discourse around the turn of the century. The dichotomous and hierarchical divide between colonizer and colonized based on the supposed racial superiority of the European colonizer gave way to a more flexible racial discourse informed by Social Darwinism. This discourse inscribed difference less in terms of a fixed racial hierarchy than in terms of the levels of development of cultures. Bringing history into the equation, economic competition was conceptualized as a competition among cultures that found themselves at different stages of development. Thus discourses concerning Europeanization, modernization, colonization and economic development were part of a larger project of expanding the field of European governance in an age of "colonial globality".[9] Such reinscriptions of race as cultural difference legitimated European hegemony on the basis of claims concerning Europe's technological, economic and cultural advancement over other regions and cultures. The implication of this discursive shift was that if European hegemony was not absolute, then it had to be maintained through constant struggle since non-European cultures could conceivably advance and challenge European dominance.[10]

These shifting ideologies of European hegemony also corresponded to the rapidly changing global order in the age of high imperialism. Siberia and the Russian Far East were situated on the borders of one of the key sites of imperial rivalry in the Pacific, with American, Japanese and European imperial powers (including Russia) attempting to gain access to Chinese markets and territory.

---

[7] Voigt 1994, pp. 88–111.

[8] Wolff 1994, p. 7. Most scholars now view the invention of eastern Europe as having occurred in the mid- to late-nineteenth century, see Adamovsky 2005, pp. 591–628; Struck 2004, pp. 504–524; Lemberg 1985, pp. 48–91.

[9] Conrad 2006, pp. 41–44.

[10] Zimmerman 2001, pp. 38–61, 201–216; Zimmerman 2006, pp. 53–79; Adas 1989, pp. 271–342. As Zimmerman observes, this discourse bears a number of similarities with the discourse of neoracism that accompanies contemporary globalization.

Although European imperialism had predominantly focused on overseas domination, technological developments in transportation and communications such as the railroad, steamship and telegraph had made it possible to expand and develop the interior of continents, populating sparsely settled territories and extracting previously inaccessible natural resources. Railways were at the centre of these regimes of "modern territoriality," both as the means and as symbols of these developments.[11] Chinese encouragement of settlement in neighboring Manchuria awakened Russian interests in developing Russian Asia and settling Russian populations in Siberia. The completion of the Canada-Pacific Railway in the 1880s shortened the distance between Asian markets and Europe and provided the British with a faster means of transporting troops to the Pacific. The construction of the Trans-Siberian Railway, including a concession to build the Chinese Eastern Railway through Chinese territory in Manchuria, thus had both economic and military importance for Russia in its policy to develop the territory and to ensure that Vladivostok, its main Pacific port, was protected against imperial rivals.[12] In addition, by linking Siberia to Europe, the railway also provided opportunities for locals to expand their production and engage in global trade.[13]

Contemporary German and Russian elites and commentators on these developments shared fears concerning the danger of an "awakening Asia" as China and especially Japan attempted to modernize their countries. As Sebastian Conrad has demonstrated, Germany's acquisition of the colony of Jiaozhou in 1897 elicited a sense of possibility concerning Germany's expansion of its colonial empire in East Asia and its dominance over Chinese markets. The opening of new markets for German industry in China, however, was also accompanied by fears that German and European culture might be flooded by Chinese laborers and even that a modernizing China might develop the potential to compete with European countries.[14] Russian anxieties concerning the "yellow peril" were more directly related to preserving its territorial integrity in Asia. Russian officials feared that the sparsely populated territories of Siberia might be an attraction to Chinese settlers or Japanese imperial advance. Policies of encouraging settlement in Siberia were thus in part shaped by these desires to populate the territory with loyal Russian subjects.[15] Such fears intensified after the Japanese defeat of Russia in the Russo-Japanese war in 1905, an event that was viewed by contemporaries as a victory of an Asian nation over a European power and one that called into question the "global domination of the white race," as one German expert on Siberia put it.[16]

Although there was common ground between Germany and Russia in terms of their mutual participation in Europe's civilizing mission, German economic

---

[11] Maier 2006, pp. 44–46; see also Ewing's paper in this volume.

[12] Marks 1991, pp. 28–45; Glatfelter 1991, pp. 137–144; Stolberg 2004, pp. 165–170.

[13] Krahmer 1897, pp. 96–98, 103; Marks 1991, pp. 28–30, 46–47.

[14] Conrad 2006, pp. 168–173, 180–187.

[15] Stolberg 2004, pp. 165–169; Gollwitzer 1962.

[16] Goebel 1953, p. 171; Aydin 2007, pp. 213–219.

development was increasingly shifting the power balance between the two countries in favor of the former. The German Empire was an integral part of turn-of-the-century economic globalization, second only to Great Britain in terms of its integration into the world economy. Historians of modern Germany have increasingly come to view the processes of globalization and nationalization not as conflicting processes, but rather as ones that work in dialectical relationship to each other. Indeed, there is a growing consensus among historians that the creation of the German nation-state needs to be viewed in the context of a broader wave of national consolidation that was very much a response to and an attempt to assert national sovereignty in an increasingly competitive and globally interconnected world.[17] The German national economy neither predated nor developed separately from the world economy. Rather, the two emerged in tandem with each other, and indeed, Germany's economic strength was very much dependent on this economic entanglement with the wider world.[18] As Germany was transformed into an industrial power, Germany's economy increasingly became oriented towards the export of manufactured goods abroad and German industry became more dependent on the import of raw materials and foodstuffs. To be sure, for contemporaries, Germany's colonial possessions had political importance as a measure of Germany's status as a "great power". However, Germany's informal imperialism was much more significant in advancing German power, including its economic hegemony in eastern and southeastern Europe.[19]

Germany's rapid change of status as an expanding industrial power was a concern to Russian elites. Russia's policies of industrialization, railway construction and reform were aimed at transforming the old empire to make it more competitive with other European empires, following similar strategies to Austria-Hungary or the Ottoman Empire. But Russia's industrialization was highly dependent on foreign trade and capital investment. Germany had become Russia's largest trading partner in the years before the First World War, capturing 35 % of the Russian market for imports by 1902, a figure that increased to 45 % by 1913 in part as result of favorable trade treaties. As a trading partner, Russia ranked behind Great Britain and Austria-Hungary in terms of the size of its market, accounting for about 9 % of Germany's total exports. But the Russian market had the highest potential for growth and was particularly profitable for new industries such as the chemical industry, electrical industry and manufacturers of finished goods and machinery including motor vehicles. Germany was also Russia's largest export market, accounting for 30 % of its total exports by 1913, mostly consisting of grain, foodstuffs and raw materials.[20] German foreign capital investment accounted for

[17] Geyer 2004, pp. 77–79; Conrad 2006, pp. 316–333; Maier 2006. My reading is also in line with Löhr and Wenzlhuemer's argument that globalization produces dynamics of integration *and* fragmentation, see their Introduction to this volume.

[18] Petersson 2004, pp. 49–61.

[19] Blackbourn 2003, pp. 249–254; Conrad 2006, pp. 44–46.

[20] Spaulding 1997, pp. 86–88.

approximately 20 % of the total foreign capital investments in Russia, placing Germany in third place behind Great Britain and France. German capital was particularly well represented in areas such as metal processing and machine building, banking, mining and metallurgy, and municipal electrical and lighting companies.[21] While Russia's efforts to reform and modernize its economy contributed to increasing its productivity, these efforts at the same time made it more dependent on other European countries and the United States.[22]

German observers did not just view Russia as existing in stagnant Asia, but rather as engaged in substantial transformations. Russia appeared to them both as a reforming European imperial power in Asia but also as an early model of a developing country.[23] Indeed, what is particularly striking about German academic writing and coverage of Siberia in the German press is that Siberia's entry into the global economy – what contemporaries termed *Weltwirtschaft* – allowed Siberia, Russia's largest colonial territory, the potential to become more advanced than Russia itself. German observers recognized that Russia's attempts at reform and modernization were making progress toward greater integration of the empire into the modern global economy. However, in their view, it was only on Russia's eastern frontier that it would truly be capable of doing so, contributing to a broader European "civilizing mission" in Asia.

## Reform, Resettlement and the Making of Peasants into Independent Farmers

The recent imperial rivalries in the Far East, the Russian Revolution of 1905, and the reforms that followed served as catalysts for the growth of German interest in Russia. Most experts viewed the reforms introduced after 1905 by Russian Prime Minister Pyotr Stolypin in a positive light and believed that, if they were successful, they would place Russia on a path of transition to European modernity. Economist Kurt Wiedenfeld drew an analogy between Russia's geographical position spanning Europe and Asia and its economic development, viewing Russia as "representative of an enormous region of transitions".[24] Similarly, the historian Otto Hoetzsch, who founded and edited the journal *Osteuropa* and who would become one of the most important experts on Russia between the wars, also saw the political and agricultural reforms in Russia as part of Russia's "transition to the modern conditions of a European state".[25] German experts on Russia often drew parallels between Russia's

[21] Ol' 1983 [1922], pp. xi–xii, 91.

[22] Domosh 2010, pp. 427–444.

[23] Cf. Shanin 1985, pp. 124–133.

[24] Wiedenfeld 1913, p. 249.

[25] Hoetzsch 1913, p. 86; on Hoetzsch, see Voigt 1978.

contemporary social, economic and political transformations and the stages that Prussia had undergone over the course of the nineteenth century.

For German observers, Russia thus occupied not only a different space but also existed at a different stage of historical development from western Europe. In thinking about how German scholars viewed Russia, Johannes Fabian's concept of the "denial of the coevalness" of the Other is useful (1983, 30). In contrast to the views of the more reactionary Russophobic voices in the German academy and press, Russia was not seen as backward and incapable of development. Rather, in its efforts to enact reform, Russia was attempting to catch up and replicate social transformations that other European societies had undergone over the course of the nineteenth century. Although there was certainly some debate as to whether these reforms would be successful given the extent of the social and economic problems in Russia and the perception of the lower level of cultural development of its peoples, German commentators were convinced that the path of reform was necessary and that the continued existence of a stable Russian state was important to German interests in extending economic hegemony over Russia. However, they also expressed fears that Russia might be able to bridge the temporal gap between its own development and European modernity, a prognosis that could have significant implications for Germany.

The main issues on which observers focused their attention were agricultural reform and the process of settlement of Siberia. These issues were interconnected: German commentators viewed the 1905 Revolution largely as a product of the Russian state's failure to address problems in Russian agriculture, one of the most important sectors in the Russian economy and one in which most of the population was employed. For many observers, the very existence of the Russian state and its ability to maintain political control over its vast empire was at stake in the reforms; their failure could have a significant impact for the German economy. The contemporary Russian efforts to colonize and settle Siberia were related to these issues of agricultural reform. More land for settlement in Siberia would provide an outlet for surplus agricultural populations in Russia proper while contributing to increasing agricultural productivity in Siberia. This project would also be in Russia's national interest and in the interest of Europe's civilizing mission in Russian Asia. For German observers, reliable Russian settlers were central to the project of preventing Siberia from falling into the hands of emerging Asian powers.

German interests in Siberia at the turn of the century were shaped by Russia's own policies of developing the territory. Siberia had long been integrated into the Russian Empire, but it was only in the 1890s that a concerted program of Russian settlement began in earnest. This program combined both national and imperial ambitions, as it aimed to find an outlet for social problems in Russia proper but also to foster Russian imperial interests in Asia. Serfdom had of course long inhibited the freedom of movement of peasants and even after its abolition in 1861, the peasants' legal ties to the village commune made large-scale migration difficult. Illegal migration began to increase in the 1880s as peasants moved east searching for better economic conditions and attracted by the freedom Siberia offered.[26] In the 1890s, at the same time as the beginning of the construction of the Trans-Siberian Railway, the state began to systematically encourage and attempt to actively manage the migration of Russian peasants, founding a Resettlement Administration in the Interior Ministry in 1896 that was responsible for overseeing and encouraging the settlement of Siberia. In 1906, the Resettlement Administration was moved to the recently renamed agricultural ministry Chief Administration of Land Settlement and Agriculture, which would become the central institution involved in Stolypin's ambitious agricultural reforms under the direction of A.V. Krivoschein, an institution that one historian has provocatively argued had the potential to develop into the Russian equivalent of a colonial office for all of Asiatic Russia.[27] State support and the opening of the railway increased the numbers of settlers, with over 3.5 million Russian settlers arriving in Siberia between 1897 and 1911.[28]

Settlement of Siberia was also connected to the larger issue of agricultural reform in Russia. In the aftermath of the Revolution of 1905, which particularly affected rural areas, Stolypin was appointed Prime Minister and introduced land reform legislation that attempted to restructure Russian agricultural ownership and encourage the transformation of peasants into individualistic and independent landowning farmers. Given that most peasants still lived in the traditional village commune and land was held in communal tenure, this program entailed a radical restructuring of the social relations of the peasantry. However, Russian officials believed these reforms were necessary in order to modernize agriculture and avoid further social unrest. Legislation was passed that permitted peasants to leave the village commune and keep their land, which ideally would become an enclosed farm. The reforms also reduced peasants' tax obligations and abolished the redemption payment for serfdom. As Judith Pallot observes, the policy of reform relied on a binary opposition between what reformers saw as backward village communes and the modern individualistic and independent farmer. For the reformers, the latter embodied the ideals of modernizing agriculture and would serve as the avant-garde for the further transformation of Russian society.[29]

Russian reformers, and especially Stolypin, placed particular emphasis on the benefits of encouraging the settlement of Siberia as part of the transformation of Russia along the lines of other European colonial empires.[30] The settling of Russian peasants in Siberia would contribute to the general project of agricultural reform by providing some relief for peasants and Russian agriculture in central Russia. Stolypin and Krivoschein regarded the migration as benefiting the development of Siberia itself. In their view, as conveyed in a report they co-authored after an

[26] Forsyth 1992, pp. 190–192; Lincoln 1994, pp. 257–262; Treadgold 1957, pp. 67–81.

[27] Treadgold 1957, pp. 120–130; Sunderland 2010, pp. 120–127.

[28] Lincoln 1994, p. 257.

[29] Pallot 1999, pp. 1–6, 31–69; Kotsonis 1999, pp. 57–61.

[30] Sunderland 2010, pp. 120–127.

official visit to observe the developments in Western Siberia in 1910, what Siberia lacked in order to develop the territory was people. Thus the migration of Russian settlers to Siberia was considered to be the main force driving modernization and development of the territory, overcoming the traditional "plunder economy" of the old settlers and the "primitive economy of the nomads".[31] For Russian elites, the settlement of Siberia with Russians would contribute to the territory's development and the integration of this peripheral region into the core of the Russian empire. In the process, it would also continue to push the boundary line between Europe and Asia further to the East while providing firmer borders with Russia's neighbors, a project that German observers also recognized as being in a common European interest.[32]

The reforms that were taking place in Russia drew the interest of an interdisciplinary group of German social scientists, economists and historians who challenged the dominant Russophobic tendencies of experts on Russia such as Theodor Schiemann. Max Sering, a professor of economics with a specialization in agriculture at the University of Berlin, and Otto Auhagen, by this time a professor at Berlin's Agricultural College, published a collection entitled *Russlands Kultur und Volkswirtschaft* in 1913.[33] The essays were based on presentations given on a high-profile tour of Russia that the Berlin-based Vereinigung für staatswissenschaftliche Fortbildung had organized the year before for 108 German academics, civil servants and judges to visit administrative, cultural, industrial and agricultural sites in Russia.[34] One of the most important issues discussed in these contributions was Russia's agricultural reforms. There was general agreement among the organizers that the social habits and mentalities of the Russian peasants – shaped by centuries of serfdom and collective life in the village communes – needed to be transformed in order to make the peasants more productive and to allow them to develop into modern independent farmers. Sering, for example, held that the Russian peasants' "agrarian collectivism . . . paralyzes the strengths of the individual and gives the members of the all too parochial local community that herd-like character that makes the Russian peasant appear to us like a person from the middle ages."[35]

German observers viewed Stolypin's agricultural reforms positively. Sering considered the Russian legislation of 1906 and 1910 that introduced the privatization of agricultural communities and allowed individual peasants to leave the village communes as having provided "that individualistic foundation upon which European culture rests". Sering believed that a farmer who possessed his land as private property would value the land and work to make it more

[31] Stolypin and Kriwoscheïn 1912, p. 3; Treadgold 1957, pp. 153–183; Steinwedel 2007, pp. 128–147.

[32] Remnev 2007, pp. 440–445; Stolberg 2004.

[33] For Sering's biography, see Nelson 2009, pp. 65–93; Stoehr 2002, pp. 57–90.

[34] Sering 1913, pp. iii–vi; Voigt 1994.

[35] Sering 1913, p. iv.

productive. German observers shared with Russian officials many of the Social Darwinist assumptions regarding the potentials of the reforms to transform Russian society. Socio-economic competition among the peasantry would lead to social differentiation producing an elite of productive landowning farmers and better conditions for the rest of the peasants who would work the land. Sering held that such a transformation in the peasantry – which made up the majority of Russia's population – would inevitably result in broader social transformations in Russian society. Increasing agricultural productivity would lead to stronger demand for consumer goods that would also strengthen Russia's industry. In the process, German observers believed that Russian mentalities would also be transformed, replacing "the spirit of comfortable carelessness and melancholy dreams" with the "virtues [of] ... discipline and initiative at all levels of society".[36] German commentators were well aware that the reforms would be disruptive to Russian social life and even contained the potential to spark another revolution, but most shared in the view that they were also necessary. As one expert put it, the agricultural reforms were a "painful operation" that "had to be undertaken" if Russia was ever to develop along western European models.[37]

Many of these observers' prescriptions for Russia to turn its peasants into modern independent farmers drew on contemporary debates on the issue of the internal colonization of the Prussian East, discussions which were followed by Russian officials in the Resettlement Office.[38] The topic of internal colonization was central to German national culture and occupied the attention of historians, social scientists, economists and civil servants from the 1880s to the outbreak of the First World War. A number of nationalist intellectuals, most famously, Max Weber, took a strong interest in the issue, which they hoped would deal with a variety of social problems that had accompanied the processes of industrialization and urbanization in Germany. Those involved in the debates were concerned with two broader issues: the supposed danger that free labor posed to the German economy (leading to an expanding proletariat that might challenge bourgeois hegemony) and the threat of Polish seasonal workers to German national culture, which in their view might lead to the Polonization of the Prussian East and eventually even the loss of this territory. Supporters of internal colonization held an ideal of a free and independent German farmer who would be settled in the land and take ownership over his production, thereby increasing productivity and contributing to the Germanization of the Prussian East. These utopian nationalist ideas often collided with the interests of Prussian landowners who wanted to continue to utilize seasonal labor from Russian Poland because of the lesser expense (some even entertained the idea of replacing Polish laborers with agricultural workers from China).[39] But these

[36] Sering 1913, p. v; cf. Auhagen 1913, pp. 142–143.

[37] Hollmann 1913, p. 319.

[38] Sunderland 2004, pp. 194–196. The transnational discussion of inner colonization is another example of the cultural transfer among experts, as Dittrich describes in his paper in this volume.

[39] Zimmerman 2006, pp. 57–63; Nelson 2009, pp. 65–69; Conrad 2006, pp. 124–167.

ideas were nonetheless central to shaping policies and the national imaginary at the turn of the century.

In their discussions, German observers also drew on the example of the other continental empire, the United States of America. Indeed, both Germans and Russian commentators drew parallels between the development of the Siberian "Wild East" and the American "Wild West". Tsarist officials in the nineteenth century had imagined Siberia as the Russian frontier, a space for future settlement and growth of the Russian people, parallel to the westward expansion of the United States in the Americas.[40] The liberal Decembrists and later exiles who opposed tsarist autocracy developed a counter-image of Siberia as America, which valorized the Russian settlers as living in conditions that were more free and natural than those of the old country of Russia. For them, Siberia represented a utopia of how life in Russia might be if Russians were freed from tsarist autocracy and the burdens of serfdom.[41] Frontier mythology was a transnational discourse and one which German observers shared. Many observers of Russia – especially those who were proponents of internal colonization in the Prussian East – had the American example of the colonization of a continent in mind when they imagined Russia.[42] Works about Siberia written for a general audience often drew comparisons between the colonization of Siberia and North America, portraying the Russian settlers as "pioneers" who brought the 'evils of civilization', alcohol and syphilis, with them thus contributing to the eventual extinction of the native peoples of Siberia.[43]

Commentators on Russia's development of Siberia were also engaged in more general debates about the emergence of world powers at a moment when it became possible to imagine the globe as a space of action. Increasingly, with the expansion of railways making it possible for markets to penetrate the interiors of continents, Europeans considered the continental powers of America and Russia as having the potential to become the world powers of the future.[44] For example, in his influential *Political Geography*, Friedrich Ratzel, geographer and founder of geopolitics, described the expansion of Russia into Siberia and Central Asia as one of the most important instances of the colonization of contiguous territory on a continental scale. Much like the United States after westward expansion, if developed, Siberia could give Russia the potential to become a world power with a global reach, one that could challenge the dominance of the British Empire.[45] German scholars could also claim these acts of colonization as achievements for the German nation, since

[40] Bassin 1999; Stolberg 2004; Weiss 2007.

[41] Bassin 1991, pp. 775–779.

[42] Nelson 2009, pp. 65–70; Steinweis 1999, pp. 56–69.

[43] Stirne 1912, p. 18.

[44] Groh 1988; Neitzel 2000.

[45] Ratzel 1923, pp. 114–116, 257.

German emigrants to both countries contributed to the process of expansion, even if their efforts benefited other states.[46]

Drawing on such examples from the Prussian East and the American West, German observers argued that in Siberia, Russian settlers would be freed from the old constraints that bound them in Russia proper and could become independent and more productive citizens, while also maintaining their loyalty to the tsar. This idea of unleashing the productive powers of the people – apparent in contemporary discussions of the Americas and Siberia – was central to the prescriptions that German observers held for Siberia. Observers also maintained that an ethnic Russian population was necessary to secure Russia's vast Asian territory from competitors in the region, an issue that became all the more pressing after Russian defeat in the Russo-Japanese War.[47] Thus settlement and colonization would ensure that the economic development of the territory would benefit the Russian state and indirectly Europe. At the same time, the Russian settler population would also serve as a demographic barrier against future migrations of populations from Asia. By remaining part of Russia, Siberia would also be preserved for Europe allowing Germany to profit from its resources.

## Siberia and the Civilizing Mission of the Global Economy

Among the German observers of Russian developments was Otto Goebel, one of the foremost experts on the condition of the Siberian economy before World War I. Goebel had worked in St. Petersburg as an engineer and later studied economics at the University of Berlin. He was a trade attaché for the German consulate in St. Petersburg from 1905 to 1910. During this time, he traveled on two official expeditions to Siberia resulting in two book-length studies published under the auspices of the German Interior Ministry.[48] These works solidified his reputation in both Germany and Russia as an expert on Siberia.[49] In addition to his academic publications, Goebel made considerable efforts to popularize knowledge about the recent developments in Siberia in the public sphere, publishing two travel accounts about Siberia before the war. The publisher's preface to one of them placed the completion of the Trans-Siberian Railway in a long line of western expansion to the east, from Alexander the Great's conquest of Persia to Vasco da Gama's voyages to the Indian Ocean and the Pacific. The completion of the railway was heralded as offering the "fastest connection between Europe and the Far East," outpacing the Suez Canal and allowing for the "opening up of virgin territory to human culture".[50]

[46] Hoetzsch 1904, p. 169.

[47] Cf. Krahmer 1897, p. 11; Goebel 1914, pp. 11–13, 60–61.

[48] Goebel 1910b *Westbaikalischen*; Goebel 1910a *Ostbaikalischen* 1910.

[49] Cf. Goebel 1953, pp. 250–252.

[50] Goebel 1914, p. 3.

Goebel himself also viewed the colonization of Siberia as an event of world historical importance, "one of the greatest migrations of people of all times," but one which most Germans knew little about. For Goebel, the colonization of Siberia was squarely in the civilizing mission of Europe in the world:

> The last great act in the settling of the non-tropical zones of the earth by the Indo-Germanic race . . . the last of the peaceful penetrations that together with advancements in mechanical engineering and transportation have transformed the conditions of humanity in the nineteenth century greater than in any earlier era.[51]

German observers viewed Russia's efforts to settle and develop its territory in Siberia as part and parcel of a broader European colonial project in which the Russians were employing similar methods to other European and North American empires. And yet, despite his celebration of the colonization of Siberia, Goebel regretted that the Russians did not possess the colonizing abilities of other Europeans: "The Russians are indeed passable agricultural colonizers, but [they are] not comparable with the Germanic-Romanic elements that have colonized the moderate [climate] zones in the rest of the world."[52] Thus, for Goebel, Russians were participants in a broader European civilizing mission to colonize Siberia, but they were not quite as civilized and capable of colonization as western Europeans.

This ambiguity of Russia's status was not limited to Goebel's work. Kurt Wiedenfeld, an economist trained at the University of Berlin and active observer of Russian affairs, was similarly struck by these tensions. Wiedenfeld had written his dissertation on the construction of the Trans-Siberian Railway and its effects on the Russian economy.[53] Upon his appointment as a professor at the Handelshochschule in Cologne in 1904, Wiedenfeld abandoned his research interest in Prussian internal colonization to focus on the study of industrial policy and development. He continued to maintain his interest in Russia, becoming a foreign trade advisor for the foreign office in the early years of the Weimar Republic and also serving as a representative of the German government in Moscow from 1921 to 1922.[54]

As an observer of Russia, Wiedenfeld was particularly interested in how economic development was transforming the country. Although he viewed western Russia as the most advanced area, he still considered it as an extension of the German economy since German investment in the region and German industry's demands for raw materials had a strong influence on its economy. Thus Russia appeared as an object of German economic power and was clearly less developed than its western neighbors. However, Russia's "transitional character" was most apparent when one looked to the east where countries such as Persia and China appeared "nearly as objects of its economic expansion" and where Japan had only secured the right to be considered a "subject in a mutual relationship" with Russia

[51] Ibid., pp. 60–61.

[52] Ibid., p. 61.

[53] Wiedenfeld 1900.

[54] See Wiedenfeld 1960, pp. 14–21, 51–109.

through its victory in the Russo-Japanese War.[55] This tension reveals more generally the ambiguous position of Russia in the German (and European) imagination: in relation to the East it was a bastion of European power, participating in the civilizing mission in Asia. In relation to the West, by contrast, it was increasingly being reduced to an object of European economic domination despite Russia's military might. Thus for contemporaries, the level of integration into the global economy also spoke to the level of civilization of different regions of the world.

The civilizing mission inherent in Siberia's entrance into the global economy was evident in Kurt Wiedenfeld's discussion of Russia's economic development. He viewed Russia as a "country in transition" which was characterized by considerable regional differences in terms of the level of integration into the global economy. Wiedenfeld considered economic history to be shaped by a developmental trajectory in which progress was measured by the extent to which a particular country or world region was incorporated into the world economy (*Weltwirtschaft*). Grain exports made up the largest portion of Russia's contributions to world trade and clearly agriculture was well integrated into global markets. However, Wiedenfeld still considered most peasants to be living in a state of *Naturalwirtschaft* or natural economy, basically a subsistence economy in which the consumption of imported items was limited to luxury goods (tea being the most prominent in the Russian case). Much like the civilizational development implied in transforming *Naturvölker* to *Kulturvölker* in anthropological terms,[56] the economy could advance from *Naturalwirtschaft* to *Weltwirtschaft*.

Wiedenfeld considered Russia's economic development, however, to be very uneven, varying from region to region and even within regions. Russia's western provinces that bordered Germany – the Baltic and Poland – were well integrated into the world economy and were the most industrialized regions of Russia. In fact, Wiedenfeld viewed them less as a part of the Russian economy than as an extension of the German economy. By contrast, he considered central and eastern Russia, with the exception of Moscow and the other administrative centers of the empire, as still possessing "the character of a natural economy".[57] The Russian peasant lived almost completely from his or her own production – food, clothes, even housing. The need to pay taxes was the only external motivation for the peasant to produce more than what was needed for subsistence. The different levels of economic development also corresponded to the cultural development of the inhabitants of these regions.

Siberia, however, was a different case. While most contemporaries associated Asia with stagnation and backwardness, Wiedenfeld considered "Asiatic Russia" including Siberia and Turkestan to be much more integrated into the world economy than central Russia. One of the main factors that Wiedenfeld saw as contributing to this was Russia's investment in the transportation infrastructure.

[55] Wiedenfeld 1913, p. 271.

[56] Cf. Zimmerman 2001.

[57] Wiedenfeld 1913, pp. 249–251, cit. 251.

In particular, the Trans-Siberian Railroad in its few years of existence had had an enormous impact having "already transformed large parts of the whole area into world economic bodies".[58] This was particularly evident in Siberia's big cities that had grown at "American speed" to become administrative centers for gold mining, machinery import, the butter trade and other industries. Wiedenfeld considered the cities of Siberia to be completely integrated into the global economy.[59] Despite this substantial evidence of progress, Wiedenfeld was still hesitant to label Siberia, aside from the large cities, as an actual "global economic body".[60] Even with the modernizing impulse of the butter trade, agricultural regions outside the urban centers still found themselves in a state of transition. In addition, Wiedenfeld found areas inhabited by the indigenous peoples of Siberia to be at an even lower level of development, which to him represented a natural economy that was untouched by modernity. For Wiedenfeld, these cultural and economic disparities also made it politically difficult for the Russian state to rule the territory.[61]

The integration of Siberia into the global market and the cultural advancement that followed was also evident in Wiedenfeld's discussion of the transformation of the traditional trade fair into a modern market. Wiedenfeld considered the traditional trade fairs that had been commonplace in Europe since the medieval period to have been primitive economic formations that allowed isolated groups or tribes to come together on an annual basis to exchange goods with peoples from another region. Although these had for the most part lost their economic function in Europe with the growth of the stock market, in Russia they still played a large role in trade in central Russia and in parts of Russian Asia, especially in the steppes of western Asia and the northern tundra.[62] For Wiedenfeld, transportation was the impetus that transformed the trade fairs into modern markets. Before the railway, climate conditions had limited transportation to particular times of the year. Even after its completion, in the sparsely settled territories of Russia with primitive transportation infrastructure, it was often difficult if not impossible to transport goods, especially in the winter months or after the spring floods. For Wiedenfeld, the trade fair corresponded to the primitive transportation infrastructure and subsistence economy.[63] He experienced a taste of this when he visited an annual fair in the steppes, which he presented as a journey back in time to a primitive stage of development. Observing the Kirghiz tribes gathering together to bring their herds to market, Wiedenfeld was particularly struck by the initial slow pace of the market, where the traders spent a long time looking at all of the goods and beasts for sale before making a purchase, exhibiting an "oriental patience" so strange for the western

[58] Ibid., p. 252.

[59] Ibid., p. 256.

[60] Ibid., p. 255.

[61] Ibid., pp. 255–257.

[62] Ibid., p. 257.

[63] Ibid., p. 261.

European visitor.[64] The railways would challenge this slow pace and do away with the market, as the regular and reliable schedule made it possible to establish stores in towns that would serve the function that fairs once had for trading goods.[65] Thus Wiedenfeld viewed the railway as transforming the economies of the regions it touched, shrinking the distances to European markets and accelerating the pace of life to correspond to European norms.

The wide frontier spaces and the transportation infrastructure that the Russian government was developing in Siberia were also transforming the populations of Russian settlers. Most German observers viewed the Russian peasantry as being hampered by the mentalities of the peasant commune and the oppressive relationship with the Russian state. They were considered to be less culturally and economically developed than their counterparts in Western Europe or the United States. But in Siberia, which in many respects observers saw as a laboratory for Russian reform efforts, Russian peasants were being transformed into modern productive citizens. To be sure, many German observers still viewed the Russian peasantry as not quite at the same level as European or North American farmers, and indeed, some even attributed the slower development in Siberia in comparison to the United States to the backward qualities of the Russian peasantry who were slow to change even in the new surroundings.[66] But in general, they tended to view the modern conditions and access to global markets as forces that were having a transformative impact on Russian peasants in Siberia and that were providing them with the potential to become more productive, even if they were still behind western European developments.

Wiedenfeld in particular was impressed by the qualities of the Russian settlers in Siberia. He saw Siberian farmers as "colonists" who possessed "an increased drive and desire for innovation".[67] Liberated from the social constraints and collective mentalities that burdened peasants in European Russia, Siberian farmers could employ such traits to take advantage of the improved transportation infrastructure (both the railway and steamboats) to bring their goods to international markets. Not bound by the traditions of the village commune, freed from certain tax burdens such as redemption payments (which had only recently been abolished in European Russia), and with abundant land and untapped resources with which to work, Siberian farmers were more productive and better able to produce for the global market. As individual landowners, they possessed more wealth and demonstrated greater initiative in managing their holdings. This increase in productivity also meant that they had more money to spend on imported consumer goods, especially tea which Wiedenfeld mentions was consumed at four times the quantities of peasants in European Russia.[68]

---

[64] Ibid., p. 258.

[65] Ibid., p. 262.

[66] Auhagen 1902, p. 8; id. 1913, pp. 143–144; Goebel 1914, pp. 80–81.

[67] Wiedenfeld 1913, p. 253.

[68] Ibid., pp. 252–254.

One example that attracted particular attention for German observers, including Wiedenfeld, was the Siberian butter trade. Butter production had begun in western Siberia in the 1890s with considerable support from the state which provided loans, equipment and training for workers, and sent experts to help educate the peasants. Eventually, dairy cooperatives (*arteli*) were organized along the Kurgan line of the Siberian railroad. The dairy industry was oriented primarily towards export and its production rose rapidly, reaching 3,500,000 Russian poods in 1907, a figure that corresponded to almost the entire butter export for the Russian Empire that year.[69] Wiedenfeld considered the butter trade in western Siberia to be one of the most impressive examples of the entrance of Siberia into the world economy, since production in this area was completely oriented towards export and not local consumption. Siberian dairies used some of the most modern separator equipment and machinery and shipped the finished product by rail packaged in ice to consumers in western Europe. Commenting on the lack of understanding in Germany about the extent of Germany's dependency on imports but also on the quality of Siberian wares, Wiedenfeld wrote that "only a few housewives have an idea of how much Siberian butter is regularly consumed in the large cities of Germany, and not only for cooking purposes but also as table butter".[70]

Despite the acknowledgement of the progress that was being made in Siberia, many German observers still tended to see much of the advancement of Russia as a product of German culture and labor. Wiedenfeld noted the role of Germans in the economic development of the country: "For Russia, contact with the outside world in earlier times as in the present was organized mainly by German merchants."[71] Goebel, who had extensive experience in his role as a trade advisor in trying to make inroads for German investors and business people in Russia, frequently pointed out the value of having German-speaking populations in Russia for German economic interests:

> The German Russians are of importance for Germany's economic relations with Siberia. One meets large numbers of their sons in the cities as white-collar employees or even as independent shopkeepers. Their language abilities and often their inclination towards Germany make them born mediators between the distant country and us.[72]

Indeed, in his explorations of Siberia and his time in Russia more generally, Goebel benefitted from German-speaking Russians who served as his guides and interpreters and who had a strong impact on what he saw and how he interpreted social conditions in Russia.[73] Commenting on German farmers, Goebel stated that:

---

69 Treadgold 1957, p. 179; Kotsonis 1999, pp. 140–153; Larsen 2003, pp. 329–348.

70 Wiedenfeld 1913, p. 253.

71 Ibid., p. 257.

72 Goebel 1913, p. 21.

73 Ibid., pp. 98–128.

> Nowhere else has the superiority of the German as colonizer appeared to me so directly as here [in Russia] where in the same climate and under the same transportation conditions the German villages thrived, while the Russian ones sank into poverty and filth.[74]

This sense of the development of Russia as in part a product of German cultural work was part of a larger colonial discourse that saw the work of *Auslandsdeutschen* or Germans abroad as contributing to a European civilizing mission, even if they were not citizens of Germany.

Goebel was aware of the possibilities inherent in Siberia and was also carried along by the great expectations of what might be done with this massive territory. For example, when traveling near the Kuznetsk Alatau mountain range, he fantasized about how a (presumably German) capitalist overseer might transform the region and its inhabitants by connecting the rich soil and abundant natural resources to the railway. However, Goebel was also skeptical about the Russians' ability to realize such ambitions. To be sure, he recognized a greater sense of individual initiative among the peoples of Siberia than among those in European Russia, but when looking at the people of the region, who lacked "the sense for time management and organization, for acquisition and possession," Goebel concluded that "[n]o American and no German development will arise out of such people". The development of Siberia would be dependent on the impact of foreign investors, but the Russians made the conditions for investors difficult, preventing Siberia from seeing the development of a country like Canada.[75] Goebel's accounts thus portrayed Russia as having the resources and populations to become modern, but as requiring foreign and ideally German assistance to realize its full potential.

With the outbreak of the First World War, the hoped-for gains of the development of Siberia as a "land of the future" as the Norwegian explorer Fridtjof Nansen labeled it, did not come to pass. Although German armies never set foot in Siberia, other than as prisoners of war, German observers' interest in Siberia as a market for German goods and as a source for raw materials did not wane. Most of the experts on Russia used their knowledge to contribute to the war effort by writing propaganda, managing the war economy and contributing to the economic and demographic planning of the occupation zones, including plans to Germanize territory newly acquired from Russia.[76]

---

[74] Goebel 1953, p. 243.

[75] Goebel 1914, pp. 80–81.

[76] Wiedenfeld and Goebel both worked together under Sering's leadership in the Scientific Commission of the Prussian War Ministry (Goebel 1953, pp. 300–301; Wiedenfeld 1960, pp. 51 ff.); Sering saw the war as a chance to expand the scope of internal colonization from the Prussian East to newly annexed territories from Russia (see Stoehr 2002). Goebel's knowledge of Siberia was also put to use in the prisoner-of-war camp at Zossen where he was in charge of trying to win over Muslim prisoners of war for a "Holy War" against the Allies; he organized a Ramadan service for 10,000 prisoners of war that was led by the pan-Islamist Siberian Tartar Ibrahim Abdul Rashid; Goebel claimed that the event made quite an impression on the Kalmuck and Kirghiz prisoners from Siberia (Goebel 1953, pp. 284–287).

Siberia continued to figure in some of these activities. For example, Kurt Wiedenfeld published a study on the economy and culture of Siberia in 1916 with the aim of providing the German public with knowledge about the "eastern enemy".[77] Many of the arguments that he and others had made concerning the value of the independent and individualistic land-owning farmers continued to resonate, as Wiedenfeld claimed that German soldiers had discovered the superiority of Siberians over their European Russian counterparts in battle. Unlike the peasants from European Russia who had failed to withstand the "demands of modern war," Wiedenfeld observed that

> the Siberian, who is further advanced along the path of human development, demands to be taken seriously and at the same time shows what soldierly power can be gained from the Russian peasant as soon as the free ownership of open land begins to lead the individual to consciousness of his own self.[78]

Wiedenfeld argued that this apparent success of Russian policy to colonize Siberia was also an indication that the Russian Empire might have been better off had it continued to concentrate its energies on its eastern frontier rather than waging a war on its western one, territory that, as Wiedenfeld maintained, had long been a part of Germany's sphere of influence.[79]

Wiedenfeld and Goebel's pre-war and wartime writings on the potential of Siberia also informed Werner "Daya" Karfunkelstein's 1918 publication on Russian Asia as a German war aim. Daya, a writer and engineer in Berlin, saw the Peace Treaty of Brest Litovsk as having inaugurated "a new era of our world-political development and thus of our world-political thinking".[80] He emphasized that while before the war Germans had viewed "Russia" and "the East" as one and the same, with the peace settlement with Russia the boundaries of "the East" had expanded significantly to include "the whole Eurasian landmass from the western border of Russia to the coast of the Japanese Sea". With the demise of the autocratic Russian state, Germany had regained its "freedom of movement" in the East and could develop a "continental policy" and exert its economic and political muscle in Asia.[81] Daya did not see this move as detracting from Germany's overseas colonial policy. Rather, he thought it would strengthen it by providing a firmer foundation for Germany's bid to become a world power. According to him, Germany was in a strong position to help Russia. Indeed, he viewed German and Russian interests as complementary: as an "agricultural state," Russia was in need of "capital and organization" that the "industrial state" Germany could provide so that Russia could rebuild after the devastation of war.[82]

---

[77] Wiedenfeld 1916, p. 4.

[78] Ibid., p. 2.

[79] Ibid., p. 86.

[80] Daya 1918, p. 1.

[81] Ibid., pp. 1–2, cit. 2.

[82] Ibid., pp. 3, 12, 15.

Siberia was the pivot for Daya's project of expanding German power in "the East". Similar to earlier observers, he perceived Siberia as a utopian space with rich fertile soil, ample land for raising animals, and numerous untapped natural and mineral resources. He also believed that Siberia had the potential to develop its own industrial production and export goods to markets throughout central Asia. Drawing on the work of Wiedenfeld and Goebel, Daya noted the remarkable transformation that had taken place in the Siberian economy in the years before the war, and believed that Siberia was on the cusp of "a development in which under the guidance of a modern western European state it can follow the path of the United States or Canada" becoming one of the largest producers of both agricultural products and industrial goods in the world.[83] With Germany's defeat in the war, however, such fantasies would remain unrealized. But many of these ideas concerning the importance of thinking in continental terms would continue to resonate in the radically transformed circumstances of the post-war years.

## Conclusion

In defining nations as "imagined communities," Benedict Anderson observed that they were imagined "as both inherently limited and sovereign".[84] With the rise of the nation-state form in the nineteenth century, an important component of defining sovereignty was its application within clearly demarcated territorial boundaries.[85] Although in pre-war Europe the nation remained largely an "aspiration" as Edward Ross Dickinson has provocatively observed,[86] the desire for national autonomy was always in conflict with the reality of a nation's political, economic and cultural entanglement in the wider world. Discussions by German observers of Russia's development of Siberia in the decades before the First World War thus illuminate some of these tensions inherent in the transnational horizon of the nation. Although they fantasized about organizing and restructuring Russian society and bringing the resources of Siberia into the global market, their ability to realize these ambitions was limited, as the territory always remained outside of their control.

In making prescriptions concerning Russian policy in Siberia, German observers' were attempting to govern Siberia and to shape its development to coincide with German interests in expanding its markets in the region. Drawing analogies between the colonization of Siberia and the internal colonization of the Prussian East or the settlement of the American West, German observers also thought that in Siberia Russian settlers would be freed from the old constraints that bound them in Russia proper and could become independent and more

[83] Ibid., p. 21.

[84] Anderson 1991, p. 6.

[85] Maier 2006, pp. 34–36.

[86] Dickinson 2008, pp. 143–144.

productive citizens. This unleashing of the productive powers of the Russian people in Siberia would have the added benefit of providing an ethnic Russian population to ensure that Siberia remained in the hands of a European power. Thus in their discourse concerning Russia's development of Siberia, national and imperial ambitions were not separate, but interconnected and intertwined.[87] For German observers, Russia's path to modernity lay in reforms that would help transform it by colonizing and nationalizing the peripheral regions of the empire.

German observers were also fascinated by the potential Russia possessed in Siberia to develop as a continental empire, much like its American counterpart. Thus they looked to Siberia as a utopian space upon which they could project their own fantasies of what Germany might do if it, too, possessed the resources and land of a continental empire. Increasingly, in their imagining of the future political order, German observers and commentators on Russia viewed large continental territories that could mobilize the powers of their populations as being better able to contend with and – in Social Darwinist terms – survive in a world of competing global powers, attitudes that certainly would come to inform German policies towards eastern Europe and Russia during the two World Wars. While beyond the scope of this chapter, these tensions in German observers' imaginings of Siberia also suggest that it may be fruitful to pay more attention to German informal imperialism or *Weltpolitik* when thinking about the origins of the catastrophes of the twentieth century.

## Bibliography

Adamovsky, Ezequiel. 2005. "Euro-Orientalism and the Making of the Concept of Eastern Europe in France, 1810–1880." *The Journal of Modern History* 77, no. 3, 591–628.

Adas, Michael. 1989. *Machines as the Measure of Men: Science, Technology, and Ideologies of Western Dominance*. Ithaca: Cornell University Press.

Anderson, Benedict. 1991. *Imagined Communities: Reflections on the Origin and Spread of Nationalism*, London: Verso.

Auhagen, Otto. 1902. *Zur Besiedlung Sibiriens. Berichte über Land- und Forstwirtschaft im Auslande*. Berlin: Dt. Landwirtschafts-Ges.

Auhagen, Otto. 1913. "Zur Beurteilung der russischen Agrarreform." In *Russlands Kultur und Volkswirtschaft. Aufsätze und Vorträge im Auftrage der Vereinigung für Staatswissenschaftliche Fortbildung zu Berlin*, edited by Max Sering, 115–145. Berlin: Göschen'sche Verlagshandlung.

Aydin, Cemil. 2007. "A Global Anti-Western Moment? The Russo-Japanese War, Decolonization, and Asian Modernity." In *Competing Visions of World Order: Global Moments and Movements, 1880s–1930s*, edited by Sebastian Conrad and Dominic Sachsenmaier, 213–236. New York: Palgrave.

Bassin, Mark. 1991. "Inventing Siberia: Visions of the Russian East in the Early Nineteenth Century." *American Historical Review* 96, no. 3, 763–794.

---

[87] See also Akami's paper in this volume.

Bassin, Mark. 1999. *Imperial Visions: Nationalist Imagination and Geographical Expansion in the Russian Far East, 1840–1865*. New York: Cambridge University Press.

Blackbourn, David. 2003. *History of Germany, 1780–1918: The Long Nineteenth Century*, 2nd ed. Malden: Blackwell Pub.

Conrad, Sebastian. 2006. *Globalisierung und Nation im Deutschen Kaiserreich*. Munich: Beck.

Daya, Werner. 1918. *Der Aufmarsch im Osten. Russisch-Asien als deutsches Kriegs- und Wirtschaftsziel*. Dachau: Einhorn-Verlag.

Dickinson, Edward Ross. 2008. "The German Empire: an Empire?" *History Workshop Journal* 66, no. 1, 129–162.

Domosh, Mona. 2010. "Uncovering the Friction of Globalization: American Commercial Embeddedness and Landscape in Revolutionary-Era Russia." *Annals of the Association of American Geographers* 100, no. 2, 427–443.

Forsyth, James. 1992. *A History of the Peoples of Siberia: Russia's North Asian Colony*. Cambridge: Cambridge University Press.

Geyer, Michael. 2004. "Deutschland und Japan im Zeitalter der Globalisierung. Überlegungen zu einer komparativen Geschichte jenseits des Modernisierungs-Paradigmas." In *Das Kaiserreich Transnational: Deutschland in der Welt 1871–1914*, edited by Jürgen Osterhammel and Sebastian Conrad, 68–86. Göttingen: Vandenhoeck & Ruprecht.

Geyer, Michael. 2006. "Where Germans Dwell: Transnationalism in Theory and Practice." *German Studies Association Newsletter* 31, no. 2, 29–37.

Glatfelter, R. Edward. 1991. "Russia, the Soviet Union, and the Chinese Eastern Railway." In *Railway Imperialism*, edited by Clarence B. Davis et al., 137–154. New York: Greenwood Press

Goebel, Otto. 1910. *Volkswirtschaft des Ostbaikalischen Sibirien ums Jahr 1909. Berichte über Landwirtschaft*. Berlin: Paul Parey.

Goebel, Otto. 1910. *Volkswirtschaft des Westbaikalischen Sibirien. Berichte über Landwirtschaft*. Berlin: Verlagsbuchhandlung Paul Parey.

Goebel, Otto. 1913. *Vom Ural bis Sachalin*. Berlin: Dietrich Reimer.

Goebel, Otto. 1914. *Über Sibirien nach Ostasien St Petersburg und Moskau Tscheljabinsk-–Mandschuria Wladiwostok und Dairen*. Frankfurt am Main: M. Hendschel.

Goebel, Otto. 1953. *Ein buntes Leben im zweiten Deutschen Reich*. Bad Harburg: F.A. Taubert.

Gollwitzer, Hans. 1962. *Die Gelbe Gefahr. Geschichte eines Schlagworts*. Göttingen: Vandenhoeck & Ruprecht.

Groh, Dieter. 1988. *Rußland im Blick Europas 300. Jahre historische Perspektiven*. Frankfurt am Main: Suhrkamp.

Hoetzsch, Otto. 1904. *Die Vereinigten Staaten von Nordamerika*. Bielefeld: Velhagen & Klasing.

Hoetzsch, Otto. 1913. "Die innere Entwicklung Russlands seit 1905." In *Russlands Kultur und Volkswirtschaft. Aufsätze und Vorträge im Auftrage der Vereinigung für Staatswissenschaftliche Fortbildung zu Berlin*, edited by Max Sering, 63–88. Berlin: Göschen'sche Verlagshandlung.

Hollmann, Anton Heinrich. 1913. "Die Agrarreform und innere Kolonisation in Russland." *Archiv für innere Kolonisation* 5, no. 10, 313–344.

Jenkins, Jennifer. 2004. "German Orientalism: Introduction." *Comparative Studies of South Asia, Africa, and the Middle East* 24, no. 2, 97–100.

Koenen, Gerd. 2005. *Der Russland-Komplex. Die Deutschen und der Osten 1900–1945*. Munich: Beck.

Kontje, Todd. 2004. *German Orientalisms*. Ann Arbor: University of Michigan Press.

Kotsonis, Yanni. 1999. *Making Peasants Backward: Agricultural Cooperatives and the Agrarian Question in Russia, 1861–1914*. New York: St. Martin's Press.

Krahmer, Gustav. 1897. *Sibirien und die grosse sibirische Eisenbahn*. Leipzig: Zuckschwerdt.

Larsen, Inge Marie. 2003. "Da smør var guld. Andelsmejeribevægelsen i Vestsibirien, 1902–1908." *Nordisk Øst-forum* 17, no. 3, 329–348.

Lemberg, Hans. 1985. "Zur Entstehung des Osteuropabegriffs im 19. Jahrhundert. Vom 'Norden' zum 'Osten' Europas." *Jahrbücher für Geschichte Osteuropas* 33, no. 1, 48–91.

Lincoln, Bruce W. 1994. *The Conquest of a Continent: Siberia and the Russians*. New York: Random House.

Liulevicius, Vejas Gabriel. 2009. *The German Myth of the East: 1800 to the Present*. New York: Oxford University Press.

Maier, Charles. 2006. "Transformations of Territoriality 1600–2000." In *Transnationale Geschichte. Themen, Tendenzen, und Theorien*, edited by Gunilla Budde et al., 32–55. Göttingen: Vandenhoeck & Ruprecht.

Marks, Steven G. 1991. *Road to Power: The Trans-Siberian Railroad and the Colonization of Asian Russia 1850–1917*. Ithaca: Cornell University Press.

Meyer, Klaus. 1956. *Theodor Schiemann als Politischer Publizist*. Frankfurt am Main: Rütten & Loening.

Neitzel, Sönke. 2000. *Weltmacht oder Untergang: die Weltreichslehre im Zeitalter des Imperialismus*. Paderborn: Schöningh.

Nelson, Robert L. 2009. "The Archive for Inner Colonization, the German East, and World War I." *Germans, Poland, and Colonial Expansion to the East: 1850 through the Present*, 65–93. New York: Palgrave Macmillan.

Ol', Pavel Vasil'evich. (1922) 1983. *Foreign Capital in Russia*. Translated by Geoffrey Jones and Grigori Gerenstain. New York: Garland.

Paddock, Troy. 2006. "Creating an Oriental Feindbild." *Central European History* 39, 214–243.

Pallot, Judith. 1999. *Land Reform in Russia, 1906–1917: Peasant Responses to Stolypin's Project of Rural Transformation*. New York: Oxford University Press.

Petersson, Niels P. 2004. "Das Kaiserreich in Prozessen ökonomischer Globalisierung." In *Das Kaiserreich Transnational: Deutschland in der Welt 1871–1914*, edited by Jürgen Osterhammel and Sebastian Conrad, 49–67. Göttingen: Vandenhoeck & Ruprecht.

Ratzel, Friedrich. 1923. *Politische Geographie*. Munich: R. Oldenbourg.

Remnev, Anatolyi. 2007. "Siberia and the Russian Far East in the Imperial Geography of Power." In *Russian Empire: Space, People, Power, 1700–1930*, edited by Jane Burbank et al., 425–454. Bloomington: Indiana University Press.

Sering, Max. 1913. "Geleitwort." *Russlands Kultur und Volkswirtschaft. Aufsätze und Vorträge im Auftrage der Vereinigung für Staatswissenschaftliche Fortbildung zu Berlin*, iii-vi. Berlin: Göschen'sche Verlagshandlung.

Shanin, Teodor. 1985. *The Roots of Otherness: Russia's Turn of the Century, vol. 1: Russia as a 'Developing Society'*. London: Macmillan Press.

Spaulding, Robert Mark. 1997. *Osthandel and Ostpolitik: German Foreign Trade Policies in Eastern Europe from Bismarck to Adenauer*. Providence: Berghahn Books.

Steinwedel, Charles. 2007. "Resettling People, Unsettling the Empire: Migration and the Challenge of Governance, 1861–1917." In *Peopling the Russian Periphery: Borderland Colonization in Eurasian History*, edited by Nicholas B. Breyfogle et al., 128–147. London: Routledge.

Steinweis, Alan E. 1999. "Eastern Europe and the Notion of the 'Frontier' in Germany to 1945." *Yearbook of European Studies* 13, 56–69.

Stirne, A. 1912. *Sibirien: Eindrücke und Betrachtungen aus Natur und Politik*. Leipzig: Verlag von Otto Wigand.

Stoehr, Irene. 2002. "Von Max Sering zu Konrad Meyer – ein 'machtergreifender' Generationenwechsel in der Agrar- und Siedlungswissenschaft." In *Autarkie und Ostexpansion. Pflanzenzucht und Agrarforschung im Nationalsozialismus*, edited by Susanne Heim, 57–90. Göttingen: Wallstein.

Stolberg, Eva-Maria. 2004. "The Siberian Frontier Between 'White Mission' and 'Yellow Peril,' 1890s–1920s." *Nationalities Papers* 32, no. 1, 165–170.

Stolypin, P.A. and A.W. Kriwoscheïn. 1912. *Die Kolonisation Sibiriens: Eine Denkschrift*. Translated by Carl Erich Gleye. Berlin: Paetel.

Struck, Bernhard. 2004. "Auf der Suche nach Osteuropa. Zur Wahrnehmung Polens und Frankreichs in vergleichender Perspektive, 1770–1850." *Zeitschrift für Ostmitteleuropa-Forschung* 53, no. 4, 504–524.

Sunderland, Willard. 2004. *Taming the Wild Field: Colonization and Empire on the Russian Steppe*. Ithaca: Cornell University Press.

Sunderland, Willard. 2010. "The Ministry of Asiatic Russia: The Colonial Office That Never Was But Might Have Been." *Slavic Review* 69, no. 1, 120–150.

Thum, Gregor. 2006. *Traumland Osten. Deutsche Bilder von östliche Europa im 20. Jahrhundert*. Göttingen: Vandenhoeck & Ruprecht.

Treadgold, Donald W. 1957. *Great Siberian Migration: Government and Peasant in Resettlement from Emancipation to the First World War*. Princeton: Princeton University Press.

Voigt, Georg. 1978. *Otto Hoetzsch 1876–1946. Wissenschaft und Politik im Leben eines deutschen Historikers*. Berlin: Akademie-Verlag.

Voigt, Georg. 1994. *Rußland in der deutschen Geschichtsschreibung. 1843–1945*, Berlin: Akademie Verlag.

Weiss, Claudia. 2007. *Wie Sibirien 'Unser' wurde: Die Russische Geographische Gesellschaft und ihr Einfluss auf die Bilder und Vorstellungen von Sibirien im 19. Jahrhundert*. Göttingen: V & R Unipress.

Wiedenfeld, Kurt. 1900. *Die wirtschaftliche Bedeutung der sibirischen Bahn*. Berlin: Julius Springer.

Wiedenfeld, Kurt. 1913. "Rußlands Stellung in der Weltwirtschaft." In *Russlands Kultur und Volkswirtschaft. Aufsätze und Vorträge im Auftrage der Vereinigung für Staatswissenschaftliche Fortbildung zu Berlin*, edited by Max Sering, 247–281. Berlin: Göschen'sche Verlagshandlung.

Wiedenfeld, Kurt. 1916. *Sibirien in Kultur und Wirtschaft*. Bonn: Marcus & Weber.

Wiedenfeld, Kurt. 1960. *Zwischen Wirtschaft und Staat. Aus den Lebenserinnerungen von Kurt Wiedenfeld*. Berlin: W. de Gruyter.

Wolff, Larry. 1994. *Inventing Eastern Europe: The Map of Civilization on the Mind of the Enlightenment*. Stanford: Stanford University Press.

Zimmerman, Andrew. 2001. *Anthropology and Antihumanism in Imperial Germany*. Chicago: University of Chicago Press.

Zimmerman, Andrew. 2006. "Decolonizing Weber." *Postcolonial Studies* 9, no. 1, 53–79.

# Chapter 11
# Nationalism and the Catholic Church: Papal Politics and 'Nationalist' Clergy in Border Regions (1918–1939)

**Thies Schulze**

**Abstract** The Roman Catholic Church was highly ambivalent regards the emergence of modern nation states. On the one hand, several ideological and structural aspects underscored the church's universal nature, whereas nationalisms, on the other hand, also had a strong impact on its development. Rather than generally questioning transnational structures within the church, this article aims to analyse the limits of Catholic universalism in the interwar period, focusing both on Vatican politics and on conflicts between the church and nation states in border regions. The article demonstrates that the church's universal claims only partially contributed to bridging the borders of the existing nation states.

## Introduction

Of all transnational institutions, the Roman Catholic Church is certainly one of the most traditional and perhaps most complex organizations. Ever since the French Revolution, the emergence of nation-states had an increasing influence on the Vatican's moral views and political decisions. Particularly after the Vatican's loss of territory in 1870, the question of how to deal with the various European nation-states became vital for its own identity. Although the Catholic Church was essentially based on transnational networks, it had to take the existence of nation-states just as much into account and to adapt its inner structure to the European state system. Seen from that perspective, Catholicism had both a national and a

I owe many thanks to Johannes Schnocks and Gregor Klapczynski for their comments and helpful hints concerning passages from the Old and New Testaments.

T. Schulze (✉)
EXC "Religion and Politics in Pre-Modern and Modern Cultures", University of Münster, Münster, Germany
e-mail: tschulze@uni-muenster.de

I. Löhr and R. Wenzlhuemer (eds.), *The Nation State and Beyond*, Transcultural Research – Heidelberg Studies on Asia and Europe in a Global Context,
DOI 10.1007/978-3-642-32934-0_11, 

transnational dimension.[1] How then did the Catholic Church deal with this ambivalent situation? And did the Vatican establish a general way of dealing with nationalist movements?

Until now, historiography has not given sufficient answer to the question of what extent the Roman Catholic Church contributed to nationalism.[2] For a long time, historical research concerning the Church-state relationship was focused on rather narrow and specific aspects. A large number of historians, for example, have discussed the Vatican's diplomatic relations with individual nation-states,[3] whereas relatively few studies deal with the Church's relation to nationalist movements.[4] Protestantism, at least in the context of German history, is frequently regarded as one of the driving forces of nation-building,[5] whilst historical studies tend to underestimate the role played in this by Catholicism. There is a similar shortcoming in studies on transnational networks: although in recent research work on transnational networks the Roman Catholic Church has often been mentioned as an example of international institutions, a relatively small number of publications actually examine the Catholic Church as a transnational organization.[6]

The origin of the term "transnational" can be traced back to the mid-nineteenth century. It developed only after the emergence of modern nation-states,[7] as a reaction to the growing significance of nationalisms all over the world. In that sense, it implies the existence of nations as a precondition to transnational activities: without nation-states, "transnationalism" would lose its significance. As nationalism, in the context of the long history of the Roman Catholic Church, is a rather young phenomenon, the task of exploring its transnational effects is inevitably linked to the question of to what extent the Church itself had been affected by the emergence of modern nation-states.

Providing an answer to such a question, however, turns out to be complex. The reason for this complexity primarily lies in the inner structures of the Church, which, as a result of its development in history, can hardly be reduced to *one* structure consisting of the Vatican, dioceses, parishes etc.[8] Alongside – and within – this structure, there was a wide range of different personal networks, such as Catholic

---

[1] Altermatt 2007, p. 16.

[2] There are, however, various studies which have discussed particular aspects of this topic: Alix 1962; Altermatt 2005, 2009; Altgeld 2001; Birke 1996; Conzemius 1994, pp. 234–262. Analyzing the relations between nationalism and Catholicism in Germany: Richter 2000; for the Hapsburg Empire: Gottsmann 2006; id. 2007; id. 2010, pp. 28–34; for the relations between nationalism and religion, cf. for instance: Graf 2000; Haupt and Langewiesche 2004; Langewiesche 2009; Mergel 2008; O'Brian 1988.

[3] Stehlin 1983; Latour 1996b *La Papauté*.

[4] Altermatt 2007, pp. 15–33.

[5] Langewiesche 2000, pp. 145–147.

[6] Religious networks are rather briefly mentioned in Herren 2009, pp. 43 f., Lyons 1963, pp. 245–261; for the so-called "black international" see Lamberts 2002.

[7] Saunier 2009, p. 1047.

[8] Cf. Conzemius 1985, p. 12; Altermatt 2009, p. 23.

laymen associations, congresses, missionary organizations, Catholic party organizations and religious congregations.[9] These organizations could to some extent (or entirely) be regionalized or nationalized, but also spread over various nation-states and thus act in a "transnational" way transferring ideas, personnel, normative orders etc. across borders. Some institutions, such as national bishop conferences, were directly related to the existence of nation-states, while others, such as the Jesuit Order, were rather marginally affected by processes of nationalization. It may thus be more appropriate not to look upon the Roman Catholic Church as a predefined "transnational" organization, but rather to focus on the various ways in which its inner structures could, in the corresponding contexts, contribute either to nationalizing or to denationalizing processes.[10]

This article, therefore, does not primarily aim to explore the Catholic Church's inner structures, but rather asks *how* these structures (might have) worked in certain political and social circumstances. In consequence, rather than attempting to provide a theoretical framework or a global explanation of this topic, it will discuss how conditions of extreme nationalism might have influenced the relations between the Roman Catholic Church and the nation-states. Instead of making any general challenges to the "transnational" effects the Church's personal networks may be found to have had, it explores their limits in order to discuss some of the main problems of the relationship between the Church and the nation-states. After a brief sketch of some major aspects of the Vatican's political attitude towards nationalisms in the inter-war period, it will focus on the political situation of the Catholic Church in border regions. Based on examples taken from Alsace-Lorraine and South Tyrol, it will explore to what extent the Church contributed to reinforcing or bridging the existing borders. Although these conflicts cannot be taken as representative for all cases in which the Church's universal claims collided with processes of identity construction as undertaken by the nation-states, they nevertheless demonstrate the possibilities and limits of the Roman Catholic Church in the context of encouraging transnational exchange.

## The Vatican: Motives and Intentions of the Holy See's Attitude Towards Nationalism

Examining the Vatican's view on nationalism is no easy task. This is partly down to the source material from the Vatican's Secret Archive, since documents usually refer to very specific historical contexts and only rarely contain references to 'nationalism' as a general phenomenon. Moreover, it would be oversimplifying to speak of the Vatican's politics as something homogeneous; among the cardinals of the Roman Curia and the members of the Vatican's Congregations there was a

[9] There are in fact many studies that are dedicated to similar organizations. Cf., for example, Habermas 2008, p. 658 and Altermatt 2009, pp. 209–226.

[10] Cf. Heather Ellis in this volume.

variety of opinions, which – as Thomas Brechenmacher has pointed out[11] – are only partly reflected within the archival sources. As it appears to be problematic to give a complete and conclusive overview of the relation of the Roman Curia towards nationalism in general, the following part of this article will concentrate on a few aspects of this topic, primarily discussing the Curia's ideological convictions, pragmatic considerations and personal backgrounds.

Unquestionably, the Vatican's stance on nationalism was influenced by ideological concerns, although a general guideline on this phenomenon did not exist. Universalism was an important element of its self-perception. The Church's universal claims basically resulted from its task of providing spiritual welfare to all Christians, and were justified by quotations from the Bible such as the words of Jesus to St. Peter: "Feed my sheep" (John 21:17).[12] This passage appeared to legitimize the task of the Popes (as the successors of St. Peter) in their paternal guidance of all Catholics in moral and religious concerns, without making any distinction between the Catholics of different national origins. The Great Commission of Jesus to his disciples also appeared to confirm the universal mission of the Catholic Church: "Go therefore and make disciples of all nations, baptizing them in the name of the Father and of the Son and of the Holy Spirit [...]" (Matthew 28:19).[13] It is no wonder that the Catholic Church referred to these and other quotations from the Bible when affirming its universal nature. In the fourth session of the First Vatican Council, the universal mission of the Church was explicitly confirmed: "To satisfy this [the Pope's] pastoral office, our predecessors strove unwearyingly that the saving teaching of Christ should be spread among all the peoples of the world."[14] Even more explicitly, the encyclical *Immortale dei* (1885) emphasized that Christian religion was unconfined both regarding time and space.[15] As an element of Catholic ideology, the universal nature of the Church led by the Holy See expressed itself in many different contexts. When, in 1917, the *Codex Iuris Canonici* was published as a codification of the existing Church laws, Papal supremacy over the Roman Catholic Church was established in the legal as well as in the moral and religious fields.[16] Whilst there is no intention here to focus on matters of the construction of Catholic religious identity – or on how much 'nationalized' elements of religious manifestations could counterbalance the

---

[11] Brechenmacher 2005, pp. 596 f.

[12] This passage corresponds to the Old Testament's Psalm 100:3: "Know that the LORD, he is God!/It is he who made us, and we are his;/we are his people, and the sheep of his pasture."

[13] In this translation, the term "nation" is used for "έθνοςτΘ," which, in the Greek text, has a much broader sense and could also be translated as "peoples" or (in the New Testament) as "pagans"; this term could not therefore be applied to the phenomenon of modern nationalism, although modern translations provide a basis for respective (mis-)interpretations.

[14] "Concilium Vaticanum I.," 1990, p. 815.

[15] Leo XIII 1903, p. 17.

[16] CIC 1917, Can. 218; cf. Scholder 1977, p. 66.

Pope's universal claim[17] – this dimension of Papal universalism was nevertheless fundamental for the Vatican's self-perception. Many Catholic priests and laymen considered the universal mission of the Vatican as a central element of Christianity. Most prominently, Catholic ultramontanism gained an influential role in many European countries during the nineteenth century. Ultramontanists tended to promote Catholic conservatism, and emphasized the leading role of Rome within the Catholic Church. However, ultramontanism was anything but uncontested within the Church, and remained a point of issue into the twentieth century.[18]

This, of course, does not mean that the Holy See regarded nation-states as something illegitimate. On the contrary, when Pope Leo XIII supported the idea of Social Catholicism at the end of the nineteenth century, it was fundamental for the pontiff to make the theoretical separation between the Church's sphere and the sphere of the states in order to design a general concept of social welfare. Correspondingly, encyclicals such as *Immortale dei* (1885) and *Rerum novarum* (1891) explicitly referred to the modern state as an institution that formed part of an ideal world order.[19] The Papal encyclicals which were published after the pontificate of Leo XIII, however, only rarely mention the term "nation", *natio*. They often made reference to "states", *res publica* or *civitas*, or, in some cases, to "peoples", *populi* or *gentes*.[20] Pope Pius XI, on the other hand, still under the impression of World War I, made a somewhat ambiguous statement about nationalism in his first encyclical *Ubi arcano dei*:

> "Patriotism – the stimulus of so many virtues and of so many noble acts of heroism when kept within the bounds of the law of Christ – becomes merely an occasion, an added incentive to grave injustice when true love of country is debased to the condition of an extreme nationalism, when we forget that all men are our brothers and members of the same great human family, that other nations have an equal right with us both to life and to prosperity, that it is never lawful nor even wise, to dissociate morality from the affairs of practical life."[21]

---

[17] Although it could be argued that religious processions or church services contributed common "transnational" sets of 'Catholic' experiences and memory, one should also take into consideration that even seemingly apolitical issues such as liturgy can contain 'national' peculiarities; cf. Gottsmann 2006, pp. 441–450; Gottsmann 2010, pp. 38–46.

[18] Cf. Fleckenstein and Schmiedl 2005; Weiss 1978, pp. 821–877.

[19] Leo XIII 1963, pp. 18–22, § 26–30; Leo XIII 1903, pp. 7–15. *Immortale dei* explicitly referred to Matthew 22: 21: "Give to Caesar what is Caesar's, and to God what is God's", thus transferring a concept originally applied to the ancient Roman Empire to modern nation-states; Leo XIII 1903, p. 23.

[20] However, some of the translations of the encyclicals did not match the Latin original literally; the German translation of the encyclical "Divini illius magistri" (1930), for example, translated "societas civilis" with "Volksgemeinschaft", a term which was employed by most of the political movements in the Republic of Weimar, but also belonged to the key vocabulary of National Socialism; Pius XI 1930, pp. 26–27. Cf. Wildt 2009.

[21] Pius XI 1923, p. 26, translation according to: Pius XI 1922, paragraph 25; "patriotism", here, is used as a translation of "caritas patriae", whereas "nationalism" is a rather free translation of "immoderatum [. . .] nationis amorem".

According to this statement – which was to be confirmed by semi-official publications from the Vatican some years later[22] – there was a good and an evil kind of nationalism: the former was moderate and inspired by Christian values, whilst the latter was exaggerated and ignorant of both religious principles and the moral authority of the Catholic Church. Any kind of conflict between nation-states could as a result be attributed to a lack of moderation and Christian spirit, whilst, on the contrary, the Catholic doctrine was seen as a basis for the peaceful and harmonious coexistence of nations. This utopian approach, of course, ignored much of the belligerent nature of nationalism.[23]

Nevertheless, the impact of 'universalist' ideology on the Vatican's politics should not be overestimated. For practical politics the concept of 'good' and 'evil' nationalism provided no information on where to draw the line between the two. For the Vatican's policy, this vagueness turned out to be of some advantage, as political pragmatism was vital for putting forward the Church's interests on many occasions.[24] The Holy See's pragmatism, in fact, owed much to history, and especially to its experiences during the nineteenth century. Secularization had become one of the Papacy's major fears ever since the French Revolution, and in various contexts modern nation-states turned out to actively support the Church's loss of influence. Most visibly, the Vatican was challenged by the emerging Italian national movement; during the revolutionary years of 1848/1849, an insurrection in the Papal State forced Pope Pius IX into exile for several months, and after the process of Italian unification (1859–1871) the Holy See lost all of its territory to the Italian state. The idea of being "prisoners" of the Italian state remained a central element of Papal self-perception in the following decades, and only the concordat settled with Mussolini in 1929 solved the highly symbolic "roman question".[25] Alongside this very specific dimension of the Vatican's experiences with nation-states, the "culture wars" of the late nineteenth century impressively demonstrated to the Holy See that it was extremely important to come to agreement with national governments over controversial topics such as education policy, civil marriage, the rights of religious congregations and the financing of the Church.[26]

Concordats were one of the answers to this challenge, although those concordats concluded in the nineteenth century had already demonstrated that any agreement with national governments would force the Vatican into taking up positions with respect to conflicts between nationalities. The concordat of the Vatican with Montenegro (18/08/1886), for instance, contained a paragraph which introduced Slavic liturgy into Church services. The Vatican, as a consequence of the concordat,

[22] Anonymous 1924.

[23] Cf. Langewiesche 2000, pp. 45–54.

[24] For the following sketch of the motives of Papal politics, cf. Brechenmacher 2005, pp. 597–604.

[25] Moos 2007, pp. 242–250.

[26] For an overview of the European dimension of the conflicts between Churches and nation-states, see Rémond 2000, pp. 125–168, 189–205; for the 'culture wars' in a European perspective, see Clark 2002, pp. 7–37.

had to face some severe criticism from the royal court at Vienna, which regarded the paragraph as a concession to Slavic nationalist movements within the Empire.[27] Although the Vatican generally considered the Hapsburg Monarchy as an ally for defending the Catholic faith in Central and Eastern Europe, several examples demonstrate that the Vatican's diplomacy was partly guided by pragmatism.[28] The concordats, many of which were concluded in the 1920s,[29] frequently contained compromises between the Church and the nation-states, which could be interpreted as a concession on the part of the Holy See to national governments at the expense of other nationalities.[30] As the Holy See regarded the concordats primarily as a measure for guaranteeing a maximum of 'liberty' to the Church, the compromising nature of the Vatican's foreign policy was a necessary precondition for this purpose.[31]

By concluding concordats, the Holy See aimed to avoid conflicts with modern nation-states. As a consequence, it could concentrate its efforts primarily on religious tasks.[32] This motivation was in fact equally important for the Vatican's willingness to extend its diplomatic network. Between 1914 and 1922, the number of nunciatures increased from 6 to 18, and particularly in the 3 years following the peace treaties of Paris, the Holy See notably extended its presence in the world. Nunciatures were consequently established in Paraguay and Poland (1919), Germany, Hungary, Romania, Switzerland, Czechoslovakia and Yugoslavia (1920), and in Salvador (1922).[33] Under the pontificate of Pius XI, the Vatican continued to expand its diplomatic network[34] and in the 1920s, even states such as France and Italy, which were known for their rejection of the Roman Catholic Church, exchanged ambassadors with the Holy See.[35]

There were, of course, several additional motives for the pragmatic attitude of the Vatican. Since, under the pontificate of Benedict XV, the Vatican's diplomacy increasingly saw its mission as mediating between the states involved in the war, this function of Papal foreign policy implied the idea of the strict neutrality of the Holy See. Although the peace initiative launched by the Papal secretariat of state in 1917 was unsuccessful,[36] the Vatican's claim of being impartial continued to be an

---

[27] Gottsmann 2007, pp. 457–466.

[28] Gottsmann 2006, pp. 409–418.

[29] Brechenmacher 2009, p. 181.

[30] For instance, the Polish Concordat concluded in February 1925 was also valid for the Free City of Danzig (Article III), which was the subject of claims made by the German nation-state; Concordato con la Polonia, 1954, in: Mercati 1954, p. 31; Stehlin 1983, p. 416. Likewise too the Concordat concluded with Prussia in April 1929 was challenged by Polish nationalists because of the enhancement of the Diocese of Wroclaw; Concordato con la Prussia (14.4.1929), in: Mercati 1954, p. 135; cf. Stehlin 1983, p. 423.

[31] For the concordats, cf. Feldkamp 2000, pp. 54–61.

[32] Brechenmacher 2005, pp. 600 f.

[33] Latour 1996b, Papauté, p. 301.

[34] Chiron 2004, p. 152.

[35] Cholvy and Hilaire 1986, pp. 273–276; Moos 2007, pp. 246–250.

[36] Cf. Chenaux 2003, pp. 85–121.

important motive in Papal foreign policy. The way in which this policy was implemented, however, depended a lot on the prevailing political situation and could differ considerably from one situation to another according to who was involved in the different conflicts.[37] Nevertheless, the claim of impartiality was still to play an important role during World War II.[38] Of course, neutrality was more a self-imposed ideal than a reality, and the Holy See in its diplomatic actions often had to defend itself against accusations of taking sides. In reality, aims to be "neutral" and of exerting influence on international politics were hardly compatible. "Impartiality", as a consequence, remained a rather unspecific way of affirming the Holy See's moral superiority over the various nation-states.

Alongside such ideological and strategic considerations, personal issues concerning the Vatican's congregations also affected the Holy See's relationships with single nation-states. This was by no means a novelty, as many examples from early modern history demonstrate that the political sympathies of Popes and cardinals of the Roman Curia could play an important role in their politics.[39] Whilst loyalties like these cannot be understood in terms of modern nationalism, the matter of emotional ties with states and their sovereigns or representatives remained important up until the twentieth century. Within the Vatican's inner circles, the national affiliation of high Church officials towards single nation-states was anything but balanced. Still more than half of the Curia cardinals, in 1926, were born in Italy.[40] As the relationship between Italy and the Holy See was particularly complicated until the Lateran treaties of 1929, this cannot be taken as an indication of any general sympathy towards the Italian nation-state.[41] However, at least in terms of language and culture, Italian identity was widespread within the Roman Curia. Moreover, some members of the Curia, and, above all, of the Roman Congregations, were known for their sympathies towards particular nation-states. In December 1916, the Pope appointed three French cardinals, and although he was anxious to affirm that the appointments were meant as a personal recognition and not as a gesture towards France as a nation,[42] German diplomacy was keen to obtain similar titles for German and Austrian Church representatives.[43] In 1929, the German foreign ministry even planned to provide stipends for young German clergymen in order to enable them to start a career in one of the Roman Congregations by establishing a special training programme for priests. The foreign ministry had developed this project after having consulted Mgr. Giuseppe Pizzardo, who was a member of the Papal Congregation of Extraordinary Ecclesiastical

[37] Ibid., p. 121.

[38] Brechenmacher 2009, pp. 184–190.

[39] For example, the Barberini Pope Urban VIII (1623–1644) was widely known for his sympathies towards the French state; cf. Seppelt and Schwaiger 1964, p. 328.

[40] *Annuario Pontificio* 1926, pp. 31–57, 457–485.

[41] Moos 2007, pp. 241–250.

[42] Latour 1996a, "De la spécificité", p. 353.

[43] Stehlin 1983, p. 7.

Affairs and was known to be sympathetic to the wishes of the German government.[44] Although the ministry only partly managed to put its plans into effect, it was evident that the German government considered the cardinals and members of Roman Congregations as representatives of their respective nation-states. When the last remaining German cardinal of the Curia, Franz Ehrle, died in 1934, the German ambassador to the Holy See, Diego von Bergen, wrote:

> It is extremely important to have an appropriate representation in the highest senate of the Roman Catholic Church by a cardinal residing in Rome. His position offers him the possibility of promoting the interests of his country by using his personal influence on the prefects of the congregations and on the Pope himself, to whom he has access at any time. This is of a particular importance in cases in which it would be unreasonable for the Embassy to intervene directly.[45]

Of course, this point of view was unlikely to be shared by Vatican officials. And yet, at least in Bergen's view, the "international network" of the Roman Catholic Church was woven with national threads. Since Vatican diplomacy had to interact with single nation-states, it can hardly be any surprise that the concept of nationalization did not leave Rome unaffected.

So far it has been shown that the Vatican's stance on nationalism has been more complex than it might have appeared at first glance. To a certain extent, trans- or internationality derived from Catholic ideology, but they only partly found their way into the Holy See's decisions, structures and internal processes. Although the Church disposed of transnational networks, significant parts of it had been nationalized. In order to discuss similar developments on a local level, the following part of this article will examine to what extent the challenge of nationalism has affected the Catholic Church in border regions, emphasizing in particular the example of educational politics.

## Border Regions: Educational Politics, Faith and National Identities

Examining the regional implications of the Church's stance on nationalism is by no means less complex than analyzing the Vatican's perspective on it. Border regions with large national minorities provide a striking example of how conflicts between ethnic groups could affect the inner structures of the Catholic Church.

---

[44] Anger 2007; Klee to Bergen (11.4.1930), in: Politisches Archiv des Auswärtigen Amtes (Berlin), Bestand Rom-Vatikan 1067: Deutsche in Kongregationen und Päpstlichen Behörden (1928–1938); Bergen to Grünau (21.2.1933), Politisches Archiv des Auswärtigen Amtes (Berlin), Bestand Rom-Vatikan 1067: Deutsche in Kongregationen und Päpstlichen Behörden (1928–1938).

[45] Bergen to AA (6.4.1934), in: Politisches Archiv des Auswärtigen Amtes (Berlin), Bestand Rom-Vatikan 440, p. 2.

When, after the end of the First World War, the borders of central Europe were redrawn, both Alsace-Lorraine and South Tyrol came under the rule of victorious nation-states. As a former part of the Hapsburg Empire, the southern part of Tyrol was put under Italian rule after the peace treaty of St. Germain. The political rights of the German minority group were in the main respected up until Mussolini's "March on Rome" in 1922. When the Fascist government succeeded in installing a dictatorship in Italy during a process that ended in 1929,[46] the civil rights of the German-speaking minority group in South Tyrol were conspicuously threatened and increasingly diminished by national and local government institutions.[47] Whereas political and civil liberties in South Tyrol were profoundly affected by the Mussolini Regime, Alsace-Lorraine was governed by a parliamentary democracy. The two provinces, which had formerly been part of the French state, since 1871 had been directly governed from Berlin as a "Reichsland" before passing back to France after the end of the Great War. Alsace, however, maintained its strong regional identity, which was strongly influenced by Catholic culture, the German-Alsatian dialect and an anti-centralistic spirit that had developed under German rule.[48]

In South Tyrol, the reshaping of borders had its consequences for the inner structures of the Church. When, after the First World War, the newly established boundaries between Austria and Italy cut the prince-bishopric of Brixen into two parts, many observers expected the territory of the diocese to be adapted to the boundaries of the nation-states. In fact, there were many examples of this kind of nationalization of Church boundaries; in Ticino, for example, the Holy See had created a bishopric in 1888 according to the state borders between Switzerland and Italy,[49] and the bull *Vixdum poloniae unitas* (1925) established a whole system of dioceses which, to a great extent, corresponded to the borders of the Polish nation state.[50] For the diocese of Brixen, however, the Vatican refused to make a similar decision. Although an apostolic administrator was nominated for the larger Austrian part of the prince-bishopric, and the diocese was thus divided into two administrative entities, a definitive confirmation of the separation of the Church territory was not made until 1964. The Vatican's decision to formally oppose the creation of a new Austrian diocese was at least partially motivated by its reluctant attitude towards the peace treaty of St. Germain, which had confirmed the break-up of the Catholic Hapsburg monarchy.[51] Undoubtedly, this decision encouraged transnational activities, as the diocese of Brixen had to share institutions (such as seminaries for priests) with the apostolic administration of Innsbruck-Feldkirch,

---

[46] Cf. Lyttelton 1973.

[47] Cf. Lill 2002, pp. 69–118.

[48] For Alsatian regional identity cf. Fisch 2002; Dreyfus 1969; Dreyfus 1979; Harvey 2001. For Catholicism in Alsace-Lorraine cf. Baechler 1982; Schulze 2010.

[49] Cf. Altermatt 2009, p. 85.

[50] Marschall 1980, p. 158.

[51] Gelmi 1984; Dörrer 1955, p. 68.

thereby intensifying personal ties between the South Tyrolean and the Austrian clergy.[52] Only gradually did the apostolic administration manage to establish its own diocesan institutions, thereby reinforcing the separation from Brixen.[53]

Just as they applied at the level of international Vatican diplomacy, personal issues were far from being of marginal importance for the dioceses. Some bishops did not support any nationalist tendencies while others were themselves convinced nationalists. All bishops were dependent on the Roman hierarchy and – in the event that diplomatic relations had been established – on their nuncio. They were appointed through different procedures according to concordats of the nation-states with the Vatican, or – if no concordat had been concluded – by canon law. If the appointment required consent between Church and government institutions, this could result in conflicting loyalties for bishops. Charles Ruch, for example, was nominated in 1919 according to the Napoleonic concordat of 1801, which was still valid in Alsace-Lorraine. As a consequence, he was appointed by the French head of government and confirmed by the Papal secretariat of state. It is therefore no wonder that Ruch became known for his close ties to the French state, said nationalistic prayers for French soldiers at commemorative church services and was one of the major Alsatian promoters of the worship of Joan of Arc.[54] The Prince Bishop of Brixen (South Tyrol), Johannes Raffl had on the contrary been appointed in April 1921 according to canon law after a 3-year vacancy of the bishopric. Although the Holy See's relations with the Italian nation-state were seldom uncomplicated, the Italian government, for pragmatic reasons, did not oppose his candidacy. Nevertheless, the case demonstrates that, even if nominated according to canon law, a bishop might well have explicit sympathies for a particular nation-state. Raffl, who was born in Austria, strongly identified with German culture, though he was anxious not to upset the Italian inhabitants of his diocese.[55] One can conclude from these and other[56] examples that, at least under the conditions of extreme nationalism within border regions, bishops could hardly be regarded as 'neutral' in their national affiliation.

In many cases, therefore, the nomination of bishops had significant implications for the way conflicts between nationalities developed within border regions. Generally, personal issues were an important factor within conflicts between the

---

[52] Memorandum of the Vatican's Secretariat of State (24.1.1921), Archivio Segreto Vaticano (Rome), Affari Ecclesiastici Straordinari, Austria, 3. Per., Pos. 1408, fasc. 566, 28r–32r.

[53] For instance, the Tyrolean boys' boarding school in Schwaz was founded in 1927 as an equivalent of the diocesan institution "Vincentinum" at Brixen (South Tyrol); Apostolische Administratur Innsbruck-Feldkirch to Sibilia (13.7.1926), in: Diözesanarchiv Brixen, Bestand Hamherr, no. 1.

[54] Lorson 1948, pp. 135–156; Schulze 2010, p. 174; prayer read by Mons. Charles Ruch (24.11.1928), in: Politisches Archiv des Auswärtigen Amtes (Berlin), R 30201a: Elsass-Lothringen A: Die Stellung Elsass-Lothringens im französ. Staat sowie die elsass-lothring. Autonomiefrage, Bd. 2: März 1928–März 1934, p. 77.

[55] Cf. Gelmi 1984, p. 262.

[56] For the case of the Upper Silesian plebiscite of 1921, cf. Besier and Piombo 2004, pp. 72–78.

Catholic Church and the nation-states over topics such as the regional structure of religious congregations, the language of Church sermons or the Catholic local press. Primary schooling was one of the major points at issue, as nation-states often tended to standardize education programmes on a national level, while the Church aimed to guarantee religious instruction in the mother tongue of the pupils in order to better explain its teachings. In border regions, the Catholic Church thus advocated school-teaching in the language of the national minorities.[57] As a result, national governments often accused the Catholic Church of being biased in favour of the national minorities.

In South Tyrol, the Mussolini government published a series of decrees after 1923 in which all primary schools were obliged to use the Italian language. The Prince Bishop of Brixen resolutely opposed these measures, arguing that it was essential for the children to understand the contents of Catholic doctrine and that consequently children had to receive religious instruction in their mother tongue.[58] Even the Prince Bishop of Trent, Celestino Endrici, who was a native Italian and had advocated the cultural rights of the Italian minority under the Hapsburg Empire,[59] actively supported the principle of religious instruction in the mother tongue, though he was more reluctant in doing so than the Bishop of Brixen. In one of his reports to the Vatican's secretariat of state, he wrote:

> What, however, directly affects the Church is the fact that it has been made impossible for children of the first year to follow [the subject of] religious instruction. In reality, they do not know a single word of Italian. How to teach them the catechism in Italian? For this reason, the whole region is aroused, and the clergy does not know what to do.[60]

Endrici certainly kept his distance from the German-speaking minority in South Tyrol, but he nonetheless promoted the Church's interests in the field of religious instruction, since he considered the comprehension of Catholic doctrine as something fundamental which could not be subjected to the interests of a nation-state. In doing so, he subordinated his sympathies towards the Italian nation to the Vatican's point of view. Inadvertently, therefore, his way of arguing favoured the German minority, although many of its members were considerably less than enthusiastic about the bishop and his Italian roots.[61]

---

[57] During World War I, the Roman Catholic Church showed a similar attitude concerning linguistic conflicts in Quebec: Epistola Benedikt XV to Card. Bégin (8.9.1916), in: *Acta Apostolicae Sedis (AAS)* 8 (1916), pp. 389–442; Epistola Benedikt XV to Kard. Bégin (7.6.1918), in: *Acta Apostolicae Sedis (AAS)* 10 (1918), pp. 439–442.

[58] Raffl to secretariat of state (25.11.1923), Archivio Segreto Vaticano (Rome), Affari Ecclesiastici Straordinari, Italia, 4. Per., Pos. 542, Fasc. 5, 7r-8v.

[59] Undated letter of the South Tyrolean clergy to the Pope, Archivio Segreto Vaticano (Rome), Affari Ecclesiastici Straordinari, Italia, 4. Per., Pos. 644, Fasc. 72, 30r-31r, at 30r.

[60] Endrici to Gasparri (28.11.1923), Archivio Segreto Vaticano (Rome), Affari Ecclesiastici Straordinari, Italia, 4. Per., Pos. 542, Fasc. 5, 21r-22v, at 22v.

[61] In some of the existing historiographical studies about this subject, Endrici is regarded as an opponent of the claims of the German minority. Cf. Marzari 1974, p. 55.

Although the Vatican generally tended to avoid conflicts with the Italian government over South Tyrol, it insisted that religious instruction should be given in the mother tongue of the children. When the Fascist state, in 1928, tried to introduce Italian as obligatory for religious teaching, the dioceses of Brixen and Trent, with the Vatican's permission, withdrew all teachers from public schools and organized their own teaching programmes within the parishes.[62] Despite this arrangement, conflict between state institutions and the South Tyrolean dioceses continued into the 1930s, and both the Italian government and local authorities made several attempts to establish religious education in primary schools as a subject organized and taught by state employees.

Originally, the demand for school-teaching in the mother language of the children came from below – parish priests and local church officials signed several petitions which were sent directly to the Papal secretariat of state. In contrast to the Vatican, they did not hesitate to express their national solidarity alongside religious convictions. In 1932, for example, one of these petitions claimed that Germans had a historical right to call South Tyrol their *Heimat*. "With the permission of God", the petition stated, "a foreign people came and took away our *Heimat*, her wealth and all her characteristics. The foreign people took away our laws and rights; they even took away the names of the deceased."[63] Southern Tyrolean parish priests also tried to indirectly influence the Vatican's politics by asking the Austrian episcopate to direct a petition to the Pope. In their petition, which explicitly criticized plans by the Italian government to send Italian-speaking school-teachers to South Tyrol, the Austrian bishops asked the Holy Father to ban Italian priests from teaching in South Tyrolean primary schools:

> By these measures a holy natural right is being violated; unquestionably, every people, every family has the inviolable right of religious education and religious instruction being given in the mother tongue of the children – as it was clearly and plainly articulated many times by the Holy See as the defender of all rights. [. . .] The Austrian bishops as the closest neighbours observe this new major religious distress and danger for the worthy and honest people of former South Tyrol. We know, however, that in this matter we cannot do anything on our own. Therefore, we appeal in even greater faith to the paternal benevolence of Your Holiness presenting the invocation that Your Holiness may provide help and consolation to the beleaguered in all the ways the enlightened insight of Your Holiness considers as appropriate.[64]

The Austrian episcopate thus did not openly refer to any political implications of the parish priests' claims, concentrating the argument primarily on religious principles. Nevertheless, with its reference to the "worthy and honest people of

---

[62] Lill 2002, p. 113.

[63] Letter of the catholic priests and laymen to the Pope (undated copy), Archivio Segreto Vaticano (Rome), Affari Ecclesiastici Straordinari, Italia, 4. Per., Pos. 644a, Fasc. 83, 80r-85r, at 80r-81r; the last sentence refers to a decree of the South Tyrolean local authorities (1927) to Italianize the German names carved on tombstones; Lill 2002, p. 112.

[64] Riederer to Pius XI (31.10.1932), Archivio Segreto Vaticano (Rome), Affari Ecclesiastici Straordinari, Italia, 4. Per., Pos. 644, Fasc. 76, 89r-92r, at 91rv.

former South Tyrol", the letter alluded to the fact that the diocese of Brixen had been affiliated to the Austrian Archdiocese of Salzburg before the end of World War I. Since the intervention of the Austrian episcopate could easily be interpreted as a threat to the existing borders and could therefore provoke the Italian government, the petition of the Austrian bishops was a political affair and was criticized by members of the Papal secretariat of state for exactly that reason.[65] However, a large part of Brixen's clergy apparently were inclined instead to identify with the Austrian rather than with the Italian Church hierarchy and had no difficulty in demonstrating this. When, in 1934, the Bishop of Acqui, encouraged by Fascist officials, decided to send a delegation of three Italian priests to South Tyrol for the purpose of school-teaching, the Bishop of Brixen did not hesitate to let the priests know that they were *not* welcome.[66]

In Alsace-Lorraine, the question of which language should be used for religious instruction was less controversial than in South Tyrol. After the First World War, the French government had guaranteed the rights of Alsace-Lorraine to maintain the traditional denominational school system, which had been established in France in 1850 and abolished in the 1880s when Alsace-Lorraine was under German rule.[67] In municipalities with a German-speaking majority, religious instruction was usually given in German,[68] whilst school-teaching generally was converted into French. This, of course, did not resolve all the conflicts about which language was used in primary schools, but a different type of conflict concerning primary schools played a much more prominent role during the 1920s. Whilst the Catholic Church in Alsace-Lorraine, in contrast to the rest of France, had retained particular legal privileges,[69] with primary schools continuing to be denominational, this regional peculiarity was called into question by Socialist governments.

In 1924/1925, the Socialist government of Edouard Herriot attempted to introduce French law standards into Alsace-Lorraine, giving permission to local administrations to change denominational schools into interdenominational institutions. Apart from other measures taken by Herriot, this decision caused major discontent amongst the Alsatian population. The Bishop of Strasbourg, Charles Ruch, who was known for his sympathies towards French culture, supported the protest movement right from the beginning in order both to prevent the government from abolishing regional privileges and to secure the leadership of

[65] Letter of the secretariat of state to Ignaz Rieder, Archbishop of Salzburg (undated draft), Archivio Segreto Vaticano (Rome), Affari Ecclesiastici Straordinari, Italia, 4. Per., Pos. 644, Fasc. 76, 88rv.

[66] Geissler to secretariat of state (3.12.1934), Archivio Segreto Vaticano (Rome), Affari Ecclesiastici Straordinari, Italia, 4. Per., Pos. 644, Fasc. 79, 19r-20r, at 19r; Mutschlechner to unknown addressee (2.12.1934), Archivio Segreto Vaticano (Rome), Affari Ecclesiastici Straordinari, Italia, 4. Per., Pos. 644, Fasc. 79, 23r-27r, at 25r-27r.

[67] Schulze 2010, p. 176; for French primary instruction cf. Klaus Dittrich in this volume.

[68] Various authors 1930, p. 281.

[69] Alsace and Lorraine were in fact the only provinces of France in which the Napoleonic concordat of 1801 was still valid; Schulze 2010, p. 170.

the protest movement.[70] In July 1924, Ruch published a proclamation which appealed to all Catholics in the region to 'defend' their religious convictions as a part of Alsatian regional identity.[71]

Under the direction of the diocese of Strasbourg, public protest demonstrations were organized; after Herriot's first government statement concerning the religious question in Alsace-Loraine, large protest demonstrations took place in Strasbourg, Colmar and Mulhouse. When the government's plans to create an interdenominational school system became more definite, the Diocese of Strasbourg organized a school strike. On March 15th, 1925, more than half of the Alsatian families kept their children from going to school to express their disapproval of the government's plans.[72] All these demonstrations were supported by the local clergy, which was largely influenced by German culture and its historical ties to the Zentrumspartei. Looking back at a demonstration in Strasbourg, one of the region's German-speaking Catholics described the following scene:

> At the end the crowd gathered at the Kleberplatz, where Hon. Michel Walther laid a wreath at the Kleber statue, saying: "Let us adopt the saying of this great son of Alsace, which is carved in these stones, and let us say to the sectarians: 'To such an insolence, one can only respond with a victory!'" Finally [the crowd sang] the Marseillaise, which, however, was unfamiliar to many of the participants, and the tremendous "Great God, we praise you!", which was powerfully refracted by the fronts of the terraces.[73]

Clearly, those taking part in the demonstration were predominantly German-speaking Catholics, who nevertheless had no objection to honouring a general of Napoleon's army and to singing the French national anthem. As both the German-speaking clergy and the French bishop of Strasbourg supported the protest movement, the dispute over primary schools in Alsace acquired a regionalist rather than a nationalistic character. Regionalism and Catholicism were both traditionally strong in Alsace,[74] and thus provided a basis for weakening nationalist attitudes. One of the German-language local Catholic newspapers noted in one of its articles: "If the Herriot government desires to intervene against Bishop Ruch, it may do so: however, in that case it would not only have to face the bishop's resistance, but the resistance of the whole Catholic people of Alsace."[75] Although the protests were supported by a large majority of German- and French-speaking Alsatian Catholics, they only succeeded in reversing the government's plans to create more interdenominational schools, and left the existing institutions unaffected. As the Catholics in Alsace tended to interpret the existence of denominational schools as part of their regional identity, the question of which language should be used for religious instruction never became part of the discussions. In this respect, the

---

[70] Cf. Baechler 1985, p. 297.

[71] Ruch 1924, p. 291.

[72] Defensor 1926, p. 125.

[73] Rossé et al. 1936, pp. 671 f.

[74] Cf. Harvey 2001.

[75] Ein Schulplebiszit in Colmar, in: *Elsässer Kurier* 28 (16.03.1925) no. 63, p. 2.

Catholic Church in Alsace opposed the ideal of national conformity promoted by the Socialist government without supporting German nationalism.

Even so, the spirit of agreement amongst the Alsatian Catholics turned out to be precarious. Only a few years later, the clergy split over the question of regional autonomy and Bishop Ruch, because of his sympathies towards the French state, became one of the most unpopular clerics in his own diocese. Paradoxically, the new conflict among Alsatian Catholics had its roots in the protest movement of 1924/1925, since the demonstrations against the government's educational plans implicitly affirmed that the denominational school system was an element of Alsatian regional culture. This type of anti-centralism, in fact, was to cause major unrest in the following years. As the appeal for Alsatian autonomy within the region grew significantly during the second half of the decade, the French government attempted to strengthen its rule, provoking protests against centralistic tendencies. Under these conditions, conflicts over the question of local autonomy arose as well within the Catholic regional party, the Union Populaire Républicaine (UPR), which, in December 1928, split into an autonomist mainstream and a 'pro-French' Action Populaire Nationale d'Alsace (APNA) that tolerated centralism. The division of the UPR had serious implications for the life of the diocese of Strasbourg, since a large part of the local clergy sympathized with the autonomists, whilst Bishop Ruch openly supported the newly founded pro-centralist APNA movement.[76] The quarrels about regional autonomy demonstrate that the bridge-building effect of local Catholic politics was limited to a short period of time. Although the major part of Alsatian autonomists were anything but sympathetic towards the German nation-state,[77] the Church, during the 'autonomist crises', took a significant part in reinforcing the conflicts.

## Conclusion

This article has discussed certain aspects of the Catholic Church's stance towards conflicts between nationalities. With regard to the Vatican's policy, but also at the level of dioceses, much more research must be undertaken in order to explain the complex relationship between Catholicism and nationalisms in the first half of the twentieth century. Even so, it has been shown that the transnational structures within the Roman Catholic Church only partly contributed to weakening the importance of nation-states. Some examples, on the contrary, have shown that, under the conditions of an extreme nationalism, nationalist attitudes and mentalities have been spread within and through the Church.

Although the Vatican regarded itself as a universal institution, and based its religious identity as well as its task of providing spiritual welfare on its authority

[76] Cf. Schulze 2010, pp. 183–192.

[77] Epp 2004, pp. 430 f.; Harvey 2001, pp. 152–162.

over Catholics of all origins, in the era of nation-states these ideals turned out to be difficult to put into practice. As an actor on the international political stage, the Holy See had permanently to deal with nation-states of all possible kinds and was seldom able to abstain from nations' interests. Since the cardinals of the Roman Curia as well as the members of the Vatican's congregations were not only affiliated to the Church, but at the same time citizens of a single nation-state, it was hardly possible for Church officials to ignore the factor of national identities. Alongside personal loyalties and cultural concepts of identity, some of the Holy See's ideological convictions and political objectives also favoured the inner process of nationalization of the Vatican; since the pontificate of Leo XIII the Vatican increasingly regarded modern nation-states as a natural element of a God-given world order.

On a regional level, the nationalization process has seriously affected the local structures of the Roman Catholic Church. In fact, some of the examples demonstrate that its actions were even interpreted as a confirmation of nationalist attitudes. The Vatican's position within the South Tyrolean conflict over the language used in primary schools for the subject of religious instruction, however, tended to favour the German national minority. The bishops and most of the clergy of the dioceses of Brixen and Trent interpreted the statements of the Holy See as a confirmation of minority rights, ignoring the fact that the Vatican argued almost exclusively in terms of religious principles. By taking up a position which conflicted with the interests of the Italian nation-state, the opinion of the Catholic Church – at least indirectly – coincided with the claims of German nationalists.

Of course, it could be argued that the existence of a strong regional and religious identity, in combination with national minorities, might reduce the power of a centralized nation-state, giving room for cultural transfers between two nationalities. This line of argument could be applied to the case of educational policy in Alsace-Lorraine, although the Catholic protest movement of 1924/1925 did not in the end lead to a long-lasting arrangement between German- and French-speaking Alsatians. In general, however, it appears to be highly questionable whether, in border regions, the diocesan networks of the Roman Catholic Church generally worked in favour of transnational exchange between conflicting groups of different nationalities. At least in the case of South Tyrol, the Church's transnational structures favoured the exchange of ideas with Austria, but by no means did they improve contacts between German- and Italian-speaking inhabitants. In that sense, the Catholic Church rather acted against the separation of Tyrol than in favour of cultural transfers.

Finally, the complexity of the question discussed in this article results from the multitude of perspectives within the Catholic Church. It was not only inside the Vatican that the cardinals and prelates differed in their attitude towards nationalism, but also on a regional and local level a wide range of opinions concerning nation-states can be observed among Church officials.

## Bibliography

Alix, Christine. 1962. *Le Saint-Siège et les nationalismes en Europe 1870–1960. Histoire et sociologie de l'Église 1*. Paris: Sirey.

Altermatt, Urs. 2005. "Das komplexe Verhältnis von Religion und Nation: Eine Typologie für den Katholizismus." *Schweizerische Zeitschrift für Religions- und Kulturgeschichte* 99, 417–432.

Altermatt, Urs. 2007. "Katholizismus und Nation. Vier Modelle in europäisch-vergleichender Perspektive." In *Religion und Nation. Katholizismen im Europa des 19. und 20. Jahrhunderts (Religionsforum 3)*, edited by Urs Altermatt and Franziska Metzger, 15–33. Stuttgart: Kohlhammer.

Altermatt, Urs. 2009. *Konfession, Nation und Rom. Metamorphosen im schweizerischen und europäischen Katholizismus des 19. und 20. Jahrhunderts*. Stuttgart: Huber

Altgeld, Wolfgang. 2001. "Christentum, Revolution, Nation. Geschichtliche und zeitgeschichtliche Auseinandersetzungen in der Formierung des deutschen Katholizismus." *Historisches Jahrbuch* 121, 501–512.

Anger, Gunnar. 2007. "Giuseppe Pizzardo." *Biographisch-Bibliographisches Kirchenlexikon*, vol. XXVIII, coll. 1268–1272. Nordhausen: Bautz.

*Annuario Pontificio*. 1926. Rome: Libreria Editrice Vaticana.

Anonymous. 1924. "Il nazionalismo e le presenti lotte politiche." *Civiltà Cattolica* 75, vol. 4, 97–108.

Archivio Segreto Vaticano (Rome), Affari Ecclesiastici Straordinari, Austria, 3. Per., Pos. 1408, Fasc. 566.

Archivio Segreto Vaticano (Rome), Affari Ecclesiastici Straordinari, Italia, 4. Per., Pos. 542, Fasc. 5.

Archivio Segreto Vaticano (Rome), Affari Ecclesiastici Straordinari, Italia, 4. Per., Pos. 644, Fasc. 72, 76, 79.

Archivio Segreto Vaticano (Rome), Affari Ecclesiastici Straordinari, Italia, 4. Per., Pos. 644a, Fasc. 83.

Baechler, Christian. 1982. *Le parti catholique alsacien 1890–1939. Du Reichsland à la République Jacobine*. Paris: Ophrys.

Baechler, Christian. 1985. "Les relations entre Mgr Ruch et le Clergé alsacien lors de la crise autonomiste de 1925/1929, vues à travers un mémorandum de décembre 1929." *Archives de l'Église d'Alsace* XLIV, 297–320.

Besier, Gerhard and Francesca Piombo. 2004. *Der Heilige Stuhl und Hitler-Deutschland. Die Faszination des Totalitären*. Munich: Deutsche Verlags-Anstalt.

Birke, Adolf M. 1996. "Nation und Konfession. Varianten des politischen Katholizismus im Europa des 19. Jahrhunderts." *Historisches Jahrbuch* 116, 395–416.

Brechenmacher, Thomas. 2005. "Teufelspakt, Selbsterhaltung, universale Mission? Leitlinien und Spielräume der Diplomatie des Heiligen Stuhls gegenüber dem nationalsozialistischen Deutschland (1933–1939) im Lichte neu zugänglicher vatikanischer Akten." *Historische Zeitschrift* 280, 591–645.

Brechenmacher, Thomas. 2009. "Der Papst und der Zweite Weltkrieg." In *Die Katholiken und das Dritte Reich. Kontroversen und Debatten*, edited by Karl-Joseph Hummel and Michael Kißener, 179–195. Paderborn: Ferdinand Schöningh.

Chenaux, Philippe. 2003. *Pie XII. Diplomate et pasteur*. Paris: Cerf.

Chiron, Yves. 2004. *Pie XI (1857–1939)*. Paris: Perrin.

Cholvy, Gérard and Yves-Marie Hilaire. 1986. *Histoire religieuse de la France Contemporaine, vol. 2: 1880/1930*, 273–276. Toulouse: Privat.

Clark, Christopher. 2002 "Kulturkampf in Europa im 19. Jahrhundert." *Comparativ* 12, no. 5–6, 7–37.

*Codex Iuris Canonici (CIC) 1917*. Can. 218, ed. Libreria Editrice Vaticana. Accessed 11.11.2011 (http://www.jgray.org/codes/cic17lat.html).

"Concilium Vaticanum I." 1990. In *Decrees of the Ecumenical Councils, vol. 2: Trent to Vatican II*, edited by Norman P. Tanner SJ., 801–816. London: Sheed & Ward.

Conzemius, Victor. 1985. "Kirchen und Nationalismen im Europa des 19. und 20. Jahrhunderts." In *Katholizismus, nationaler Gedanke und Europa seit 1800* (Beiträge zur Katholizismusforschung), edited by Albrecht Langner, 11–50. Paderborn: Schöningh.

Conzemius, Victor. 1994. "Nationalismus und Katholizismus." *Theologisch-praktische Quartalschrift* 142, 234–262.

Corsini, Umberto. 1988. "Die Zeit der Militärregierung und des zivilen Generalkommissariats: November 1918 bis Oktober 1922." *Südtirol 1918–1946,* 45–114. Bozen: Autonome Provinz Bozen-Südtirol.

Defensor. 1926. *Elsass-Lothringen im Kampfe um seine religiösen Einrichtungen 1924–1926.* Schwerdorff: Verlag und Expedition: Sekretariat des Lothringer Volksbundes.

Diözesanarchiv Brixen. Bestand Hamherr, no. 1.

Dörrer, Fridolin. 1955. "Bistumsfragen Tirols nach der Grenzziehung von 1918." In *Südtirol. Land europäischer Bewährung. Kanonikus Michael Gamper zum 70. Geburtstag*, edited by Franz H. Riedl, 47–88. Innsbruck: Wagner.

Dreyfus, François G. 1969. *La vie politique en Alsace 1919–1936.* Paris: A. Colin.

Dreyfus, François G. 1979. *Histoire de l'Alsace.* Paris: Hachette.

Epistola Benedikt XV to Card. Bégin (8.9.1916). In *Acta Apostolicae Sedis (AAS)* 8, 389–442.

Epistola Benedikt XV to Card. Bégin (7.6.1918). In *Acta Apostolicae Sedis (AAS)* 10, 439–442.

Epp, René. *Histoire de l'Église Catholique en Alsace des origines à nos jours. Avec la collaboration de René Pierre Levresse et Charles Munier.* Rome 2004.

Feldkamp, Michael. 2000. *Pius XII. und Deutschland.* Göttingen: Vandenhoeck & Ruprecht.

Fisch, Stefan. 2002. "Der Übergang des Elsass vom Deutschen Reich an Frankreich 1918/19." In *Das Elsass. Historische Landschaft im Wandel der Zeiten*, edited by Michael Erbe, 147–152. Stuttgart: W. Kohlhammer.

Fleckenstein, Gisela and Joachim Schmiedl, eds. 2005. *Ultramontanismus. Tendenzen der Forschung. Einblicke 8.* Paderborn: Bonifatius.

Gelmi, Josef. "1984. Johannes X. Raffl." *Die Brixner Bischöfe in der Geschichte Tirols*, 262–265. Bozen: Athesia.

Gottsmann, Andreas. 2006. "Konkordat oder Kulturprotektorat? Die Donaumonarchie und die diplomatischen Aktivitäten des Hl. Stuhls in Südosteuropa, 1878–1914." *Römische Historische Mitteilungen* 48, 409–464.

Gottsmann, Andreas. 2007. "Papst Leo XIII. und die 'jugoslawische' Versuchung. Montenegro, San Girolamo und die südslawische Frage in der Diplomatie des Hl. Stuhls." *Römische Historische Mitteilungen* 49, 457–510.

Gottsmann, Andreas. 2010. *Rom und die nationalen Katholizismen in der Donaumonarchie. Römischer Universalismus, habsburgische Reichspolitik und nationale Identitäten 1874–1914. Publikationen des Historischen Instituts beim österreichischen Kulturforum in Rom 1.* Vienna: Verlag der Österreichischen Akademie der Wissenschaften.

Graf, Friedrich Wilhelm. 2000. "Die Nation – von Gott 'erfunden'? Kritische Randnotizen zum Theologiebedarf der historischen Nationalismusforschung." In *'Gott mit uns' Nation, Religion und Gewalt im 19. und frühen 20. Jahrhundert*, edited by Gerd Krumeich and Hartmut Lehmann, 285–317. Göttingen: Vandenhoeck & Ruprecht.

Habermas, Rebekka. 2008. "Mission im 19. Jahrhundert – Globale Netzwerke des Religiösen." *Historische Zeitschrift* 287, 629–679.

Harvey, David Allen. 2001. *Constructing Class and Nationality in Alsace 1830–1945.* DeKalb: Northern Illinois University Press.

Haupt, Heinz-Gerhard and Dieter Langewiesche, ed. 2004. *Nation und Religion in Europa. Mehrkonfessionelle Gesellschaften im 19. und 20. Jahrhundert.* Frankfurt am Main: Campus Verlag.

Herren, Madeleine. 2009. *Internationale Organisationen seit 1865. Eine Globalgeschichte der internationalen Ordnung.* Darmstadt: Wissenschaftliche Buchgesellschaft.

Lamberts, Emiel, ed. 2002. *The Black International 1870–1878. The Holy See and Militant Catholicism in Europe (Kadoc-Studies 29)*. Leuven: Leuven University Press.
Langewiesche, Dieter. 2000. *Nation, Nationalismus, Nationalstaat in Deutschland und Europa*. Munich: C.H. Beck.
Langewiesche, Dieter. 2009. "Nation und Religion." In *Europäische Religionsgeschichte. Ein mehrfacher Pluralismus*, vol. 2, edited by Hans G. Kippenberg et al., 525–553. Göttingen: Vandenhoeck & Ruprecht.
Latour, Francis. 1996. "De la spécificité de la diplomatie vaticane durant la grande guerre." *Revue d'histoire moderne et contemporaine* 43, 349–365.
Latour, Francis. 1996. *La Papauté et les problèmes de la paix pendant la Première Guerre Mondial*. Paris: Harmattan.
Leo XIII. 1903. *Sanctissimi Domini nostri Leonis Divina providentia Papae XIII epistola encyclica de civitatum constitutione cristiana*. Freiburg im Breisgau: Herder.
Leo XIII, "Über die Arbeiterfrage." 1963. *Leo XIII., Pius XI., Johannes XXIII., Die sozialen Enzykliken. Rerum Novarum, Quadragesimo anno, Mater et magistra, Pacem in terris, mit einer Einleitung von Johannes Binkowski*, 1–35. Villingen: Ring-Verlag.
Lill, Rudolf. 2002. *Südtirol in der Zeit des Nationalsozialismus*. Constance: UVK-Verl.-Ges.
Lorson, Pierre. 1948. *Charles Ruch. Evêque de Strasbourg*. Strasbourg: Le Roux.
Lyons, Francis. 1963. *Internationalism in Europe 1815–1914* (European Aspects, Series C, No. 14). Leyden: A.W. Sythoff.
Lyttelton, Adrian. 1973. *The Seizure of Power. Fascism in Italy 1919–1929*. London: Weidenfeld and Nicolson.
Marschall, Werner. 1980. *Geschichte des Bistums Breslau*. Stuttgart: K. Theiss.
Marzari, Walter. 1974. *Kanonikus Michael Gamper. Ein Kämpfer für Glauben und Heimat gegen Faschistenbeil und Hakenkreuz in Südtirol* (Aus Christentum und Kultur 3). Vienna: Hollinek.
Mercati, Angelo, ed. 1954. *Raccolta di concordati su materie ecclesiastiche tra la Santa Sede e le autorità civili, vol. II: 1915–1954*. Vatican City: Tipografia poliglotta vaticana.
Mergel, Thomas. 2008. "Dauernde Zugehörigkeiten. Überlegungen zum Verhältnis zwischen Nation und Religion im 19. und frühen 20. Jahrhundert." In *Kirchengeschichte. Alte und neue Wege, Festschrift für Christoph Weber*, vol. 2, edited by Gisela Fleckenstein et al., 867–885. Frankfurt am Main: Lang.
Moos, Carlo. 2007. "Kirche, Staat und Nation in Italien." *Religion und Nation. Katholizismen im Europa des 19. und 20. Jahrhunderts* (Religionsforum 3), edited by In Urs Altermatt & Franziska Metzger, 241–254. Stuttgart: Kohlhammer.
O'Brian, Connor Cruise, *God Land. Reflections on Religion and Nationalism*, Cambridge/Mass. 1988.
Pius XI. 1922. "Ubi arcano dei consilio. Vatican encyclicals." Accessed 17.11.2009 (http://www.vatican.va/holy_father/pius_xi/encyclicals/documents/hf_p-xi_enc_23121922_ubi-arcano-dei-consilio_en.html)
Pius XI. 1923. *Sanctissimi domini nostri Pii divina providentia Papae XI litterae encyclicae. De pace christi in regno christi qvaerenda*. Munich: Theatiner-Verlag.
Pius XI. 1930. *Sanctissimi domini nostri Pii divina providentia Papae XI litterae encyclicae. De Christiana Iuventutis Educatione*. Freiburg im Breisgau: Herder.
Politisches Archiv des Auswärtigen Amtes (Berlin). Bestand Rom-Vatikan 440.
Politisches Archiv des Auswärtigen Amtes (Berlin). Bestand Rom-Vatikan 1067: Deutsche in Kongregationen und Päpstlichen Behörden (1928–1938).
Politisches Archiv des Auswärtigen Amtes (Berlin). R 30201a: Elsass-Lothringen A: Die Stellung Elsass-Lothringens im französ. Staat sowie die elsass-lothring. Autonomiefrage, Bd. 2, March 1928–March 1934.
Rémond, René. 2000. *Religion und Gesellschaft in Europa Von 1789 bis zur Gegenwart*. Munich: C.H. Beck.
Richter, Reinhard. 2000. *Nationales Denken im Katholizismus der Weimarer Republik. Theologie 29*. Münster: Lit.

Rossé, Joseph, et al. 1936. *Das Elsass von 1870–1932, vol. I: Politische Geschichte*. Colmar: Verlag Alsatia

Ruch, Charles. 1924. "01.07.1924. Lettre de l'Évêque de Strasbourg à Messieurs les Doyens et Curés du diocèse, à Monsieur le Président Général et à Messieurs les Présidents Paroissiaux de la Ligue des Catholiques." *Bulletin Ecclésiastique du Diocèse de Strasbourg* XLIII, no. 13, 290–292.

Saunier, Pierre-Yves. 2009. "Transnational." In *The Palgrave Dictionary of Transnational History*, edited by Akira Iriye and Pierre-Yves Saunier, 1047–1055. New York: Palgrave Macmillan.

Scholder, Klaus. 1977. *Die Kirchen und das Dritte Reich, vol. 1: Vorgeschichte und Zeit der Illusionen 1918–1934*. Frankfurt am Main: Ullstein.

"Ein Schulplebiszit in Colmar." 1925. *Elsässer Kurier* 28, 16 March, no. 63.

Schulze, Thies. 2010. "Bischof in einem fremden Land. Der Straßburger Bischof Charles Ruch zwischen Katholizismus und Nationalismus, 1919–1931." *Francia* 37, 167–194.

Seppelt, Franz Xaver and Georg Schwaiger. 1964. *Geschichte der Päpste. Von den Anfängen bis zur Gegenwart*. Munich: Kösel.

Stehlin, Stewart. 1983. *Weimar and the Vatican 1919–1933. German-Vatican Diplomatic Relations in the Interwar Years*. Princeton: Princeton University Press.

Haegy, Xaver and Joseph Rossé, ed. 1930. *Im Dienste der Kirche und des Volkes. Festschrift zum 60. Geburtstage des H. Abbé Haegy*, Colmar: Ed. Alsatia.

Weiss, Otto. 1978. "Der Ultramontanismus. Grundlagen – Vorgeschichte – Struktur." *Zeitschrift für bayerische Landesgeschichte* 42, 821–877.

Wildt, Michael. 2009. "Die Ungleichheit des Volkes. 'Volksgemeinschaft' in der politischen Kommunikation der Weimarer Republik." In *Volksgemeinschaft. Neue Forschungen zur Gesellschaft des Nationalsozialismus*, edited by Frank Bajohr and Michael Wildt, 24–40. Frankfurt am Main: Fischer.

# Index



I. Löhr and R. Wenzlhuemer (eds.), *The Nation State and Beyond*, Transcultural Research – Heidelberg Studies on Asia and Europe in a Global Context, DOI 10.1007/978-3-642-32934-0, © Springer-Verlag Berlin Heidelberg 2013

The manufacturer's authorised representative in the EU is Springer Nature Customer Service Centre GmbH, Europaplatz 3, 69115 Heidelberg, Germany. If you have any concerns regarding our products, please contact ProductSafety@springernature.com

Printed and bound by CPI Group (UK) Ltd, Croydon, CR0 4YY
01/10/2026
02225951-0012